Ethnolinguistic Chicago

Language and Literacy
in the City's Neighborhoods

Ethnolinguistic Chicago

Language and Literacy
in the City's Neighborhoods

Marcia Farr
Ohio State University
Columbus, OH

LAWRENCE ERLBAUM ASSOCIATES, PUBLISHERS

2004   **Mahwah, New Jersey**   London

PART III: COMMUNITY SPACES

Foreword

Dell Hymes

This book is both rewarding and challenging. Rewarding, first of all, to people interested in Chicago. There are accounts of Chicago as a city from various standpoints: its architectural history (Vergara & Samuelson, 2001), or its variety of churches (Johnson, 1999), but not, so far as I know, from the standpoint of its variety of languages, old and new. This work should stimulate further inquiry in Chicago, and analogous studies throughout the country.

Many are aware that people from European communities retained the languages of those communities for some time after settling in the United States. Probably few are aware of how long such retentions have survived, let alone of how complex this can sometimes be. Not far from Chicago, in northwestern Indiana (Allen County), the Old Order Amish speak a dialect of German (Alsatian). Within their community, English and Pennsylvania German are significant as well, and some know Bernese Swiss and Standard German. (Thompson, 1994).

What this book makes clear is that diversity of language is not merely a matter of retention. There are new arrivals as well, some from Africa, some from Asia, and some, of course, from elsewhere in the New World. (The forthcoming companion volume to this one, *Latino Language and Literacy in Ethnolinguistic Chicago*, will take up the complex story of Mexicans and Puerto Ricans.)

Furthermore, diversity is not a matter only of named languages. The chapters in this book describe diverse genres: "signifying" and "loud-talking," personal storytelling, sermons, invocations, various forms in an accountant's office, a style of speech called *bella figura,* how to argue, Chinese books, and Japanese newspapers. Clearly, each of the many communities involved has ways of speaking of its own, and there is more to be learned about them.

I grew up knowing that Carl Sandburg had christened Chicago in terms of meat. Clearly, it has a strong claim to being christened the polyglot capital of Middle America, and there is much still to be learned about the way we live now in terms of languages and ways of using languages. A recent study focuses on a surge of ethnic eating in Quebec City, "seemingly in answer to a growing desire to experience cultural difference" (Turgeon & Pastinelli, 2002; p. 262). The study says nothing about another essential use of the mouth, talking. Perhaps people most often seek out settings for speaking that will be familiar, comfortable, although the growth of occasions for performance poetry needs to be noted.

Some years ago, the diversity of rural North Dakota was studied under the heading "Prairie Mosaic" (Sherman, 1983). "Mosaic" seems an apt term for what Marcia Farr and her colleagues are bringing to light, an apt term for the objects of such study: urban mosaics.

REFERENCES

Johnson, E. (1999). *Chicago churches: A photographic essay.* Chicago: Uppercase Books.

Sherman, W. C. (1983). *Prairie mosaic: An ethnic atlas of rural north Dakota.* Fargo: North Dakota Institute of Regional Studies.

Sherman, W. C., & Thorson, P. V. (Eds.). (1988). *Plains folk: North Dakota's ethnic history.* Fargo: North Dakota Institute for Regional Studies at North Dakota State University in cooperation with the North Dakota Humanities Council and the University of North Dakota, 1986.

Thompson, C. (1994). The languages of the Amish of Allen County, Indiana: Multilingualism and convergence. *Anthropological Linguistics, 36*(1); 69–91.

Turgeon, L., & Pastinelli, M. (2002). "Eat the World": Postcolonial encounters in Quebec City's ethnic restaurants. *Journal of American Folklore, 115,* 247–268.

Vergara, C. J., & Samuelson, T. (2001). *Unexpected Chicagoland.* New York: The New Press.

Preface

Marcia Farr

This book, along with its forthcoming companion volume, *Latino Language and Literacy in Ethnolinguistic Chicago*, fills an important gap in research on Chicago and, more generally, on language use in globalized metropolitan areas. Although Chicago has been fairly well studied by scholars interested in ethnicity, including sociologists (e.g., Massey & Denton, 1993; Wilson, 1987) and historians (e.g., Holli & Jones, 1977/1984/1995), no one has focused on language and ethnicity. This is so despite the well-known fact that Chicago is one of the most linguistically diverse cities in the United States and often is cited as a quintessential American city. Certainly, Chicago is, and always has been, a city of immigrants (and migrants arriving from other parts of the United States). Moreover, language is unquestionably central to social identity, because how we talk constructs for ourselves and others who we are.

Arriving in Chicago in August of 1982, I was fascinated by its mosaic of ethnic neighborhoods, even though the often neat separation of populations into neighborhoods or community areas illustrated the results of segregation and racism as much as ethnic vitality. Discovering that sociologists in Chicago had provided abundant demographic profiles, based on census data, of each community area of the city in a periodically published Local Community Fact Book (in 1938, 1949, 1953, 1963, 1984, and 1995), I began to plan a research program investigating language use in local neighborhoods all over the metropolitan area. Thus the research on language in various ethnic communities builds upon the demographic profiles provided by what has evolved into the Chicago Fact Book Consortium. My own research on language and literacy practices within transnational Mexican families in several community areas on the south side of the city is one part of this program (Farr, 1993, 1994a, 1994b, 1994c, 1998, 2000a, 2000b, forthcoming). Other contributions to the larger program were made by graduate students whose dissertations I have directed over the past decade and a half. This volume contains not only many chapters by those former graduate students, but also a number of chapters by colleagues carrying out similar studies in Chicago.

Most of the chapters in this book are based on ethnographic studies of language as called for by Hymes (1974), although several provide historical narratives as well. Because an ethnographic perspective requires attention to local-level, "insider" meanings rather than those imposed from the outside by researchers, what has surfaced as important varies thematically from study to study. This book, then, instead of being composed of similarly structured chapters (e.g., the historical and contemporary linguistic context of particular ethnic communities, itself a valuable endeavor), provides a more richly diverse set of portraits whose central themes emerged inductively from the research process and the communities themselves. Despite this diversity of themes, however, all the chapters nevertheless emphasize language use as centrally related to ethnic, class, or gender identities (see Introduction). As such, this volume should be of interest to anthropologists, sociologists, linguists, historians, educators and educational researchers, and others whose concerns require an understanding of "ground-level" phenomena relevant to contemporary social issues.

The book is structured into three parts. After this Preface and the Foreword by Dell Hymes, whose work inspired many of the studies represented here, Part I contains an Introduction to the volume by myself and Rachel Reynolds and a history of language policy in Illinois by Elliot Judd. Part II of the book comprises studies carried out Within the Family Circle, with chapters by Marcyliena Morgan on African Americans, by Grace Cho and Peggy Miller on middle- and working-class European Americans, and by Lukia Koliussi on Greek Americans. These chapters share the context of family and home. Part III of the book is composed of chapters located in "Community Spaces" in various neighborhoods. These chapters include African American churches (Beverly Moss), an African immigrant association (Rachel Reynolds), an Arab accountant's office (Sharon Radloff), varieties of Swedish (Carl Isaacson), an Italian American club (Gloria Nardini), Lithuanian and English language use (Daiva Markelis), a working-class White bar (Julie Lindquist), Chinese language use (John Rohsenow), and Japanese print media (Laura Miller). The chapters in this third part of the book include those based in specific community locations, as well as those that provide an historical or contemporary overview of language and/or literacy practices within a particular ethnic community. Finally, an Afterword by Robert Gundlach speculates on the processes of language retention and change illustrated in the preceding chapters, as well as on the relation of this work to other realms of language study.

ACKNOWLEDGMENTS

I acknowledge a number of people whose support made this book possible. I thank the Spencer Foundation for providing me with Mentor Network funds that enabled many graduate students to carry out their dissertation studies. I especially thank former Spencer Foundation Program Officers Rebecca Barr and Catherine Lacey, who have supported my work over the years in various ways.

It seems equally appropriate here to thank my wonderful graduate students over the years. Together we have made a reality of research plans hatched in innumerable conversations in graduate seminars and over dissertations and co-authored articles (Farr & Guerra, 1995; Farr & Nardini, 1996; Guerra & Farr, 2002). I am particularly grateful to Rachel Reynolds, who not only furnished a chapter based on her dissertation and co-authored the Introduction, but also provided invaluable help as a research assistant in myriad ways, including tirelessly searching for potential contributors to fill in population gaps and communicating with authors over the course of the development of the manuscript.

I also thank the editors at Lawrence Erlbaum Associates, Naomi Silverman (who grew up in Chicago) and her assistant Erica Kica, for all their attention to detail and for their vision of the importance of the larger project. Dell Hymes, who rendered a painstakingly detailed review of all the chapters and then an elegant foreword to the volume, is also due many thanks. Finally, I thank my husband Michael Maltz and my daughter Julianna Whiteman for providing the kind of emotional support and guidance that can come only from a loving family.

REFERENCES

Chicago Fact Book Consortium. (1984). Local Community fact book: Chicago metropolitan area. Based on 1970 and 1980 Censuses. Chicago: Chicago Review Press.

Chicago Fact Book Consortium. (1995). *Local Community fact book: Chicago.* 1990 metropolitan area. Chicago: Academy Chicago Publishers.

Farr, M. (1993). Essayist literacy and other verbal performances. *Written Communication, 10 (*1), 4–38.

Farr, M. (1994a). *En los dos idiomas*: Literacy practices among *Mexicano* families in Chicago. In B. Moss (Ed.), *Literacy across communities* (pp. 9–47). Cresskill, NJ: Hampton Press.

Farr, M. (1994b). Biliteracy in the home: Practices among *Mexicano* families in Chicago. In D. Spener (Ed.), *Adult biliteracy in the United States* (pp. 89–110). McHenry, IL and Washington, DC: Delta Systems and Center for Applied Linguistics.

Farr, M. (1994c). *Echando relajo*: Verbal art and gender among *Mexicanas* in Chicago. In M. Bucholtz, A. C. Liang, L. A. Sutton, & C. Hines (Eds.), *Cultural performances: Proceedings of the third women and language conference, April 8–10, 1994* (pp. 168–186). Berkeley, CA: University of California.

Farr, M. (1998). *El relajo como microfiesta*. In H. Pérez (Ed.), *Mexico en fiesta* (pp. 457–470). Zamora, Michoacán, Mexico: El Colegio de Michoacán.

Farr, M. (2000a). *¡A mí no me manda nadie!* Individualism and identity in Mexican *ranchero* speech. In V. Pagliai & M. Farr (Eds.), [Special issue] *Pragmatics, 10,* 1: Language, Performance, and identity (pp. 61–85).

Farr, M. (2000b). Literacy and religion: Reading, writing, and gender among Mexican women in Chicago. In P. Griffin, J. K. Peyton, W. Wolfram, & R. Fasold (Eds.), *Language in action: New studies of language in society* (pp. 139–154). Cresskill, NJ: Hampton Press.

Farr, M. (Forthcoming). *Rancheros* in Chicagoacán: Ways of Speaking and identity in a Mexican transnational community.

Farr, M., & Guerra, J. (1995). Literacy in the community: A study of *mexicano* families in Chicago. [Special Issue] *Discourse Processes*: Literacy Among Latinos, 19 (1), 7–19.

Farr, M., & Nardini, G. (1996). Essayist literacy and sociolinguistic difference. In E. White, W. Lutz, & S. Kamusikiri (Eds.), *The politics and policies of assessment in writing* (pp. 108–119) . New York: Modern Language Association.

Guerra, J., & Farr, M. (2002). Writing on the margins: Spiritual and autobiographic discourse among *Mexicanas* in Chicago. In G. Hull & K. Schultz (Eds.), *School's out! Literacy at work and in the community* (pp. 96–123). New York: Teachers College Press.

Holli, M. G., & Jones, P. d'A. (Eds.). (1977/1984/1995). *Ethnic Chicago: A multicultural portrait.* Grand Rapids, MI: William B. Eerdman.

Hymes, D. (1974). *Sociolinguistics: An ethnographic approach.* Philadelphia: University of Pennsylvania Press.

Massey, D. S., & Denton, N. A. (1993). *American apartheid: Segregation and the making of the underclass.* Cambridge, MA: Harvard University Press.

Wilson, W. J. (1987). *The truly disadvantaged: The inner city, the underclass, and public policy.* Chicago: University of Chicago Press.

I

INTRODUCTION AND BACKGROUND

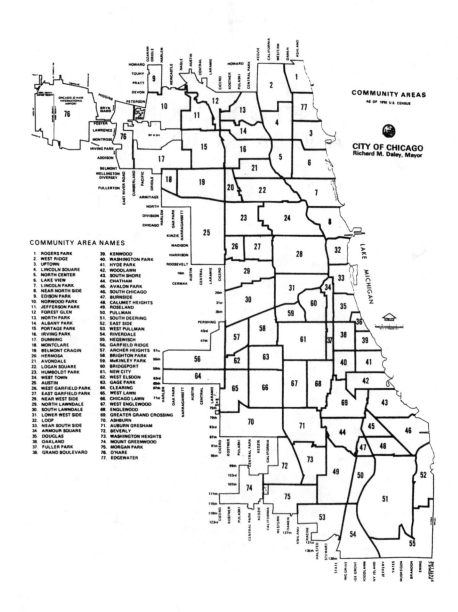

COMMUNITY AREAS
AS OF 1990 U.S. CENSUS

CITY OF CHICAGO
Richard M. Daley, Mayor

COMMUNITY AREA NAMES

1. ROGERS PARK
2. WEST RIDGE
3. UPTOWN
4. LINCOLN SQUARE
5. NORTH CENTER
6. LAKE VIEW
7. LINCOLN PARK
8. NEAR NORTH SIDE
9. EDISON PARK
10. NORWOOD PARK
11. JEFFERSON PARK
12. FOREST GLEN
13. NORTH PARK
14. ALBANY PARK
15. PORTAGE PARK
16. IRVING PARK
17. DUNNING
18. MONTCLARE
19. BELMONT CRAGIN
20. HERMOSA
21. AVONDALE
22. LOGAN SQUARE
23. HUMBOLDT PARK
24. WEST TOWN
25. AUSTIN
26. WEST GARFIELD PARK
27. EAST GARFIELD PARK
28. NEAR WEST SIDE
29. NORTH LAWNDALE
30. SOUTH LAWNDALE
31. LOWER WEST SIDE
32. LOOP
33. NEAR SOUTH SIDE
34. ARMOUR SQUARE
35. DOUGLAS
36. OAKLAND
37. FULLER PARK
38. GRAND BOULEVARD

39. KENWOOD
40. WASHINGTON PARK
41. HYDE PARK
42. WOODLAWN
43. SOUTH SHORE
44. CHATHAM
45. AVALON PARK
46. SOUTH CHICAGO
47. BURNSIDE
48. CALUMET HEIGHTS
49. ROSELAND
50. PULLMAN
51. SOUTH DEERING
52. EAST SIDE
53. WEST PULLMAN
54. RIVERDALE
55. HEGEWISCH
56. GARFIELD RIDGE
57. ARCHER HEIGHTS
58. BRIGHTON PARK
59. McKINLEY PARK
60. BRIDGEPORT
61. NEW CITY
62. WEST ELSDON
63. GAGE PARK
64. CLEARING
65. WEST LAWN
66. CHICAGO LAWN
67. WEST ENGLEWOOD
68. ENGLEWOOD
69. GREATER GRAND CROSSING
70. ASHBURN
71. AUBURN GRESHAM
72. BEVERLY
73. WASHINGTON HEIGHTS
74. MOUNT GREENWOOD
75. MORGAN PARK
76. O'HARE
77. EDGEWATER

1

Introduction:
Language and Identity in a Global City

Marcia Farr
Ohio State University

Rachel Reynolds
Drexel University

At the onset of the 21st century, the words "global" and "globalization" have begun to appear everywhere: in academe, in the popular press and electronic media, and even in everyday conversation. Like the words "multiculturalism," "democracy," and "community" (Urciuoli, 1999), the word "globalization" is best examined for meaning in specific contexts, wherein it may signify, among other things, a push for free market economic practice across the globe, the spread of American iconic images through media and products, or a growing sense of Western responsibility for economic and political effects on people and the environment planet-wide. Some treat "the global" as a sociological term, expressing the blended or hybrid nature of people, goods, and cultural practices that has resulted from the dissolution of traditional boundaries regarding gender, nationality, ethnicity, and politics. The politically intense aspects of globalization are especially immanent now, in the wake of the September 11, 2001 terrorist attack on the World Trade Center in New York, a symbol not only of the United States, but also of Western economic and cultural globalization.

Although the chapters in this book are not specifically about globalization, the worldwide processes that comprise it do pervade the chapters. Globalization provides a backdrop, a context, within which the people represented in these chapters live (or lived) their lives. More than globalization, however, much of the work in this book is embedded in transnationalism. Globalization often is contrasted with transnationalism. For some, the latter is a subordinate term, both chronologically and structurally (Kearney, 1995). That is, nation building is seen as preceding the transfer of goods and people across borders, so transnationalism is presumed to be a historical precursor to globalization. Transnationalism is seen as a small piece of global processes, as deterritorialization involves "new kinds of political actors," among whom the economic and political intersections between ethnic groups and the state are recast (Guerra, 1998; Kotkin, 1993, p. 5; Sassen, 1998; Stack, 1981). Thus people become "deterritorialized" as they move and work across nation–state borders. With worldwide air travel, telecommunications, and ever-more-rapid flows of information, the deterritorialization of national and ethnic groups becomes even more intense. That is, movement of people across the globe has increased (Harvey, 1990; Giddens, 2000). One outcome of these new and large-scale migrations is the need to study the predicaments of deterritorialization, particularly for immigrants (Basch, Glick-Schiller, & Szanton-Blanc, 1994; Holtzman, 2000).

Many of the chapters in this volume take as their subject of inquiry the ethnolinguistic practices of those people who experience deterritorialization. Other chapters, which focus instead on the ethnolinguistic practices of class or racialized groups, similarly trace a movement through the social landscape marked by deeply felt group affiliation (and sometimes exclusion). Unlike theories of globalization, which assert that the new world order involves the erosion of ethnic group identities, the groups represented in this volume have strongly felt affiliations, struggling less with hybrid identities than with adaptive responses to the trials of life as immigrants or as groups whose practices and self-perceptions are outside the dominant mainstream. (Other types of ethnic formation include blended identities and the development of new ones that replace the old, but these are topics to be treated elsewhere.) Indeed, a central theoretical bias of this volume, and of the methods used to generate the social and linguistic data presented here, is that despite the movement toward a "global monoculture," implied and sometimes seen in studies of free market capital and international media marketing, a typical response to globalization often is the entrenchment of highly marked ethnic, class, and religious identities. The eloquent and complex ways in which people of varying class, ethnic, and racial groups (including "mainstream" groups) express their multiple identities here in Chicago is a testament to how much more we need to study class and ethnic formation on the ground.

"Borderlands" studies, focusing on the interface between peoples as they move across borders, provide another relevant context in which to view the work in this volume. Extrapolating from the 2,000-mile U.S.–Mexican border, scholars now use the term "border" metaphorically: A border exists wherever differing "social practices and cultural beliefs" confront each other "in a contemporary global context" (Alvarez, 1995, p. 448). Staudt and Spener (1998) viewed the border "as an ongoing dialectical process which generates multiple borderland spaces" (p. 2) some of which are quite distant from actual international boundaries. Rouse (1991), studying a transnational community located in Redwood City, California, and Aguililla, Michoacán, Mexico, saw "a proliferation of border zones" and the eruption of "miniature borders" throughout both Mexico and the United States (p. 17).

Chicago evidences these multiple miniature borders both in contemporary and historical terms. It could be argued, in fact, that Chicago has always been a global city with transnational populations (Holli & Jones, 1977/1995) confronting each other, creating "miniature borders" all over the city. Certainly, Chicago is known for its cultural and linguistic diversity, its mosaic of ethnic neighborhoods, but just as clearly, this is a scene that now has become characteristic of many more U.S. regions and cities. Furthermore, the social geography of immigration is developing in complex new ways. Professional immigrants from Asia and Africa are settling increasingly in far-flung suburban neighborhoods, choosing to locate near employment rather than move de facto into ethnic enclaves. Not living in close proximity, these groups then often create new institutions (e.g., ethnic associations) and channels of communication (e.g., the Internet) in which to come together and share a common heritage.

The chapters presented in this volume thus ask and begin to answer the following questions: How did these groups come to live in Chicago? Have they maintained their "traditional" identities, their own ways of speaking, dialects, and languages? Alternatively, have they recreated or transformed these social and cultural practices, including linguistic ones? How does communication change from one generation to the next? Why does language use across the generations change, and what does this mean as the demographic and linguistic composition of the United States continues to change? How do Chicago's historical ethnic enclaves compare with current ethnically segregated neighborhoods, particularly in relation to the creation of ethnic literature and other writing? How do changing political relationships "back home" appear in ethnic discourse in Chicago? How are immigrants and class groups adapting their linguistic practices to aspects of globalization, including the worldwide women's rights movement, and the increasing use of English as a global language, as well as the English-only movement in the United States? Does the increasing compression of space and time through communication and travel technology affect language maintenance and group identity? What impact do different communicative practices have on people in multicultural work spaces, or in our public and private schools, and how can we be more intelligent about the issues that disrupt that communication and cross-cultural understanding?

NON-ENGLISH TONGUES AND THE UNITED STATES

Despite a multilingual and multicultural history that dates back to the founding of the country, the United States has had an ambivalent relationship with cultural diversity in general, and with non-English languages and nonstandard English dialects in particular. Although nation building has been entwined with insistence on the official status and dominance of English, non-English languages nevertheless have been used regularly throughout U.S. history in government agencies, courts, newspapers, schools, and other public contexts (Ferguson & Heath, 1981).

Current national debates over such diversity invoke and repeat earlier debates in the second half of the 19th century over German language and culture, and in the early 20th century over heavy migration from Eastern and Southern Europe. Some claim that the fervor in recent decades against non-English languages and their speakers is intensified by the experience of language loss in earlier generations of European immigrants, especially by the numerous German speakers in this country up until World War I (Baron, 1990; Judd, this volume). After that, German was quickly dropped by its speakers and in school curricula. Yet because of the broad range of ethnic groups and their numerical strength in the history of

Chicago, conflict over linguistic and cultural diversity has been more muted here than elsewhere in the United States, at least in recent years. Consequently, Chicago presents an interesting contrast to California or Florida, for example, where such conflict is more publicly salient. The recent debate over bilingual education in Chicago, for example, questioned the length, not the existence of, bilingual programs in the public schools. (Official policy now limits bilingual education to 3 years.)

Chicago has a long history of economic vitality and diversity, and it remains an attractive destination for people ready and willing to work in a variety of industries. For example, Lithuanians, Poles, and African Americans came here to work in the stockyards at the turn of the 20th century, and Mexicans arrived in droves in the 1920s to sustain the iron and steelworks located in south Chicago. Today, highly educated South Asians, East Asians, and Africans are vital to the western suburban technology corridor, while the African American middle class and Mexican working class continue to arrive here. Other ethnic groups are part of the long trajectory in which Irish, Greeks, Poles, Italians, and others continue to flow into the working- and middle-class neighborhoods that their forbears found welcoming.

If the numerous ethnic groups in Chicago's historic neighborhoods have created a somewhat more tolerant ambience toward diversity, or at least a more realistic acceptance of it, they also have anticipated the cultural and linguistic diversity now evident across the entire United States, especially, but not entirely, in urban areas. As noted earlier, an increasingly globalized world economy has fomented migratory streams all over the world (Rosenau, 1997; Sassen, 1998; Wallerstein, 1974). In this hemisphere, the United States is the primary destination of these migrant labor forces, followed by Canada and Argentina (United Nations, 1988). Atlanta and other southern locales, for example, now host a substantial number of Mexicans, disrupting the traditional black–white racial dichotomy (Murphy, Blanchard, & Hill, 1999). Such populations increase not only because of economic "push and pull" factors (e.g., the wage differential between Mexico and the United States; pressures from U.S. businesses for minimum-wage workers), but also through the reconstituting, over time, of virtually entire villages in the United States (Farr, 2000, forthcoming; Rouse, 1992).

Most chapters in this volume arose from ground-level studies within social networks. Transnational social networks (i.e., groups of family and friends both "back home" and in the destination site) facilitate the communication that feeds transnational movement and growth. Migration to the United States probably has always proceeded through family networks and transnational communication. For example, the massive German migrations throughout the 19th century were stimulated at least in part by family networks, letters, emigration handbooks, and newspapers (Kamhoefner, Helbich, & Sommer, 1991; Trommler & McVeigh, 1985).

Furthermore, once settled in American neighborhoods, families rely on social networks to carry out ethnic socialization of youth born in the United States, with some groups maintaining a sense of heritage and a network of foreign social ties that last for several generations—a phenomenon that we are only beginning to understand (Constantakos & Spiridakis, 1997; Gans, 1999, p. 1304). Our understanding of ethnic formation or "ethnification" is something that may change as jet travel and telecommunications facilitate constant contact between ethnic groups and their home countries. Indeed, the fact that transnational mechanisms are markedly more extensive now than a century ago may cause significant changes in how ethnic formation comes about in the United States (Friedman, 1999). Even so, the contemporary diversity in the United States no doubt has its origins in U.S. history, even while apparently unique in pace and heterogeneity, with people now coming from all over the world. The studies in this volume explore this diversity through a focus on language use in a city that is both diverse and archtypical of the larger United States.

This volume is the first of a pair. It focuses on ethnolinguistic variation among groups with origins in Europe, the Middle East, Africa, and Asia. Because of the recent intense growth in Spanish-speaking populations, the second volume focuses entirely on Mexicans and Puerto Ricans, the two largest Latino groups in Chicago and in the United States. The studies in both volumes together contribute to our understanding of ethnolinguistic diversity by showing how it is woven into the fabric of daily life in Chicago, both historically and currently, and how it is an inevitable aspect of human life. Although important work has documented the history of various ethnic Chicago enclaves (Holli & Jones, 1977/1995), and sociologists have abundantly studied numerous "community areas" (Chicago Fact Book Consortium, 1995), the role of language, either oral or written, in these diverse communities has not yet received systematic attention. Garcia and Fishman's (1997) *The Multilingual Apple: Languages in New York City* is a notable exception, although it does not address variation within languages, only between them. Although researchers in the field of sociolinguistics have long studied regional and social dialect variation (see, for example, recent work on African American vernacular English in Baugh, 1999, 2000; and Rickford, 1999), ethnographic approaches to this kind of variation have been fewer. These two volumes begin to address this lacuna by presenting "slices of language life" involving both multilingualism and within-language variation in specific home and community settings.

LANGUAGE AND IDENTITY: ETHNICITY, CLASS, AND GENDER

Although most people have experienced the intensely felt tie between language and ethnicity, they commonly think of language with a capital "L," referring holistically, for example, to individual languages such as Spanish, Hebrew, or Navajo (Fishman, 1997). Language diversity, according to this definition of "language," simply means multilingualism, or the use of several different languages in one society or group. In contrast, the researchers whose work appears in these volumes view language diversity more broadly, and include attention to variation within languages. For example, monolingual Americans routinely use one or more varieties of English. That is, they may speak a more standard variety of American English (acquired perhaps in school) along with a regional, class, or ethnic dialect. Their shifting from one variety of English to another roughly parallels the code switching that is characteristic of multilingual populations.

The speakers in the various chapters of this volume evidence one or the other pattern of diversity, and sometimes both. They may, for example, speak multiple languages such as Arabic, Spanish, and English (see Radloff's chapter), and in some cases, groups of people speak multiple varieties of these languages, perhaps both a rural variety of their home language and its standard counterpart. Furthermore, as they learn English in Chicago, they may code switch between their home language and English, or when more than one vernacular variety of the home language exists in Chicago, they may blend varieties. Ultimately, they often borrow English words and phrases and incorporate them into the home language, as did the Swedes (see Isaacson's chapter) and the Greeks (see Koliussi's chapter). Thus "Swinglish" and "Greeklish" parallel contemporary "Spanglish" (see the forthcoming volume on Latinos).

These studies also analyze stylistic dimensions of language use, or "ways of speaking" (Hymes, 1974b), along with practices involving written language or literacy. Indeed, more attention is paid in these studies to the uses or functions of language, oral and/or written, in the daily life of these groups than to the structural or formal characteristics (e.g., pronunciation or syntactic patterns) of the language varieties they speak. Shifting between and among these language varieties, whether from language to language or from one dialect of a language to another, often is about social attachment, signifying group membership and solidarity. Although, of course, language use does in a certain sense begin at the level of the individual who uses the tool of language toward individually motivated ends, the studies in this volume look at how individuals with similar backgrounds and interests create, reinforce, and share mutual interests with each other through language. As Tabouret-Keller (1997) pointed out, our language use creates our social identities, whether that language use involves one or more varieties of one language, code switching between two languages, or new varieties of language created by combining elements from various languages or dialects. For monolingual Americans, language use most often involves one or more varieties of one language (e.g., the use of Standard American English along with a regional or ethnic dialect). More often in this volume, speakers code switch between two languages, or they transfer stylistic patterns, (e.g., of joking and storytelling) from an "ethnic" language to their new language, English (Gumperz & Cook-Gumperz, 1982).

Most of the language represented in this volume is a non standard variety of a "capital L" Language. In fact, the works in this volume show that immigrants rarely use the standard variety of their language. For example, the Lithuanian and Swedish immigrants represented in the historical studies presented all spoke regional, non standard dialects of their respective languages at home. Many in these populations had to choose to learn standard varieties of their home languages in the United States in order to communicate with each other and to share standardized ethnic institutions such as newspapers and schooling. These processes have implications for a new shift toward the codification of ethnic culture through culturally sensitive curricula and standardized language varieties (see also King, 2001 for a discussion on Quichua standardization). The ways that immigration has contributed to the standardization of languages "abroad" warrants further investigation.

Upon arrival here, many immigrants must attain competence in the English varieties to be accepted amicably by their neighbors, employers, or customers. For some immigrants, that may also mean learning Mexican Spanish or African American English. Immigrant speakers of English are acutely aware that their new American neighbors label them by their imperfect use of the standard, or that even if they speak the most "proper" (i.e., grammatically standard) English, English spoken with a nonnative "accent" (i.e., pronunciation) instantly evokes the ethnic difference between them and their U.S.-born neighbors.

Furthermore, it is not only the surface features of language use, such as simplified grammar or nonnative phonology, that mark immigrants as different. Favored genres and other ways of speaking also distinguish culture groups, and many immigrants use culturally specific rhetorical devices such as Italian *bella figura* (see Nardini's chapter) as a performance of solidarity. That culture-specific literacy and orality practices are often at odds with dominant standards is also a source of trouble for immigrant children who must adapt to standard English forms and uses in school. For example, the ideology embedded in essayist modes of writing (notably the five-paragraph composition class essay and other genres promoting an "objective" tone that removes the personal voice of the author) often runs counter to the linguistic expectations of the home culture to which immigrant students and nonstandard dialect-speaking students belong (Farr, 1993).

If we identify ourselves and others by the way we speak, we also use other markers. Language is only one means of identity differentiation in semiotic systems that include neighborhood boundaries, clothing, food, types of houses and decor, and even kinesthetics (i.e., how people move their bodies through space). Given the persistence of identity differentiation, we can assume that semiotic markers will "place" people in terms of various identities, and, moreover, that language will be a central means of placement, whether that placement is generated from inside the group or imposed from the outside. Certainly, language, in addition to other markers, delineates White and non-White groups in the United States, for example in the cases of Native American English (sometimes called Indian English), African American English, and Spanglish (Spanish-English codeswitching). Recently developed conceptualizations of language ideology explicitly link beliefs about language, including both vernacular and standard varieties, to broader sociocultural and political processes (Kroskrity, 2000; Philips, 1998; Schieffelin, Woolard, & Kroskrity, 1998). As Woolard (1998) noted, language ideologies are never just about language. They also involve such notions as personhood and group identity vis à vis others. As people from different cultural groups establish conventional ways of using language, they simultaneously organize relations among people and define "us," as opposed to "them," in terms of specific moral, aesthetic, and other qualities.

In addition to ethnic identities, language also expresses and constructs class identities. Thus vernacular varieties of English, whatever the ethnicity or race, identify speakers as working class. For example, class is quite salient for people of "mixed" European ethnicities in Chicago, but it is omnipresent even when more implicit than explicit. Lindquist's chapter explores just this dynamic in its analysis of argumentative rhetoric in a White working-class bar on the south side of Chicago. Here people identify, and are identified, as "White," a privileged category. More implicitly, however, especially in their rhetorical use of language, they are marked as, and construct themselves as, working class, an unprivileged category that is less salient in daily life than their "racial" status, but nevertheless disempowering. Cho and P. Miller's chapter provides another example of how class is implicitly constructed through speakers' use of language, focusing in this instance on differential preferences for a particular oral genre. When interviewed in their own homes, mothers from a White, working-class neighborhood told three times as many stories of personal experience as their counterparts from a middle-class neighborhood. The working-class women not only privileged personal storytelling, but also used this genre to construct a perspective that spotlighted the hardships and challenges of family life and the harsh realities that children would face. Both of these chapters are based in Chicago neighborhoods composed of "old" rather than "new" immigrants (i.e., descendants of immigrants rather than contemporary immigrants) who speak only English, and who have few continuing ties to Old World countries. In contrast, U.S. contexts provided for Swedish (and Lithuanian) peasants, for the first time, a means by which to transcend class affiliations. As Isaacson's chapter explains, the complex struggle between Swedish immigrants to use four different language varieties (proper Swedish, country Swedish, American Swedish, and English) demonstrates the social turbulence within a migration order that is forming new class affiliations in the New World.

Gender is also an inextricable part of language use, and, like class and ethnicity, it is not only expressed but also constructed linguistically. Women's favored genres often differ from those of men, and for many immigrant groups, gender roles change over the generations with the move from, for example, a traditional agrarian context to a modern urban one in the United States. Such changes include norms for appropriate female behavior, including linguistic behavior. Tensions that arise over such changes, as well as their sometime resolution, are evident in the language practices of both women and men (Farr, 1994). Nardini's chapter on Italian American women and their use of the rhetorical strategy of *bella figura* to wrest power from their men is an example of this. Koliussi also deals with this dynamic, including in her analysis the interaction between Greek men and women, as some women promote gender changes discursively during female gatherings. Morgan's chapter also focuses on changes in gender through time, but instead of presenting a context of migration, she describes African American women settled for many generations in Chicago. As these women of a single generation age, they practice and adapt their rhetorical presentation of the self to the times and to a changing self-image.

When the topics or contexts of talk are specifically about class, ethnic, or gender identity, these are, following Susan Philip's discussion of an idea developed by Stuart Hall, "key sites" for these highly marked linguistic practices. Philips uses the notion of "site" to highlight those situations in which ideology is most punctiliously brought up and instantiated, as hot spots in which "powerful ideological work" is being done (Philips, 2000, pp. 232–233). For example, the choice of a writing system, a language, or a particular dialect of a language may signify an entirely different ideology and identity in the new immigrant context, as opposed to "back home" (see the chapters by Rohsenow, Miller, and Isaacson in this volume). Such key sites are methodologically distinct from the ways in which linguists use the term "context", (i.e., an analytical unit based on real-time speech and real gatherings of people).

In the chapters of this volume, the investigators have chosen either contexts of verbal performance (oral or written) or group-specific ways of speaking because they are key sites of identity construction, or reconstruction, in terms of class, ethnicity, or gender. These include public spaces and institutions such as an accountant's office, a bar, and ethnic newspapers, as well as informal, intimate, and private spaces and genres such as a family kitchen or personal letters.

Sometimes what is meaningful in key sites, then, emerges from the forms and uses of speech, and not from overt topics of discussion. Language thus expresses and constructs identities either subconsciously through the choice of dialects, standards, or culturally marked rhetorical styles, or consciously through overt ideological talk that groups use to define themselves. Because such issues are best studied ethnographically, most of the work in these two volumes on ethnolinguistic diversity was undertaken within the framework of the ethnography of communication (Hymes, 1974a). Those chapters that are not explicitly ethnographies of communication are nevertheless compatible with this framework. In the next sections, we discuss this framework and its methodology.

METHODOLOGY

Chicago provides an abundance of fertile natural settings in which identities are linguistically constructed. Because so much identity formation emerges in felt contrasts with others (Barth, 1968; Cohen, 1978), the diversity of the city, and its multiple "miniature borders," makes it particularly productive for research on this topic. The chapters in this book, and in its companion volume, rely on the assets of the city as well as methodological resources in a variety of ways.

First of all, because insider or "emic" understandings of various communities are fundamental to valid understandings of the ways identities are constructed in language, most of the chapters rely on ethnographic methods and perspectives in their research. That is, they rely on participant observation, deep listening, a holistic focus, and, implicitly or explicitly, a comparative sense. Even those chapters not based on ethnographic fieldwork, for example, those that are historical or descriptive in focus, nevertheless are compatible with ethnography in spirit. Long-term involvement and familiarity with the communities studied and careful attention to local, not just researcher-generated meanings, then, characterize all the work. Moreover, the discourse analysis used in many chapters documents the ways people use language to construct, or reconstruct, social and cultural realities, including their identities.

Second, because all of these chapters are centered on language, either in its spoken or written mode, material samples of language have been gathered for analysis. Oral language has been tape-recorded (with the permission of the speakers), selected, transcribed, and studied in different ways. Written language has been collected as artifacts (e.g., newspapers, magazines, and letters). Both modes of language have been explored for local meanings through oral interviews. All these instances of language in use, however, even augmented by the understandings generated from interviews, would be incomplete without broader (and deeper) ethnographic understandings of the contexts in which they occurred naturally. In what follows we selectively present key concepts developed within an ethnographic approach to the study of language that contribute to a comprehensive understanding of language, both oral and written, and its constitutive role in social and cultural life. These concepts are utilized differentially across the chapters.

THE ETHNOGRAPHY LANGUAGE

Dell Hymes' call four decades ago for an anthropology of language was intended to fill an important gap: the study of language grounded equally in linguistic and cultural realities. He argued that the study of culturally situated language was falling into a gap between disciplines. On one hand, linguistics focused on cognitive rather than social aspects of language, and on the other, anthropology, although carried out through language, often through a language nonnative to the researcher, ignored language almost entirely. His original conceptualization of the ethnography of speaking (Gumperz & Hymes, 1964, 1972/1986) eventually broadened to the ethnography of communication (Saville-Troike, 1989) and spawned the ethnography of literacy (Street, 1984, 1993; Szwed, 1981). Much work following this latter tradition has been stimulated by social concerns regarding inequities in education and literacy. Important though such studies are, they unfortunately increasingly have ignored the relevance of oral language practices to these concerns, even though understandings of literacy are deepened and enriched by attention to oral practices among populations learning or using literacy (Farr, 1993), despite serious critique of an orality–literacy dichotomy (Collins & Blot, 2003; Street, 1984). In spite of the fact that Heath's (1983) seminal research relied centrally on oral language patterns to illuminate educational and literacy issues, much other work has not been equally grounded in a deep understanding of language as the base from which literacy springs. Notable exceptions in this regard are the studies of Besnier (1995), Boyarin (1992), and Finnegan (1988). The studies in this book, and in its companion volume on Latinos in Chicago, attempt to redress this imbalance by attending to both modes of language use in the daily life of Chicagoans.

Attention to both oral and written language has flourished in the field that Hymes, Gumperz, and others invigorated (Bauman & Sherzer, 1974/1989; Duranti, 1997, 2001; Gumperz, 1982a, 1982b), showing how language, carefully studied, can illuminate other aspects of social, cultural, and political life. Sherzer (1987), quoting Boas (1911), pointed out that "language pat-

terns are unconscious and provide access to unconscious cultural pattern-
ing otherwise inaccessible to researchers" (p. 295). Some aspects of social
and cultural life cannot be understood simply by asking people about them,
as Briggs (1986) showed, although this is how most social science, including cultural anthropology, proceeds. Briggs argued that we need to treat the
interview instead as a communicative event, a social practice negotiated by
interviewer and informant. This methodological insight has far-reaching implications for researchers concerned with cultural and linguistic variation.
For example, Cho and Miller demonstrate in their chapter that interviews
take systematically different forms in the two communities they studied, reflecting variation in local communicative practice. In particular, although
their interviews focused on the topic of storytelling, only the working-class
women spontaneously demonstrated their affinity for narrative by enacting
it, carrying the whole interview in a narrative direction.

Sherzer (1987) showed how discourse, which he defines as language
use, oral or written, brief (e.g., a greeting) or lengthy (e.g., a novel or oral narrative), is "the nexus, the actual and concrete expression of the language–culture–society relationship" (p. 296). Thus through discourse
analysis researchers can illuminate social and cultural patterns. Discourse
then is constitutive: both culture and language are created, recreated, and
changed through language use or discourse. Furthermore, particular kinds
of discourse are especially fertile for this:

> It is especially in verbally artistic discourse such as poetry, magic, verbal du-
> eling, and political rhetoric that the potentials and resources provided by
> grammar, as well as cultural meanings and symbols, are exploited to the full-
> est and the essence of language–culture relationships becomes salient.
> (Sherzer, 1987, p. 296)

Poetics and Performance

The study of verbal art, or ethnopoetics, as developed by Hymes (1975,
1981), Bauman (1977/1984, 1986), Bauman and Briggs (1990), Tedlock
(1983), Sherzer (1987, 1990), Tannen (1989), and others, has developed
cultural analysis via discourse analysis with notions of poetics and verbal
performance, including speech play. Performance can occur in formal,
scheduled, public events (in which primarily males perform in most cultures), or it can emerge spontaneously in everyday conversation (a frequent province of female performers). Bauman (1977/1984) set out the
empirically observable characteristics of verbal performance, which he

sees as the unifying thread tying together various artistic genres in a unified conception of verbal or spoken art as a way of speaking:

1. There is a "focus on the message for its own sake" (Jakobson, 1960, p. 356); that is, the form of the message is important beyond the need for communication. The function of the particular discourse is, then, poetic, in Jakobson's terms. Various linguistic devices can be used to accomplish this, a central one being parallelism, the "empirical linguistic criterion of the poetic function" (Jakobson, 1960, p. 358). Parallelism involves repetition, sometimes with variation of semantic, syntactic, or phonological (including intonational) structures, and seems to be a fundamental, possibly universal, characteristic of verbal art. More recent work shows how oral narrative can be considered a kind of poetry, in that spoken lines from speeches and personal narratives are organized in terms of verses, stanzas, scenes (Hymes, 1999; Hymes, 2002; Ochs & Capps, 2001).

2. Performance reframes "usual" or ordinary language use that often fulfills a referential function in which words carry "literal" meaning. That is, hearers are signaled that words are to be understood in some special sense. Linguistic devices that signal a performance frame include, but are not limited to, a change in code (language), figurative language (e.g., metaphors), parallelism, and paralinguistic features, (e.g., pitch contour, rate of speaking, loudness) (Tedlock, 1983).

3. Performance is the authoritative display of communicative competence by a "performer" that is evaluated by an "audience." That is, there is a shared assumption among participants that hearers will judge those who verbally perform as good or not-so-good storytellers, jokers, preachers, and the like.

4. Performance is marked as available for "the enhancement of experience" in the present moment. That is, there is a "special intensity" on the part of the audience (e.g., bodies and faces turn towards the performer and other talking ceases).

Performance, then, makes language highly "noticeable." That is, linguistic devices used to make a particular stretch of language a "performance" (e.g., the telling of a joke or story) also make a "text" stand out from surrounding speech. Language that "stands out" in this way facilitates its own critical examination:

> Performances move the use of heterogeneous stylistic resources, context-sensitive meanings, and conflicting ideologies into a reflexive arena where they can

be examined critically. . . . Performance . . . provides a frame that invites critical
reflection on communicative processes. (Bauman & Briggs, 1990, p. 60)

Thus performances of verbal art are not just interesting aesthetically, but
also are particularly salient sites for the creation, recreation, and transformation of culture and society. Farr (1994, 1998, forthcoming), for example,
showed how Mexican women, during a way of speaking they call *echando
relajo* (joking around), challenge traditional gender roles through performances of verbal art. These verbal poetics, performed in all-female contexts, serve to build support for and affirm the kinds of changes they are
making in their now transnational lives. Such "play frames . . . provide settings in which speech and society can be questioned and transformed"
(Bauman & Briggs, 1990, p. 63) and so have ramifications for reconfiguring
social relations.

Genre

The concept of genre itself has been central in considering the interrelationships between language and culture (Briggs & Bauman, 1992; Hanks 2000;
Philips, 1987) and in studies of verbal art. A persistent aspect of work on genre
revolves around the question of how to define the concept itself, key defining
features being characteristics of form (i.e., how the writing or speech is organized in jokes, stories, plays, letters, and so on). Equally important as defining
features, however, are shared frameworks for reception and interpretation,
as well as the larger sociocultural context in which concrete instances of genres are actualized (Hanks, 2000).

Genre as used in studies in this volume, then, involves not only aspects
of form, but also the dimensions of function and reception—that is, how
audience and performer come together in a specific context to share the
meaning of a performance and to accomplish a particular function. Thus
local understandings of concrete instances of genres rely not only on form,
but also on the broader context in which they occur and the specific functions these instances serve.

A final aspect of work on genre concerns the organization of genres
themselves within particular local communities and the ideological implications of this organization. For example, the association of genre and gender when genres are organized hierarchically affirms the hierarchy of
genders in social relations. In addition, it can be important to note for particular communities which genres have local names (e.g., for praying, joking,
gossiping) and which do not (e.g., making *bella figura* is important to Italian

Americans but is not named as such; see the Nardini chapter) and why this might be so. In some languages, moreover, the etymological source of a genre name can be revealing (Hymes, personal communication).

Although, as Briggs and Bauman (1992) observed, genre has been associated with order for quite some time in Western thought, in actuality, the organization of genres and their boundaries in real discourse are much less ordered and neat. Communities differ in the extent to which their genres are organized, and the "messy underside of people's speech" (Briggs & Bauman, 1992, p. 140) is more the rule than the exception. This "messiness" in people's real speech is due to the lack of fixed and discrete (empirical) boundaries of genres. Instead, genres sometimes overlap one another, and often are found in complex shapes in which some genres "absorb and digest" other genres (Briggs & Bauman, 1992, p. 145; Bakhtin, 1986). Cho and Miller's chapter shows that the genre of personal storytelling pervaded the whole interview for working-class women but not for middle-class women. Working-class speakers repeatedly returned to particular stories and produced cascades of interlinked stories, transforming the interview into a narrative task. Thus genres do not always occur as discrete texts in daily life. That is, they are not fixed, timeless structures. Rather, they are general frameworks, or sets of expectations, according to which people generate and interpret discourse for specific social, cultural, and political ends. These expectations are shared assumptions that have formal, functional, and contextual characteristics. That is, people associate certain features of form (e.g., the framing device associated with jokes: "Have you heard the one about . . ."), function (e.g., understanding that joking is not to be taken seriously), and context (e.g., joking sessions are associated with informal and private rather than public and formal settings) with specific genres (in our examples here, jokes as a genre).

Speakers and hearers then draw on these general sets of expectations as they organize discursive life, and in turn, daily discourse can create, recreate, or change generic expectations. That is, the use of genres is a two-way street: Shared understandings of culturally specific genres organize our linguistic and social life, but these same genres change through use and time, just as they are used either to maintain or to change aspects of our social order. When the performance of artful verbal genres, themselves already highly changeable by nature, is conjoined to the ways that immigrants negotiate their way through multiple cultures and culture change across generations, these forms become even richer sites for experimentation with language and identity.

In what follows, we provide an overview of the chapters in this volume, paying special attention to the ways in which they utilize the themes, concepts, and issues we have reviewed so far in this Introduction. All the chapters deal with language and identity, whether that identity is national (Judd, Markelis, Rohsenow, & L. Miller), ethnic (Moss, Reynolds, & Radloff), class affiliated (Cho & P. Miller, Isaacson, & Lindquist), or gendered (Koliussi, Nardini, & Morgan). Most of the chapters echo and implicate questions of transnationalism and globalization (all except Morgan, Cho and P. Miller, Lindquist, and Moss). In terms of language itself, all of the chapters focus either on oral genres and the performance of verbal art (Cho & P. Miller, Koliussi, Nardini, Morgan, Moss, Reynolds, & Lindquist), or on a broader treatment of both oral and written language use (Judd, Radloff, Isaacson, Markelis, Rohsenow, & L. Miller).

OVERVIEW OF CHAPTERS

For groups long settled in Chicago, four historical chapters describe the multigenerational processes of adjustment, acculturation, accommodation, and assimilation. What is striking about these chapters is the focal status that literacy institutions such as ethnic newspapers, ethnic schools, and immigrant novels all reflect in the negotiation of a new identity that is partly Old World and partly New World. As these immigrant groups begin their lives in Chicago, the acquisition of literacy is central to the negotiation of new class formations, in which among other things, ethnic newspapers provide proscriptive guidelines for proper modern behavior to a former peasant class, and many ethnic publications debate questions of language and politics. The literary work of historical figures in Isaacson's chapter especially exposes the fault lines that arise when immigration is crossed with class ascension. Isaacson's Swedish American writers are faced with three linguistic choices. Some choose to use Standard Swedish from the Old World despite the fact that its use signals class prejudice back in Sweden, in marked contrast to most Swedish immigrants' use of rural dialects. Other pundits attempt to forge a progressive Swedish American identity in which an updated and hybrid blend of Swedish and English is used as an ideological tool to celebrate and promote the ways American egalitarianism will allow former peasants to own land and businesses. It is, however, the Swedish domestic maids' acquisition of standard American English (and literacy) that is emblematic of those immigrants' ability to evade Swedish class politics even while stepping up the American class ladder, at least symbolically and for that generation.

In another ethnohistorical chapter, Markelis reconstructs the political history of Lithuanians through their literacy and orality practices in a Chicago neighborhood. As for the Swedes studied by Isaacson and the Chinese studied by Rohsenow, Lithuanian language standardization politics back home had important implications for cultural and linguistic preservation abroad. Markelis notes that as soon as Russian political persecution against the Lithuanian language stopped when Lithuania gained its independence in 1918, the language immediately became less important for Chicago Lithuanians. This phenomenon raises the question touched on in Rohsenow's chapter as to how peace between Taiwan and The People's Republic of China might have an impact on Chinese ethnic formation and language maintenance in the United States. Markelis also examines class dimensions among Lithuanians whose cooperative sense of literacy (in the workplace, in the home, on the streets) and commitment to community education maintained a vibrant Lithuanian community into the second and third generations.

Markelis' chapter parallels Judd's historical discussion of American immigrants' struggles to maintain bicultural and bilingual lives. One of the most peculiar and long-term political problems in the United States results from the incorrect assumption that immigrants (willfully) do not learn English. English-only movements in the United States, for example, at best work under the presumption that immigrants need a push to learn English, whereas laws that proscribe the use of non-English languages are xenophobic and carry with them punitive dimensions. These presumptions seem particularly ironic, considering that nearly half of mainstream Anglo-Americans descend from German immigrants in the 19th Century. As Judd points out with reference to the linguistic effects of World Wars I and II in the United States, "We can see how delicate linguistic freedoms are and how in times of crisis, real or imaginary, some people begin to equate linguistic diversity with disloyalty" (Judd, this volume).

What monolingual Americans do not always realize is that nearly all immigrants do indeed learn English, and that the acquisition of English literacy is in and of itself a special social practice, as Markelis' chapter illustrates. The French, Lithuanians, Swedes, and Germans who populate the historical chapters of this volume absorbed English on the streets, through the media, and in schools, acquiring literacy with it. Furthermore, every immigrant group represented in these chapters demonstraties two shared features of American immigrants: first, immigrant children are nearly always raised as (near) native speakers of English. Second, immigrants have clear incentives to learn English and move up in the world. Notably, in this volume four of the authors are bilingual and bicultural first- or second-generation immigrants who not only learned English, but also achieved high levels of literacy in it, although raised in bilingual environments.

Rohsenow's chapter explains in intricate detail how politics abroad and intergroup politics in the United States have had a deep impact on its Chinese American community. For example, even the very choice of scripts taught in local heritage language schools has become politicized. Schools funded by supporters of Taiwan claim the authority of tradition by providing written teaching materials printed in old-style, nonsimplified Chinese characters, as opposed to materials printed in the simplified script used in the Peoples Republic of China after the 1950s. Additionally, many people of Chinese origin are secondary or tertiary immigrants with rich social and interethnic connections across Southeast Asia. They are in large part the driving force behind business development in a mixed-ethnic Asian community on the north side of Chicago. The extraordinarily long history of Chinese immigration to the United States, including the separatist tradition between the Chinese and the Americans, until recently reinforced the extreme boundedness of Chinese neighborhoods. For example, this history has created very tightly knit Cantonese (Guangzhou) enclaves from an older era of immigration dating back to the 1860s. The speech of the old timers contrasts not only with speakers of other Chinese dialects (from other areas of China), but also with that of more recent immigrants. In Chicago's Chinatown, contemporary Canton (Guangzhou) and Hong Kong city dialects of Chinese (including their fashionable slang) and the new immigrants who speak them are supplanting the older Cantonese Toisan dialect spoken by elderly and second-generation immigrants and their descendants. Thus, Rohsenow's chapter develops historical perspective on how ethnicity and language use in Chicago neighborhoods is shaped not only by local politics, but also by changes "back home," and by multiple waves of immigration.

Another fruitful element in the historical chapters is the question they raise as to whether assimilation to the American scene is really an earlier form of globalization. Chapters such as these allow us to compare ethnic formation and maintenance today with that of the past. For example, do contemporary immigrants differ from earlier waves of immigrants, because today's groups are more likely to be affected by global time–space compression? Indeed, the chapter by Reynolds begins to look at how ethnic actors are forming a sense of identity across global contexts. As a small and just-beginning wave of immigrants, these African people are setting the stage for future immigrants. The speech genre, prayers of invocation, that Reynolds explores involves mental and linguistic acts of space–time compression. The prayers use poetic speech to minimize the distance between Nigeria and the United States in terms both of time and space, in service of ethnic cohesion. In other words, instead of being "postnational," this group of Igbo immigrants may be the first in a line of global Africans, groups who use communication technology and travel opportunities to maintain strong ethnic and national affiliations across extreme distances without regard to actual physical borders. Likewise, the ideological constructs with which they express immigrant identity are iconic of the shrinkage of time–space, mending the disjunctures of deterritorialization with symbolic words. Yet one cannot raise children on the telephone or on the Internet, and Reynolds' informants must struggle together with questions of maintaining ethnicity, of imparting cultural competence, to a younger generation growing up without in-depth social exposure to Igbo neighborhoods, schools, and churches.

Like Reynolds' chapter, Radloff's chapter involves describing the activities of a specific network of immigrants. But her description of an Arab Palestinian's accounting office also provides unique entry into the everyday problems of Arab people who run myriad businesses in the Chicago area. Radloff's richly descriptive chapter invites us to see the complexity of the work of one focal immigrant whose job is not merely to file tax returns, but to translate between two cultures, two languages, and two print systems. She explains, for example, the problems with transliterating written Arabic, which uses only diacritics to indicate vowels, into English and how the differences in writing systems recursively create differently spelled names for individuals (Mohamed, Muhammad, Mohammad, and the like), who must then attempt to reconcile their status with the government vis-à-vis their different documents. At a larger level too, Radloff explains how cultural perceptions of the individual, the collective, and the state vary between Arab and U.S. business cultures. These differences are borne out in linguistic problems, and the Arab accountants in her study end up mediating between very different systems, often making important decisions for clients simply by how they choose to explain a business problem across cultures. Radloff's chapter is particularly striking in that her descriptions reflect the need for any community to have highly skilled culturally competent individuals and institutions like the accounting office in focal positions. That is, speakers with varying levels of oral and literate competence in Spanish, Arabic, Hindi, and English frequently come together in this very office, among people of many different backgrounds, in service of the larger Arab community.

Laura Miller's chapter on Japanese abroad raises more questions about contemporary global culture. Miller deepens the questions surrounding print and ethnic maintenance by asking how print media contribute to "enclaving" or the creation of key sites that are so highly nationalized and ethnicized as to be virtually nonintegrative. To do so, she takes us on a tour of a key site for Japanese identity practices abroad, the Asahiya bookstore within a Japanese shopping complex in the Chicago suburbs. These professional Japanese in Chicago are true sojourners, whose return to Japan is imminent, and whose professional work abroad can be seen as a direct link between the Japanese economy and the United States, but not as a direct link between Japanese and Americans. They have little reason to integrate fully into the American spaces around them, and even more reason to use literacy as a personal and collective means of losing themselves in the nexus of personal and cultural expression from back home. And yet, at Asahiya Bookstore, the stock does not include only those items typical of a Tokyo bookstore, but also "survival" books and books for professional women and wives abroad, signs of a small "global" Japanese circuit. This is evidenced even more strikingly by the absence, in Chicago, of the popular genre of Japanese sociology studies. As Japanese sojourners experience deterritorialization, one can see again how less-than-constant contact with a home community makes everyday concerns from home less pressing. Miller also shows how immigrant culture differs from that of sojourners by outlining the peculiar (and sentimental) blend of immigrant community news and symbolic news from home that *nissei, sansei* and *yonsei* (second-, third-, and fourth-generation) Chicagoans read about in *Chicago Shimpo.*

Several chapters examine the interrelationships between performing oral genres and creating gender identities. In Nardini's chapter, making *bella figura* is unquestioned, since this traditional Italian speech genre is, Nardini claims, central to Italian identity. Here it is used to challenge traditional gender identities, or rather to challenge the power dynamics inherent in those identities. First of all, the people studied here must understand the social importance of the genre and accept the basic idea that a discussion about money is not really a discussion about money. They must also have knowledge of the various poetic devices and speech acts, such as questioning and teasing, that can sequentially build up to the spectacle of *bella figura*. This shared knowledge is known as communicative competence (Hymes, 1974a), or the knowledge of and ability to practice the full range of language styles, varieties, and functions in a particular speech community, in this case, middle-aged first generation immigrants from Tuscany who are active members of the immigrants' association. This basic knowledge includes much that is subconscious, such as the gendered nature of who may say what and when to whom, including norms for indirection. Such aspects of communicative competence are then drawn on by interactants as they generate discourse. In turn, daily discourse can facilitate the critical examination and transformation of communicative competence. In other words, communicative competence, like culture more generally, is dynamic and changing rather than static and timeless. Hanks describes this duality of discourse in practice, incorporating language practices into the larger set of expectations Bourdieu (1977) refers to as *habitus*:

> Being grounded in cultural schemata that recur across distinct fields of action, habitus is logically prior to any actual event of practice. At the same time, it is subject to innovation and strategic manipulation in practice, such that it is a product as well as a resource that changes over time. (Hanks, 2000, p. 145)

Koliussi's chapter on Greek American women grappling with gender role changes during the genre of *gynaikoloi*, or verbally humorous gatherings of women, also illuminates transformations in communicative competence. Here one woman leads others in talking in ways traditionally inappropriate (i.e., considered "vulgar") for women, even in the presence of one of the women's husbands, who nonverbally registers his disapproval. As this woman models new gender behavior for the others, they support her with approving laughter, which seems to spur her on to provoke the husband further. She, together with the other women, skillfully manipulates traditional expectations for women's linguistic behavior such that the husband is unable even to answer without affirming their new roles himself. In one instance, by using the rural variant of a Greek word rather than its standard counterpart, she is able to align herself, and by extension the other women, upward at the husband's (male) status level. Thus Koliussi illustrates how Greek American women challenge tradi-

tional norms of communicative competence and together begin to transform them.

The final four chapters reviewed in this section are distinct from all the
others in that they focus on groups of Americans descended from those
who arrived here much earlier. Morgan and Moss both focus on African
American communities, whereas Lindquist and Cho and Miller focus on
White working-class communities. The latter especially are often somewhat "invisible" given the explicit, even celebratory, acknowledgment of
ethnicity in the United States and the comparatively ignored dimension of
class. Both African American and working-class White communities,
however, are often disregarded in the current emphasis on globalization
and the new waves of immigration. Morgan's piece in this volume, in fact,
is unique in that she deals with changing Black women's identity and the
ways that rhetorical sophistication vis-à-vis other women is acquired
across a woman's lifetime. Yet she also, like Koliussi, looks at an older generation and their poetic expression of memories from the good old days
when they did not conform to conservative gender norms. Morgan examines how these women interpret and affirm the bygone meanings of their
lives, describing those lives "while assessing their belief that other women
did not live complete lives." Her article centers on a characteristically African American speech event, or genre, "signifying" (although other groups
use such sophisticated rhetorical devices as well), out of which emerges
the social patterns by which women understand each other competitively,
socially, rhetorically, and of course, through the filter of culture.

Just as *bella figura*, the gatherings of the *gynaikoloi*, and the complex
forms of African American women's "signifyin'" involve rhetorical negotiations of complex female selves, so the African American ministers
whose sermons Moss analyzes ride a fine line between presentation of
an educated self and a communitarian self. More than the other chapters
in this volume, Moss's chapter uses the extraordinary power of ethnography to demonstrate how the interaction of literacy (education) and ethnicity (or an African American identity) are conjoined as a unified identity
practice, however momentary. This takes place, interestingly, in a formalized community event, the African American sermon. Furthermore,
Moss weaves in a class dimension, class mobility itself being an inevitable benefit (and price) of education, showing how the dynamics of
church interaction are exacerbated by class difference. There is more
than one way to do things with words, and Moss fruitfully contrasts the
ways that two different ministers in two congregations, using two differ-

ent composing and preaching styles, can appeal to the rhetorical principle of *kairos,* or timeliness, as well as to *logos,* or the word of the people.
Notably, one minister's pulpit personality (*ethos*) involves community
building through a special form of self-representation. By implying that
his authority is derived from the strengths of the very congregational
group that created his will to become educated, the manuscript minister
establishes a sort of dialogue with the community, as an equal within it.
In that way he becomes the marked embodiment of that community,
and is part of it, even as he stands above it. In this portion, Moss's chapter
is similar to Reynolds' in the sense that those who are leaders are also
emblems of ethnic cohesion, using speech to build consensus and affection under the umbrella of their authority.

Importantly, as all the chapters in this volume suggest, Moss expands
our understanding of genre by demonstrating how blurring the boundaries
of genres and other linguistic devices (as in witnessing, call-and-response,
and use of "we" in place of "I") creates a mode of dialogue between
speaker and audience. The dialogic nature of the sermon performance
runs counter to Western academic expectations, in which the text and its
author are definitively separate entities. Indeed, if one's principal experiences with literacy and orality function to build community rather than
transmit immutable facts or philosophical abstractions, then the ethno-
centrism of Anglo-American texts becomes more readily apparent, as
does the imperative to make their nature more explicit to students not familiar with them.

Lindquist's chapter also demonstrates the distinction between Western genres of argumentation most often imparted by formal education and
community-level, nonelite genres. In her study of the rhetoric of argument
in a White working-class bar on the south side of Chicago, Lindquist ably
demonstrates how "cultural boundaries are often concretized ... through
conventional speech genres." Her informants use working-class genres of
argument as a mode of resistance to more elite genres, embodied by
Lindquist herself, who is forced to take on the role of the abstract thinker
and rhetorician associated with the outcomes of effective schooling, even
though she grew up in this very neighborhood as a member of this social
class. Furthermore, Lindquist's study melds place and practice in the creation of a highly marked working-class context. She shows how "even if a
theory of class is not present" among the patrons of the Smokehouse Bar,
"its practice is everywhere." The Smokehouse is a safe place for patrons to
play out local themes and ideologies in conflict, using working-class argu-

mentative rhetoric to share membership in a collective, even while they are challenging the ideology behind that collective identity.

Finally, Cho and P. Miller provide a capstone to the themes of ethnicity and class that continuously arise in American immigration and ethnic experience. Focusing on two neighborhoods whose European ancestors immigrated to Chicago many decades ago, Cho and Miller use an interdisciplinary approach that combines qualitative and quantitative analyses. They find that working-class mothers produced many more stories of personal experience, transforming the interview itself into a vehicle for narratives. This finding parallels that of Burger and Miller's (1999) earlier study of the same two communities, in which they found that rates of conarrated personal storytelling were much higher for young working-class children than for their middle-class counterparts. Cho and Miller also report that working-class mothers construct personal storytelling as a medium through which negative experience, child-rearing challenges, and family difficulties can be candidly aired, a strategy that is consistent with their expressed intention to forearm their children with knowledge of life's harsh realities. By contrast, middle-class mothers offer a much more sanguine representation of family life and are more likely to put a positive spin on negative events. This work builds on other research in education and psychology that explores how storytelling allows human beings to organize experience, using local resources and perspectives, here class-related ones, to particularize universal language practices.

A final comment is warranted here. There are important populations in Chicago that are not covered in this volume. As noted earlier, a second volume is devoted entirely to Mexicans and Puerto Ricans, the two largest groups of Latinos in the United States and in Chicago. Other gaps in representation, however, we were unable to fill, in spite of diligent efforts to locate studies of language among, for example, Native Americans (who numbered 10,000 in 2000), Appalachians, Poles (who comprise the largest non–English speaking-group after Mexicans), Russians, Koreans, South Asian Indians, and others. Whereas we were able to locate some studies of these groups, none of these studies focused on language use, but were more general ethnographies. It is our hope that this volume, and its companion volume on Latinos, will stimulate more such work, and that future volumes can broaden our understandings of oral and written language in a wider variety of populations.

REFERENCES

Alvarez, R. (1995). The Mexican–U.S. border: The making of an anthropology of borderlands. *Annual Review of Anthropology, 24,* 447–470.

Bakhtin, M. M. (1986). *Speech genres and other late essays.* Austin: University of Texas Press.

Baron, D. (1990). *The English-only question: An official language for Americans?* New Haven: Yale University Press.

Barth, F. (1968). *Ethnic groups and boundaries: The social organization of culture difference.* Boston: Little, Brown and Company.

Basch, L., Glick-Schiller, N., & Szanton-Blanc, C. (1994). *Nations unbound: Transnational projects, postcolonial predicaments and deterritorialized nation-states.* Langhorne, PA: Gordon & Breach Science Publishers.

Baugh, J. (1999). *Out of the mouths of slaves.* Austin, TX: University of Texas Press.

Baugh, J. (2000). *Beyond ebonics: Linguistic pride and racial prejudice.* New York, NY: Oxford University Press.

Bauman, R. (1977/1984). *Verbal art as performance.* Prospect Heights, IL: Waveland.

Bauman, R. (1986). *Story, performance, event: Contextual studies of oral narrative.* Cambridge, UK: Cambridge University Press.

Bauman, R., & Briggs, C. (1990). Poetics and performance as critical perspectives on language and social life. *Annual Review of Anthropology, 19,* 59–88.

Bauman, R., & Sherzer, J. (Eds.). (1974/1989). *Explorations in the ethnography of speaking.* Cambridge, UK: Cambridge University Press.

Besnier, N. (1995). *Literacy, emotion and authority: Reading and writing on a Polynesian atoll.* Cambridge, UK: Cambridge University Press.

Boas, F. (1911). *Handbook of American Indian languages.* (BAE-B 40, Introduction, Part I). Washington, DC: Smithsonian Institution.

Bourdieu, P. (1977). Outline of a theory of practice. Cambridge, UK: Cambridge University Press.

Boyarin, J. (Ed.). (1992). *The ethnography of reading.* Berkeley: University of California Press.

Briggs, C. (1986). *Learning how to ask: A sociolinguistic appraisal of the role of the interview in social science research.* Cambridge, UK: Cambridge University Press.

Briggs, C., & Bauman, R. (1992). Genre, intertextuality, and social power. *Journal of Linguistic Anthropology, 2*(2), 131–172.

Burger, L. K., & Miller, P. J. (1999). Early talk about the past revisited: Affect in working-class and middle-class children's conarrations. *Journal of Child Language, 26,* 133–162.

Chicago Fact Book Consortium. (1995). *Local Community Fact Book: Chicago Metropolitan Area 1990.* Chicago: University of Illinois at Chicago.

Cohen, R. (1978). Ethnicity: Problem and focus in anthropology. *Annual Review of Anthropology, 7,* 379–403.

Collins, J., & Blot, R. (2003). *Literacy and literacies: Texts, power, and identity.* Cambridge, UK: Cambridge University Press.

Constantakos, C., & Spiridakis, J. (1997). Greek in New York. In O. Garcia, Ofelia, & J. A. Fishman (Eds.), *The multilingual apple: Languages in New York City* (pp. 143–166). Berlin: Mouton de Gruyter.

Duranti, A. (1997). *Linguistic anthropology.* Cambridge: Cambridge University Press.

Duranti, A. (2001). *Linguistic anthropology: A reader.* Oxford, UK: Blackwell.

Farr, M. (1993). Essayist literacy and other verbal performances. *Written Communication, 10*(1), 4–38.

Farr, M. (1994). *Echando relajo*: Verbal art and gender among *mexicanas* in Chicago, in M. Bucholtz, A. C. Liang, L. A. Sutton, & C. Hines (Eds.), *Cultural performances* (pp. 168–186): *Proceedings of the third women and language conference,* April 8–10, 1994. Berkeley: University of California.

Farr, M. (1998). *El relajo como microfiesta.* In H. Pérez (Ed.), *Mexico en fiesta.* Zamora, Michoacán, Mexico: El Colegio de Michoacán.

Farr, M. (2000). ¡A Mí no me manda nadie! *Individualism and identity in Mexican* ranchero *speech.* In V. Pagliai & M. Farr (Eds.), Special issue of *Pragmatics, 10* (1) on Language, performance and identity: (pp. 61–85).

Farr, M. (Forthcoming). Rancheros in Chicagoacán: Ways of speaking and identity in a Mexican transnational community.

Ferguson, C., & Heath, S. B. (Eds.). (1981). *Language in the USA.* Cambridge, UK: Cambridge University Press.

Finnegan, R. (1988). *Literacy and orality: Studies in the technology of communication.* Oxford, UK: Blackwell.

Fishman, J. (1997). Ethnicity and language: The view from within. In F. Coulmas (Ed.), *The handbook of sociolinguistics* (pp. 327–343). Oxford, UK: Blackwell.

Friedman, J. (1999). Indigenous struggles and the discreet charm of the bourgeoisie. *Journal of World-Systems Research, 5*(2), 391–411.

Gans, H. (1999). Filling in some holes: Six areas of needed immigrant research. *American Behavioral Scientist, 42*(9), 1302–1313.

Garcia, O., & Fishman, J. A. (Eds.). (1997). *The multilingual apple: Languages in New York City.* Berlin: Mouton de Gruyter.

Giddens, A. (2000). *Runaway world: How globalization is reshaping our life.* New York: Routledge.

Guerra, J. (1998). *Close to home: Oral and literate practices in a transnational Mexicano community.* New York, NY: Columbia Teachers College.

Gumperz, J. (Ed.). (1982a). *Language and social identity.* Cambridge, UK: Cambridge University Press.

Gumperz, J. (1982b). *Discourse strategies.* Cambridge, UK: Cambridge University Press.

Gumperz, J., & Cook-Gumperz, J. (1982). Introduction: Language and the communication of social identity. In J. Gumperz (Ed.), *Language and social identity.* Cambridge, UK: Cambridge University Press.

Gumperz, J., & Hymes, D. (Eds.). (1964). The ethnography of communication (Part 2). *American Anthropologist, 66*(6).

Gumperz, J., & Hymes, D. (Eds.). (1972/1986). *Directions in sociolinguistics.* Oxford, UK: Blackwell.

Hanks, W. F. (2000). *Intertexts: Writings on language, utterance, and context.* Boulder, CO: Rowman and Littlefield.

Harvey, D. (1990). *The condition of postmodernity.* Oxford, UK: Blackwell.

Heath, S. B. (1983). *Ways with words: Language, life, and work in communities and classrooms.* Cambridge, UK: Cambridge University Press.

Holli, M. G., & Jones, P. d'A. (Eds.). (1977/1995). *Ethnic Chicago.* Grand Rapids, MI: Eerdmans.

Holtzman, J. (2000). *Nuer journeys, Nuer lives: Sudanese refugees in Minnesota.* Boston: Allyn & Bacon.

Hymes, D. (1974a). *Foundations in sociolinguistics: An ethnographic approach.* Philadelphia: University of Pennsylvania.

Hymes, D. (1974b). *Ways of speaking.* In R. Bauman & J. Sherzer, (Eds.), *Explorations in the ethnography of speaking.* New York: Cambridge University Press.

Hymes, D. (1975). Breakthrough into performance. In D. Ben Amos & K. Goldstein (Eds.), *Folklore: performance and communication* (pp. 11–74). The Hague: Mouton.

Hymes, D. (1981). *"In vain I tried to tell you": Essays in Native American ethnopoetics.* Philadelphia: University of Pennsylvania Press.

Hymes, D. (1999). Poetry. *Journal of Linguistic Anthropology, 9*(1–2), 191–193.

Hymes, D. (2002, May). Problems of translation, *Anthropology News, 43*(5), 23.

Jakobson, R. (1960). Closing statement: Linguistics and poetics. In T. Sebeok (Ed.), *Style in language* (pp. 350–377). New York: John Wiley.

Kamhoefner, W. D., Helbich, W., & Sommer, U. (1991). *News from the land of freedom: German immigrants write home.* Ithaca, NY: Cornell University Press.

Kearney, M. (1995). The local and the global: The anthropology of globalization and transnationalism. *Annual Review of Anthropology, 24*, 547–565.

King, K. A. (2001). *Language revitalization processes and prospects: Quichua in the Ecuadorian Andes.* Clevedon, UK: Multilingual Matters.

Kotkin, J. (1993). *Tribes: How race, religion, and identity determine success in the new global economy.* New York: Random House.

Kroskrity, P. (Ed.). (2000). *Regimes of language.* Santa Fe, NM: School of American Research Press.

Murphy, A. D., Blanchard, C., & Hill, J. (Eds.). (1999). *Latino workers in the contemporary south.* Athens, GA: University of Georgia Press.

Ochs, E., & Capps, L. (2001). *Living narrative: Creating lives in everyday storytelling.* Cambridge, MA: Harvard University Press.

Phillips, S. (1987). *The concept of speech genre in the study of language and culture.* Working Papers and Proceedings of the Center for Psychosocial Studies, no. 11. Center for Psychosocial Studies; Chicago.

Phillips, S. U. (1998). *Ideological diversity in judges' courtroom discourses: Due process rights in practice.* Oxford, UK: Oxford University Press.

Phillips, S. U. (2000). Constructing a Tongan nation state through language ideology in the courtroom. In P. V. Kroskrity (Ed.), *Regimes of language* (pp. 229–258). Santa Fe, NM: School of American Research Press.

Rickford, J. (1999). *African-American vernacular English.* Malden, MA: Oxford University Press.

Rosenau, J. (1997). *Along the domestic-foreign frontier: Exploring governance in a turbulent world.* Cambridge, UK: Cambridge University Press.

Rouse, R. (1991). Mexican migration and the social space of postmodernism. *Diaspora, 1*(1), 8–23.

Rouse, R. (1992). Making sense of settlement: Class transformation, cultural struggle, and transnationalism among Mexican migrants in the United States. Towards a transnational perspective on migration. *Annals of the New York Academy of Sciences, 645*, 25–52.

Sassen, S. (1998). *Globalization and its discontents: Essays on the new mobility of people and money.* New York: The New Press.

Saville-Troike, M. (1989). *The ethnography of communication.* London: Basil Blackwell.

Schiefflin, B. B., Woolard, K. A., & Kroskrity, P. V. (Eds). (1998). *Language ideologies: Practice and theory.* New York: Oxford University Press.

Sherzer, J. (1987). A discourse-centered approach to language and culture. *American Anthropologist, 89*(2), 295–309.

Sherzer, J. (1990). *Verbal art in San Blas: Kuna culture through its discourse.* Cambridge, UK: Cambridge University Press.

Stack, J. F. (1981). *Ethnic identities in a transnational world.* Westport, CT: Greenwood Press.

Staudt, K., & Spener D., (1998). The view from the frontier: Theoretical perspectives undisciplined. In D. Spener & K. Staudt (Eds.), *The U.S.–Mexico border: Transcending divisions, contesting identities* (pp. 1–4). Boulder: Lynne Riener Publishers.

Street, B. (1984). *Literacy in theory and practice.* Cambridge, UK: Cambridge University Press.

Street, B. V. (Ed.). (1993). *Cross-cultural approaches to literacy.* Cambridge, UK: Cambridge University Press.

Szwed, J. (1981). The ethnography of literacy. M. F. Whiteman, (Ed.), *Writing: Functional and linguistic–cultural variation* (pp. 13–23). Hillsdale, NJ: Lawrence Erlbaum Associates.

Tabouret-Keller, A. (1997). Language and identity. In F. Coulmas (Ed.), *The handbook of sociolinguistics* (pp. 315–326). Oxford, UK: Blackwell.

Tannen, D. (1989). *Talking voices: Repetition, dialogue, and imagery in conversational discourse.* New York, NY: Cambridge University Press.

Tedlock, D. (1983). *The spoken word and the work of interpretation.* Philadelphia: University of Pennsylvania Press.

Trommler, F., & McVeigh, J. (Eds.). (1985). *America and the Germans.* Philadelphia: University of Pennsylvania Press.

Wallerstein, I. (1974). *The modern world system.* New York, NY: Academic Press.

Woolard, K. A. (1998). Introduction: Language ideology as a field of inquiry. In B. B. Schieffelin, K. A. Woolard, & P. V. Kroskrity (Eds.), *Language ideologies: Practice and theory* (pp. 3–47). New York, NY: Oxford University Press.

United Nations. (1988). *World population trends and policies.* Monitoring Report Population Studies No. 103. New York, NY: United Nations Population Division.

Urciuoli, B. (1999). Strategically deployable shifters in college marketing, or just what do they mean by "skills" and "leadership" and "multiculturalism"? *Language and Culture: Symposium [on-line], 5,* http://www.language-culture.org/colloquia/symposia/urciuoli-bonnie / Accessed: 4/5/2001.

2

Language Policy in Illinois:
Past and Present

Elliot L. Judd
University of Illinois at Chicago

The State of Illinois has always been a multilingual entity. From the time of its admission into the Union, and prior to that, residents of Illinois have spoken many languages. Today, the multilingual tradition of Illinois continues in all parts of the state, in both urban and rural areas. Clearly, English is the dominant language of the state of Illinois and always has been. Yet, there have always been speakers of other languages who have resided in the state, and whose language use has posed an issue for the English-speaking majority. Should languages other than English be tolerated in public domains? Should state policy promote the use of languages other than English? Should there be policies to restrict such languages? Should there be limited use in certain domains and restrictions in others?

This chapter discusses the language policy of Illinois from initial statehood until the present. Various periods are highlighted to illustrate the tensions between English and non-English languages, and how these tensions were handled by policymakers. At the end of the chapter, I try to tie together the various periods in order to reconcile what may seem to be a very inconsistent and contradictory history of language policy in the state of Illinois.

Before proceeding, certain parameters need to be drawn. The term "policy," as used in this essay, refers to official, governmental actions (Judd, 1992; Kaplan, 1992). Such policy can be enacted by the state legislature, declared and promulgated by the governor, or enunciated by the courts. Policy proclamations can be found in the state constitution, in bills that have been enacted by the legislature, in court rulings, and in documents printed by state agencies (i.e., the School Code, the Secretary of State's Office, and so on).

Additionally, language policy in Illinois is subsumed under federal language policy of the United States because any policy passed in Illinois must be constitutional within the legal boundaries of the federal system. That is, no language policy measure in Illinois may violate constitutional provisions of the United States, as interpreted by the courts, for example, constitutionally guaranteed provisions for freedoms of the press, speech, and religion. This article, however, deals only with state issues, not wider federal issues.

Finally, it is important to remember that there are many areas of language use that are currently beyond the area of language policy as defined earlier. Such areas include the use of non-English languages in private schools, the media (private presses, newspapers, radio, and television), religious worship, private commerce, and daily interactions among individuals. Non-English languages are, and always have been, used in these areas in Illinois and create a rich multilingual heritage for the state. The other chapters in this volume attest to this diversity in a variety of domains. Here, however, I concentrate on the treatment of language in state policy.

FROM STATEHOOD TO THE PRESENT

English has not always been the dominant language of Illinois. Prior to Illinois statehood (1818), the earliest documents governing the Northwest Territory all were written in English, and there is no mention of other languages (Baron, 1990a, p. 14). However, this does not mean that speakers in Illinois and the rest of the territory all were English speakers. It has been estimated that in 1790 there were 1,000 French speakers and 300 "other whites" in Illinois (Kloss, 1977, p. 164). Although this figure itself clearly shows that English speakers were in the minority at this time, three important things need to be added to this earliest language census. First, in the "other whites" category, it is not clear that all of the speakers were English users and, in fact, they probably were not because colonial America included speakers from many other European languages.

Second, in both the French and non-French classifications, there is no indication of any bilingualism. It is reasonable to assume that some of the French speakers knew some English and that some of the non-French speakers knew some French because there were occasions in which groups needed to communicate across language barriers.

Finally, there is no mention of Native American languages. Although it is clear that there were numerous Native American languages spoken in the Northwest Territory, including Illinois, they were not mentioned in the census, owing to the ignorance of and disdain for of Native Americans within colonial America. No doubt there was also some bilingualism among Native Americans and speakers of European languages.

While English was the dominant language in Illinois during the period of the Northwest Territory, there was a tension between French and English, and both languages were used (Kloss, 1977, pp. 164–166). Territorial laws were translated into French so that judges could administer justice, and French courts were set up in the towns of Kaskaskia and Cahokia in the 1790s. Additionally, for 1 month a year, a French school was set up in Cahokia so that French children could receive some limited education (Baron, 1990a, p. 14; Baron, 1990b, pp. 113–114). Although 1 month of education may seem very limited by today's standards, it was not uncommon for rural and poor children not to have any formal schooling at all or to study only with the aid of a hired tutor.

The first constitution of the state of Illinois, written in 1818, makes no mention of language. English was not declared the official language, nor was English required for any specific function, nor was there any ban against the use of other languages. Because the constitution and other early laws of the state were written in English, it may be argued that this granted English "semi-official" status (Baron, 1990b, p. 113). On the other hand, legislators must have been cognizant of the number of citizens who spoke languages other than English, as evidenced by later state constitutions.

The 1845 School Law designated English to be the medium of instruction in all public schools. The Law stated that "No school shall derive the benefit from the public or town funds unless said schools shall be in the English language, nor unless the common medium of communication in said schools shall be in the English language" (Baron, 1990a, p. 16). The fact that the law was passed suggests that in some places schools were teaching in languages other than English while being supported by public funds. Such was the practice in other Midwestern states where bilingual education was supported, especially education in German (Andersson, 1971). The law, however, did not ban foreign language education at any level, and thus left open the possibilities of teaching other languages in some form. In 1869, the State Legislature reaffirmed the right to teach modern languages in public schools throughout Illinois (Baron, 1990a, p. 16).

In 1848, a new constitution was enacted. Schedule 18 of the constitution mandated that "all laws of the State of Illinois, and official writings, and the Executive, Legislative and Judicial proceedings, shall be conducted, preserved, and published in no other than the English language" (State of Illinois, 1847, p. 571). This marked the first time that English was constitutionally accorded a primary role in Illinois. However, the state legislature also decreed that the new constitution be published and disseminated in German, while rejecting the printing of the constitution "in the Irish and French languages" (Baron, 1990a, p. 16). By proposing such bills, legislators were tacitly acknowledging the existence of a substantial population of people who did not speak or read English, although the linguistic knowledge of the legislators may be questioned in the case of "Irish" as a language, which is a term that was never clearly explained. The English provision of the Constitution was reaffirmed in the 1870 Constitution of Illinois, which however stated that "oral testimony, depositions, or documentary evidence" could be given in languages other than English (Baron, 1990b, p. 117). It was also mandated that 30,000 copies of this new Constitution be printed in English, 15,000 in German, 5,000 in French, and 5,000 in "Scandinavian," but rejected printing the Constitution in Italian (Baron, 1990a, p. 16; Kloss, 1977, p. 166). Again, legislators felt the need to communicate with their constituencies in their native languages. Neither Constitution forbade the reprinting or translation of state laws in non–English-language newspapers, as apparently such republications were quite common throughout the period.

Linguistic tolerance was also legislated in the city of Chicago. In 1863, the City Council granted discretionary power allowing the publication of proceedings, ordinances, and public notices in both English and German newspapers. This law was amended in 1867 to require the publication of these official pronouncements in English and German newspapers (Kloss,

1977, p. 84). Clearly, the elected municipal officials felt the need to communicate with the large number of Germans living in Chicago. Yet, in 1891, in the case of *McCoy v. City of Chicago* (136 Ill .341 [1891]), the Chicago law was overturned, and the state court ruled that all laws and ordinances in Chicago must be in English. The ruling stated that since Chicago lost its home rule status in 1871 and was thus governed by the same state laws as the rest of the state, the city of Chicago must comply with the 1848 Constitution with respect to laws and ordinances being published only in English.

Beginning in the 1880s, a series of anti-German moves occurred in both the legislative and judicial arenas. In 1881, the Illinois Supreme Court heard the case of *Powell v. Board of Education* (97 Ill. 375 [1881]). The case was a challenge to the 1-hour daily instruction in German in St. Clair County schools, which was voluntary for 80% to 90% of the student population. The Court ruled that modern language teaching was legal and did not violate the 1848 School Law, which mandated instruction in English. This ruling was based on the premise that it was not within the domain of the judiciary to ban modern languages from the school system; such a move could only come from the legislature (Baron, 1990a, p. 16).

In 1889, the Republican-controlled legislature enacted the Edwards Law, which was named after the then Superintendent of Education. The bill decreed that all instruction in reading, writing, arithmetic, American history, and geography in every public and parochial school must be in English (Baron, 1990a, pp. 17–18; Baron, 1990b, pp. 119–121; Kloss, 1977, p. 69). The bill was clearly aimed at the large German-speaking population in the state, both Lutherans and Catholics, who had established German-speaking parochial schools throughout Illinois. Republican supporters claim that the Democratic opponents were against English instruction because they were seeking to gain votes from non-English speakers, and that Democrats were enemies of public education in Illinois. Opponents of the Edwards Law "were objects of violent anti-Catholic, anti-Democratic, and anti-German attacks in the press" throughout the state (Baron, 1990a, p. 17).

In reaction to the Edwards Law, a coalition of Democrats, German Catholics and German Lutherans, the latter of whom generally voted Republican, united to support the Democratic candidacy of John P. Altgeld in the 1890 election. Altgeld made the school issue a key part of his gubernatorial campaign. The Democrats, under Altgeld, were victorious and ended a twenty-year Republican control of the state government. In 1893, the Edwards Law was repealed (Baron, 1991a, pp. 17–18; 1990b, pp. 199–121).

During World War I, many states, especially in the Midwest, enacted a series of laws and proclamations declaring English to be the official language and banning the teaching and use of German and other foreign languages. These xenophobic measures were mainly directed at Germans living in the United States, who were suspected of being a subversive element and disloyal citizens (Kloss, 1977; Leibowitz, 1969, 1971). These laws were eventually ruled unconstitutional by the United States Supreme Court in the case of *Meyer v. Nebraska* (262nU.S. 390 [1923]). Illinois, however, was not one of the states that enacted such legislation.

Despite the lack of explicitly anti-German statutes in Illinois, there were a series of legal rulings that restricted non-English language use and could be considered as being anti-German in intent. In 1916, the Attorney General of Illinois issued an opinion that all charters and names of domestic insurance companies must be in English, and that such companies must have English names. This ruling was quickly followed by two cases decided by the Illinois Supreme Court. In 1916, in the case of *Perkins v. Board of County Commissioners of Cook County et al.* (271 Ill. 449 [1916]), the court decreed that notices and ordinances published in English, but in foreign-language presses, were disallowed because they were not really "published" in the normal sense as defined by the Illinois Constitution of 1848. Because a forest preserve levy had been published in a German newspaper in English, Perkins was not subject to payment because it had not been "officially" published. Perkins further claimed that the existence of German-language newspapers was evidence of how reluctant Germans were to assimilate into American society. Similarly, in 1917, in the case of *People v. Day* (277 Ill. 543 [1917]), the Illinois Supreme Court decided that Day was not subject to a tax levy because it had been published only in a German newspaper, which again violated the Constitution of Illinois (Baron, 1990a, pp. 15–16; 1990b, pp. 116–117).

These rulings are significant in several respects. First, they marked the end of an era in which there was a large degree of linguistic tolerance toward non-English speakers within Illinois. With the exception of the short period of the Edwards Law, non-English languages were for the most part tolerated by the general populace. Clearly, English was assumed to be the dominant language, both legally and otherwise, but there were few concerted attempts to muzzle other languages. Second, we can see how delicate linguistic freedoms are, and how in times of crisis, real or imaginary, some people begin to equate linguistic diversity with disloyalty. Germany was the enemy during World War I, and for some, anyone who was of German origin became suspect. Although the reactions in Illinois were not as harsh as in some other Midwestern states, it is clear that those of German origin felt the hatred.

This was true not only at a policy level, but throughout daily life. Many businesses changed their names from German to English-sounding names, and many people Americanized their family names in an effort to avoid charges of being un-American, and in an attempt to escape the anti-German sentiments that were sweeping across the United States during and immediately after World War I. Illinois was not alone in this respect. This was a national trend. Furthermore, the repression of linguistic rights in times of perceived crisis has occurred elsewhere in the United States, as with Spanish speakers in the Southwest, and with the Chinese and Japanese on the West Coast (see Leibowitz 1969, 1971, for a fuller discussion).

The impact of both the legal measures and the generally antiforeign sentiments extended beyond specific language groups and created a general xenophobic attitude throughout the entire country. In 1919, a bill was introduced in the Illinois legislature to ban all foreign language instruction in elementary schools, but it was tabled (Baron, 1990b, p. 121). However, many other states began to curtail the study of foreign languages in both elementary and secondary schools. German, which had been the most studied foreign language, ceased to be so after World War I, and foreign language studies in general plummeted after World War I.

Also, in 1919, the legislature revised the Illinois School Code, and reinstituted the requirement of English in all public and parochial schools. The wording of Section 276a of the School Code embodied the belief that English was the key to good citizenship and loyalty to the country:

> Because the English language is the common as well as official language of our country, and because it is essential to good citizenship that each citizen shall have or speedily acquire, as his natural tongue, the language in which the laws of the land, the decree of the courts, and the proclamations and pronouncements of its officials are made, and shall easily and naturally think in the language in which the obligations of his citizenship are defined, the instruction in the elementary branches of education in all schools in Illinois shall be in the English language. (Baron, 1990b, p. 121)

The wording of this pronouncement is quite interesting in several respects. First, English was not the "official" language of the United States then, nor is it today (Baron, 1990b; Judd, 1987; Marshall, 1986). There is no legal official language in this country, although de facto English is clearly the dominant language. Second, the ability to think about citizenship and other obligations is not restricted to English; people can comprehend information in any language. Finally, there is no evidence that those who do not speak English, either at all or only partially, are less law abiding or loyal than those who speak it fluently. Yet the statement from the School Code manifests the thinking of the times and the suspicions of the legislation's supporters.

Throughout the United States, there was an intense effort to "Americanize" immigrants and to restrict further immigration. Thus, on the federal level, new immigration laws were passed, reducing the number of immigrants allowed into the country and setting quotas that favored those from Western Europe while restricting those from other parts of Europe and the rest of the world. It was felt that these "foreign" elements were endangering the fabric of American society and subverting the quality of American life. In 1919, Illinois too joined this movement by passing a bill to provide for the teaching of English to adults "in order to Americanize the foreign-born and minimize work-related accidents (Baron, 1990b, p. 121).

From 1920 until 1922, Illinois held another constitutional convention to revise the state's constitution. The delegates passed a requirement that all appointed and elected officeholders be able to speak, read, and write English. Some opponents feared that the measure would bar certain racial and ethnic groups from assuming offices. Nevertheless, it passed by an overwhelming majority of 52 to 2. The convention also debated a move to establish a literacy requirement for voting in elections. Proponents favored the establishment of this requirement as a way of counteracting the votes of new immigrants, but opponents argued that the bill would disenfranchise some who had just defended the country during World War I as well as "colored voters." Furthermore, it was unclear as to how to measure exactly the criteria for literacy. The motion was eventually withdrawn from the floor. Additionally, there was a motion to require English as the language in all Illinois private and public schools. This too did not pass as it was argued that the School Code already contained such a provision. Finally, and in contrast to previous constitutions in Illinois, no authorization was given for printing the new constitution in any language other than English (see Baron, 1990a, pp. 19–21; Baron, 1990b, pp. 123–127, for more specific discussions).

The Constitutional Convention represented a symbolic attempt to proclaim English as the dominant language of Illinois. It was important symbolically rather than linguistically, and represented the prevailing mood of the entire country. English was already the dominant language and had been so since the earliest days of statehood. Yet, there was a strong anti-immigrant mood, and foreigners were perceived as alien elements and feared by the majority. They were linked, often without much basis in fact, with revolutionary ideas that were perceived to undermine the country, as evidenced by the Red scares of the early 1920s. Illinois participated in this nationwide sentiment. It was not in the forefront of the movement, but did not abstain from it either. The message was clear: Americanize, give up your language and culture, and speak English.

In 1923, State Senator Frank Ryan sponsored, and the legislature passed, a law making "American" the official language of the State of Illinois.. The bill was really an attack on British colonial policy and had great appeal among the Irish of the state. It also reflected a view that a language should be named after the country in which it is spoken, so that one should speak "American" to be considered a true American (Baron, 1990b, 128–130). The fact that English was being taught in the schools and was a requirement for officeholders and public notices, according to the ruling of the courts and the state Constitution, went unnoticed until 1928. Then, in the case of *Leideck v. City of Chicago* (248 Ill. App. 545 [1928]), the Illinois Appeals Court ruled that the American language law did not conflict with laws mandating English because the languages were "in legal effect and intendment … the same thing."

In 1969, the legislature amended the 1923 statute to make "English" the official law of Illinois (State of Illinois, 1969 Public Act 76–1464), thus ending the anomaly of Illinoisians officially speaking "American" rather than English, as in the rest of the United States. In actuality, the Ryan law, in either its original or amended versions, was a symbolic gesture that had little impact on later laws and practices in Illinois. There has never been serious enforcement of its provisions to guarantee that all in Illinois use English, nor has it prevented politicians from passing laws and regulations that allow the use of non-English languages for official state functions.

Like numerous other states during the late 1960s and early 1970s, the state of Illinois passed a bill endorsing bilingual education in 1973. Because the federal government had already passed its own bilingual education bill (The Bilingual Education Act of 1968, Title VII of the Elementary and Secondary Education Act), and because the Supreme Court had ruled in the case of *Lau v. Nichols* (414 U.S. Report 563 [1974]) that non–English-speaking children require specialized education programs (often interpreted as meaning bilingual education) in order to receive equal educational opportunities, the Illinois bilingual bill was in line with the current educational trends nationally. Bilingual education in Illinois was of a transitional nature; children were to be in such programs only until the time when they had mastered enough English so that they could be "mainstreamed" with other children. In other words, the home language and culture of children were not viewed as valuable assets. Rather, they were seen as obstacles that impeded the assimilation of children into the dominant English-speaking mainstream and should be eliminated as soon as educationally feasible.

As of 1988, the wording of the School Code with respect to the education of non-English speakers was written as follows:

> Instruction in all public elementary and secondary schools of the State shall be in the English language except in second language programs and except in conjunction with programs which the school board may provide, with the approval of the State Board of Education pursuant to Article 14c, in a language other than English for children whose first language is other than English. (State of Illinois, 1988 Public Act 85–1389)

That is, the school code currently in effect mandates that English is the only language of the schools except in cases of foreign language education and bilingual education for non- English–or limited English–speaking children.

In 1998, the Chicago Public School (CPS) Board restricted the time allowed for bilingual education. Students are allowed only 3 years of bilingual education, and then must be transitioned into regular classes. If the student does not attain English fluency in 3 years, an extension of 1 year is allowed upon the recommendation of the school, subject to parental approval. Students in regular classes will continue to receive English as a second language (ESL) support if they require it. At the same time, CPS stated their intention to expand "dual language" programs into preschools, so that "English-speaking and Spanish-speaking children can learn each other's language." Paul Vallas, the CPS's Chief Executive Officer, voiced the assimilationist position that "our first responsibility is to make certain that all students master English so they will have access to a good education, college, jobs and a decent life" (Chicago Public Schools, 1998). This limitation on bilingual education applies only to programs within Chicago, not to the rest of Illinois. The Chicago policy does not contradict state or federal law on bilingual education; it merely restricts the time allowed in such a program. It further represents a trend in several states to restrict further or gradually eliminate bilingual education (Judd, 1999).

CURRENT POLICIES IN ILLINOIS

At present, there are several language policy areas in which the state of Illinois is involved. They can be classified into two major areas: educational and noneducational. Each is presented and analyzed separately.

As mentioned earlier, according to the School Code of Illinois, it is legally permissible to have programs in another language to teach children English as long as those children are classified as being limited English proficient (LEP). Each school district in Illinois is required to identify LEP students by using a home language survey that indicates the language(s) that each child speaks and the language(s) used in the child's home. Then, for all students identified as coming from a non-English language background, an individual language assessment measurement must be administered. The measurement evaluates the child's skills in listening, speaking, reading, and writing English. To be eligible for bilingual education, the child's score

> must be below the 50th percentile on a "nationally normed English-language proficiency test," or
>
> must be at or above the 50th percentile on a nationally normed test, but with "other performance indicators" that show that the child is "more than one year behind the average of district age/grade level peers in any required subject," or
>
> in cases wherein there does not exist a nationally normed test, "a review of other indicators" must indicate that such children cannot "succeed in English-only classes or are more than one year behind the average of district/grade level peers in any required subject." (Illinois State Board of Education, 2000a, p. 3)

Two types of program exist: transitional bilingual education (TBE) and a transitional program of instruction (TPI). As mandated in the 1973 legislation, TBE occurs in school districts "whenever there are 20 or more LEP students with a common native language enrolled in one school." A TPI program is "in lieu of a TBE program whenever there are fewer than 20 LEP students of a common native language at an attendance center," and "must always be made available to any LEP student if a TBE program is not otherwise available" (Illinois State Board of Education, 2000a, p. 1). In short, all LEP children in Illinois must receive some kind of specialized educational program, with transitional bilingual education being the preferred option. Again, it is important to stress that this bilingual education is "transitional," a way of using the home language up until the time the child masters enough English to enter "regular" English classes. It is not designed to foster or maintain the child's home language, nor to develop literacy in that language.

The total number of children in TBE and TPI programs in Illinois, according to the figures for fiscal year 1998–1999, was 137,717. The majority of students, 72,490 (52.64%), are enrolled in the Chicago Public School system, with an additional 29,009 (21.06%) in the rest of Cook County, excluding Chicago. An additional 29,720 (21.58%) reside in the "collar" counties (those surrounding Cook County) of DuPage, Kane, Lake, McHenry, and Will. The remaining 6,498 (4.72%) live in other parts of Illinois (Illinois State Board of Education 2000a, p. 8). Although 107 different languages were identified in fiscal year 1999, by far the largest language group comprises Spanish speakers, accounting for 106,555 (77.37%) of the students. The next nine largest groups of students are Polish (6,620, 4.81%), Urdu (2,259, 1.64%), Arabic (2,210, 1.60%), Serbian/Croatian/Bosnian (1,921, 1.39%), Korean (1,793, 1.30%), Gujarati (1,761, 1.28%), Cantonese (1,507, 1.09%), Russian (1,337, 0.97%), and Vietnamese (1,260, 0.91%) (Illinois State Board of Education, 2000a, pp. 5–6). These demographic data attest to the continued linguistic diversity in Illinois, and probably are representative of the general linguistic diversity among children and adults throughout the entire State.

In addition to providing public funds for the education of LEP children, the state funds or administers federal money for programs in adult education. In fiscal year 1999, there were 110, 603 students in state adult education and literacy programs. Of these, 57,756 (52.2%) were enrolled in ESL classes. This compares with 30,916 (30.7%) learners in Adult Basic Education, 3,116 (2.8%) in High School Credit, 16,417 (16.3%) in General Education Development (GED), and 2,398 (2.4%) in Vocational Training (Illinois State Board of Education, 2000b, p. 1). These figures are actually an underrepresentation of the number of nonnative English speakers in these programs, because ESL speakers also are in the other categories of adult education, but not separated out from other groups. For example, students in Illinois can take the GED exam in Spanish, and those numbers are counted in the GED category, not ESL. Suffice it to say then that at least 50% of the public funds for adult education in Illinois go to nonnative English speakers. These funds are designed to provide classes for people to master English, as well as other skills, and are parallel with policies in elementary and secondary schools in which the goal is transitional English instruction.

In addition to the educational areas just discussed, the state of Illinois provides other services for speakers of non-English languages. The Secretary of State publishes the "Rules of the Road" booklet for drivers in both Spanish and Polish, as well as in English. At certain testing centers, the written test for the driver's license is given in Spanish or Korean. Additionally, a person taking the written or road test is allowed to bring an interpreter, but the expense for such a person is assumed by the test taker. The availability of all these language services applies only to a regular diver's license, not to commercial or other types of licenses granted by the Department of Motor Vehicles. In other areas of state licensure, the general policy in Illinois has generally been English only, yet there are several exceptions. The state examinations for barbers, barber teachers, and cosmetologists are given in both Spanish and English (State of Illinois 2000; personal communication).

Several current statutes within Illinois allow the use of non-English languages. The Mental Health Hispanic Interpreter Act (405 ILCS 75) mandates that in all state-operated facilities for mental health and disability in which 1% of the total admissions for outpatient or inpatient care are Spanish speakers, qualified interpreters must be provided and funded by state funds. The Illinois Notary Public Act (5 ILCS 312) states that all "fee schedules shall be written in English and in the non-English languages in which notary services were solicited." Finally, in the Criminal Proceeding Interpreter Act (725 ILCS 140), any person accused of a misdemeanor or felony who is to be tried in any state court, upon the motion of the court, the defense or prosecution must be examined to determine the person's ability to understand English or to express him- or herself clearly in English to the court, counsel, or jury. "If the court finds the accused incapable of so understanding or so expressing himself, the court shall appoint an interpreter for the accused whom he can understand and can understand him." (All the preceding statutes can be accessed via the internet at http//:www.legis.state,il.us).

Finally, within the city of Chicago, information about state rules and regulations through the office of the Secretary of State of Illinois are provided by staff members in English, Spanish, Polish, and Hebrew (State of Illinois 2000, personal communication). The case for Spanish and Polish is obvious because they represent the two largest non–English-speaking groups within Chicago. As for the use of Hebrew, it can also be explained as a symbolic, if useless, political gesture toward Jewish voters within the city. Ironically, there are very few speakers of Hebrew within Chicago, even among Jewish residents.

CONCLUSIONS

How can we best summarize Illinois' language policy? First, Illinois has always had non–English-speaking residents, and such a linguistically heterogeneous population has posed dilemmas for policymakers. English has consistently been the dominant language, and Illinois' language policies have clearly established English as the prime language of schools and governmental institutions. Baron (1990a) stated that, within Illinois, "English is the one essential badge of Americans" (p. 13). In fact, today English (or its original form "American") is the official language of the state. Yet, as noted throughout this chapter, state officials have recognized the existence of other languages by printing official materials in several languages, granting licensure in other languages, and allowing transitional bilingual education. Historically, however, in other periods, there have been attempts to restrict non-English language use and bar all other languages.

Is there a contradiction between the "official" English statute and other state policies that allow for the use of other languages? Marshall (1986) claimed that:

> the establishment of an official language … has had little effect upon the supplying of state services in other languages, where the recognition of the rise of language rights has led to legislation *circumventing* the official language statute, making it meaningless. (p. 58, italics added)

However, this explanation assumes that the state legislators were both actively aware of the official English statute and actively trying to ignore it. There is little evidence for this overstatement.

Baron (1990b), on the other hand, described Illinois's language history in more pragmatic terms. He stated:

> Language has been both a symbolic and a practical issue. The Illinois language laws have reflected public linguistic and ethnic prejudice, though, as in most states, its legislation has avoided the extremes of nativism and racism that conflict with federal constitutional practices. Illinois language law is also typical in that it has proved flexible enough to accommodate shifting attitudes or public policies toward language and education. (p. 132)

This analysis seems closer to the real picture in Illinois. Legislators and other state officials respond to the immediate issues of the day and are not often aware of how today's policies conflict with those previously enacted. Implicit in the Baron's statement is the notion of change and shifting philosophy. What Illinois history has shown is that language policy is subject to wider forces in the society. When groups are perceived as a threat, as in the case of the Germans and others before and after World War I, legislators are likely to respond with efforts to curtail linguistic freedom in favor of restrictive English-only policies. If groups are viewed as deserving of special help and not as politically menacing, then policymakers are willing to aid them by allowing the use of non-English languages, as long as the dominance of English is maintained.

At the time of this writing, we are in a period in Illinois when the role of English is quite secure and the use of non-English languages is tolerated in certain arenas. Whether or not this situation will continue is difficult to predict. In other states (e.g., California and Arizona), there have been recent policy initiatives against bilingual education and against the use of Spanish and other languages in public domains. Some states have passed restrictive English-only laws that go far beyond Illinois' symbolic declaration of English as the official language. Some, like Arizona, have tried to forbid the use of any language but English in the state's official business. The constitutional legality of such legislation has yet to be decided by the Supreme Court.

Furthermore, on the federal level, since the early 1980s, there has been a series of proposed legislation to declare English the nation's official language, to curtail or discontinue bilingual education, and to ban bilingual ballots. To date, no such legislation has been enacted, and the impact of such initiatives on policy in Illinois has been minimal. Yet, the history of language policy in Illinois demonstrates that the state has followed other states in enacting restrictive policy during periods when xenophobia was high, and so would not be immune from passing such legislation if the mood of the state turned anti-immigrant again. The message for those of us who value linguistic diversity is to monitor language policy within the state, realize that it can shift directions quickly, and be on the alert against policies that deprive linguistic minorities of the rights and benefits to which they are entitled.

REFERENCES

Andersson, T. (1971). *Bilingual education: The American experience.* Eric Document ED048581.

Baron, D. (1990a). The legal status of English in Illinois: Case study of a multilingual state. In Harvey A. Daniels (Ed.), *Not Only English: Affirming America's Multilingual Heritage,* (pp. 13–26). Urbana, IL: National Council of Teachers of English.

Baron, D. (1990b). *The English-only question.* New Haven: Yale University.

Chicago Public Schools. (1998). *School Board Adopts New Policy for Bilingual Education.* Chicago: Chicago Public School System.

Illinois State Board of Education. (2000a). *Transitional Bilingual Education and Transitional Program of Instruction Evaluation Report: Fiscal Year 1999.* Springfield, IL: Division of Research.

Illinois State Board of Education. (2000b). *FY 1999 Adult education and literacy: Report to the Governor and General Assembly.* Springfield, IL: Business Community and Family Partnership.

Judd, E. (1987). The English language amendment: A case study on language and politics. *TESOL Quarterly, 21,* 113–135.

Judd, E. (1992). Language-in-education policy and planning. In W. Grabe & R. B. Kaplan (Eds.), *Introduction to applied linguistics* (pp. 169–188). Reading, MA: Addison-Wesley.

Judd, E. (1999). California, here we go—again. *TESOL Journal, 8,* 4.

Kaplan, R. B. (1992). Applied linguistics and language policy and planning. In W. Grabe & R. B. Kaplan (Eds.), *Introduction to applied linguistics* (pp. 143–166). Reading, MA: Addison-Wesley.

Kloss, H. (1977). *The American bilingual tradition.* Rowley, MA: Newbury House.

Lau v. Nichols, 414 U.S. Reports 563 (1974).

Leibowitz, A. (1969). English literacy: Legal sanctions for discrimination. *Notre Dame Lawyer, 45,* 7–67.

Leibowitz, A. (1971). *Educational policy and political acceptance: The imposition of English as the language of instruction in American schools.* ERIC Document ED 047321.

Leideck v. City of Chicago, 248 Ill. App. 545 (1928).

Marshall, D. F. (1986). The question of an official language: Language rights and the Official Language Amendment. *International Journal of the Sociology of Language 60,* 7–75.

McCoy v. City of Chicago, 136 Ill. 344 (1891).

Meyer v. Nebraska, 262 U.S. 390 (1923).

People v. Day, 277 Ill. 543 (1917).
Perkins v. Board of Commissioners of Cook County, 271 Ill. 449 (1916).
Powell v. Board of Education, 97 Ill. 375 (1881).
State of Illinois. (1847). *Journal of the Convention Assembled at Springfield*, June 7, 1847, Springfield, IL.
State of Illinois. (1969). *Illinois Public Act 76–1469,* Springfield, IL.
State of Illinois. (1988). *Illinois Public Act 85–1389,* Springfield, IL.
State of Illinois. (2000). Office of the Secretary of State. 2000. Personal Conversation.

WITHIN THE FAMILY CIRCLE

3

Signifying Laughter and the Subtleties of Loud-Talking: Memory and Meaning in African American Women's Discourse

Marcyliena Morgan
Harvard University

> *Lord, this bitter earth*
> *Yes, can be so cold.*
> *Today, you're young.*
> *Too soon, you're old*
> *But while a voice*
> *Within me cries,*
> *I'm sure someone*
> *May answer my call*
> *And this bitter earth*
> *May not be so bitter*
> *After all.*
> (Clyde Otis 1959)

Whenever I think of Chicago, my memories—of its neighborhoods, politics, culture, and institutions—always focus on the city's African American women, their families, and their music.[1] As a young girl growing up on the South Side, I always marveled—and feared—Black women shaking their heads in response to some act they deemed incredibly stupid or ironic. My amazement was not because they passed harsh verdicts on

51

people and events, but that they were always so confident in their assessments. The daily lives of Chicago's Black women were wrapped in layers of contradictions, and they knew it. Yet they celebrated it. And they agonized over it too.

In the midst of their everyday experiences, Black women often concerned themselves with sexism, racism, and Chicago politics. Sometimes they buried their real fears and stories of discrimination in hilarious tales of adventure. At other times, the realities were revealed in retrospect—when one finally grasped in astonishment that what seemed out of place in a story was actually what was "really" going on. Getting the "real story," or at least more of the real details from women who have an incredible story to tell, is complicated, and not only because these stories are often painful and humiliating. It is also especially challenging to uncover these narratives because Black women are too often dismissed as difficult and irrelevant to a full understanding of African American culture. Their stories are often trivialized as inconsequential, ordinary, emotional and argumentative.[2] Yet, when African American women are considered unimportant, those who dismiss them obtain only a superficial appreciation of African American culture. Thus it is impossible to understand Black Chicago without recognizing the Black women who are at its core.

This chapter addresses the complexity of African American women's stories by exploring how language and interactions frame and reveal the buried truth, depth, and richness of African American women's lives. I focus on the body of linguistic and symbolic resources they employ to express their ideas, identities, roles, and relations to each other.[3] Through narratives, conversations, and interviews I analyze two generations of women's language and cultural practice, especially as they negotiate their race, gender, class, and sexuality. In particular, I focus on what Erving Goffman (1978/1981) called response cries. Response cries are instances of what appear to be self-talk in conventional conversations that also functions as a reference to beliefs outside of the talk. In studying African American women's discursive practices, I pay close attention to direct and indirect discourse, and verbal genres such as instigating, conversational signifying, and signifying laughter.[4]

Over the years that I have conducted research on African American women in Chicago, their music has served as a constant refrain. It has never been just background noise, even when I scarcely heard voices over the songs playing on the radio and stereo. Instead, music has represented attitude and commentary, the answer to questions answered and unanswered. The most loved singers of my mother's generation were Dinah Washington and Billie Holliday—two women who infused critically conscious hopefulness into every note they sang. Her favorite Dinah Washington song was *This Bitter Earth,* and it could be heard billowing from windows as the women raised their voices and their children, cleaned their homes, and the homes of others. My mother would say she loved Dinah because "she said what she wanted to and didn't care what anyone thought," and Billie, because "She knew what it meant to suffer."

DISCOURSE AND VERBAL REPERTOIRE: IDEOLOGY AND INTERACTION IN THE BLACK SPEECH COMMUNITY

The discourse and verbal genres enjoyed by African American children and young adults have been explored previously in both folklore and anthropology. These styles of talk are part of interaction rituals that represent the linguistic identity and socialization of African American youth. These rituals include the game of signifying—he-said-she-said—and instigating (Abrahams, 1976; Goodwin, 1990; Kochman, 1972; Mitchell-Kernan, 1973; Morgan, 1996, 1998, 1999, 2002).

Signifying is a fast-paced game of indirection played by mainly adolescent males who exchange verbal insults that highlight and place in jeopardy cultural symbols and capital (e.g., Your mama is so old when she reads the bible she reminisces).[5] As part of their growing up lesson, young girls reconcile disputes about power, gossip, loss of privacy, and insults through he-said-she-said episodes (Goodwin, 1990). Throughout neighborhoods and schoolyards one can hear girls impugning others by saying things like: "Wanda said that Christine said that you said that [my hair won't grow!]." In resolving these disputes, girls focus on the content of previous and future interactions and what someone actually said, could say, or would say if given the opportunity. Finally, teenage girls are less interested in who said something and more interested in investigating and evaluating instances of instigation. They have a finely developed sense of friendship, loyalty, and privacy, and seek to determine whether someone who reports that someone said something behind her back is a true friend.

Predictably, the preceding styles of speaking are considered inappropriate beyond the teenage years. Yet these childhood verbal games and interactions, having served their purpose, are not tucked away and forgotten. On the contrary, African American women incorporate and transform the knowledge accrued in playing childhood games, resolving interactions, and learning the difference between speaking African American English (AAE) and other dialects as well as the rewards and punishments for speaking AAE. Because vestiges of these practices remain in adult interactions, it seems that they are not lost but regenerated in women's conversations and narratives that take into consideration the speaker's intentionality, social face and the importance of coauthorship. Thus, signifying is replaced by indirect reference to cultural symbols in verbal interactions among adults. Women discourage he-said-she-said discourse and instead focus on a woman's right to represent herself and to tell her own story without interference from others (Morgan, 1996, 1999, 2002). Adult women also find instigators and talking about someone behind her back devious and juvenile. They constantly proclaim that grown women say things to your face!

As a direct result of the aforementioned childhood and adolescent verbal play, by the time they are adults, women have developed an elaborate analysis of interaction and social face and skills in evaluation and communication. In fact, it is assumed that for adult women, the spoken word is only one aspect of what is being said. This is because in the African American speech community, hearers and audience members construct meaning and intention along with the speaker. The cultural logic requires that individuals be aware of the consequences of their words. As a result, personal, cultural, social, and political factors must be considered along with the speaker's relationship to these factors and to footing (Goffman, 1981). As an actor and observer, one's social stance and social face are defined as how others understand the speaker as part of a community of cultural and social actors. Thus one's social footing or standing and the positions and roles one assumes in interactions are the foundation of talk. The African American community is not simply "one nation under a groove" as the popular song says, but a nation that grooves on evaluating and creating words and talk that represent individuals and ideas. Of course, one can establish and sustain his or her social stance and footing in numerous ways. It is possible to presume a cool social face and maneuver positive social standing. Correspondingly, depending on the content and social context, African American women's discourse can be direct, indirect, and directed (Table 3.1).

As a form of talk, direct discourse is typical of institutional settings, in which the event or context prescribes speaker intent as identical to the task (e.g.,

TABLE 3.1
Discourse and Context

	Focus	Social Context
Indirect discourse	Local knowledge, situated knowledge	Includes persons aware of local discourse practices
Direct discourse	Activities, procedures	Any hearers
Directed discourse	Clarification	Any hearers that think they are the target

school, work). It is often the form of discourse that reflects the speaker's most standard speech. Because of its association with formal and regulated settings, direct speech serves an instrumental function and is not considered indicative of speaker intentionality (Morgan, 1996). In contrast, indirect discourse involves the speaker's intentional representation of her desire to establish footing and social face through linguistic form and discursive style. For indirect discourse to be successful, the speaker must pay close attention to the locality of a shared audience who may serve as intended recipients, targets, and overhearers as well as those remembered and imagined. Thus indirect discourse incorporates local, social, and historical knowledge as well as knowledge of rules of discourse and AAE. Finally, directed discourse (Morgan, 1998) is marked by the absence of indirection, audience collaboration, and a disregard for social context. It highlights a hearer's responsibility and presence in the construction of social stance. Because of this challenge to the audience, directed discourse is often used to make what is implicit explicit, and to determine truth, knowledge, and power.

These forms of discourse appear in conversations and narratives of women in Chicago's African American community, and each style conveys the speaker's attitude toward the topic being discussed and toward participants described in the interactions and narratives. For indirect discourse to be successful, audience and participants must share local knowledge about African American culture. In contrast, neither direct nor directed discourse requires a knowledgeable audience. Direct discourse may include, but is not constructed around, speaker intent. Rather, the delivery of the message or information is considered appropriate for any hearer. Within this system, directed discourse makes explicit the local knowledge of indirect discourse and calls attention to the general audience typical of direct discourse. In this way, the speaker signals that she intends for both appropriate and inappropriate hearers to understand exactly what she means. It is because the type of discourse indexes speaker intent that the dialogic relation between style and content conveys what a person "really" means in a conversation.

In the examples in this chapter, African American women of different ages use and manipulate these styles to represent their lives, opinions, and realities. The narratives and interactions described in the following sections reflect the language ideology of the African American community. As Kathryn Woolard (1998) noted:

> Ideologies envision and enact ties of language to identity, to aesthetics, to morality, and to epistemology. Through such linkages, they underpin not only linguistic form and use but the very notion of the person and the social group. (p. 3)

This ideology is enmeshed in cultural beliefs of fairness and equality—about life and expectations in conversations. It is not surprising that at the core of Black communities are women prepared and compelled to confront injustice fearlessly because of a belief in principles of fairness. There are rewards for women who are adept at handling discourse, and there is punishment for those who are naïve and fail to recognize the power they have over their words.

GOING TO CHICAGO—SORRY BUT I CAN'T TAKE YOU

Chicago was founded by a Black man. Jean Baptiste Point de Sable (also spelled DuSable) established a trading post along the Chicago River about 1790, and from that location the city was born. Although most Black Chicagoans know the story of DuSable, especially students of DuSable High School, that knowledge did not protect Chicago's emerging Black community from racial discrimination. Chicago's Black population growth was a part of what is often described as the Black Exodus or Great Migration. This was the large-scale migration of Blacks from the southern United States to the North that accelerated around World War II. This migration was in response to the social, economic, and political conditions under which southern Blacks of the time lived. After slavery's official end in 1863, Blacks in the South enjoyed a brief legal respite from White supremacy during the reconstruction period that lasted from 1867 to 1877. By 1880, however, the life of the southern Black was characterized by a peonage system of sharecropping, lynching, and widespread disenfranchisement.

As they fled to northern urban areas for better jobs and to escape discrimination, the Black population of the South decreased from 77% in 1940 to 53% by 1970 (Jaynes & Williams, 1989, p. 60). The resulting expansion of Chicago's Black community was unrelenting and embodied the life, joy, and struggle of urban African American communities throughout the United States.

In 1890, Chicago was a city of 1 million people in which 75% percent of the population was foreign born or second-generation foreign born (Drake & Cayton, 1945). In 1910, Chicago's 2 million inhabitants included more than 40,000 Blacks who migrated from the South to escape the repercussions that marked the end of reconstruction and the reintroduction of laws protecting White supremacy. Between 1910 and 1940, its population increased eightfold (Patillo-McCoy, 1999). With the outbreak of World War I, European migration ceased, and more than 50,000 southern Blacks rushed into the city to meet the labor demands of the war. As immigrant neighborhoods declined, Blacks began settling in (Braden, 1995). While the foreign-born population of Chicago decreased during the depression by 20%, the Black population responded to their decline with a 20% increase in population (Drake & Cayton, 1945). In 1920, the Black population of Chicago had increased to more than 100,000; by 1940 it had increased to nearly 350,000. In 2000, the U.S. Census reported that the Black population of Chicago exceeded 1 million, which was 37% of the city's total population (Grossman, 1995). From DuSable's earlier expedition, a rousing Black Chicago had been born, and as it grew, the people laid claim to their city, nicknamed "Chitown."

The Black Belt of Chicago's South Side had absorbed 10,000 migrants at the turn of the century, but the same area could not hold the growing masses fleeing the South. St. Claire Drake and Horace Cayton conducted the first major sociological study on the Black community of Chicago in the 1940s. Their publication *Black Metropolis* (1945) identified the Douglas, Grand Boulevard and Washington Park communities as the core of what was called Chicago's Black Belt. Although the growth of Chitown was celebrated throughout the northern communities of the United States, it was not without its problems. Duncan and Duncan (1957) and Drake and Cayton (1945) reported that prior to the waves of migration, Blacks often lived in mixed immigrant neighborhoods, but the rapid increase in the population resulted in a steady push into working-class Irish communities and middle class areas (Spear, 1967). Tensions from the movement into White ethnic enclaves resulted in the race riots of 1919. The race riots lasted 5 days and were sparked by Whites drowning a Black youth on a South Side beach. In the end, 37 lives were lost; more than 1,000 people were homeless; and $250,000 worth of property was destroyed (Drake & Cayton, 1945). Today, the African American community stretches throughout Chicago's near Westside and the South Side, bordering Lake Michigan and Western Boulevard and stretching from 22nd Street to 127th Street and beyond.

By the time the steady flow of Blacks from the South had subsided, Chicago was brimming with a diverse African American community united by a common experience and shared attitudes and beliefs. The Black women who called Chicago their home represented all aspects of southern and northern society. Some were exslaves who were from both rural and urban southern areas. Some were men and women rural and urban born, who had been free before emancipation. Others were exslaves who had lived in northern rural and urban areas before emancipation, whereas still others, were free men and women who were born in rural and urban northern areas. By the middle of the 20th century, these four groups of men and women found themselves clustered together in Chicago, having taken part in one of the greatest internal migrations this country has ever witnessed. The urban Black community that they formed reflected both their similar beginnings and the diverse directions that were their fate. Moreover, for African Americans it was a community recognizable not simply by skin color, but by values, norms, expectations, a shared reality, and way of talking about the world around them.

SPEAKING UP AND STEPPING OUT:
PLEASURE AND PROPRIETY IN CHITOWN

To many who live there, Chicago is as Joe Williams sang in "Goin' to Chicago Blues": "a real down city—full of good folks who come from home." Its African American community is known nationwide for its oral creativity. From singer Lou Rawls describing "The Hawk"—the community's name for the city's bitter winds—to verbal toasting and blues storytelling, verbal skill is celebrated. For the women of Chicago, verbal skill is a force of both celebration and contestation as their identities and ethics of the past and present are negotiated through discourse. Among those born after World War I, stories about life in Chicago invariably incorporate the conflicts over moral issues regarding the role of women, race, migration from the South, the church, and work in general. This generation of women enjoyed their youth within the piety of strict religious doctrine and the enticing rhythms of the era's big jazz bands such as those of Duke Ellington and Count Basie. Thus it comes as no surprise that many of the older participants in the study (65–80 years old) mentioned the conflict and excitement in Black Chicago when the bands were in town. The conflict over whether one should dance to the big bands or sing in the church choirs were also questions about the role and status of

TABLE 3.2
Key to Dialog

CAPITAL LETTERS indicate some form of emphasis which may be signaled by changes in pitch or amplitude.

BOLD CAPITAL LETTERS indicate loud-talking.

A period (.) indicates a stopping fall in tone, not necessarily the end of a sentence.

A comma (,) indicates a continuing intonation, not necessarily between clauses of sentences.

An ellipsis (...) indicates that the sound just before the period has been lengthened.

A question mark (?) indicates a rising inflection, not necessarily a question.

An exclamation point (!) indicates an animated tone, not necessarily an exclamation.

A single dash (–) can indicate a (1) short untimed pause, (2) halting, abrupt cutoff, or when multiple dashes hyphenate the syllables of a word or connect strings of words, the stream of talk so marked has (3) a stammering quality.

All overlapping utterances, including those which start simultaneously are marked with a single left bracket ([).

The point where overlap stops is marked with a single right bracket (]).

=When there is no interval between adjacent utterances, the second being latched immediately to the first, the utterances are linked together with equal signs. They are also used to link different parts of a single speaker's utterance when those parts constitute a continuous flow of speech that has been carried over to another line to accommodate an intervening interruption.

(.)A period within parenthesis indicates a one second pause.

( )When intervals in the stream of talk occur, they are timed in tenths of a second and inserted within parentheses either within an utterance or between.

*(( ))*Double parentheses in italics provide description of quality of talk and activity related to talk.

women. Whenever I asked the older women whether they saw any of the jazz performers, none of the women offered simple yes or no responses, although their degree of exposure varied widely based on their experiences and moral belief systems. Rather, they either launched into a discussion about their youth or began a narrative describing their experiences. Surprisingly, irrespective of the style of discourse used, whether women attended the jazz clubs and dances correlated with whether they used direct or indirect discourse. For example, when I asked Crystal Hawthorne (age 67 years) whether she ever went to a jazz club when the big bands came to town, she responded with direct discourse exclusively. (All names are fictitious. The women included in this discussion were interviewed in 1991.)

```
 1  MM:    Did you ever get involved in any of the music in Chicago or
 2         anything like that?
 3  CH:    Just uh–I used to direct the choir at uh Sangamon at
 4         Christ's Church and I uh–sang in the choir so—that's
 5         what I did at the time. And when I was in–at Christ's
 6         Church But I (3-s pause) started going out here after we
 7         moved out here and I had problems with transportation
 8         going backwards and forwards so I started going–My
 9         children had join church out here so–I started going out
10         here and uh–wasn't going to my church too much. So I
11         decided I would make my own church out here–so I
12         could go regular. I could walk there if necessary.
```

Mrs. Hawthorne's response to my question is detailed and informative, but she does not say whether she attended jazz clubs. Instead, she responds by explaining that she used to direct a church choir. Besides a 3-s pause in line 6, Mrs. Hawthorne does not show any animation or variation in her speech. In fact, if this episode were not preceded by a question about jazz clubs, it would appear that she was responding to a question about going to church because she never utters the words "jazz club"! Like Mrs. Hawthorne, Irma Washington and Judy Murray's discussion of jazz in Chicago also reflects the values and attitudes of families and women. These two women had been friends for more than 40 years at the time of the interview, although they never socialized together until they were adults. In contrast to Mrs. Hawthorne, their description of the importance of jazz clubs includes various styles of speaking as well as insight into how they were viewed by the community at large.

1 IW: OK *((laughs))*, I went to the average teenage dance
2 *((laughs))* OK but they–we, we did have a center on 19th
3 and Archer. And every weekend we would have dances
4 there. (.3) Then a few **OTHER** times? we would sneak out?
5 MM: What were the names of some of the places you went to?
6 IW: Crown Propeller, was one. And, *((laughs))* and let's see it
7 was one, one called–I think it was the Peps—48th Street.
8 MM: That's for dancing right? They danced a lot there?
9 IW: Yeah. That was it!
10 JM: What did you think of the Peps?
11 IW: Wi … ld. That's where—that was my style. Wi … ld. It was
12 always crowded. You know, it was nice, it was nice.
13 That's where all the high school kids went.
14 MM: So you never went to the Peps? *((to JM who shakes her*
15 *head))*
16 IW: Na … w? *((looking at JM)* How you miss that? *((looking at*
17 *MM))* And she living right in the **HEART** of the city.
18 JM: My mother wouldn't **LET** me go!
19 IW: **DIDN'T YOU HEAR ME SAY** we was **SNEAKING** out?

Irma Washington responds to the question about going to jazz clubs by framing her statement in line 1, "I went to the average teenage dance," with laughter. Laughter is a special category in indirect reference and serves an indexical function in interactions by highlighting the speakers' critical attitude toward a situation or topic. Indexicality is an important concept because it incorporates all aspects of context to construct referential systems of signs and symbolism—the core ingredients for ambiguity and indirection.[7] Through indexicality we manage to understand what is being said within a framework of the social, cultural, local, political, imagined, and artistic world. Thus indexicality may not only reveal and display cultural knowledge, beliefs and practices, but may also serve as an endorsement to cultural insiders that a particular set of interpretative beliefs and practices are in play. Similarly, what I call "the Black woman's laugh" (Morgan, 2002), can seem out of context if one does not possess the interpretive framework to recognize and respond to that which is implicit and indexed and that which is explicit. This is because the Black woman's laugh often occurs within narratives and discussions of bigotry, patriarchy, paternalism, social class privilege, sexism, and other situations that may also be responded to with outrage and indignation. Consequently, in conversations and narratives, African American women's laughter often signals an indirect critique on situations in which injustice and the exercise of power highlight the event under discussion.[8]

This laugh is easily misinterpreted because it occurs as a reflex within discourse that is tragic or may have dire consequences for the speaker, who never provides an explanation for why she is laughing. As a response cry, it is meant to be overheard and aligns speakers with events. Yet this form of self-talk also aligns the speaker with a competing or contradictory assessment of the discourse. In this way, the laugh becomes representational self-talk in which the speaker indexes historical and social events and situations of power inequity that contrast and expose the speaker's—and culture's—attitude toward talk. Similarly, Goffman (1981) described how self-talk helps index that an alternative view, community, or the like may be represented:

> Its occurrence strikes directly at our sense of the orientation of the speaker to the situation as a whole. Self-talk is taken to involve the talker in a situationally inappropriate way. It is a threat to intersubjectivity; it warns others that they might be wrong in assuming a jointly maintained base of ready mutual intelligibility among all persons present. (p. 85)

Thus the contextually inappropriate response in the form of self-talk marks the laugh as indicative of a strong and positive social face of the speaker (Morgan, 1996). It represents a negative, sarcastic, or ironic attitude of the speaker toward her own remarks, the person who asked a question, or the situation as a whole. In this way, the laugh not only signals that the statement is misleading, but also it simultaneously indicates that the speaker is no fool and questions whether the questioner or listeners might be! Considering all of these factors, it is likely that Mrs. Washington has much more to say about the "average" teenage dances that she attended in her youth than she is revealing.

Although she does not come forward with the full details about her excursions into the jazz scene, Mrs. Washington does acknowledge that at times she would sneak out to attend dances (line 4). And after naming a few more of her favorite dance clubs, she laughs again and names another club (lines 6–7). Although her friend Judy is present during the interview, she is surprisingly silent and does not confirm anything her friend is saying. Instead, in line 10 Judy asks Irma Washington what she thought of Peps. Mrs. Washington responds

> Wi ... ld. That's where—that was my style. Wi ... ld. It was always crowded. You know, it was nice, it was nice. That's where all the high school kids went.

Mrs. Washington's description of Peps ranges from "wi ... ld" to "nice" and ends with the unassuming explanation that "all the high school kids went" there. Yet, her use of vowel lengthening on wild contrasted with her repeated saying how nice it was suggests that some part of the story remains untold. What's more, when I indicated to Judy in line 14 my understanding that she never went to Peps, she confirmed it, much to her friend's surprise. The way Irma Washington handles Judy Murray's statement addresses the conflict during the period between the secular and sacred life. First, Mrs. Washington asks Mrs. Murray how she missed the clubs and then signifies in line 17 when she begins to talk about Judy Murray—to me. Mrs. Murray responds with a statement that indexes the piety of the period " My mother wouldn't LET me go!" Finally, Mrs. Washington uses directed discourse, employing loud-talking in line 19 in response to Judy Murray's insistence that her mother wouldn't let her attend the jazz club. According to Mitchell-Kernan , loud-talking always signals that what is meant is not being directly stated:

> That is to say, it assures that intent will be imputed beyond the surface function of the utterance, which might be to seek information, make a request, make an observation, or furnish a reply to any of these. (p. 329)

Mrs. Washington responds to Mrs. Murray's statement about maternal—and moral—restrictions on her social life by stating, "**DIDN'T YOU HEAR ME SAY** we was **SNEAKING** out?" Her loud-talking is meant not only to critique Mrs. Murray's lack of deceptive dexterity as an adolescent. It is also her self-protective response to Mrs. Murray's implied censure regarding Mrs. Washington's lack of maternal and moral guidance, and it is something more.

To determine what part of the story Irma Washington did not reveal, and its importance within the local culture of Black Chicago at that time, I reviewed the interaction of Ruby Stokes, another woman who also went to Peps. When I asked her about jazz clubs and dancing, Mrs. Stokes discussed her favorite entertainers and then began talking about visiting the clubs. Included in the following conversation are Ruby Stokes' cousins, Judy Murray (Irma Washington's aforementioned friend) and Rae Murray (Judy's older sister).

1	Ruby:	But Savoy was great to dance. And those Count Basie—the
2		Big Band, OH MAN! Those WAS the days! As BIG as I
3		was—you know—we used to be doing—they called it the
4		jitter bug then right? *((in very fast and excited speech))* And
5		I be doin' my little dance and they would THROW me up in
6		the air over they head and come down on the floor and
7		COME ON UP! Baby I was GETTIN' IT! One dance (.2) and
8		I'd bé re … al wet! I'd be almost ready to go home. I didn't
9		get but maybe a couple dances out of the night. I'd be too
10		wet!—from da … ncin' and sweatin'. And you know? I
11		never lost a pound! (2–5 pause) As **MUCH** as I used to
12		dance and skate, I never lost a pound. Just **ATE** too much.
13		You know I was **HU … GE!** didn't hurt me at all–right. And
14		Rae used to go–Rae would go off and I'd be **DANCIN'!**–
15	Rae:	I knew all the dances.
16	Ruby:	I used to **MAKE** you dance with me. She say, "Ruby I'm
17		too"–She say (*in a mock hyperfeminine voice*), "Quit look-
18		ing at me! Quit lookin' at me like that!" I say "Well you
19		gotta look like **THIS** when you dancin'. You gotta have
20		**THIS** kinda look (*makes a serious face*). Oh Lord ! but that
21		was fun. Those was MY good ole days.
22	Rae:	We had some good times.
23	Judy:	Ruby used to go to the Peps to dance
24	Ruby:	**A … LL NIGHT!**
25	Judy:	And I couldn't go.
26	MM:	What? Pimps?
27	Judy:	Peps. The Peps.
28	Ruby:	Oh yeah that's the joint. That's a famous joint on 47th street,
29		47th and St. Lawrence. Didn't nothin' go up there but reefer
30		heads. See … we didn't have co**CAINE** heads in those days
31		—we only had **REE**fer heads. Bunch a **REE**fer heads hung
32		out up there. The fellows, the girls always went up there to
33		dance and be cute–see. Judy wasn't that cute yet–see.

34 Judy: No I was cuter.
35 Ruby: No you wasn't that cute! But of course **YOU** couldn't dance. I
36   could dance, you know. And I danced a ... ll night long. And
37   I'd come in the house 3, 4 o'clock in the morning and they'd
38   say, *((sarcastic voice))* "That **TRAMP'S** home." Isn't that ter-
39   rible to say that about Rae? *((laughs)))* "Ruby, your feet are
40   dirty!" **WHO CARES!?** ((very animated)) **DIDN'T NOBODY**
41   **ASK ME FOR NO FEET! They asked me to DANCE!**

Ruby Stokes' enthusiastic story of her youth includes both indirect and directed discourse. She begins with an animated narrative description of her exceptional dancing ability—in spite of her size—and then brings Rae into the conversation. However, Mrs. Stokes' inclusion of Rae Murray is strategic. Although Mrs. Murray says she knew the dances too (line 15), Ruby Stokes quickly reveals that it is she who taught Rae Murray to dance and imitates or marks Rae Murray's speech (lines 17–18). To mark someone, a speaker imitates a language variety associated with another context or a variety of speech style not preferred in the African American community. Thus the marking is attributable to a "type" of person who is different from the speaker, intended hearers, or both (Mitchell-Kernan, 1972).

Judy Murray identifies Peps as the name of the club where Ruby Stokes used to dance (line 27), and Mrs. Stokes quickly agrees by loud-talking her response: "all night." Judy Murray repeats the plight she described in Mrs. Washington's interaction and simply states that she couldn't go (line 25). Then Ruby Stokes describes Peps, using loud-talking to reveal that reefer (marijuana) was used regularly at the club (lines 31). Mrs. Stokes ends her description by using conversational signifying when she tells me—in the presence of Judy Murray—that girls went there to dance and be cute, and that Judy wasn't cute enough to go (lines 33–35). Note that this is the first time that Ruby Stokes addresses Judy Murray's statement in line 25. She implies that Judy Murray's absence was not because she couldn't go (as Judy Murray argued to Irma Washington), but that Judy Murray didn't go to Peps because she couldn't dance and she wasn't cute enough! Ruby Stokes actually states that belief in line 35. She then returns to a description of her nights out dancing and loud-talks on the word tramp as she imitates how her family responded to her nights out. Ruby Stokes then says to me "Isn't that terrible to say about Rae?" in Rae Murray's presence and laughs (line 39). This laugh accomplishes two things. As a response cry, it signals that her statement is contradictory. Thus it was not said to Rae Murray but Ruby Stokes. Also, it implicates Rae Murray as the person who said the terrible thing as well.

The laughter of older women exists in relation to both the content of the discourse and the social context in which it occurs. Because both indirect and directed discourse requires the presence of targets and those who can serve as the targets' surrogates, a speaker can say something for someone to hear rather than respond to. Thus in cases wherein Ruby Stokes talks to me about Rae and Judy Murray, they say nothing. This is typical in baited indirectness (Morgan, 1996), in which to respond is to acknowledge the truth in what the speaker has said. Mrs. Stokes quotes what is said to her: "That **TRAMP'S** home." "Ruby, your feet are dirty!" Then Ruby Stokes loud-talks again after she imitates Rae Murray's criticism of her dirty feet. And in lines 40 to 41 she loudly proclaims, **"WHO CARES! DIDN'T NOBODY ASK ME FOR NO FEET! They asked me to DANCE**!" Later Mrs. Stokes explained to me privately: "You know, your feet get dirty cause you be dancin' on them dusty floors you know." This statement once again invokes the conflict between pleasure and propriety exposed in Mrs. Washington's statement about sneaking out as opposed to being let out. Although Ruby Stokes, like Mrs. Washington, is not ashamed of having a good time, she does not want me to think of her or her feet as dirty—physically or morally.

I JUST HAD TO LAUGH

The response cries of Irma Washington and Ruby Stokes both function to signal that something significant is not being said in the interaction that is important to an understanding of what the women are actually saying. These cries suggest that the hearer listen closely and use her knowledge of the situation and culture. This form of signifying laughter is also a part of Rae Murray and Nora Snyder's discourse. They were in their late 70s at the time of our 3-hour discussion about their lives as friends and cousins in Chicago. Before the following exchange, they had been talking about migrating from Mississippi to Chicago when they were young and about the freedoms of women in the North compared with to the South. Their use of the laugh is structured around information about the life of women in general and the lack of equality in the home.

```
 1  MM:    Uh-huh now in terms of changes—and the—and the—as
 2          Black—Black women, what are some of the—the things
 3          that you see that are different now—first—that you like.
 4  Rae:    Being Black women?
 5  MM:     In terms of what's happened to Black women.
 6  Rae:    I LIKE it because they are more outspoken than they were
 7          when I was coming along. Aaahh they weren't allowed to
 8          say they vie … ws in front of their HUSbands! Most of the
 9          time they DID, they KNOCKED you down.(.) You know.
10  MM:     Do you remember ever seeing that happen?
11  Rae:    Uh no—like if you disaGREED - I mean—ah like if some-
12          thing was sai … d and you said "Oh NO it wasn't like
13          that"—you know- uh—YOU not supposed to say that!
14          Long as the—man of the house say it was this way—it's
15          got to be that way.
16  NORA:   And if it wasn't you [hit the floor
17  RAE:                          [And don't you forget it
18  All:    ((laughter))
```

This story is the beginning of a long episode in which Rae Murray and Nora Snyder talk about the abuse women suffered before the women's liberation movement. They use loud–talking and laughter as a device of indirect critique to indicate that they do not agree with the abuse women suffered. Thus in describing what happened when a woman spoke her mind, Rae Murray loudly says the word knocked (line 9). When I asked her if she had ever witnessed this, she begins to say no in line 11, but continues with her description of what happened.[9] She stresses her negative attitude toward the treatment of women by contrasting the words and syllables she speaks with loud-talk and those she expresses in a normal voice.

When she provides an example of what happened when a woman had an opinion that was different from that of her husband, she again loud-talks, focusing on the words disagreed, no, you and say. Through this form of directedness Rae Murray is able to convey that she doesn't care who knows or hears her negative attitude toward the way things were regarding women in the good old days. The accuracy of her description is supported and collaborated when she and Nora Snyder overlap in lines 16 and 17 as Nora describes women being knocked down by their husbands (hit the floor) if they didn't do as their husbands suggested and as Rae collaborates with "And don't you forget it" followed by laughter. Their laughter at the end is a scathing commentary on the period and signals how much they are at odds with the description they have actually given.

These segments illustrate both the use of indirect verbal styles and the significance of local knowledge in interpreting discourse. The three segments about jazz clubs in Chicago reveal that women do not participate in conversations about things they did not experience firsthand. To do so would be to speculate and talk about others, and they do not speculate about something that they did not do. Thus Crystal Hawthorne only mentions church, whereas Judy Murray only says that she was not allowed to go. In many respects, Crystal Hawthorne was a religious and good woman and Judy Murray was an obedient and good one. Both Irma Washington and Ruby understand how their club forays are interpreted within this world. Thus Mrs. Washington represents herself as wild and nice, whereas Ruby Stokes constructs herself as just wild. But their description of their lives includes a critique of prudery and an assessment that the other two women did not live complete lives. Irma Washington and Ruby Stokes use laughter, loud-talk, marking, and pointed indirection to convey their recognition of the cultural conflicts of their generation. It also takes the full arsenal of discourse styles for Nora and Rae to describe the lives of women in Chicago at the turn of the century. They are confident and adept at waiting to develop intricate indirect references and responses. Through the use of these styles, they are able to present a general, personal, and personalized account of life for Black women in Chicago.

OH NO SHE DIDN'T!

The complex skills of older women is even more remarkable when one recognizes the difficulty young adult novices face when navigating social face, footing, cultural norms, discourse rules, and power. I have observed that whereas older women use indirectness with facility, younger women continue to struggle with this form in conversation and tend to be more directed. This may be because younger women continue to resort to instigating, testing loyalty, and determining both whether one's ambiguity is purposeful and how to mediate it. For example, one evening four young women 18 to 25 years old visited me after they had returned from celebrating one of their birthdays.[10] They laughed and talked for more than an hour. As they were preparing to leave, one of the women (Josie) whispered to me

> Can you believe what Lori said? I kept thinking, "Oh NO! Oh No she didn't!" AND I DIDN'T SAY ANYTHING because you were there and we had such a good time. It wasn't time to hurt nobody's feeling.

When Josie confided in me, I wasn't aware that anything had happened in the conversation that she might find offensive. Later, I reviewed my notes on the conversation, noticed the flow of talk, and assessed whether targets seemed to shift. I discovered that the offensive segment began in reference to Lori's new hair extensions and her sudden tendency to fling her hair around.[11] African American hair texture and hairstyles can be complex signifiers of cultural, political, and social values. Since the texture of African American hair varies widely from very tight curls to straight hair, it is sometimes the case that tighter, natural curls are associated with African sensibilities and standards of beauty, and straight hair is associated with European standards. Thus flinging straight hair, in particular, is seen as extremely problematic and conceited, and is often ridiculed as non–African American.

```
1  Lori:    ((directed to MM)) Yeah, they hatin' on my hair but I under-
2           stand. I would hate true beauty too if I didn't have it! But I
3           just say, "Don't hate the beautiful—hate yourSELF you ugly
4           people" ((everyone laughs)). 'Cause I KNOW that girl in
5           Krispy Kremes was hating on my hair. That's why she had
6           an attitude—but I just let it go 'cause—you know—be kind
7           to those who have not ((everyone laughs)).
8  Josie:   Girl you KNOW you a fool.
9  Lori:    Hatin' on me? That's OK! I know I look good. ((long pause))
```

10 Gwen: I can't believe what we did at the club!
11 Josie: I didn't do anything. I was the only one who laid back.
12 Lori: *((looking at Kesha))*. Yeah, girl, **YOU** were laid back. Just
13   like you were when that guy came up to talk to me and
14   you thought he was talking to you! Well—anyway, I for
15   one had a **GREAT** time.
16 Josie: Well anyway–I had fun.

As stated earlier, although younger women use the same discursive resources as more experienced women, they often do so in different ways and with less facility. As with the older women, a strong positive face is necessary, but it is negotiated with the audience, who may not confirm the self-assessment. Thus Lori uses loud-talking to refer to herself—and her newfound long hair—as beautiful. Everyone considers this humorous, and the directed loud-talking implies that she doesn't care what people think, and that she may not really be serious about what she has said. But there is a problem here. The powerful social face being presented is actually a fragile façade replete with cracks—cracks that when touched, bring the whole act down.

Lori's suspicion that her social standing may be in dispute is signaled in lines 12–15 when she loud-talks Josie and uses indirection as she addresses Kesha about something that Josie actually did. This is the same strategy that Ruby Stokes used with me earlier, to talk about something that Rae Murray did. Kesha knows and acts out the social rules when something is said to her, but about someone else—say nothing and behave as if you are not being targeted. That it was Josie whom Lori is targeting and not Kesha is apparent from Kesha's lack of response and from Josie's response that was not in reference to what Lori said. Thus, whereas Lori conversationally signifies by using Kesha as the intermediary, Josie does not address Lori's remarks. In some respect, the signifying seems more personal than that of the other women because it is not based on what someone obviously did, but rather on what Josie may have intended to do. This may be because they are unable to use successfully the multiple forms of indirection at their disposal. Because Lori uses this style without clear provocation, she damages her social footing among the group, who later described her as too sensitive and immature.

JUST LIKE ME: EMPATHY AND SYMPATHY IN WOMEN'S DISCOURSE

Desiré was 23 years old when I met with her to talk about assisting me with my research on youth who participate in Chicago's poetry circles. She interrupted our discussion of her assignment to tell me about a shooting in my old neighborhood in the city. The beginning of her story was confusing for me because I initially thought she was directly involved in the incident in some way.

1   Desiré: Did you hear about the girl that got shot in the car who was
2   **JUST LIKE ME**!
3   MM: No. What happened?
4   Desiré: *((fast paced))* Well, see this policewoman killed this girl
5   and I think she did it on purpose. Now that's the word on
6   the streets and **STREETS** don't lie!
7   MM: What?
8   Desiré: See, because she knew him and knew she was with her
9   man. *((fast paced))* Well, not really her man.—See, she
10   wanted him, and he didn't see it that way, so when she
11   came up on her she wasn't expecting it.
12   MM: What?
13   Desiré: 'Cause she didn't know.
14   MM: Didn't know what?
15   Desiré: The girl, who was shot and killed by a police officer—a fe-
16   male police officer.
17   MM: What??!! Did you know her?
18   Desiré: *((talking fast and excitedly))* This man and this woman
19   were together. And they were in his car. And he saw police
20   lights flashing and he started trying to get away. He fled—on
21   foot. But he fled because he said he was afraid of the police
22   *((rolls eyes))* and the girl in the car didn't know she was a
23   policewoman. *((laughter))* When they were chasing them,
24   they called their sergeant and he said, "Don't pursue. DON'T
25   PURSUE!" But they did anyway. And when he stopped the
26   car, he got out and ran. She just sat there. And the police-
27   woman walked up to her and said something and then shot
28   her as she sat there. She wanted to get her purse because it
29   was behind her and when she tried she got shot.
30   MM: How did they find that out?

31 Desiré: I **TOLD** you it was **ME**! *((laughs))* That's what I would have
32   done! Now this was a **GOOD** woman my age! She had gone
33   to my school and **EVERYTHING!** She didn't know that he
34   had been out with her! And the word on the street is always
35   true. And everybody's saying she just shot her because she
36   was jealous! And that's why it happened. *((in a soft voice))*
37   *Nothing more and nothing less.–And she got off!*

Desiré's story is an important example of a young woman's earnest, although not always effective, attempt to use indirect and directed discourse. In many ways, it reveals by contrast how seamlessly the older women use these speech styles and what they accomplish. Whereas the older women's attitude and position are enmeshed in their exploitation of indirection, Desiré's attempt to invoke her personal stance and attitude appears awkward and unsophisticated. She is very disturbed about the death of the young woman and serves to place herself as the hypothetical victim. That she empathizes with the young woman who was shot is evident when she doubles herself and considers the victim's jeopardy as Black, woman, and in love as her own. She uses loud-talking to clarify how she viewed the tragedy in line 2—"**JUST LIKE ME!**"[12] She also suggests that many people in the community agree with her in line 6 when she loudly proclaims, "streets don't lie!" Her emotional involvement in the topic is obvious as she tells her tale with increasing speed. Although she knows I no longer live in Chicago and have no knowledge of the tragedy, she does not consider my outsider status or use indirection to signal alternative audiences as the older women likely would. Instead, she aligns with me in my knowledge of police brutality, excessive force and racism as well as my knowledge of what can happen when a lover is scorned. Her story, therefore, is one of injustice and lover's revenge. It is about the relationship between the young woman who was killed, the police who shot her and the boyfriend who fled.

Desiré rolls her eyes (line 22) to convey that she does not believe the boyfriend's reason for running away from imminent danger. Her laughter and response cry in line 23 serves as a confirmation that it is true that he knew the police following him was his girlfriend. Although Desiré does offer more background information about what happened, she continues to insert herself into the story, causing me continuous confusion about who did what to whom and—more importantly—why (lines 8–11). She uses directed loud-talking in a way that stresses that she finds the story troubling and that it could have happened to her. Yet she does not provide local references or use me to convey her indirection to highlight the event. Laughter is her only indirect device in spite of my attempts to get clarification on the tragedy, and the laughter in line 31 suggests that Desiré is not particularly interested in whether she is telling me a factual story with all of the details. What is important to her is that I understand that this story is her story too.

CONCLUSION

African American women's discourse is a part of the chorus of the culture. Many of the women described in this chapter would argue that their use of indirectness and laughter is the result of growing up in a city where people love the power of their language and their laugh. They are right, but there is more to the story. African American women are well aware that they have paid and continue to "pay their dues," and their discourse joins in with their nonvocal cues such as the hand on the hips—or in your face—and the slow rolling of the eyes. The system of indirectness described in this chapter produces powerful speech in that it comments on and references all aspects of social life. It provides attitude and constant assessment. Yet these women's discourses are not the secret handshake of a group wrapped in hidden ritual. Instead, they are discursively layered critiques by Black woman in Chicago and America who want us to know what they think, know, and feel—if we are willing to acknowledge their symbols, histories, social realities, and joys and pains first.

Although I have focused on women's interactions, both men and women who are socialized within the African American experience share their ideology of language use. These women's discourse styles provide insight into how language embodies who a person is as well as how people consider language to be a tool to represent and index their ideas and culture. It is a window into the complexity of representation and meaning and the elaborate constructions on which speakers rely to express lives deeply layered in memory, rights, family, politics, art, culture and music. It is a particular view of Black Chicago that includes the details of its history and politics and the glory of getting the story told so that it reveals and celebrates culture, life and hope.

ENDNOTES

1. In fact, many of my taping sessions include the background music of the women as well as pleas to cut off the tape so they could enjoy a favorite song.

2. See Morgan (1999, 2002) for a critique of research on African American women.
3. This chapter is based on ethnographic fieldwork conducted from 1989 to 1999. It includes interviews and conversations that were audiotaped and videotaped.
4. I do not discuss the use of African American English (AAE) and general English contrast (Morgan, 1996, 2002) to index the language ideology of the speech community in this chapter, although I am aware that the women incorporate them in their discourse.
5. Signifying is also known by the regional names of "sounding," "the dozens," "joning," "snapping," "busting," "capping," "bagging," and "ranking."
6. The blues and jazz singer Joe Williams recorded "Goin' to Chicago Blues" while a singer with the Count Basie band.
7. See Peirce (1955), Hanks (2001), Silverstein (1976) for further discussion of indexicality.
8. Men also use this laugh but within the culture it seems to occur more frequently among women without additional comment. See Morgan (2002).
9. In fact she later tells a story about seeing this happen to her mother.
10. This event occurred in 1998 when they were celebrating the youngest woman's birthday.
11. This occurred during the second hour of their visit. I took notes on the conversation and taped some segments. I did eventually return to Josie who confirmed my observations.
12. She was teary-eyed throughout the narrative and did not know the young woman who was killed.

REFERENCES

Abrahams, R. (1976). *Talking Black*. Rowley, MA: Newbury Press.

Braden, W. (1995). Chatham: An African-American success story 1995: African-American migration to Chicago. In M. G. Holli & P. d'A. Jones (Eds.), *Ethnic Chicago: A multicultural portrait* (pp. 340–345). Grand Rapids, MI: Eerdmans.

Drake, S., & Cayton, H. (1945). *Black metropolis*. New York: Harcourt, Brace and Company.

Duncan, O., & Duncan, B. (1957). *The Negro population of Chicago*. Chicago: The University of Chicago Press.

Goffman, E. (1981). *Forms of talk*. Oxford, England: Basil Blackwell.

Goodwin, M. (1990). *He-said-she-said: Talk as social organization among black children*. Bloomington, IN: Indiana University Press.

Grossman, J. (1995). African-American migration to Chicago. In M. G. Holli, & P. d'A. Jones (Eds.), *Ethnic Chicago: A multicultural portrait* (pp. 303–340). Grand Rapids, MI: Eerdmans.

Hanks, W. (2001). Indexicality. In A. Duranti (Ed.), *Key terms in language and culture* (pp. 119–121). Oxford, England: Blackwell.

Jaynes, G., & Williams, R. (1989). *A common destiny: Blacks and American society*. Washington, DC: National Academy Press.

Kochman, T. (Ed.). (1972). *Rappin' and stylin' out: Communication in urban Black America*. Urbana, IL: University of Illinois Press.

Mitchell-Kernan, C. (1972). Signifying, loud-talking, and marking. In T. Kochman. (Ed.), *Rappin' and stylin' out: Communication in urban Black America* (pp. 315–335). Champaign, IL: University of Illinois Press.

Mitchell-Kernan, C. (1973). Signifying. In A. Dundes (Ed.), *Mother wit from the laughing barrel* (pp. 310–328). New York: Garland Publishing.

Morgan, M. (1996). Conversational signifying: Grammar and indirectness among African-American women. In E. Ochs, E. Schegloff, & S. Thompson (Eds.), *Interaction and grammar* (pp. 405–433). Cambridge: Cambridge University Press.

Morgan, M. (1998). More than a mood or an attitude: Discourse and verbal genres in African-American culture. In S. S. Mufwene, J. R. Rickford, G. Bailey, & J. Baugh (Eds.), *African-American English: Structure, history, and use* (pp. 251–281). London/New York: Routledge.

Morgan, M. (1999). "No woman no cry": Claiming African American women's place. In M. Bucholtz, A. C. Liang, & L. A. Sutton (Eds.), *Reinventing identities: From category to practice in language and gender* (pp. 27–45). Oxford: Oxford University Press.

Morgan, M. (2002). *Language, discourse, and power in African American culture*. Cambridge: Cambridge University Press.

Otis, C. (1959 & 1960). *This Bitter Earth* (song lyrics). Play Music. (Copyright renewed 1987 & 1988 by Iza Music Group.)

Patillo-McCoy, M. (1999). *Black picket fences: Privilege and peril among the Black middle class*. Chicago: University of Chicago Press.

Peirce, C. S. (1955). Logic as semiotic: The theory of signs. In J. Buchler (Ed.), *Philosophical writings of Peirce* (pp. 98–119). New York: Dover Publications.

Silverstein, M. (1976). Shifters, linguistic categories, and cultural descriptions. In K. Basso & H. Selby (Eds.), *Meaning in anthropology* (pp. 11–55). Albuquerque, NM: University of New Mexico Press.

Spear, A. (1967). *Black Chicago: The making of a negro ghetto 1890–1920.* Chicago: University of Chicago Press.

Woolard, K. (1988). Introduction: Language ideology as a field of inquiry. In B. Schieffelin, K. Woolard, & P. Kroskrity (Eds.), *Language ideologies: Practice and theory* (pp. 3–50). Oxford: Oxford University Press.

Photograph by Michael Maltz

4

Personal Storytelling: Working-Class and Middle-Class Mothers in Comparative Perspective

Grace E. Cho
Peggy J. Miller
University of Illinois at Urbana-Champaign

Several strands of sociolinguistic research indicate that personal storytelling flourishes in many European American and African American working-class communities. Labov and Waletzky's (1967) classic analysis of stories of personal experience was based on a corpus of stories told by adults who had not finished high school and who came from a variety of urban and rural areas, including Harlem, the Lower East Side of New York City, and Martha's Vineyard. Bauman's (1986) influential work on highly performed oral narrative focused on working-class men from rural Texas. In addition, several studies attest to the narrative skill of working-class adolescents (Labov, 1972; Goodwin, 1990; Shuman, 1986). Most remarkably, this proclivity for narrative is detectable at a very early age. Several studies show that 2-year-olds from working-class communities—in Baltimore

(Miller, 1994; Miller & Moore, 1989; Miller & Sperry, 1988), in the Piedmont Carolinas (Health, 1983), in the Black Belt of Alabama (Sperry & Sperry, 1996)—not only inhabit home environments that are densely populated with personal stories, but participate routinely in telling such stories.

This evidence raises the possibility that the affinity for personal narrative is stronger in working-class communities than in middle-class communities. Surprisingly, however, there is very little empirical work that actually compares personal storytelling in working-class and middle-class communities. The study reported in this chapter extends a line of research that attempts to remedy this omission by comparing personal storytelling in two predominantly White communities in Chicago: one working-class community and one middle-class community.

TWO CHICAGO NEIGHBORHOODS

Daly Park (a pseudonym)[1] is a stable, predominantly Catholic, working-class neighborhood settled originally by Irish immigrants in the 1830s. The area quickly became an industrial center, supporting a steel mill, meatpacking plants, and brickyards. These employment opportunities drew German, English, Welsh, Swedish, Polish, and other European immigrants to the neighborhood. Daly Park reached its peak population in the 1920s, and has experienced a gradual decline in population since then. At the time of data collection in the late 1980s and early 1990s, many residents struggled with factory closings and other economic hardships. In recent decades the ethnic composition of the neighborhood has changed as Mexican families have moved into the neighborhood. However, families of European descent still predominate.

Although Daly Park is located only a few miles from the Loop, one city newspaper called it, "one of those hidden secrets." Another referred to its residents as "a forgotten people." Like many working-class enclaves in urban areas, Daly Park is somewhat invisible to outsiders. Many residents live only a few blocks from where they grew up. Several of the families in our study rented modest two-flats, which they shared with grandparents or another relative. Only one family owned their own home. Most of the parents in our sample were high school graduates. The fathers worked in blue-collar jobs (e.g., construction and maintenance), and some of the mothers occasionally held part-time jobs as clerks or waitresses. In Daly Park, a strong sense of neighborhood identification is reflected in civic association membership. Moreover, like many residents in Daly Park, the families in our sample were active in local churches and sent their children to parochial schools located in the neighborhood.

Longwood (a pseudonym) has been a home to Irish Americans for nearly a century. Although it remains predominantly Irish Catholic, a sizeable minority of African American families reside in the neighborhood. St. Patrick's Day is observed with great enthusiasm and includes an annual neighborhood parade. Longwood is a prosperous neighborhood of spacious, single-family dwellings situated on quiet, tree-lined streets. The neighborhood is known locally for the beauty of its streets and houses, several of which are on the National Register of Historic Places. All the families in our Longwood sample owned their homes. Although Longwood has a much more suburban flavor than many Chicago neighborhoods, several of the parents in our study felt it was important to resist the homogenization of the nearby suburbs. Civic organizations have worked actively to preserve the special character and small-town ambiance of the neighborhood.

Like Daly Park, many Longwood residents have strong intergenerational roots in the community, with extended family members living nearby. Houses in Longwood are almost never placed on the real estate market, being sold instead by word of mouth. One of the families in our study lived in the house in which the mother had grown up. In another family, the father refused a job promotion that would have required moving from the neighborhood. All the parents were college graduates. The fathers worked in professional positions (e.g., finance, law). Most of the mothers had worked outside the home as teachers or researchers before they had children, but all had chosen to be full-time homemakers when their children were young. In parallel to Daly Park, many of the families were active in local churches and sent their children to the local parochial schools.

COMPARING PERSONAL STORYTELLING IN DALY PARK AND LONGWOOD

Previous research conducted in these two neighborhoods by Miller's research team focused on co-narrated personal storytelling with young children (Burger & Miller, 1999; Wiley, Rose, Burger, & Miller, 1998). That is, we recorded naturally occurring episodes of talk, in which the child and one or more family members together narrated past events from the child's life. We found that these co-narrations occurred much more frequently in the working-class neighborhood of Daly Park than in the middle-class neighborhood of Longwood. When the working-class children were 3 years old, they produced nearly three times as many stories as their middle-class counterparts.

In addition to differences in frequency, Burger and Miller (1999) found a complex pattern of similarities and differences in the content of personal storytelling in the two communities. Although story content was skewed in the positive direction in both communities, working-class children and their families told stories about more extreme negative experiences and produced more negative emotion talk. Like the working-class families in South Baltimore (Miller & Sperry, 1987), the Daly Park families also used more dramatic language for conveying negative emotional experience.

In this chapter, we explore further the meanings and discourses associated with personal storytelling in these two Chicago neighborhoods. Instead of examining observations of young children and their families, we draw upon a complementary data source from the same ethnographic study, namely interviews with mothers concerning personal storytelling. We approach these interviews from two angles: as sources of information about mothers' folk theories or ideologies and as communicative events or social practices.

MOTHERS' BELIEFS AND VALUES ABOUT STORYTELLING

Within cultural psychology, the mothers' beliefs and values about personal storytelling can be construed as parental folk theories or ethnotheories (Bruner, 1990, 1996; Harkness & Super, 1996). Within linguistic anthropology, these beliefs and values fall under the rubric of language ideologies (Hanks, 1996; Schieffelin, Woolard, & Kroskrity, 1998). Both of these disciplinary viewpoints converge on the idea that it is not possible to appreciate the full meaning of a cultural or linguistic practice without taking into account the participants' "informal" theories or commonsense understandings and evaluative stances toward that practice. These ideologies may be explicitly discussed, but are often deeply taken for granted and implicit in the practices themselves. In the current study, there were various aspects of their families' narrative practices—memories from childhood and reflections about current practices—that the mothers talked about easily and at length, providing ready access to some components of their folk theories.

INTERVIEWS AS CULTURAL-LINGUISTIC PRACTICES

We also approached the interviews from a second angle, namely as communicative events or cultural–linguistic practices in their own right (Briggs, 1986). From this perspective, interviewing is an observable social activity in which ethnographer and informant participate. The interviews will vary, depending on how the two parties negotiate their joint activity. This raises the possibility that interviews will take systematically different forms in different communities, reflecting variation in local norms of communication. The interviews thus provide an opportunity to examine not only what people say, but when and how they say it—and what they do not say. In the current study, this approach led us to analyze the storytelling that the mothers spontaneously produced during the interviews.

In other words, in this study we examined the mothers' talk about storytelling and their enactments of storytelling. Both provide insight into the mothers' folk theories and practices of narrative. Four specific questions, derived from these complementary perspectives, provide the focus of this chapter: (a) How did mothers from working-class Daly Park and middle-class Longwood characterize their family's storytelling practices? (b) How frequently did mothers from the two communities tell personal stories during the course of the interviews? (c) How were these stories sequenced relative to one another? (d) What were these stories about?

THE INTERVIEWS

In the larger comparative project, of which this study is a part, we combined ethnographic fieldwork with extensive audio- and video-recorded observations of naturally occurring talk in the home (Burger & Miller, 1999; Miller, Fung, & Mintz, 1996; Miller, Wiley, Fung, & Liang, 1997). The study unfolded in three phases over the course of at least 2 years: an initial fieldwork and get-acquainted phase, a longitudinal observation phase, and an interview phase.

The findings reported in this chapter are based on interviews with six Daly Park mothers and six Longwood mothers. The focal children were balanced by gender, and had a mean age of 3 years and 9 months in Daly

Park and 4 years in Longwood at the time of the interviews. All the families in both communities were two-parent families of European descent, with the mothers as the primary caregivers. In each family, at least one parent had grown up in the community, and extended family members lived nearby.

Because the interviews were conducted during the final phase of the study, the mothers and researchers knew each other well. The interview took place in the home, and children were often present during the interview. The interview protocol consisted of 29 questions, but the researchers did not necessarily follow a preset order. They were encouraged to adapt the wording as necessary and to follow the mother's lead as much as possible. Topics included memories of storytelling from childhood, good storytelling, narrative practices within the current family, and storytelling to, with, and by children.

The interview was designed to be open-ended and informal, and the mothers were encouraged to elaborate on their responses, examples, and stories as much as they wanted. Most interviews lasted 1 to 2 hours. All the interviews were transcribed verbatim by a trained research assistant and subsequently checked for accuracy by a second transcriber.

MOTHERS' REFLECTIONS ON STORYTELLING

In analyzing the interviews, our first question was, how did the Daly Park and Longwood mothers characterize their families' personal storytelling practices? To answer this question we reviewed and re-reviewed the mothers' responses throughout the interview, paying particular attention to the following questions: Can you remember hearing people tell stories when you were growing up? How often did they tell stories? Were there some people in your family or community who were really good storytellers? Do children listen to adult storytelling? Are there some topics that you feel are inappropriate for children? Following the procedures for deriving descriptive schemes in qualitative analysis (Bloom, 1974; Gaskins, Miller, & Corsaro, 1992), we looked for patterns in the mothers' attitudes toward personal storytelling, their memories of personal storytelling when they were growing up, and their reflections on current family practices. We then compared the patterns for Daly Park and Longwood.

We found that mothers from both communities responded positively to questions about storytelling. The overwhelming consensus among both groups of mothers was that storytelling was avidly practiced by themselves, their husbands, parents, grandparents, and other relatives. Mothers had little difficulty naming the "good storytellers" in their families. When asked whether she could remember hearing people tell stories when she was growing up, Janet, a Longwood mother, enthusiastically responded, "All the time. All the time. The first person that popped into my mind … was my older brother … just all the time would tell stories … but all of us. We just must love to tell all about whatever happens to us because we do anecdotes, we still do it. We go out to eat, the brothers and sisters, and we tell anecdotes. I tell anecdotes all the time, my kids, tell anecdotes; we do that constantly." Like many of the mothers in both communities, Janet began by talking about her memories of personal storytelling, but then volunteered that this kind of storytelling remains an important part of her family life in the present. Pamela, another Longwood mother said, "Oh yeah, and we always begged them [parents and grandparents] to tell more … We knew the story, had heard it a million times, but we asked to hear it a million more!"

Similarly, Mabel, a Daly Park mother, said, "I had this one great great grandma … She was born in 1888. And oh, the stories. We would just sit there and she would, you know, tell us about, you know, how it was … and that was fun." Sharon, another Daly Park mother, repeatedly exclaimed what great storytellers her in-laws were in between sharing multiple examples of those stories, "OH! I could be there for DAYS! And that's all … that's all they do is they TALK! I mean seriously, you could sit there and I mean, I could make tons and tons of coffee, and they [would] never leave. I mean you could talk about things now, but they go straight to the back. That's all they do.… I mean they can go on for hours. They are the biggest storytellers, Ed's side of the family, than anything!"

Mothers remembered storytelling in their families as a positive experience, an entertaining experience, a cathartic experience, and a bonding experience. As Martha, a Daly Park mother, thoughtfully put it, "I think this is what helps keep our family close and together, is the continuous reminiscing…if you don't have a past to hold on to, what kind of a future do you have?"

All of the mothers from both neighborhoods agreed that children listen when adults tell stories to one another, but estimates of the age at which children begin to listen varied from 1 to 5 years. When asked if there are certain narrative topics that young children should not be exposed to, the Daly Park caregivers said that it was important to be "very open and talk about things" with their children, although several said that certain topics (e.g., weird sexual practices) should be off-limits to children. One mother, Mabel, stressed that she would never hide the truth from her children about the realities of life and death, and did not believe in making things "rosy" for her children. She said, "I think that they will handle, they will grow up and handle things better." Another Daly Park mother, Martha, also voiced the importance of being open and honest with children. "My kids can tell you things that will blow your mind ... from listening to us talk. Nothing is hidden. There's no, I mean good and bad, there's nothing hidden.... I think it helps kids mature-wise to accept situations because nothing's hidden."

By contrast, the Longwood mothers placed more emphasis on sheltering children from inappropriate topics."Heavy" topics, such as death and sex, were thought to frighten them, and parents were concerned that children would not be able to understand or know how to deal with them. One Longwood mother, Patty, explained that she and her husband tried to shield their daughter from "adult worries" when a family member fell ill. "Things that they just don't need to think about. I mean that was one of the things we tried to tell her was that she didn't need to have adult worries, or, you know, that, that she was a child and there was a time in her life when she would have to accept those things but that for now she should just go on." Another Longwood mother voiced her struggles and concerns about how to gauge the appropriateness of negative topics. "I don't think entire topics should be avoided but, you know, there are levels that, at which the discussion can be held. I mean, there are certainly things that are too intense for them to cope with at a young age."

Thus, although mothers from both neighborhoods believed that some narrative topics should be censored on behalf of children, the Daly Park mothers emphasized the importance of exposing children to life's harsh realities, whereas the Longwood mothers emphasized the need to protect children.

STORY ENACTMENT: FREQUENCY OF STORIES

Considering that all the mothers valued storytelling, how frequently did they actually engage in storytelling during the interview? In answering our second question (as well as the remaining questions), we examined all the stories of personal experience that the mothers told over the course of the entire interview.

Following Burger and Miller (1999) and Miller and Sperry (1988), we defined a story of personal experience as an episode of talk containing three or more utterances that referred to a nonimmediate past event or class of past events.[2] In keeping with Labov and Waletzky's (1967) classic definition, a story had to have temporal ordering and an evaluative dimension provided by the narrator. Boundaries of stories were assessed by identifying the first and final utterances that referred directly to the past event.[3] Once the stories were identified, we tallied them separately by participant and community. The length of narratives was determined by counting the number of utterances contained within the boundaries of each story. We then tallied these figures separately by participant and community as well.

In both communities, every mother told stories, yielding a total of 499 narrations. However, the overall pattern of storytelling differed markedly between working-class Daly Park and middle-class Longwood. As shown in Table 4.1, Daly Park mothers produced more than three times as many stories as their middle-class counterparts. The average figures were 65 stories per interview in Daly Park, as compared with 18 stories in Longwood. Moreover, there was no overlap in the distributions of the two communities: Every mother in Daly Park told more stories than the mothers in Longwood.

Another striking finding, also displayed in Table 4.1, is that the Daly Park families told longer stories. Again, the distributions for the individual mothers were distinct: All but one Daly Park mother exceeded the Longwood mothers in the length of their stories.

STORY ENACTMENT: SEQUENCING OF STORIES

The third research question focused on the sequencing of mothers' stories over the course of the interview. Repeated review of the transcripts revealed three qualitatively different story sequences. Although these types all occurred in each community, the Daly Park mothers produced more frequent and elaborate versions of each.

Repeated Stories

Repeated stories were those narrated in response to one interview question and then later brought up again in response to another question. Many of the repeated stories elaborated on the initial rendition of the story, providing details that were relevant to other interview questions. All the mothers in Daly Park and four mothers in Longwood repeated or elaborated on at least one story. For example, when the researcher asked what kinds of experiences people talked about, Janet, a Longwood mother, responded

TABLE 4.1
TABLE 4.1
Frequency and Length of Narrations

Participant	Number of Narrations	Total Utterances	Utterances per Narration	
			Mean	(Min/Max)
Daly Park				
Lynn	41	752	18.3	(4/96)
Mabel	55	979	17.8	(5/48)
Margie	29	270	9.3	(3/42)
Martha	84	1870	22.3	(5/60)
Sharon	100	1446	14.5	(3/104)
Silvia	82	1403	17.1	(5/74)
DP Mean	65	1120	17.2	
DP Total	391	6720		
Longwood				
Diana	19	226	11.9	(4/23)
Janet	21	212	10.1	(4/25)
Monica	11	140	12.7	(6/38)
Pamela	21	265	12.6	(5/47)
Patty	14	85	6.1	(3/11)
Sarah	23	251	10.9	(4/20)
LW Mean	18	196.5	10.9	
LW Total	108	1179		
Grand Total	499			

Note. Community mean utterances were calculated using the total number of utterances over the total number of narrations for that community. Individual mean utterances were calculated using the total number of utterances over the total number of narrations for that individual.

with a story about her 2-year-old son, who climbed behind the wheel of his father's car and rammed it into the neighbor's garage. Later, she brought up the story again to illustrate how other relatives made her feel better about her son's mishap by sharing similar misdeeds.

Associated Chain Stories

In associated chain stories, the first story in the sequence was told in response to an interview question, then followed by a series of self-generated stories, which unfolded one right after another without any intervening prompts or questions from the interviewer. For example, when the researcher asked Martha, a Daly Park mother, if she ever found herself talking about something over and over again, she responded with a story about a car accident she was involved in 3 years before in which a person died. She then immediately launched into another story about how her aunt had died of a heart attack in her arms earlier that year, and how she could not stop replaying the tragic incident in her head. This reminded her of a neighbor who had suffered a heart attack on her way home from work. And remembering the deaths of loved ones prompted her to relate how her daughter had dealt with the death of her aunt, comforting others at the funeral and yet being unable to grieve herself. These stories unfolded in uninterrupted succession, like links in a chain. Associated chain stories occurred more frequently in Daly Park. Most Daly Park interviews included multiple chains linking three to six stories per chain, whereas most Longwood interviews included only a few chains linking two or three stories per chain.

Umbrella Stories

Umbrella stories were similar to associated chain stories except that the stories fell under the same encompassing theme, thus providing an even stronger association with each other. For example, Sharon, a Daly Park mother, spoke of her concerns about her sister Laurie, who was estranged from the family. In the process, Sharon related stories involving attempts to get in contact with Laurie after Laurie had an argument with their mother and other sisters, letters sent to Laurie that were sent back, and arguments with her other sisters about contacting Laurie when their mother fell sick and nearly died. Although these stories shared the same overarching theme, (i.e., Laurie's estrangement from her family), we considered them to be self-contained stories because each met the definitional criteria for stories and contributed unique events and details to the umbrella theme.

All the Daly Park mothers and four of the Longwood mothers told umbrella stories, but the Daly Park mothers offered many more umbrella stories.

In summary, our analysis suggests that both groups of mothers used stories to supplement and elaborate on their responses to the interview questions. The Daly Park mothers, however, were much more inclined to volunteer multiple stories to illustrate their points and to create complex links among stories.

STORY ENACTMENT: CONTENT OF STORIES

Our starting point for analysis of narrative content was a coding scheme developed by Burger and Miller (1999) and Miller and Sperry (1988) for use with young children's stories. However, this scheme had to be elaborated significantly for use with the much more complex content of adult stories.

The primary content codes that we used included 14 negative categories, which are listed in Table 4.2, 10 positive categories (vacations and family trips, positive family history, positive holiday memories, positive [nonholiday] get-togethers, bonding and good relations, good storytelling ability, accomplishments, gifts and generosity, positive community change, and other positive themes), and 8 neutral categories (neutral family history, neutral holiday memory, neutral historical event, neutral storytelling, ordinary and routine activities, odd occurrences, fictional stories, and other neutral themes).[4]

Although some stories were given only one primary content code, the content of other stories could not be accurately captured by using only one code and were thus double-coded. For instance, a story about the narrator's injury and how she was mistreated at the hospital was coded as both "injury" and "conflict."

Once these primary codes were applied, we tallied the data in terms of the global valence of stories, (i.e., the number of stories that fell into negative content, positive content, and neutral content categories). Then, we tallied the data separately in terms of the individual content categories within each global valence category (e.g., transgressions and conflict were individual categories within the negative global valence category).

In addition to the primary content codes, we also developed four secondary content codes to draw out more nuances from the stories. In the results that follow, we present these codes only as they apply to the negative stories because negative stories accounted for the majority of the data, and because negative stories strongly differentiated between the two communities. Further details on the complete analysis of secondary codes can be found in Cho (2001).

We applied the following four codes to the negative stories: (a) *family* if the protagonist was a family member, (b) *positive spin* if the narrator portrayed a past experience as negative but then reversed the valence of the story (see Example 4 later), (c) *didactic* when the narrator conveyed that it was used to teach a lesson, and (d) *rated "R"* when the story was explicitly reported as being withheld from children because of its inappropriateness.[5]

Global Valence of Stories

Turning first to the global tallies, negative stories accounted for at least half of the stories for all the mothers in both communities. However, the preponderance of negative stories was especially striking in Daly Park, accounting for an average of 76% of the stories, as compared with 56% in Longwood. On the other hand, the Longwood mothers produced substantially more positive stories (mean, 27%) than the Daly Park mothers (mean, 14%), and somewhat more neutral stories (mean, 18%) than the Daly Park mothers (mean, 10%).

Positive and Neutral Categories

Analysis of the individual primary content codes revealed that the types of positive and neutral content were similar in the two communities. In Daly Park, the most frequently narrated positive stories were about bonding experiences or good relationships among family members (6%), followed by stories of good storytelling experiences (3%), such as fond memories of sitting on a grandmother's lap listening to her tell stories and positive stories of the family's history (3%). In Longwood, good storytelling experiences were told most frequently (16%), followed by bonding experiences (6%) and stories about family trips and vacations (5%). All other positive and neutral themes occurred infrequently (less than 3%) in both communities. Further details of this analysis can be found in Cho (2001).

Negative Categories

On the other hand, the pattern with respect to negative stories proved to be highly divergent between the two neighborhoods (Table 4.2). One of the most striking discrepancies between the communities occurred with re-

TABLE 4.2
Frequency and Proportion of Negative Themes in Narrative Content

Negative Theme	Daly Park		Longwood	
Childrearing challenges	118	(0.30)	10	(0.09)
Family challenges	26	(0.07)	0	(—)
Emotional strain	26	(0.07)	0	(—)
Conflict/fight/argue	95	(0.24)	2	(0.02)
Mental/sexual/physical abuse	10	(0.03)	0	(—)
Illness	40	(0.10)	3	(0.03)
Accidents/injuries	13	(0.03)	13	(0.12)
Death/funerals	38	(0.10)	5	(0.05)
Past hardships	43	(0.11)	15	(0.14)
Recent hardships	19	(0.05)	0	(—)
Transgressions	55	(0.14)	15	(0.14)
Scary experiences	17	(0.04)	6	(0.06)
Separation from family	16	(0.04)	2	(0.02)
Other negative	34	(0.09)	3	(0.03)

Note. Proportions were calculated using the total number of narrations for each community as the denominator (Daly Park = 391; Longwood = 108). Proportions do not sum up to 1.0 because the positive and neutral categories were not represented, and some narrations received multiple codes.

spect to childrearing challenges. In Daly Park, all the mothers told numerous stories about the challenges they faced or the struggles they experienced in raising their children, including, for example, dealing with rambunctious children or overly sensitive children whose feelings were easily hurt, trying to get their children to do their homework or dress correctly or eat their breakfast, and persuading their children to open up and share feelings or problems, such as teasing, that they faced at school. Other stories focused on promoting positive sibling relationships, teaching children to respect their elders, helping children to avoid succumbing to peer pressure, and teaching children to respect the value of a dollar. Childrearing challenges represented the single most frequent theme in Daly Park, accounting for 30% of the mothers' stories ($n = 118$), as compared with only 9% in Longwood ($n = 10$). Only 12% of the Daly Park stories were narrated with a positive spin, and only 2% were rated R. Similarly, all but one Daly Park mother narrated stories of family challenges and emotional strain (e.g., having the responsibility of being the person to whom family members and friends turned with their problems), whereas none of the Longwood mothers narrated these types of experiences.

Equally striking was the contrast in conflict stories. Conflict was the second most frequent theme in Daly Park. Every mother shared numerous conflict stories (e.g, children hitting, kicking, and biting each other; adults fighting over inheritances; disputes between spouses; hurt feelings over harsh words). Stories about conflict, arguments, fights, and the history behind bad feelings accounted for 24% ($n = 95$) of Daly Park stories. Most of these conflicts (94%) were experienced by family members. Only 6% were narrated with a positive spin, and 11% included a didactic lesson. The following provides a good example:

> *Example 1* (Martha, Daly Park mother)
> (R: Do you remember any stories that upset [you] or, like you know, [made you] angry or scared, or you know, heard growing up?) My mother and father getting into a fight at a dinner party or something like that. And every once in a while that story will come up, but I remember it like yesterday it happened because I remember my mother jumping out of the car and grabbing me and she told my father she was walking home. He jumped the sidewalk, jumped over the curb, over the grass, and pulled her and I up against the garage and says, "You ain't goin no where." [story continued]

In marked contrast, there were only two conflict stories in the entire Longwood corpus, and both were told by the same mother. One of these stories was told with a positive spin (her son's singing and dancing around the house drives the older kids crazy, but she and her husband think it's great), and the other was narrated about a nonfamily member and for didactic purposes (the narrator once broke up a fight between two girls and now uses that example to teach her own children about forgiveness).

Stories of child and spousal abuse, as well as mental, sexual, and physical abuse were also told with surprising candor by the Daly Park mothers. Some mothers referred to these stories as "skeletons that were let out of the closet" and accepted these incidents as unfortunate parts of their family history, lessons to be learned, or merely hard facts of life. Half of the Daly Park mothers but none of the Longwood mothers told stories of this sort.

The mothers in both communities narrated stories about accidents, physical injuries and illnesses. The Longwood mothers told proportionately more accident and injury stories, whereas the Daly Park mothers told more illness stories. However, the experiences narrated by the Longwood mothers tended to be relatively minor. The following exemplifies a typical illness story:

> *Example 2* (Monica, Longwood mother)
> (R: What kinds of stories would you tell him?) When he had chicken pox, you know, I remember telling him about my chicken pox and how I didn't, you know, tried not to scratch and that I did scratch, and I got a big scar and that kind of thing, and, you know, tried not to. And uh, you know you, you just, I don't know, I just felt that you, you actually tell him stuff that, or I actually tell him stuff that I think will help him cope better in certain situations.

Note that this story was told succinctly and with the didactic purpose of "help[ing] him cope better in certain situations."

Conversely, injury and illness stories in Daly Park were narrated in great detail, often with painful, graphic descriptions of tragic accidents or complicated medical procedures. Only 15% of the Daly Park stories were told with positive spin, and none were considered rated R. The Daly Park stories included car accidents resulting in hospitalization and death, a nephew hit by a van while riding his bicycle, family members who had suffered from various cancers, strokes, neurologic disorders, and heart attacks. In the following example, Sharon narrates an incident in which her son suffered from a seizure.

> *Example 3* (Sharon, Daly Park mother)
> William had a seizure. (R: William had a seizure?) Seizure, and he just blacked out on us and Ned was—had to give him CPR. (R: Really?) Yeah, and that was … I just, I'm the type where I can't … I want to help, but I just freak out more than I want to help.
> (R: Right.) And Ned's walking up and downstairs and William's face is pitch white and his head, his eyes are like, you know, rolled back, and Ned's mom says, "You better breathe in him, Ned." And they all did that in the bathroom, and I called the ambulance, and instead the fire department came, and then the ambulance came, and then we rushed William to the hospital. And they said the outside felt cool on William. When I felt William, every time I felt William, I kissed his head and everything, but the inside of William was burning up more than the outside was. So he had an internal temperature of 104. (R: Wow.)

Often, tragic accident or illness stories in Daly Park were followed by stories of funerals and deaths. Some examples included an aunt who suffered from childbirth complications and died giving birth and an uncle who had been an alcoholic for years and died of cancer of the pancreas. Every Daly Park mother told at least one story about a death or funeral, accounting for 10% of the Daly Park stories, the majority about deceased family members. On the other hand, only half of the Longwood mothers narrated a death or funeral experience (5% of the Longwood stories), the majority about nonfamily members (e.g., a dog that had to be put to sleep, a TV news story about a girl in Texas who had been murdered).

Interestingly, although the Daly Park mothers were much more likely than the Longwood mothers to invoke extreme negative experience, some of the Daly Park narrators framed such stories as humorous, inviting comparison with their working-class counterparts in South Baltimore, who told disaster stories with high hilarity (Miller, 1994; Miller & Sperry, 1987). The following example shows that even funeral stories could be told with a positive spin:

Example 4 (Lynn, Daly Park mother)
I don't think there is ever a glum meeting. There's never. There's never a time that we've gotten together to besides … Even wakes, even my dad's wake. We laughed our heads off the day that he died. We were like, "Okay, now where do we go for clothes?" 'cause the guys, the standing joke was that the guys never had suits. They had a lot—the guys are all into business that don't require having a suit … even though we were devastated.… But the older ones [older siblings in the family], I mean, they couldn't even go to work because they [were so devastated]. When we were together we made big jokes.… We said, "Jesus, dad." He's layin in a coma for three months, he gave us all this opportunity to go buy clothes and none of us got the clothes, (Lynn and R laugh), you know. So, then he said, "Shit on you guys, I'm dyin. I don't have any more time. You know, you better get your act together." (Lynn and R laugh).

The mothers from the two communities told similar stories about their families' past hardships. Most of these focused on their grandparents' poverty upon immigrating to this country or their parents' struggles to make ends meet during the Great Depression. However, whereas all the Daly Park mothers shared stories of recent hardships (e.g., stressful job experiences, monetary struggles), none of the Longwood mothers produced such stories. Considering the occupational differences between the two communities, this finding is not surprising. The blue-collar jobs held by the Daly Park parents (e.g., construction work, gravedigging) entailed a harsher and more dangerous work environment and provided less job security than the professional jobs held by the Longwood parents. In the following example, Margie, a Daly Park mother who worked part-time as a waitress reenacts scenes from a negative work experience.

Example 5 (Margie, Daly Park mother)
Where I was working. It was like 12:15. The party was supposed to be over at 12. And my boss was saying, "Clear your tables," and the lady who ran this cotillion was saying, "I get another half hour. The man downstairs told me." So anyway, I had four of my five tables cleared, and I was letting these

women talk before I pulled the tablecloth from under them, you know? (R: Uh huh. Laughs) So I was waiting to see if they're done and I was like this (Margie reenacts how she was waiting with hands in pockets). And this owner grabbed my arms and he said, "Hands out of your pockets please! Is that how you work?" (R: laughs) I said, "Don't touch me again!" (laughs) (R: laughs) "Is this how you work? Go on. Punch out. Get outta here!" (imitates her boss). I said, "Goodbye." And I'm walking out and I think he said, "You're not gonna get paid for tonight." (R: laughs) So he saw me turn into the kitchen and instead of going out the stairs, I was going to get my purse. So he followed me in there raving and I said, "I work hard and you don't appreciate anybody." And uh, I left—and I'm curious to see if I get my pay this coming Monday. (R: Yeah.) And I'll never work there again.... I've never met such a rotten human being in my whole life.

Transgression stories accounted for 14% of the stories in each community. However, most (75%) of the transgression stories in Daly Park described unambiguous transgressions (e.g., lying, stealing, disobeying a parent) that were taken seriously, as compared with only 40% of the transgression stories in Longwood. Furthermore, whereas 95% of these unambiguous transgressions in Daly Park were committed by family members (e.g., son lied to her, brother got arrested), 67% of the Longwood unambiguous transgressions were committed by nonfamily members (e.g., an elementary school classmate lied, a stranger robbed her grandfather). Instead, the Longwood mothers narrated minor misdeeds with a positive spin, stories that were celebratory and told in an entertaining manner (e.g., practical jokes, hilarious stories of youthful hellraising).

Other negative themes included separation from family, scary experiences, and property damage. These themes were relatively infrequent and showed similar patterns in both communities.

In summary, the several content analyses revealed a skewing in the negative direction for both communities, but particularly for Daly Park. Although mothers from the two communities shared similar stories about positive and neutral events, the working-class Daly Park mothers produced more stories of negative experience, narrated a wider range of negative experiences, and shared more extreme negative experiences. In keeping with this picture, the Longwood mothers were more likely than the Daly Park mothers to put a positive spin on their negative stories and to cast nonfamily members as the experiencers of negative events.

CONCLUSION

In this study we used interview data to explore personal storytelling as practiced in two neighborhoods in Chicago. Building upon an earlier study

(Burger & Miller, 1999) in which we compared personal storytelling as practiced with young children in these same communities, we examined mothers' reflections on personal storytelling (what they said about storytelling) as well as their enactments of storytelling (whether and how they engaged in personal storytelling) during the course of the interviews. We found a pattern of results that parallels and extends our earlier findings, strengthening the claim that the affinity for personal storytelling is stronger in working-class Daly Park than in middle-class Longwood.

All of the mothers in both communities expressed enthusiasm for personal storytelling, recalling positive memories from childhood and reporting that they and their families continue to engage avidly in personal storytelling. However, over the course of the interview, the Daly Park mothers told three times as many stories as the Longwood mothers. This finding is especially intriguing because it mirrors Burger and Miller's (1999) findings that the Daly Park families produced three times as many co-narrations with young children as the Longwood families.

In the current study, the Daly Park mothers told longer stories and produced more complex sequences of stories: They were more likely to repeat particular stories, create chains of associated stories, and generate multiple stories that illustrated the same encompassing theme. Although both sets of mothers used stories to exemplify and elaborate on their responses to the interviewer's questions, the Daly Park mothers often "ran away" with their stories. One story would evoke another, which would flow into another and still another until that line of storytelling was exhausted and the next question could be entertained. We do not mean to imply that these mothers were resistant to the interview, that they responded evasively to the questions, or that they engaged in wild digressions. They did, however, allow themselves to do more than simply answer the interviewer's questions. In essence, the Daly Park mothers seemed to treat the interview itself as a narrative task, an opportunity not only to share their views about storytelling, but also to engage in storytelling. By following Briggs' (1986) recommendation that interviews be examined as cultural–linguistic practices, we were able to demonstrate that the Daly Park mothers responded in a systematically different way to the interview context, converting it into a forum for personal storytelling.

Because interviews are co-constructed by interviewer and interviewee, this finding raises the possibility that the interviewers, not the interviewees, slanted the interview in different directions. Perhaps, for example, the Longwood interviewer was less friendly to narrative chains, interrupting or deflecting such sequences. Or perhaps the Daly Park interviewer solicited more stories. Review of the interview transcripts, however, reveals no such patterns. In fact, the Daly Park interviewer seemed at times to be uncomfortable with some of the longer and more graphically negative stories. At one point she said, "Oh, you don't really have to go into that if you don't want to." Similarly, the Longwood interviewer was careful to ask for additional examples, but these were rarely provided.

There are two important methodological lessons to be drawn from these findings. The first is that interview guidelines granting the interviewee latitude to define the interview may be more accommodating to the communicative norms of working-class speakers. Or to put it another way, attempts to rigidly standardize the interview format, according to middle-class norms of sticking closely to the point, may in fact disproportionately impede working-class speakers, whose inclination is to take the interview in a narrative direction. Second, analytic strategies that presume self-contained and transparent "answers" to the interviewer's questions may preclude access to some of the most rich and revealing data, especially for working-class speakers.

Turning to the content of the mothers' stories, we found that negative stories predominated in both communities, but especially in Daly Park. Although Longwood mothers produced proportionately more positive stories, there was relatively little differentiation between the communities in terms of the individual positive categories.

However, the two communities showed dramatically different patterns in several of the individual negative categories. The Daly Park mothers narrated a wider range of negative experiences and shared more extreme negative experiences, a finding that parallels the findings of Burger and Miller (1999) for co-narrations with young children. Stories of family challenges, emotional strain, recent hardships, and mental, sexual, and physical abuse were told only by the Daly Park mothers. In addition, the Daly Park mothers told more stories of childrearing challenges, family conflict, illness, and death. Moreover, their illness, injury, and transgression stories dealt with more serious events than the stories of their middle-class counterparts, and they were more likely to cast family members as the experiencers of negative events. Although the mothers from both communities put a positive spin on some of their negative stories, the Longwood mothers engaged in this strategy twice as often as the Daly Park mothers.

Why is there such a strong skewing in the negative direction in Daly Park? One possibility is that the Daly Park mothers had endured more negative life experiences. This seems to be a plausible explanation for stories of recent hardship, given the stark financial and employment realities in this working-class community. This may also help to explain the large number of stories of childrearing challenges told by the Daly Park mothers. Harwood, Miller, and Irizarry (1995) reported that working-class Anglo mothers were more likely than middle-class Anglo mothers to worry about whether they could achieve their childrearing goals.

However, we doubt that this is the whole explanation. It seems highly unlikely that the Longwood children pose so few challenges for their parents and just as unlikely that the Longwood families experience almost no conflict. What is more likely is that the Daly Park and Longwood mothers hold different folk theories or ideologies about which events are appropriate or inappropriate to narrate. As Johnstone (1990) noted, shared attitudes and values are reflected through community members' choices of personal experiences to narrate and in how they tell about these events. Because the Daly Park mothers repeatedly stressed the importance of openness and candor when discussing the narrative topics to which they expose their children, and because they treated the interview as an occasion for storytelling, they may have felt more comfortable—if not obliged—to share stories of negative experiences with the researcher. Wiley et al. (1998) found that the Daly Park mothers, as compared with the Longwood mothers, were more forthright and direct when co-narrating young children's experiences.

In summary, this comparative study of two neighborhoods in Chicago adds further weight to the growing sociolinguistic evidence that working-class families privilege personal storytelling in a way that middle-class families do not. Although personal storytelling occurs routinely with young children in both communities, and although the mothers in both communities explicitly embrace personal storytelling, only the working-class Daly Park mothers transform the interview into a narrative task. What is at stake for them is not just participation in an enjoyable activity. Rather, personal storytelling provides a medium for sharing a wide array of negative experiences, and for making sure that children are forearmed with knowledge of life's harsh realities.

ENDNOTES

1. In keeping with the consent forms signed by the participants in this study, we use pseudonyms both for the names of the communities and for the names of the individual participants.

2. Utterances were defined as units that were grammatically distinct from the surrounding words, and that would be separated from the next utterance by a comma or a full stop in a standard transcript (adapted from Fisher and Tokura, 1996). More specifically, full clause statements, subordinate clauses, compound verb phrases, substantive fragments, and framing phrases before quotes were considered utterances. However, fillers (e.g. "you know," "um"), false starts (e.g. "I was, uh, she was ..."), and direct addresses attached to a thought (e.g. "Dad, come ...") were not considered separate utterances.

3. Four of the six interviews from each community were randomly selected to establish intercoder reliability estimates. From each of these transcripts, 20 pages chosen to be representative of all the questions asked during the interview were independently coded by three trained coders. Percentages of agreement ranged from 88% and 100% for identification of stories, and from 80% and 98% for boundaries of stories. Disagreements were resolved through discussion.

4. We randomly selected 30 stories from each community (five from each of the six interviews per community) to establish intercoder reliability estimates. These stories were independently coded by three coders. Intercoder reliability estimates ranged from 82% to 89%. Disagreements were resolved through discussion.

5. Intercoder reliabilities, which were established using the same aforementioned procedures described for primary content codes, ranged from 93% to 100%.

REFERENCES

Bauman, R. (1986). *Story, performance, and event: Contextual studies of oral narrative*. Cambridge: Cambridge University Press.

Bloom, L. (1974). Commentary. In F. F. Schachter, K. Kirshner, B. B. Klips, M. Friedricks, & K. Sanders (Eds.), Everyday preschool interpersonal speech usage: Methodological, developmental, and sociolinguistic studies. *Monographs of the Society for Research in Child Development, 39*(2, Serial No. 160).

Briggs, C. L. (1986). *Learning how to ask: A sociolinguistic appraisal of the role of the interview in social science research*. Cambridge, UK: Cambridge University Press.

Bruner, J. (1990). *Acts of meaning*. Cambridge, MA: Harvard University Press.

Bruner, J. (1996). *The culture of education*. Cambridge, MA: Harvard University Press.

Burger, L. K., & Miller, P. J. (1999). Early talk about the past revisited: Affect in working-class and middle-class children's co-narrations. *Journal of Child Language, 26*, 133–162.

Cho, G. E. (2001). *Personal storytelling: A comparison of working-class and middle-class mothers' folk theories and cultural practices*. Unpublished master's thesis, University of Illinois at Urbana-Champaign.

Fisher, C., & Tokura, H. (1996). Acoustic cues to grammatical structure in infant-directed speech: Cross-linguistic evidence. *Child Development, 67*, 3192–3218.

Gaskins, S., Miller, P. J., & Corsaro, W. A. (1992). Theoretical and methodological perspectives in the interpretive study of children. In W. A. Corsaro & P. J. Miller (Eds.), *Interpretive approaches to children's socialization* (New directions for child development) No. 58 (pp. 5–23). San Francisco: Jossey-Bass.

Goodwin, M. (1990). *He-said-she-said: Talk as social organization among Black children*. Bloomington, IN: Indiana University Press.

Hanks, W. (1996). *Language and communicative practices*. Boulder, CO: Westview Press.

Harkness, S., & Super, C. M. (1996). *Parents' cultural belief systems: Their origins, expressions, and consequences*. New York: Guilford Press.

Harwood, R. L., Miller, J. G., & Irizarry, N. L. (1995). *Culture and attachment: Perceptions of the child in context*. New York: Guilford Press.

Heath, S. B. (1983). *Ways with words: Language, life, and work in communities and classrooms*. New York: Cambridge University Press.

Johnstone, B. (1990). *Stories, community, and place: Narratives from middle America*. Bloomington, IN: Indiana University Press.

Labov, W. (1972). *Language in the inner city: Studies in the Black English vernacular*. Philadelphia: University of Pennsylvania Press.

Labov, W., & Waletzky, J. (1967). Narrative analysis: Oral versions of personal experience. In J. Helm (Ed.), *Essays in the verbal and visual arts* (pp. 12–44). Seattle: University of Washington Press, American Ethnological Society.

Miller, P. J. (1994). Narrative practices: Their role in socialization and self-construction. In U. Neisser & R. Fivush (Eds.), *The remembering self: Construction and accuracy in the self-narrative* (pp. 158–179). Cambridge, UK: Cambridge University Press.

Miller, P. J., Fung, H., & Mintz, J. (1996). Self-construction through narrative practices: A Chinese and American comparison of early socialization. *Ethos, 24*, 1–44.

Miller, P. J., & Moore, B. B. (1989). Narrative conjunctions of caregiver and child: A comparative perspective on socialization through stories. *Ethos, 17*, 428–449.

Miller, P. J., & Sperry, L. L. (1987). The socialization of anger and aggression. *Merrill-Palmer Quarterly, 33*(1), 1–31.

Miller, P. J., & Sperry, L. L. (1988). Early talk about the past: The origins of conversational stories of personal experience. *Journal of Child Language, 15*, 293–315.

Miller, P. J., Wiley, A. R., Fung, H., & Liang, C. (1997). Personal storytelling as a medium of socialization in Chinese and American families. *Child Development, 68*, 557–568.

Schieffelin, B. B., Woolard, K. A., & Kroskrity, P. V. (1998). *Language ideologies: practice and theory*. New York: Oxford University Press.

Shuman, A. (1986). *Storytelling rights: The use of oral and written texts by urban adolescents*. Cambridge, UK: Cambridge University Press.

Sperry, L. L., & Sperry, D. E. (1996). The early development of narrative skills. *Cognitive Development, 69*, 47–60.

Wiley, A. R., Rose, A. J., Burger, L. K., & Miller, P. J. (1998). Constructing autonomous selves through narrative practices: A comparative study of working-class and middle-class families. *Child Development, 69*, 833–847.

Photograph by Michael Maltz

5

Identity Construction in Discourse: Gender Tensions Among Greek Americans in Chicago

Lukia Koliussi
University of Illinois at Chicago

The first Greek immigrants to the United States came "with the first voyage of Columbus" (Kopan, 1995, p. 261), and they continued in eight different waves between 1821 and 1979.[1] Independence wars, world wars, and economic hardships that came with the social and political situations in the home country stimulated these waves of migration. The main motivation, however, for Greek immigration to the United States was predominantly economic. The goal of the immigrants was to gain financial freedom for themselves and their families at home, and eventually return to their motherland.

Greek settlers are known for the drive to own their own businesses and a good sense of entrepreneurship, which they pursued as soon as they arrived in the United States. Many Greeks initially worked in construction, railroad, and mining jobs, and very soon moved away from these occupations to become fruit peddlers, merchants, restaurant owners, ice cream manufacturers, florists, and the like. They also moved into the real estate business and the entertainment field (Kopan, 1995, pp. 280–281, 263). According to the U.S. Bureau of the Census (1990), there currently are a reported 1,110,373 people in the United States of Greek ancestry and an estimated 900,000 (Moskos, 1993)[2] first- through fourth-generation immigrants, with a return ratio to Greece of at least 1 in 3 of those who migrated to the United States (Kopan, 1995, p. 261).

Greeks in the United States have chosen predominantly big cities for settlement and the "establishment of their ethnic communities and institutions." "The most important Greek settlement and one of the oldest Greek communities" has been Chicago (Kourvetaris, 1997, p. 35), with its currently estimated 75,000 to 150,000 Greek Americans.[3]

The first Greek settlers arrived in Chicago in the 1840s, and Greek immigration increased especially after Chicago's great fire in 1871. Chicago attracted in particular Peloponnesian Greeks, mostly from the provinces of Laconia and Arcadia, and by 1882 the first Greek settlement of hundreds of immigrants was firmly established in the area of Clark and Kinzie streets on the Near North Side (Kopan, 1995, p. 263). There, north of the Loop, and surrounding the Randolph street produce market (where most of the immigrants worked), the first Greek communities and thus the first "Greektown" emerged. However, after the first official Greek Orthodox Church (Holy Trinity) was built in 1897 at 1101 South Johnson, more and more Greeks, and especially the newer Greek immigrants relocated to the near West Side, the new "Greektown," also known as the "Delta" (Kopan, 1995, pp. 264–267; Pappas, 1999, pp. 1–2). This vicinity, just north of the Hull House,[4] bounded by Halsted, Harrison, Blue Island, and Polk streets (where today the University of Illinois at Chicago campus is located), became and has remained until today Chicago's famous "Greektown," "the oldest, largest and most important settlement of Greeks in the United States" (Kopan, 1995, p. 266).

The second large settlement of Greek immigrants arose on the South Side of Chicago along 63rd Street between Wentworth and Cottage Grove, where the second Greek Orthodox Church (St. Constantine and Helen) was built (Kopan, 1995, p. 267). The Church was and still is the most crucial factor in the settlement of Greek newcomers to Chicago. There was, as Saloutos described, a "mania" for church building among Greek Americans because the church gave Greeks in the United States "a sense of belonging, which Greek society as a whole did for Greeks living in Greece." The church therefore played a much more important role for Greeks in the United States than it did in 19th and especially 20th century Greece

(Makedon, 1998, p. 6). Each church has a *koinotis*, (i.e., a community, named after its saint, with which Greek Americans identify, and which they use as a place of belonging (Kopan, 1995, p. 267). Thus, it is not unusual to be asked the question "which church (*koinotis*) do you belong to?" Hence, most Greek immigrants in Chicago (and elsewhere in the United States) are found in the areas of the Greek Orthodox churches. Today, there are 21 Greek Orthodox Church communities spread across the Chicago area (Kopan, 1995, p. 267). (See Fig. 5.1.)

The church was important not only for the location of Greek immigrants. More than just a sense of belonging, the church gave the Greeks a place for the preservation of Greek ethnic identity and language maintenance. Especially at a time when traveling was very difficult, it was important for them to have a place to celebrate holidays, to dance, to cook, and to teach the Greek language, especially to newborn children. Greek immigrants considered building Greek schools their top priority after building a church, and thus they are believed to be "among the most successful ethnic groups in transmitting their language and cultural heritage to their progeny" (Kopan, 1995, p. 287). Language maintenance was so important to the Greeks that in 1935 they established the Hellenic Education League, which managed to introduce Greek studies in at least 10 high schools in Chicago, that lasted for 25 years. Then in the 1970s, what is now called the Hellenic Council on Education introduced bilingual education programs, which are still in effect, although these programs have not been viewed positively by many Greeks (Kopan, 1995, p. 292). Even though there was an immense struggle for language maintenance, Greek immigrants, like other groups in the United States, could not avoid an eventual change in repertoire, which occurred by their mere living in an English-speaking country. Thus, U.S.-born Greeks developed a type of bilingualism, which resulted in the creative use of both languages. This mixed language involved loan words, borrowings, code switches, and the like, which even took place, in an alternating manner (from one language to another intersententially rather than intrasententially), in the church liturgies. Therefore, the church adapted to "the prevailing usage of those present" by having a "policy of 'flexible bilingualism,' a mixture of Greek and English" (Moskos, 1993, p. 8), in order still to symbolize a place of belonging that reflected, and still reflects, the churchgoers' language use. This mixture of Greek and English is not what some refer to as "linguistic decay" or "language deficiency," but it rather is a creative and innovative use of the wealth of two languages and, most important, it is part of being Greek

Greek Orthodox Church Communities of Chicago and Suburbs (1890-1980)

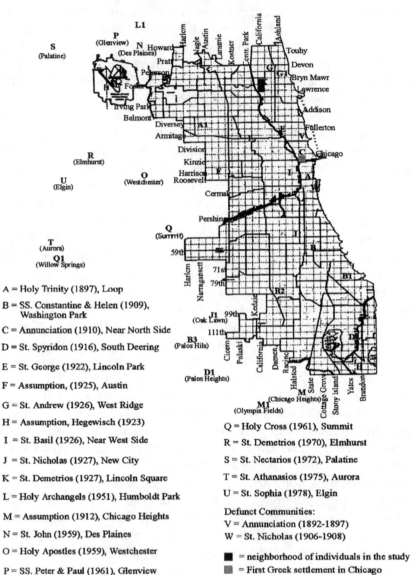

A = Holy Trinity (1897), Loop

B = SS. Constantine & Helen (1909), Washington Park

C = Annunciation (1910), Near North Side

D = St. Spyridon (1916), South Deering

E = St. George (1922), Lincoln Park

F = Assumption, (1925), Austin

G = St. Andrew (1926), West Ridge

H = Assumption, Hegewisch (1923)

I = St. Basil (1926), Near West Side

J = St. Nicholas (1927), New City

K = St. Demetrios (1927), Lincoln Square

L = Holy Archangels (1951), Humboldt Park

M = Assumption (1912), Chicago Heights

N = St. John (1959), Des Plaines

O = Holy Apostles (1959), Westchester

P = SS. Peter & Paul (1961), Glenview

Q = Holy Cross (1961), Summit

R = St. Demetrios (1970), Elmhurst

S = St. Nectarios (1972), Palatine

T = St. Athanasios (1975), Aurora

U = St. Sophia (1978), Elgin

Defunct Communities:
V = Annunciation (1892-1897)
W = St. Nicholas (1906-1908)

■ = neighborhood of individuals in the study
▓ = First Greek settlement in Chicago

KEY: Number after letter indicates move to new location.
(Source: Chicago Factbook 1990, p.XV & Ethnic Chicago, p.270)

FIG. 5.1.

American. Therefore, this code mixing or what is also known as "Greeklish" is more than just language mixture; it is who Greek Americans are; it is their identity.

With this shift in language use, many other shifts occurred among Greek Americans regarding traditions, values, gender issues, and so on, which changed with time and also adapted to the American environment. One of these issues (i.e., the gender issue), together with the tensions that come along with such change, especially among first-generation Greek immigrants, is addressed in the following section, which discusses gender-related identity/role negotiation in discourse in an attempt by the speakers to reaffirm or resist a change in gender role.

LANGUAGE AND IDENTITY

Language is the most important means of human interaction and social survival. By understanding, inferring, and relaying meaning, we creatively negotiate, construct, reconstruct, and define the norms and rules by which we live and the identities we either are "assigned" by society or choose to take in certain situations. That is, certain identities/roles are given to us by virtue of our position (based on gender, age, religion, ethnic background, and so forth) within a certain society, and thus conform to norms that are agreed upon and preexist prior to any conversational interaction, whereas other identities/roles can be constructed "locally" in specific interactions to communicate a specific meaning or intent, or to challenge the already preexistent identity and attempt to transform it.

Many studies have focused on the negotiation of identities and the way people use discourse for self-portrayal (Auer, 1998; K. Gergen, 1987; Gergen & Gergen, 1988; Goffman, 1959, 1974, 1981; Gumperz, 1982a, 1982b, 1985; Harre, 1987; Li Wei, 1994, 1998; Myers-Scotton, 1988a, 1988b, 1998), and there has been disagreement on whether these identities are predetermined and thus preexist before conversation, or whether they are constructed in discourse and thus arise through interaction within a conversation. Hence, for example, Kerby (1991) argued that as conversation participants, we draw upon preexistent identities "from which our more explicit self-reflections are formed along their narrative threads, both retrospectively and prospectively."[5] In contrast, Taylor (1991) believed that the representation of the self emerges out of an interaction and is not formed or established beforehand.[6] In this debate, special attention has been given to narratives. However, one can expand these notions about narratives and apply them to discourse in general, because all types of talk exchanges, whether in narrative form or not, have communicative value and provide evidence of self-portrayal.

Although there is disagreement on the emergence of identities and their role in self-portrayal and presentation, there is, however, agreement on the fact that identities and role assignment or construction are a crucial factor in human conversational interaction, and thus, this "prior scholarship suggests that narrative [and not only narrative, but discourse in general] is a powerful resource through which we manage our selves and identities" (Schiffrin, 1996, p. 171).

I will build my analysis on two talk exchanges and one narrative in a conversation among members of a Greek social network in Chicago using the aforementioned notions, especially focusing on gender role negotiation, gender expectations, and gender attitude in intragenerational discourse. The conversants are between 72 and 88 years of age, and the talk exchanges that take place are mostly same-gender conversations among women, who are, however, influenced by the presence of one "passive" male participant within hearing distance, whose mere presence influences the conversations between the women and the identities they are assuming, constructing, or renegotiating.

THEORETICAL FRAMEWORK

The approach taken in this chapter is what Schiffrin (1996) calls an "interactional sociolinguistics" approach, based on two very influential bodies of work, those of the linguistic anthropologist John Gumperz and the sociologist Erving Goffman. This approach incorporates ideas from the fields of anthropology, sociology, and linguistics, and focuses more specifically on the presentation of self in discourse and society[7] and the language used to communicate meaning as a form of negotiating or constructing identities based on various cultural and social expectations. These ideas differ in orientation and analysis, but as Schiffrin (1996) pointed out, they can be used in complementary ways because the reasoning and view of the language role in discourse are quite similar in all these fields.

Specifically, I use Schiffrin's (1996) analysis of narrative as self-portrait. Schiffrin (1996) argued that identities and roles are constructed locally (p. 168) in the conversation, which are then also a presentation of the self globally because these identities and roles are negotiated and constructed on the basis of previously established (or forced by the community and society) cultural and social expectations. This concept is based on Labov's notion of *verbalization*, the verbal performance in which we engage when retelling an experience, and how this verbalization is situated both socially and culturally. In this verbalization process Schiffrin (1996) distinguished between global and local situating, explaining that in the case of the former,

> by drawing on our cultural knowledge and expectations about typical courses of action in recurrent situations, we construct story topics, themes, and points, (p. 168)

and that in the case of the latter,

> we verbally place our past experiences in, and make them relevant to, a particular "here" and "now," a particular audience and a particular set of interactional concerns and interpersonal issues. (p. 168)

Thus, Schiffrin (1996) explained identity and role negotiation as both previously existent (globally) and locally constructed.

Gumperz viewed language as socially and culturally constructed, with issues of group identity, status, and so forth, arising through meaning. This social and cultural construction influences interaction on a person-to-person level, (i.e., what one says and does), with language as a mirror of our cultural and social group identity (Schiffrin, 1994, pp. 98–102). Goffman's approach to communication was to understand form and meaning through context and to view the self or identity as an interactive construction. He placed more weight on the symbolic value of actual interaction (i.e., what one says and does) and concentrated on the social organization of involvement rather than on its creation and effect as did Gumperz. Goffman focused on frame analysis, which provides the "frame" for interpreting an utterance, and its organization, which is socially situated, arguing that by *footing* we align ourselves in a conversation to the previously uttered sentence (Schiffrin, 1994, pp. 102–107).

The main contributions of both Gumperz and Goffman are central to the issues explored in this chapter. Schiffrin's analysis provides the narrative-only approach to both conversational talk exchange and narrative situations for my analysis. The main focus is the local and global construction and reconstruction of identities, in particular, gender identities.

First, however, before I turn to my analysis, I explain my methodology in the following section. Then in the section thereafter, I provide background information about the network and the individuals discussed in this chapter.

THE STUDY

In this study, I chose four members of a Greek social network of the Greek American community in Chicago by whom I have been surrounded for several years. I tape-recorded their speech in order to analyze code-switching patterns and language use in relation to identity negotiation and construction. Thus, the data used here are mainly composed of tape-recorded conversations and my own ethnographic experience as part of the larger community. In addition, I rely on participants' explanations and interpretations, in particular those of Christina and Angela. The data provided below are parts of the conversations that took place in one social gathering. Before turning to an analysis of gender identities as constructed in these data, I introduce the community, the individuals, the neighborhood, and the social situation in which the conversations were recorded.

BACKGROUND

The Social Network

This network is a very close and well-knit community whose members are mainly Greek immigrants or Greek Americans from different generations and origins (in Greece). The four members presented in this discussion belong to the senior generation of immigrants and are from the same region in Greece, (i.e., Tripolis, Peloponnese). They were friends before they migrated to the United States. Thus, their comfort level with each other is extremely high, and they know each other very well. In this network, there are certain attitudes with regard to gender, which hold true most of the time, but to which there are certain exceptions. This older generation assumes that gender roles are separate: The male is the provider, and the female stays at home (or has a part-time job), responsible for the children and especially the food. In Greek culture, food is very important and viewed as a symbol of politeness as well as respect, (i.e., food is expected to be available and offered to visitors by the hostess). In this generation, the men (in this case, George) expect the women to take care of wifely chores and behave always in a respectful way, (i.e., swearwords are judged as disrespectful, as well as any mention of sex or other intimate behavior that should not be discussed by a woman in public, which means in the presence of men). These older women follow most of these expectations when they are with their husbands and among other men. However, in women-only conversations, they break from these social expectations and "let loose" by talking freely about any type of subjects including sexual and intimate matters, usually humorously, with husbands frequently the victims of their joking material.[8] In these situations, the women are able to get things off their chests and be themselves without having anyone judge their behavior according to prevailing social norms.

The Individuals

The individuals featured in the following discussion are Christina (age, 72 years), Maria (age, 70 years), Angela (age, 86 years) and George (Angela's husband; age, 88 years). They have been friends for a very long time, and they all come from the region of Tripolis in the Greek province of Arcadia on the Peloponnesian peninsula, which, as noted earlier, is a main area of origin of Greek immigrants in Chicago. Their language use is mainly Greek with many code switches to either English or their regional vernacular Greek dialect. Switches to the regional vernacular are scarce (especially in front of me because I do not know that dialect). However, they do occur, and when they do, there is usually a particular communicative intent. All three women are quite old-fashioned in terms of gender roles (especially in comparison with the younger generation). When I spoke with Christina, however, she said that she has tried to assimilate (as much as she thought would be necessary) to American culture in order to get away and "break free"[9] from what she calls "that χωριουδίστικο [xorioudhistiko (village)] narrow-mindedness." Therefore, she is often the instigator who challenges these gender role expectations and attitudes in front of men, and she is sometimes very eager to make them listen to her so she can change their "narrow minds" and thus reconstruct her own and the other women's gender identities. Yet the men do not listen very often nor are they interested in hearing what the women have to say. Thus, the women reconstruct their identities and establish new identities mostly "when the γυναικολόι[10] [gynaikoloi (womenfolk)] gets together"(as Christina says). In Schiffrin's terms, then, the general gender role expectations, "forced" on these women by the men of their network, are the global identities that form the cultural background of their expected behavior, on which their local construction and negotiation of their identities builds in specific situations.

The Neighborhood

The neighborhood in which these four individuals, their relatives and the rest of their social network live is the Lincoln Square area on the north side of Chicago (Chicago Fact Book, 1995). Specifically, their neighborhood covers the area bounded by Bryn Mawr, Western, Lawrence, and California avenues. They are part of the Saint Demetrios Church (see map) *koinotis* (community) and live very close to the church. This area used to be one of the new "Greektowns" after the church was established (1927). Today, many Greeks have dispersed to the suburbs, and the neighborhood has become more international. However, one can still see many Greek stores and Greek-owned businesses and hear people speaking Greek on the streets. Walking down Lawrence Avenue in this area, you can find Markelo's Bakery, Lefkos, Sparti Inc., Megalonisos, Nea Synantisi (coffee shops), Gogo's Gyros, Alpha Pharmacy, Helen's Flower Shop, Hellas Pastry, and Delphi Supermarket. Other Greek-owned businesses in this neighborhood are Nea Agora (grocery store), The Hilltop, George's restaurant, Charcoal Delights, Hub's, and many more, which give it a Greek ambiance and a feeling of belonging for the Greeks of this area.

The individuals in this study have lived in this area for more than 40 years, and frequently make use of their Greek neighborhood stores and identify themselves with the *koinotis* of St. Demetrios. According to their estimations, the Greeks who live in this area make up approximately 20% of the residents, which becomes apparent when it is considered how frequently these businesses are filled with Greeks and the amount of Greek that can be heard in the back yards on a warm summer night. The 1990 *Chicago Fact Book* records 2,665 people of Greek ancestry, 2,608 of people whom speak Greek at home in this area. Going through this neighborhood, one can often find Greek flags attached to cars in the streets, hanging from rearview mirrors, or flying from buildings or the windows of houses, usually accompanied by an American flag, signs such as "Parking for Greeks Only," or various Greek sayings. All these characteristics give the neighborhood a Greek flavor still today, and play an important role for Greeks living or visiting there in maintaining and celebrating their ethnic identities.

The Situation

The conversations I analyze were recorded in the home of one of the participants. These three girlfriends, Christina, Angela, and Maria, get together often, frequently in the company of up to six or seven other women, and create the so-called γυναικολόι-(*gynaikoloi*). This time, however, Angela brought her husband, George, along because she was not feeling well that day. Yet, even though George was there, the women were not going to give up their "down time" or "let-loose" time because this was supposed to be their own time. George, knowing that, did not even attempt at any point in the entire visit to participate in any part of the conversation. As a matter of fact, he took his newspaper and a chair, and sat in a corner of the hallway, that leads to the living room where the women were going to have their gathering. He did not want to be bothered or have anything to do with the women. As far as he was concerned, he was there because of his wife, and he had no intention to partake in their conversations. Although he was well aware of what kind of talk exchange was going to take place, he was still lifting his eyes from his reading when something "inappropriate" was mentioned by any of the women. This type of behavior, then, led Christina to want to "tease" him and challenge his "narrow-mindedness,"[11] especially after Maria fell victim to it (which we will see in the first talk exchange) and actually apologized for her *gynaikoloi* type behavior. Christina was not going to leave this behavior unnoticed and tried to provoke him, knowing that both were aware that this was the *gynaikoloi* situation in which Christina could step over her boundaries in a semijoking manner and George would most likely not react to her "teasing" in a judging way.

IDENTITY CONSTRUCTION IN DISCOURSE

Example I

Maria, Christina, and Angela discuss about the στίμη[12] [stimi-heater], and Maria tells her experience, how she had turned it off and then had to turn it on again because she realized how cold it had gotten:

| 1M: | Κι έκατσα εκει στη θέση που κάθομαι κοντά στο παράθυρο και λέω: «κάλα από πού έρχεται το κρύο», γιατί είμ' μαθημαίνει όταν σηκώνομαι το χειμώνα, κάθομαι εκεί ... εκεί είν' η θέση μου. | *Ki ekatsa ekei sti thesi pou kathomai koda sto parathyro kai leo: "kala apo pou erxetai to kryo?" giati eim' mathimeni otan sikonomai to xeimona, kathomai ekei ... ekei ein' i thesi mou.* | And I set down at that seat close to the window where I usually sit and I say: "I don't understand, where is the cold coming from?" Because I am used to sit there when I get up in the winter ... that is my seat. |

2C:	Hm, by the *stimi*.	*Hm,* by the *stimi*.
3M:	*Και δίπλα είν' η στίμη. So, μου 'ρχότανε ζέστη. Τώρα αντίς για ζέστη μου ' ρχότανε παγωνιά από την λαμαρίνα, τι θα ' ρχότανε; Σηκώνομαι κι ' γω απάνω, κοιτάζω κι ' χε φύγει απ' το 70 κι ' χε φτάσει στο εξήντααα ...επτά.*	*Kai dhipla ein' i stimi. So, mou 'rxotane zesti. Tora antis gia zesti mou 'rxotane pagonia apo tin lamarina, ti tha 'rxotane? Sikonomai ki 'go apano, koitazo ki 'xe fygei ap' to ebdomida ki 'xe ftasei sto eksidaaa ... epta.*	And next to it is the *stimi*. So was getting some heat, Now instead of heat there was coming cold (freezing cold) from the steel, what else would come out? So I get up and it (the thermostat) had left from 70 and had reached now sixtyyy ... seven.
4A:	*'Οχι, κάνει κρύοΚ No, no, noΚ*	*Oxi, kanei kryo. No, no, no.*	No that is cold.
5M:	*Στο 67 το ' χα κλείσει όμως τελείως εχθές.*	*Sto eksidaefta to 'xa kleisei omos teleios exthes.*	At 67 I had completely turned it off, though.
6A:	*Τη στίμη;*	*Ti stimi?*	The *stimi*?
7M:	*Ε, βέβαια. Εχθές το είχα κλείσει τελείως ...*	*E, bebaia. Exthes to eixa kleisei teleios.*	Of course, yesterday I had it off.
8A:	*Οχι, δεν το ' χουμε κλείσει ακόμη. Εμείς το έχουμε στο 65. Τώρα που έκανε κρύο, πιάνω τις στιμης είναι ζεστές μέσα. 'Αναψε το μασίνι.[NP]*	*Oxi, dhen to 'xoume kleisei akomi. Emeis to exoume sto 65. Tora pou ekane kryo, piano tis stimis einai zestes mesa. Anapse to masini.*	No, we haven't turned it off yet. We have it at 65. Now that it was cold these last days, I touch the *stimis* and they are warm. The thermostat is on.
9C:	Sixty-five is very low though.		
10A:	*Κατάλαβες; Ο' πάει εβδομήντα ... πάει εβδομήντα.*	*Katalabes? O', paei ebdhomida ... paei ebdhomida ...*	Do you understand? Na, it goes to 70 ... it goes to 70.
11M:	*Ανοίγω τα παράθυρα...* (Aside)	*Anoigo ta parathyra...*	[I open the windows.]
12C:	*Εβδομήντα* it should be.	*Ebdhomida* it should be.	Seventy it should be.
13M:	*Ακούς; ... Ανοίγω τα παράθυρα ...γιατί όσο και ζέστη να είναι έξω//*	*Akous? ... Anoigo ta parathyra ... giati oso kai zesti na einai ekso//*	Are you listening? ... I open the windows ... because as warm as it might be outside//

14A: //και γιατί ν'
ανοίξεις το
παράθυρο; Να πάρεις
αέρα; (laughter)

//kai giati n' anoikseis
to parathyro? Na
pareis aera?

//and why should you
open the window? To
get air?

15M: Να φύγει και καμιά
κλανιά ...

Na fygei kai kamia
klania ...

So some of the farts
can get out ...

(looks over to Angela's husband [George], who is sitting further away in
the hallway and was not paying attention until now when he raises his
eyes from what he was reading and looks at Maria,-when she replies)

ε, συγγνώμή δηλαδή

E, sygnomi dhiladhi?

Well, I'm sorry, what
can I say?

(Laughter breaks out amongst the women. Maria, then, still looking to
George continues her justification.)

Ε, μα αφού με
αναγκάζει, τι να μην
το πω;

E, ma afou me
anagkazei, ti na min
to po?

e, well, since she
makes me (I am
forced to) what, I
shouldn't say it?

(Laughter continues.)

16C: Yeah, we live in a free
country, right?

(looking at George)

17M: Με το ζορι και αυτή
να της πώ γιατί
ανοίγω το παράθυρο
... καλά δεν της είπα
κι ' γω;

Me to zori kai afti na
tis po giati anoigo to
parathyro ... kala
dhen tis eipa ki 'go?

By force she wants
me to tell her why I
open the window ...
didn't I tell her right?

18C: Living in a free
country we can say
anything we like.

In this example, we focus on turns 13 to 17, in which we can see the following. In turn 13, Angela attempts to start a joke at Maria's expense, which is not an unusual behavior in these type of *gynaikoloi* conversations. In such instances, Maria usually replies to Angela's "attack," thus turning the joke on her, and everyone laughs. This kind of talk exchange is very common, often accompanied by "socially/gender-inappropriate" remarks, and characterizes a situation like this as an "insider" women-only or *gynaikoloi* instance. Therefore, Maria's response in turn 14 ("so some of the farts can get out"), which included something vulgar (especially for a woman of her age and cultural background) is completely acceptable as a reply to the sarcastic "interrogation" of Angela because Maria, feeling as though she is put on the spot, responds in the same sarcastic fashion. However, this time her response has a different effect. Even though everyone else laughs, Maria, who noticed that George looked up from his paper, is now pursuing an apology for her vulgarity and attempts to justify her supposedly poor behavior by explaining it. Because this behavior does not meet the gender role expectation of women (i.e., not saying anything vulgar in the presence of a man), Maria apologizes by saying "Well, I'm sorry, what can I say?" and tries to realign herself with her globally predetermined identity of an appropriate and respectful woman, now seeking approval from everyone else and especially from George, who says nothing. First, she says "What can I say," which indicates that she is trying to communicate that she was forced into such a vulgar response, for which she is sorry. The other women, then, find her attempted apology even more amusing and start laughing again. This is humorous to them because they know that Maria used the vulgar expression only because she assumed that it would be fine for her to "let her guard down," but instead she found herself criticized, condemned, and exposed in front of Angela's husband with only one look of his.

Thus, at this point Maria does not care that her response caused laughter and amusement for the womenfolk (which in other same-gender instances would be a positive thing). Rather, she is trying to gain "face" by an attempt to realign her "misunderstood" identity with her socially acceptable one. Therefore, she continues (still addressing George) by saying that Angela's remark "forced" her to say something inappropriate, and then proceeds by now asking for direct approval from George with her question "what, shouldn't I say it?" The fact, that she is trying so hard to realign herself is also amusing to the other women because Maria should not even have to justify herself, at least not in this type of setting. Yet, even after her direct request for approval, George still does not acknowledge her realignment attempt and just continues to read his newspaper. This silence of George can be interpreted in two different ways. First, George might want to punish her for saying something "inappropriate" in his presence, and therefore is not accepting her realignment plea. Second, his silence could mean that maybe if he acknowledged a realignment of her global identity, then by virtue of doing that, he would also automatically have accepted her local identity. Thus, by not responding, he might be denying her *gynaikoloi* identity, which she would have newly constructed in her utterance in turn 15. By not responding to any of her pleas ("I'm sorry ... what can I say?" "What, I shouldn't say it?"), realignment is not necessary because her global identity is still intact (i.e., the expectation that she would not be vulgar is not disrupted (because he does not acknowledge the incident any further), and thus her global identity prevails.

However, Christina, the usual instigator, finally cannot refrain from breaking that cycle of "request for realignment / no answer" by saying in turn 16 "Yeah, we live in a free country, right?" and looking at George. Here, Christina is communicating to Maria that she should stop trying to justify her "inappropriate" talk because there is no reason to, denying Maria's attempted realignment with her global identity by granting her her new locally constructed identity. She also indirectly communicates to George her opinion about that gender expectation (i.e., not to be vulgar) and expresses that if he will not even grant Maria realignment (thus acknowledging an existence of a different identity), she will go a step further and grant her her local identity. Maria, however, still feels as though she needs to explain and thereby realign herself, which is understandable because she came very close to "losing face." She explains again that she was "forced" to use a vulgar expression, then turns to Christina (who has just helped her "save face" by telling her that it is all right for Maria to use vulgarity) and says in turn 17 "didn't I tell her right?" now attempting to assume her new locally constructed identity by communicating that this was the only way to "set her straight." Christina repeats her firm belief/opinion about that type of gender role expectation by saying again in turn 18 "Living in a free country we can say anything we like." Here, Christina makes sure that George heard her the first time and understood that he should not make that type of judgment again, especially not in this *gynaikoloi* setting. This time, the repetition of her belief also contains the pronoun "we" twice, which is a message to Maria that Christina finds her response completely acceptable, thereby granting Maria her identity. This pronoun use, however, is also a message to George that it is time to change these identity expectations because these women are united, and the use of the pronoun "we" shows support for change and resistance to the globally constructed gender role expectations. Christina is communicating that it is time for George to realize that "we (united) can say anything we like" and George cannot stop it. After all, Maria received her new identity with or without George's acknowledgment with Christina's help.

Example 2

Christina is now addressing George who is sitting in his corner in the hallway reading a newspaper not wanting to participate in the conversation with the γυναικολόι (*gynaikoloi*), the "womenfolk," as they call themselves. Christina attempts to bother him (this is after her remark "we live in a free country"):

1C: What you're looking
        there George?

2G: He?

3C: What you're looking
        there?

4G: *Τηράω.*[14]   *Tirao.*   I am looking (Greek
                                                              regional vernacular
                                                              for "to look").

        (with a slightly ascending and then descending voice and a singing-like
        tone indicating that he wants to be left alone)

5A: Τι βλέπεις εκει;   *Ti blepeis ekei?*   What are you looking
                                                        at there? (Standard
                                                        Greek for "to look")

6C: Τι τηράς;   *Ti tiras?*   What are you looking
                                                        at? (Greek regional
        (looking at Angela)   vernacular for "to
                                                        look")
        Ναι, τι τηράς;   *Nai, ti tiras?*

                                                        yes, what are you
                                                        looking? (again Greek
                                                        regional vernacular for
                                                        "to look")

7G: /?/E τι θες;   */?/E, ti thes?*   (?)e, what do you
                                                        want?

8C:	Χμ, ε φέρε, ντε, να δούμε τι έχειΚ	Hm, e fere, de, na dhoume ti exei.	Hm, well hand it over so we can see what's there.

(A small commotion starts; everyone is talking together and Maria finally gets the floor)

9M:	Σώσε εκεί χάμω τη ˙φημερίδα //να δούμε κι εμείς//	Sose ekei xamo ti 'fimeridha //na dhoume ki emeis//	Come on, hand the newspaper over //so we can see too// (literally: put some effort to give us the newspaper so we can see too).
10G:	//Κι εγώ εδώ πήγα ν' αδιάσω το τραπέζι ... (sarcastically)	Ki ego edho piga n' adhiaso to trapezi...	//And I almost ate all the food on the table (there was no food on the table).
11M:	Δώσε εκεί στο ... //	Dhose ekei sto...//	Give it to ... //
12G:	//γι' αυτό ήρθα ˙δω πέρα.	//gi' afto irtha 'dho pera.	//That's why I came here.
13M:	... στο στο Clark έχει ένα ... //	...sto sto Clark exei ena...//	... on on Clark there is a ... //
14G:	//Σιγά που μ' έχεις φέρει τόσες ώρες εδώ πέρα ... που εμένα να χαβαδιάζει (pointing at Angela) αλλ' το τραπέζι ... και το τραπέζι γεμάτο	//Siga pou m' exeis ferei toses ores edho pera... pou emena na xabadhiazei (pointing at Angela) all' to trapezi... kai to trapezi gemato	//You have brought me here for so many hours and she (pointing to his wife) is "bullshitting around,"[15] but the table ... and the table is full (in a very accusing tone).
15A:	Ναι θα σου˙χουμε τραπέζι τώρα.[16] Δώσ' της Χριστίνας˙ κει χάμω τώρα τη ˙φημερίδα.	Nai tha sou 'xoume trapezi tora. Dhos' tis Christinas 'kei xamo tora ti 'fimeridha.	Yeah, right, we'll have food ready for you too now. Come on, hand over the newspaper to Christina now.
16C:	I'm not ... ah, I'm not. Εγώ μιλάω απλά για να παίρνει αυτό (pointing to the tape recorder and winking to her girlfriends).	I'm not ... ah, I'm not. Ego milao apla gia na pairnei afto. (pointing to the tape recorder and winking to her girlfriends)	I'm just making conversation so this thing can record.

This example is quite interesting because there are many things happening and implied, especially by George regarding his expectation as to what the woman's role (particularly the hostess's role) should be. This is an instance in which new identities are negotiated and constructed that conflict with the global identity expectations of these women. In this talk exchange, Christina is intentionally trying to "tease" George because of his quick judgment of Maria's use of vulgarity in example 1, especially considering that this is supposed to be a women-only conversation, and he thus had no place to raise his eyes and look at Maria. Therefore, now, Christina sets out to "set George straight." In turn 1 she asks him what he is looking at even while she knows he is reading a paper. The tone of George's response and his use of the regional vernacular of the verb "to look" is a clear indication that he wants to be left alone. His wife, then asks him in turn 5 "what are you looking at?" However, she is using the standard form. George uses the vernacular in order to align his identity as an old-fashioned man, as a man who still remembers his roots and origins and understands them vis-à-vis gender role expectations. Furthermore, he uses the vernacular to distance himself from the women folk, using another language variety to elevate himself away from and above the women's level of talk. His wife, Angela, grants him this identity and the therewith-created distance between the two genders by using the standard form for "to look." Because Angela is his wife and the expectations as well as the implications are different for her if she attempts on her own to realign herself with George, she decides to acknowledge his globally predetermined and newly reconstructed identity.

However, Christina does not have to and will not give him this identity, laying claim to the only setting that gives these women a little more power than usual. Therefore, Christina tries to realign herself in turn 6 with the attempted higher status identity of George by using his choice of words: «τι τηράς;» (ti tiras?—What are you looking at?) instead of «τι κοιτάς» (ti koitas) or «τι βλέπεις;» (ti blepeis), thus using the same regional vernacular form of the verb "to look." By doing this, she elevates herself to his assumed higher level in order to achieve an equal level between the two sexes. This is especially important because Christina represents all the *gynaikoloi* uniting them through the use of the pronoun "we" in her response to George in the first example. This means that if Christina just elevated herself to the new level of George, then she elevated the entire *gynaikoloi* (including his wife), and thus is not acknowledging his local reconstruction of his global identity, which also carries certain gender role expectations with which Christina does not agree with.[17] She uses this verb very cleverly, by first asking him in the vernacular, then looking at Angela (communicating to her: "Don't worry I'll set him straight.") and then repeating her question more affirmatively.

Then, George, responds to her in turn 7 in a very annoyed tone with "what do you want?" being dissatisfied with Christina's behavior, a behavior that violates George's expectations for gender roles, and that stubbornly prevents George from gaining higher status. Christina continues elevating the role of the women by telling him next in turn 8 to hand the newspaper over, a command supported by Maria in turn 9 with "come on hand it over so we can see it too." This has a very strong communicative intent in that both Maria and Christina have not only elevated themselves through Christina's vernacular use of "to look," but they are now also attempting to claim to be able to do the same thing that George does, (i.e., to read the paper). Since education is a symbol of power, especially in this network,[18] Christina and Maria imply that they want to read the same paper so they can educate themselves too. Thus, here, not only are they steering away from the globally constructed preestablished identity, but they are also constructing and negotiating a very powerful new identity. George realizes the risk of losing his higher status identity and decides not to acknowledge their identity with his change of topic in turn 10.

However, what is interesting here is the choice of topic (i.e., that there is no food on the table, which he expresses sarcastically by saying "and I almost ate all the food on the table") with which he is trying to realign the women into their old-fashioned and globally expected gender roles. This topic choice of food is also an insult for Maria because food is very important in symbolizing a good hostess. This means that Maria is again threatened with "losing face," and because she is weaker than Christina (as we saw earlier), she is trying to change the topic completely in turn 13 by saying "on Clark there is a ..." which is an attempt to "save face." This weakness occurs after her first attempt to be strong and stand up against George in turn 11 by telling him to give the newspaper to Christina, which is interrupted by George, who tells her now what her role is and why he is there when he says "that's why I came here" in turn 12. Maria then pro-

ceeds to change the topic in order to save face after George has weak-
ened her. George recognizes Maria's weakness and continues to try to
threaten Maria's face and to realign her, and thus all three women, into
the global identity role in turn 14. He attempts also to attack his wife (by
pointing to her), thus trying to get two of the three women to assume their
expected roles and not their "revolutionary" ones. He does not dare to attack Christina because, as we have seen, she is not that easy to bend, and
she sticks to her firm beliefs. So, in turn 12 he tries to make Angela feel
bad for bringing him there and making him listen to her "bullshitting"[19]
without even having any food on the table (now referring to Maria).

Now Angela, who had not said anything until this point, has to make a
choice whether she will align herself with the globally expected identity role,
for which George is negotiating very hard or with the newly constructed identity of the *gynaikoloi*, which already has been abandoned by Maria. This is a
very important decision for Angela because she is more than just a woman;
she is also his wife, which was the reason why she initially tried to grant
George his identity. However, after following a long battle between the two
genders, she decides to grant the women their identity; after all, this was supposed to be a *gynaikoloi* conversation, and thus in turn 15 she tells George
sarcastically "yeah right, we'll have food for you too now," then continues by
"instructing" George to hand over the newspaper to Christina. It is also noticeable that, here too, Angela uses the pronoun "we" to appear as a representative of the "united front" of these three women who have won the battle of
identity negotiation. Thus, in turn 15, Angela aligns all three women with their
new identity and grants them its recognition.

Interestingly then, Christina says in turn 16 (while winking to Angela) that
she actually did not want the paper, but that she was "just making conversation" so that the tape recorder would have something to record. This sym-
bolizes that Christina's intentions were clear from the very beginning, (i.e.,
she wanted to set George straight and communicate to him that maybe
these women might have not achieved new gender role identities in everyday life, but in this *gynaikoloi* situation, they have, and thus her job is done).

Example 3

After they finally gave in to George's comment about having no food on the
table, and Maria (the hostess) got up to prepare some food for everybody
and of course especially for George,

1M: (talking to George who is dipping his bread in the salad)

Βούτα και για μένα	*Bouta kai gia mena*	dip for me too,
γιατί κοίτα	*giati koita*	because look

(showing her dress and pointing at how tight it is, indicating that she has gained weight)

2G:	*Χωράει, χωράει*	*Xoraei, xoraei*	It fits, it still fits you.

2G:	*Χωράει, χωράει* *ακόμα.*	*Xoraei, xoraei akoma.*	It fits, it still fits you.
3M:	*Δε χωράει καθόλου.*	*Dhe xoraei katholou.*	It doesn't fit at all.
4A:	*Που' ν' τα ξίγκια σου, μωρέ;*	*Pou 'n' ta ksigkia sou, more?*	Oh come on, where is your fat?
5M:	*Μ' εχει πιάσει αναισθησίαΚ*	*M' exei piasei anaisthisia.*	It's like I am numb.
6A:	*Ε, με τον μπάρμπα Τζίμη* (Maria's husband, named Jimmy) *δε μπορείς... δε μπορείς.*	*E, me ton mparmpa Tzimi de mporeis ... de mporeis.*	well, with your old man Jimmy, you can't ... you just can't.
7M:	*Είχα διαβάσει ένα βιβλίο ... μπορεί να την ξέρετε αλλά δε θυμάμαι τ' όνομα ... πως λέγεται μώρε//*	*Eixa dhiabasei ena biblio ... mporei na tin kserete alla de thymamai t' onoma ... pos legetai more//*	I had read a book ... maybe you know her (referring to the author), but I don't remember her name. ... What was her name?//
8C:	//a Greek book or an English book?		
9M:	Greek.		
10C:	Ah, a Greek book?		
11M:	Greek, *αλλά κι αυτή που το' γραψε είναι* Greek *αλλά είναι 'δω πολλά χρόνια ...*	Greek, *alla ki afti pou to 'grapse einai* Greek *alla einai 'dho polla xronia ...*	Greek, but the one who wrote it is Greek but she has been here for many years ...

(The conversation veers away about the author and about Christina going to Greece this summer and continues then going back to Maria talking about the book that she read.)

| 12M: | και ήταν ένα αντρόγυνο και η Georgia … I mean η Georgia | Kai itan ena adrogyno kai i Georgia … I mean i Georgia | and there was a married couple and Georgia … I mean Georgia |

(Angela laughs.)

Georgia is a common friend of theirs and since Maria mentioned Georgia instead of the author the conversation veers away again about Georgia and gets back to the book that Maria read after about 7 min as follows:

| 13C: | Τι έλεγες; | Ti eleges? | What were you saying? |

| 14M: | 'Ελεγα για την ιστορια …και που λες έκανε retire ο άντρας της και η γυναίκα στο σπίτι, δε θα δούλευε, so όσο δούλευε ο άντρας το μεσημέρι η γυναίκα δεν έστρωνε τραπέζι να κάτσει να φάει κανονικό lunch, έτρωγε ένα σάντουιτς και την ώρα που 'ρχόταν ο άντρας της το απόγευμα ή το βράδυ έτρωγε dinner κανονικό. 'Οταν όμως έμεινε ο άντρας στο σπίτι, πρωί breakfast/ μεσημέρι lunch/ βράδυ dinnerΚ'Ηρθε κι έγεινε η γυναίκα μμ (making a gesture to indicate size). | Elega gia tin istoria kai pou les ekane retire o adras tis kai i gynaika sto spiti, dhe tha dhoulebe, so oso dhoulebe o adras to mesimeri i gynaika dhen estrone trapezi na katsei na faei kanoniko lunch, etroge ena sadouits kai tin ora pou 'rxotan o adras tis to apogebma i to bradhy etroge dinner kanoniko. Otan omos emeine o adras sto spiti, proi breakfast, mesimeri lunch, bradhy dinner. Irthe ki egine i gynaika mm. | I was talking about this story … so, the husband retired and the wife was at home; she must have not been working, so while her husband was working the wife wouldn't set the table to have regular lunch, but she would eat a sandwich and when the husband would come home in the afternoon or the evening, she would have regular dinner. But when the husband stayed home, morning breakfast, noon lunch, evening dinner. The time came when the women became that big like a chest.[20] |

| 15A: | μπαούλο (Angela adds). | Mpaoulo. | like a chest.[20] |

| 16C: | Oh my God. | | |

17M:	*Ναι, και μπαούλο ... καλά λέει η 'Αντζη ... Ε και μια μέρα του λέει: «Ρε άντρα», του λέει «απ ΄ τονκαιρο που σταμάτησες» λέει «τρεις φορές την ημέρα σου στρώνω τραπέζι.»*	Yes, like a chest, just like Angie says ... well and one day she tells him: "My dear husband" she tells him "since the day you stopped" she says "three times a day I set the table."
	Nai, kai mpaoulo ... kala leei i Antzi ... E kai mia mera tou leei: "Re adra," tou leei "ap' ton kairo pou stamatises" leei "treis fores tin imera sou strono trapezi."	
18A:	*Ναι.*	Yes.
	Nai.	
19M:	*«Κοντεύω να γίνω» λέει «σαν φουσκίδιΚ»*	"I am near to become'" she says, "a balloon."
	"Kontebo na gino" leei "san fouskidhi."	
20A:	*Αμ, τι.*	Of course.
	Am, ti.	
21M:	So, *«να βλέπεις» του λέει, «έτρωγα και κανένα σάντουιτς, ε και πήγαινα και έξω στα μαγαζιά.»*	"Look" she tells him, "I used to eat only a sandwich or so, well, and I used to go to the stores shopping."
	So, *"na blepeis" tou leei, "etroga kai kanena sadouits, e kai pigaina kai ekso sta magazia."*	
22A:	*Ναι ... πως.*	Of course.
	Nai ... pos.	
23M:	*«και πέρναγε κι η ώρα μου»l του λέει, «και περπατούσα λίγο ... τώρα ...» λέει ... Στεναχωρέθηκε ο άνθρωπος ... το άλλο το πρωί σηκώνεται ...*	"And my time would pass by easier" she tells him "and I used to walk ... now ..." she says ... the husband got sad ... and the next morning he gets up ...
	"kai pernage ki i ora mou," tou leei, "kai perpatousa ligo ... tora ..." leei ... Stenaxorithike o anthropos ... to allo to proi sikonetai ...	
24A:	*Πάει στη δουλειάΚ*	and goes to work.
	Paei sti dhouleia.	
25M:	*... έφαγε* breakfast, *ετοιμάστηκε και λέει: «Πάω» λέεil «μια βόλτα» ... πάει στην ταβέρνα, απ ΄ τη στεναχώρια που του ΄ πε η γυναίκα του έτσι, αρχισε και ήπιε, ήπιε, ήπιε.*	He ate breakfast, got ready and says: "I am going" he says "for a walk." ... He goes to the tavern and because of his sadness about what his wife had told him, he started drinking and drinking and drinking.
	... efage breakfast, *etoimastike kai leei: "Pao" leei, "mia bolta" ... paei stin taberna, ap' tin stenaxoria pou tou 'pe i gynaika tou etsi, arxise kai ipie, ipie, ipie.*	

26A:	Ναι, έγινε τούμπανο.	Nai, egine toumpano	Yes, he got wasted.
27M:	'Εγινε τούμπανο ... δεν έβλεπε να πάει στο σπίτι, δε μπορούσε να προχωρήσει και τον παίρνει ένας αστυνομικός, τον πάει στο σπίτι ... ανοίγει η γυναίκα, βλέπει τον αστυνομικό ... λέειW «τι έγινε;» «Τίποτα», λέει, «κυρία μου, σας έφερα τον άντρα σας» ... Αυτός, εδώ να πέσει, εκεί να σηκωθεί ... λέειW «καλά τι έπαθες;» «Μα δε μου είπες", λέει, «οτι σου ΄γινα βάρος και στρώνεις τρεις φορές την ημέρα τραπέζι ...»	Egine toumpano ... dhen eblepe na paei sto spiti, dhe mporouse na proxorisei kai ton pairnei enas astinomikos ton paei sto spiti ... anoigei i gynaika, blepei ton astinomiko ... leei: "ti egine?" "Tipota," leei, "kyria mou, sas efera ton adra sas" ... Aftos, edho na pesei, ekei na sikothei ... leei: "kala ti epathes? " "Ma dhe mou eipes", leei, "oti sou , gina baros kai stroneis treis fores tin imera trapezi ..."	He got wasted. ... he couldn't see his way to go home and a police man stopped him; he takes him home. ... The wife opens the door, sees the policeman ... says: "What happened?" "Nothing," he says, "madam, I brought you your husband" ... he was very shaky on his feet and she says: "What happened to you?" "Didn't you tell me" he says "that I am a burden and you set the table three times a day ..."

(laughter)

| | «... πήγα», λέει, «κι ΄γω να ξεσκάσω αλλά παραήπια», της λέει, «και δε μπορούσα να περπατήσω» ... «όχι», λέει, «αντρα μου, κάτσε δω», λέει, «δε πειράζει», λέει, «θα πάω να πάρω άλλα ρούχα αφού δε μου κάνουν αυτά που έχω.» | "... piga", leei, "ki 'go na kseskaso alla paraïpia", tis leei, "kai de mporousa na perpatiso" ... "oxi," leei, "antra mou, katse dho," leei, "de peirazei," leei, "tha pao na paro alla rouxa afou dhe mou kanoun afta pou exo." | "... I went" he says "to get away from things, but I drank too much" he tells her "and I couldn't walk." "No" she says "my dear husband, sit down" she says "it doesn't matter" she says "I'll get new clothes if these ones don't fit me." |

(laughter)

| 28A: | Άκουσες; | Akouses? | Did you hear that? |

29M: Άκουσα....και την ώρα που το διάβαζα, με πιάσανε κάτι γέλια εμένα κι ο Τζίμης ήταν στο living room, εγώ στην κουζίνα και λέω «κοίτα», λέω, «αυτό είναι ότι πρέπει για μένα»K

Akousa ... kai tin ora pou to dhiabaza, me piasane kati gelia emena ki o Tzimis itan sto living room, ego stin kouzina kai leo "koita," leo, "afto einai oti prepei gia mena."

I did and when I was reading it I started laughing so hard and Jimmy was in the living room and I was in the kitchen and I said "look," I say, "this is just right for me."

Maria continues relating this story to her own situation and describes how she used to have more time when her husband was working and how she was thinner. At one point George decides to get up and leave (not being interested to hear any more) and Christine tells him:

30C: Where are you going?

(pointing with the finger to his empty chair telling him to sit back down)

In this example I focus only on the narrative and on the meaning of the story with regard to negotiating identity. Rather than analyze the narrative, I provide a content analysis for relating this narrative to the situation, the identity negotiation in the two first examples, the gender role expectations, and its contextualization to this situation. After the two aforementioned incidents, Maria decides to stand up to her role and identity of a "somewhat-emancipated" woman (at least in the context of the *gynaikoloi* setting) after both Angela and Christina have fulfilled their part in trying to communicate to George how important it is for them to get at least these locally constructed identities granted. Because Maria is weaker in one-on-one confrontation, she takes her approach through the narrative.

The narrative has two functions. First, it illustrates how these global/social expectations of women limit their freedom and their time, especially considering that the woman described in the story was setting the table three times a day, not because she wanted to, but because she had to, because of her husband's and society's expectations. These expectations infringe on women's rights by forcing them to neglect their own priorities in favor of serving their husbands' needs. For example, the woman in the narrative gained so much weight after her husband retired because she was expected to have the table set and to eat with him. Second, the story illustrates how even after confrontation, the husband has his way of imposing these norms and expectations on the woman.

This story reflects also to some extent the character of Maria because she too gives in and is not good with confrontation. The fact that Maria relates this story (later in the narrative) to herself indicates the second function of the story, which is to communicate the importance of their locally constructed identities to George by giving him an understanding of their everyday life through the narrative. By doing so, Maria finally assumes her local identity on her own and not only with the help of Angela and Christina. This narrative shows that all these global identity expectations apply to these women every day, except only for the times when these women get together to create their own little *gynaikoloi* environment in which they can freely reconstruct their identities forced upon them through society, from which they can "break free" for a few hours.

After Maria finishes her story, George tries again to not acknowledge these identities even after having heard this story. He signals this by getting up to leave. George is not the least bit interested in hearing any more, and has no intention to recognize such locally constructed "false" identities. Yet, again, Christina, is trying to get his recognition by saying "where are you going?" and pointing with her finger to the chair, communicating to him that he had better sit down, but George has already left the room. In this exchange, Christina tried to use her previously assumed power through the equal identity status that she had gained (as shown in Example 2), yet this power fails to work because George has decided to ignore it. Hence, we can see that the power which these women constructed locally by assuming certain identities does not last long, because, especially in the global picture (or within their social network), it is not recognized. However, this short time is better than nothing for these women, which is exactly what they tried to communicate very effectively in their talk exchanges.

CONCLUSION

In this chapter we witnessed the negotiation of preestablished and newly constructed identities with the example of three Greek women who are constantly challenged to assume only their globally (socially) predetermined identities and the expectations that come with them, but whose desired identities contrast with these expectations. Gender role expectations are imposed upon these women by virtue of their generation, their region of origin and social network, and circumstances that predetermined these identities for them. The women generally meet these expectations, except during *gynaikoloi* speech events, in which the woman can "let loose" from these expectations when they are with each other. In this situation, identities frequently are newly constructed. Sometimes then, gender identities are predetermined and globally decided and are assumed as such in the discourse (based on shared cultural knowledge), whereas at other times, they are newly constructed as part of interaction and process of negotiation. Language is central to the process either way in that it constructs meaning and intent, whatever that meaning and intent may be. In the case of contested gender identities, it is through conversational discourse that these women either accept and reconstruct preexistent identities for themselves or transform these identities as part of a negotiation process.

ENDNOTES

1. 1821–1828: wave of "Philhellenism" (Kopan, 1995, p. 261); 1873–1899: early migration; 1900–1917: great wave; 1918–1924: last exodus; 1925–1946: closed door (only about 30,000 Greeks came in these two decades); 1947–1955: postwar migration; 1965–1979: new wave; 1980–present: declining migration (Moskos, 1993).
2. In Kourvetaris, G. (1997). *Studies on Greek Americans*, pp. 24–25.
3. Exact figures do not exist. This number is taken from Kopan (1995), who argued that "Chicago never reached more than 75,000 persons," and Kourvetaris (1977), who estimated that 90,000 to 150,000 Greek Americans live in Chicago.
4. The Hull House played an important role for these first Greek immigrants of Chicago. It helped their "educational, spiritual and physical development" (Kopan, 1995, p. 295) and their psychological survival in their new country. (For more information see Kopan, A. (1995). Greek survival in Chicago. In *Ethnic Chicago*, pp. 295–299.)
5. In Schiffrin, D. (1996). Narrative as self-portrait: Sociolinguistic constructions of identity. In *Language In Society*, p. 169.
6. ibid.
7. These theorists do not focus exclusively on self-representation, but also on other important elements of discourse and society. However, self-portrayal is the only thing I focus on in this chapter.
8. Marcia Farr has analyzed a similar all-female gathering among Mexican Ranchera women, who refer to it as "echando relajo" (Farr, 1994).
9. Her own words.
10. When they talk about the times they get together, they usually say, E, μαζευτήκαμε εκεί το γυναικολόι για να τα πούμε κι εμεις λιγάκι [well, the womenfolk got together to get to talk a little bit (to get things off our chest).]
11. A word used by Christina very often. I therefore mention it frequently too so I can portray her attitude and opinion of gender role expectations.
12. Στίμη is a phonologically and morphologically integrated loanword that originated probably from the word "steamer" and is used in reference to the heater (according to their explanation because this is not a very usual loanword, and as far as I know, it is used only in this community; I asked several other Greek Americans, who also had never heard of that word before).
13. μασίνι is another loanword (but very widely used among all Greek Americans; I have heard this word from Los Angeles to

New York to Chicago) from the word "machine" and is referred to things such as machines, appliances. Here it is used for the heater, actually for the thermostat of the heater, which automatically turns it on if the temperature drops below 65°F.

14. This word is not used anymore in standard Greek, but it is rather a vernacular (especially used by people from that area [Tripoli]), yet its use is rare and occurs only in some instances. Usually, the more common word κοιτάω (I am looking) is used even in that vernacular (at least as far as I have observed in this community, George uses "κοιτάω" very often, whereas this was the first time I actually heard him use "τηράω" in the nearly 4 years that I have known him).

15. Actually, this word means something like "expressing opinion and not caring."

16. This is used to express "having someone for dinner over," or more generally it is expected from the host (especially the hostess) to have food ready for people who come over for a visit. Food is very important in expressing politeness in Greek culture, and it is especially expected from the women (especially when this generation is discussed) to have food on the table and serve it to the men.

17. None of the women actually agrees with them, yet Christina is the only one who dares to express it.

18. Jokes are constantly made (in a friendly manner) at the expense of someone who uses a word incorrectly, does not know some important political figure, or the like.

19. χαβαδιαζω (*xabadhiazo*) is "expressing opinion" (literally) without caring (i.e., without caring about the social expectations and implications).

20. A huge wooden box sometimes used by the women, especially of that generation, to keep their so-called "proika," something the husband used to get from the woman's family when marrying his new wife.

APPENDIX

Transcription Conventions

Italics	Greek
//	Overlap
[( )]	Author's comments
/?/	Not clear on tape
…	Noticeable pause

Greek Transliteration

dh = /ð/ (delta - δ), a voiced interdental fricative as in English "then."

th = /θ/ (theta -θ), a voiceless interdental fricative as in English "thick."

x = /x/ (chi -χ), a voiceless velar fricative not found in English, similar to "h" with more constriction in the throat.

ks = /ks/ (ksi - ξ), like the English letter "x" as in "ax."

ps = /ps/ (psi - ψ) as in "epsilon."

ou = /u/ (omicron upsilon - ου) as in "you."

ai = /ε/ (alpha iota - αιⱭpronounced like the English vowel "e" as in "bet."

i = /i/ (iota - ιⱭpronounced like the English vowel "i" as in "see." This pronunciation is used to represent the Greek vowels iota (ι), eta (η), upsilon (υⱭepsilon iota Ɛι), and omicron iota (οι). The three other Greek transliterations for this vowel follow.

y = /i/ (upsilon - υ), in English it can be pronounced like this too as in "gently."

ei = /i/ (epsilon iota - ειⱭas in "weird."

oi = /i/ (omicron iota - οι).

mp = /b/ (mi pi - μπ) as in the word "bread."

b = /v/ (beta – βⱭas in the word "vet."

Most of the Greek transliteration is taken from *Talking Voices*, by Deborah Tannen (1989).

REFERENCES

Abbot, G. (1909). *A study of the Greeks in Chicago*. [On-Line]. Available: http://www.greeklegacy.com/article_1.htm Accessed: 6/1/6/01.

Auer, P. (Ed.). (1998). Code-Switching in Conversation. Language, Interaction and Identity. London, New York, Routledge.

Chicago Fact Book Consortium. (1995). *Local community fact book: Chicago metropolitian area 1990*. Chicago: University of Illinois at Chicago.

Farr, M. (1994). *Echando relajo*: Verbal art and gender among mexicanas in Chicago. In M. Bucholtz, A. C. Liang, L. A. Sutton, & C. Hines (Eds.), *Cultural performances: Proceedings of the third woman and language conference*, April 8–10, 1994, (pp. 168–188). University of California, Berkeley.

Gergen K. (1987). Toward self as relationship. In K. Yardly & T. Honess (Eds.), *Self and identity: Psychological perspectives*, (pp. 53–63). New York: Wiley.

Gergen, M. (1988). Narrative and the self as relationship. In L. Berkowitz (Ed.), *Social psychological studies of the self*, (pp. 17–54). New York: Academic Press.

Goffman E. (1959). *The presentation of self in everyday life*. New York: Anchor Books.

Goffman E. (1974). *Frame analysis*. New York: Harper and Row.

Goffman E. (1981). Footing. In Forms of talk, (pp. 124–59). Philadelphia: University of Philadelphia Press.

Gumperz, J. (1982a). *Discourse strategies*. Cambridge, UK: Cambridge University Press.

Gumperz, J. (1982b). *Language and social identity*. Cambridge, UK: Cambridge University Press.

Harre, R. (1987). The social construction of selves. In K. Yardly & T. Honess (Eds.), *Self and identity: Psychological perspectives*, (pp. 41–52). New York: Wiley.

Holli, M. G., & Jones, P. d'A. (1995). *Ethnic Chicago: A multicultural portrait* (4th ed.). Grand Rapids, MI: William B. Eerdmans.

Kerby, A. (1991). Narrative and the self. Bloomington: Indiana University Press.

Kopan, A. (1995). Greek survival in Chicago. In M. G. Holli & P. d'A. Jone (Eds.), *Ethnic Chicago: A multicultural portrait* (4th ed., pp. 261–299). Grand Rapids, MI: William. B. Eerdmans.

Kourvetaris, G. A. (1997). *Studies on Greek Americans*. New York: Columbia University Press.

Li, W. (1994). *Three generations, two languages, one family*. Clevedon, England: Multilingual Matters Ltd.

Makedon, A. (1998). *The social psychology of immigration: The Greek American experience*[excerpts] [On-Line]. Available: http://webs.csu.edu/`big0ama/articles/GreekAmerican.html Accessed: 6/23/01.

Moskos, C. (1993). *Faith, language and culture*. [On-Line]. http://www. voithia.org/content/qmpfalacu.htm Accessed 6/23/01.

Myers-Scotton. (1988a). Code switching as indexical of social negotiation. In M. Heller (Ed.), *Code switching: Anthropological and sociolinguistic perspectives*, (pp. 151–186). Berlin: Mouton de Gruyter.

Myers-Scotton, C. (1988b). Self-enhancing code switching as interactional power. *Language and Communication, 8*, 199–211.

Pappas, M. (1999). *Greeks voyage to "Delta."* [On-Line]. Available: http://www. suntimes.com/century/m1910.html Accessed: 6/23/01.

Schiffrin, D. (1994). *Approaches to discourse*. Oxford, UK: Blackwell Publishers.

Schiffrin, D. (1996). Narrative as Self-Portrait. In *Language in Society*, (pp. 167–203). Cambridge, UK: Cambridge University Press.

Tannen, D. (1989). *Talking voices*. Cambridge, UK: Cambridge University Press.

Taylor, C. (1991). "The dialogical self" In David Hiley et al. (Eds.) *The interpretive turn: Philosophy, science, culture* (pp. 304–314). Ithaca: Cornell University Press.

U.S. Bureau of the Census. (1990). *Basic facts > quick table* [On-Line]. Available: http://factfinder.census.gov/servlet/BasicFactsTable?_lang=en&_vt_name= DEC_1990_ST... Accessed: 6/20/01.

PART

III

COMMUNITY SPACES

Photograph by Michael Maltz

6

A Literacy Event in African American Churches: The Sermon as a Community Text[1]

Beverly J. Moss

Ohio State University

On any Sunday morning in Chicago, large numbers of African Americans from various communities that make up this city participate in one of the most fascinating literacy traditions in this country: They participate in the worship services at predominantly African American churches. And they are participants in the most important literacy event within this tradition—the sermon. In examining a literacy event to which most members in the African American community have been exposed, I use Heath's (1982) definition of literacy event: "any action sequence, involving one or more persons, in which the production and/or comprehension of print plays a role" (p. 92). The African-American sermon fits this definition, and it is the major literacy event to which most African Americans have been exposed to in their communities, including those African-Americans who do not attend church.

Over the past few years, discussions about literacy have taken a new direction, one long overdue, that is, looking at literacy in nonacademic communities. A major tension in the discussion of literacy centers on the way literacy is defined, or more accurately, on how people perceived to be literate are characterized and how people perceived to be not literate are characterized. This issue relates to how we characterize literate behavior, literate texts, and literacy events. At the core of much of the dissension is the assumption on the part of many educators that there is one definition of literacy, a standard list of features of literate behavior, literate texts, and consequently literate peoples.

It seems, then, impossible to talk about literacy without discussing the social practices of literacy. Yet, that is precisely what happens when we ignore the cultural environment from which children come and in which children learn language outside of school. Szwed (1981) suggested that to define literacy, we must examine "the social context in which writing occurs, the participants (the writer and intended readers), the function the writer serves, and the motivation for writing" (p. 14). Street (1984) labeled this model of literacy the "ideological" model, a model that stresses the specific social practices of reading and writing. Those supporting the ideological model argue that language does not occur in a vacuum, that we cannot separate our language from its social and physical environment, be it oral or written language. The view that there are various kinds of literacies defined by various cultures and communities deserves closer examination because of its potential impact on education, particularly on writing instruction.

When literacy is examined in nonschool settings, the focus is on crucial questions: How do we determine what is valued in different cultures or in different communities within a society such as the United States? Do these values affect the way language is learned? How is language being used in particular communities or cultures? What roles do reading, writing, and speaking play in these communities? These questions are not new, particularly for anthrolopologists and sociolinguists. Of particular importance in answering such questions and in framing an investigation of the role of language in specific communities and cultures is the development of the ethnography of speaking (Hymes, 1962, 1972) and the ethnography of communication (Gumperz & Hymes, 1964). Hymes and Gumperz, in their groundbreaking work, offed a systematic way of looking at language use in the context in which it occurs. One need only look at the work of scholars such as Shirley Brice Heath to see the impact of the ethnography of communication in literacy studies. Heath (1983) addressed many of the aforementioned questions in her important work, *Ways With Words*. This study focused on literacy in three communities in the Piedmont Carolinas: Trackton, a small Black working-class community; Roadville, a small White working-class community, and the Townspeople, a middle-class integrated community.

Heath's research and other similar studies point to the importance of discovering the uses and functions of language, oral and written, in both the community and classroom, and to the importance of exploring expanding definitions of literacy. This view has prompted many scholars, before and after Heath, to explore the notion of multiple definitions of literacy in various communities (Farr 1994a, 1994b, 2000; Fishman, 1988; Moss, 1994; Philips, 1972; Scollon & Scollon, 1981; Scribner & Cole, 1981; Taylor & Dorsey-Gaines, 1988; Weinstein-Shr, 1986). This view also helped to shape my thinking about my previous research on literacy in the African American church (Moss, 1988).

DATA SOURCES

I spent approximately 10 Sundays in two Chicago area African American churches observing and collecting data through ethnographic methods.[2] The major sources of data were the five sermons I collected from two ministers. From the minister who writes a complete manuscript from which to preach sermons, I collected copies of written sermons as well as the cassette tapes of the oral performances of those written sermons, and from the minister who writes very little of his sermons, I collected audiotapes of the sermons along with any notes the preacher may have written.

As in most studies conducted from an ethnographic perspective, participant observation was a standard means of collecting data (Hymes, 1974; Spradley, 1980). I was a participant observer in each of the church's Sunday services, so I kept field notes on the services as I participated in them. Although most of these notes deal with the sermons, many of them concern other aspects of the service such as what actions, during the service made use of written sources, what actions drew the most audience response, and so on. I also conducted ethnographic interviews (see Spradley, 1979 for details about how to conduct an ethnographic interview) with each minister. I interviewed each minister before I began to collect the sermons and during the sermon collections, and in some cases after the field work was completed. The field notes and interviews provide insight and support for issues arising out of the analysis of the actual written sermons and/or transcripts of the oral sermons.

THE AFRICAN AMERICAN CHURCH AND WORSHIP SERVICE

This essay explores seemingly simple questions: What features characterize the major literacy event—the sermon? How does this literacy event in this community compare and contrast with academic literacy? Before addressing these questions, it is necessary to provide some background information on the African American church and preaching tradition, and to introduce the churches in which the highlighted literacy events took place. Geneva Smitherman (1977) stated that "the traditional African American church is the oldest and perhaps still the most powerful and influential Black institution" (p. 90). Theologian C. Eric Lincoln (1974), emphasizing the impact of the church on African American people, stated that "[their] church was [their] school, [their] forum, [their] political arena" (p. 6). Lincoln (1974) also asserted that "whether one is a church member or not is beside the point in any assessment of the importance and meaning of the Black church" (p. 115), and Mays and Nicholson (1933) asserted that the "Negro church is one of the greatest, perhaps the greatest channel through which the masses of the Negro race receive adult education. ... It becomes the center of religious, moral, and intellectual teaching" (p. 58).

Features of African American Preaching

The characteristics comprising the core of African American preaching are the very features that make this event a literacy event worthy of study and which provide more insight into literacy acquisition and functions in African American communities. These essential characteristics of African American preaching can, I believe, lead us to think more complexly about literacy, literate behaviors, and literate texts.

Henry Mitchell's *Black Preaching* (1970) is probably one of the most complete explorations of African American preaching. Mitchell suggested that African American preaching takes place only in dialogue, and he credits the congregation with "making the dialogue a normal part of the black preacher's sermon" (p. 95). Mitchell (1970) characterized the dialogue as that which occurs when a member of the congregation responds "because he identifies with something the preacher has said; ... he is at home, he is interested in what the preacher is saying because he is involved, crucially involved in the issues as the preacher shapes them with scriptural reference and skillful allegory" (p. 97). In other words, while the typical African American sermon is shaped by the preacher, he or she depends upon the participation of the congregation in completing that sermon.

This dialogic quality contributes to another essential characteristic in African American preaching: African American preachers must create a sense of community between themselves and their congregations and within their congregations as a whole. Mitchell (1970) stated that through the sermon, "one has to establish a kind of intimate fellowship" (p. 185). It is with this task of creating a sense of community or "intimate fellowship" and its connection to the sermon that I will concern myself in my discussion of features of the sermon. That is, a major feature of the sermons in the churches that I studied is that the texts are used to create and maintain a sense of community. This feature sets this literacy event apart from the essay—the major academic literacy event—because of the sermon's dependence on the participants, preacher, and congregation to be considered a successful dialogic text in the community. African American preachers, like other rhetoricians, can be successful at setting up this dialogue only if they know their audience and their needs.

Mitchell's (1970) characterizations of African American preaching can be condensed to two major points:

1. Black preachers must preach in the language and culture of their people no matter how educated the preachers are.
2. The preacher must address the contemporary man and his needs[3] (p. 29).

The first point is similar to one raised by St. Augustine[4] (Saint Augustine, 1958 translation) in *On Christian Doctrine,* who argued that preaching is a rhetorical act, and that the preacher/rhetor must, if necessary, speak the language of the people to reach them. One key difference between Augustine and Mitchell is that Mitchell sees this role as a necessity for being successful in the African American church whereas St. Augustine viewed it somewhat as a last resort. The second point stresses knowing enough about the congregation, being connected enough with them, to know what is important to them. This kind of knowledge and skill, prerequisites for building a community, makes African American preachers quite effective in reaching their congregation. The dialogic quality of the text and creation of a community through the text make the African American sermon a distinctive text.

The Ministers and Their Churches

Meeting the Manuscript Minister.   The most important distinction between the two preachers for the purposes of this study is the amount of writing they do in preparing their sermons. The minister who writes and uses a full manuscript from which he delivers his sermon is referred to hereafter as the "manuscript minister," a term used by the manuscript minister himself. The manuscript minister pastors a church located on the South Side of Chicago, which in 2 years will celebrate its 40th anniversary. This church has more than 6,000 members and a multimillion dollar annual budget. It is the largest church in the study, and at the time of the original study, to accommodate the large numbers of people who attended this church, the minister normally preached at two services, one at 8 a.m. and one at 11 a.m. Eventually, he began preaching three sermons per Sunday. However, since the completion of this study, this minister and congregation have moved into a larger, new worship complex.

Licensed to preach at 17 years of age and ordained eight years later, this minister has been a pastor since 1972. He has a B.A. in English, an M.A. in literature, an M.A. in History of Religions, a Doctor of Divinity degree and several honorary doctoral degrees. This minister's seminary training focused on academic scholarship rather than preparation to preach. He explains that this kind of training has an influence on what he preaches, specifically his understanding of the African American religious tradition in the context of world religions. In addition, he serves as an adjunct professor with the Seminary Consortium for Urban Pastoral Education.

This manuscript minister's biographical sketch gives evidence of his deep commitment to education. Also, he is deeply committed to addressing political and social issues as well as religious issues. His sermons contain many illustrations that concern politics from the local level to the global level, such as criticisms of Chicago politician Ed Vrdolyak, former United States President Ronald Reagan, and former South African President P. W. Botha. He does not shy away from relating Biblical politics to world politics, nor does he shy away from criticizing politicians from the pulpit. Some of these references to politics are impromptu, but most of them are parts of the written sermons. This minister also educates his congregation about different cultures, telling them about the cultures of the people in the countries that he visits, particularly the cultures of peoples of color. He constantly introduces Hebrew and African concepts to the congregation in the context of a particular sermon's message. His focus on the bonds between peoples of color was evident to me after 2 months of observation. In short, he is a well-educated, charismatic man whose command of language and knowledge of the Bible and religions of the world are displayed in his sermons.

Meeting the Manuscript Minister's Congregation. Some churches reflect their denomination's teachings; some reflect the congregation's wishes; and others reflect their ministers' visions. This church falls into the latter category. Many of the programs that exist in this church are a result of the manuscript minister's philosophy and ideas brought to fruition. His effectiveness as a pastor can be measured by the growth of the congregation and the church's programs since his arrival more than 25 years ago. The membership has grown from fewer than 100 members to well over 6,000 members. The church now has a federally approved credit union; a reading, writing, and math tutorial program; a day care center; a legal counseling service; a large pastoral counseling staff; an educational program that concentrates on educating the church membership about their religious and cultural roots as an African people; broadcast ministries; and much more.

The manuscript minister stresses to his congregation that they should be "unashamedly Black and unapologetically Christian." This statement is part of the oath that the congregation takes when accepting new members into the church. During the time that the data were collected, this church was always full, with standing room only. Worshipers arrive 50 min before service starts so they can get seats in the sanctuary.

The congregation of this church is viewed as middle class by many members of Chicago's African American community. However, the minister views his congregation as a mixed group. He takes pride in the diversity of the congregation. Yet, although the members of this church represent a range on the socioeconomic ladder, a large number of people in this church are professionals: judges, lawyers, doctors, educators, businessmen and -women, entertainers, and so forth. A TV documentary, which aired nationally addressed the perceived "middle classness" of this church (Keeping the Faith, 1987). It is a church that stresses education, yet it does not make the less formally educated feel uncomfortable. Its apparent upward mobility makes this church appealing to those who identify with the upwardly mobile. In fact, many members of the congregation drive to Chicago's South side from Chicago suburbs.

Despite its middle class identification, this church is rooted in the tradition of the African American church, and the minister is rooted in the tradition of African American preachers. My interviews with this minister confirmed what I had observed previously: This manuscript minister takes great pride in being identified as "in the tradition of Black preachers." He believes in making connections between the traditional African American church and the contemporary African American church, and in using the language of the African American community in his sermons. This use of the language is much more than just speaking; it is also establishing a sense of community, communicating ideas and attitudes about African American people, and promoting certain community values.

Meeting the Nonmanuscript Minister.   The second preacher in the study prepares no manuscript from which to preach and usually no written notes. He pastors a church of 800+ members located in a northern suburb of Chicago. Although the church is in a Chicago suburb, it is located just across the Northern border of Chicago and has very strong ties to the city. Like the manuscript minister, the nonmanuscript minister also preaches at two Sunday morning services, at 8 a.m. and at 11 a.m. This church, rich in history, celebrated its 130th anniversary in 2000.

This preacher initially came to this area as a faculty member at a nearby well-known seminary. He was on the faculty at this seminary for 15 years. During the latter years of his faculty appointment, he also served as senior pastor of this church, probably one of the few professors who also pastored a church full-time. In his church he is addressed by his academic title "Dr_____" rather than "Reverend_____." This minister brings to this church not only a traditional training of years of preaching experience mostly in smaller churches, but also a scholarly foundation. And while this scholarship includes the study of noted Western philosophers such as Heidegger and Kant, this minister has devoted much of his scholarship and his ministry to African American theological issues. Like the manuscript preacher, the non-manuscript preacher has a basic philosophy that guides his ministry. That philosophy, which is printed on the church bulletins, is "faith and freedom for African American people." He says that he is "unapologetically a race preacher." Committed to his people, this minister's philosophy and commitment affect his sermon preparation and consequently his sermons. Through my interviews with this minister, I learned that his experience as a preacher at a southern church and his experiences while in divinity school in the South played a major role in his training to pastor African American people. Born in a Midwestern, white-collar city, it was his experiences in the South that introduced him to the traditional African American worship patterns that so many African American preachers exemplify. He now describes the congregations of many urban churches as full of transplanted Southerners who are used to the Southern African American tradition of worship, a sentiment echoed by Davis (1985), who noted the important influence of the Southern African American church tradition on African American churches in general.

When discussing with me methods of communicating with his congregation, the nonmanuscript minister focused on verbal and nonverbal language. He relies on gestures to communicate as well as words. The nonmanuscript preacher explains that in the African American church, he reaches some people with words. He states, for instance that "celestial skies means heaven for some, but those words mean nothing to people ruled by emotions. A gesture, however, pointing upward and looking upward has the meaning of heaven for those people who attach less meaning to words." This raises the issue of how much value some people attach to words in this setting. It also raises the issue of how this minister and others identify and communicate with the multiple levels of audience that make up their congregations. This minister, as evidenced by his identification of the different kinds of language use to which people respond, has a special awareness of this multiple audience issue. More important, he seems to meet the needs of his congregation.

Finally, of great importance in discussing this nonmanuscript minister is his commitment to political and social issues. It is very obvious that he sees the pulpit as the perfect place to discuss politics. During the time that I attended services and collected data, I noted that this minister regularly discussed local, state, national, and international politics. Many times, issues of politics were used as illustrations in a sermon. Tied to political issues raised in the pulpit are social and economic issues. One sermon began with a discussion of the impact of AIDS on the African American community. The politically centered discussions focus on their impact on African American people, in keeping with this minister's identification of himself as a race preacher.

Meeting the Nonmanuscript Minister's Congregation. The oldest of the churches in this study and located in a middle-class suburb, this church's long history suggests that it serves a predominantly middle-class African American population. Indeed, many of its members fit that label. Like the congregation in the manuscript minister's church, this church has a large number of African American professionals. There are teachers, judges, lawyers, doctors, businesspeople, and corporate executives in this congregation. In addition, because this church is located very near a major university, a large number of African American college students, both on the undergraduate and graduate levels, attend this church. Unlike the other churches in the study, it is not located in an African American neighborhood. People drive from various distances to get to Sunday morning service. In spite of these facts, the minister indicated that he does not really see his church as middle class, although he recognizes that there are a large number of professionals and what he calls intellectuals in his congregation. His perception does assist him in not preaching above the heads of those who are limited in their vocabulary and educational level or who do not respond as enthusiastically to verbal stimuli.

This church's organizations are concerned not only with the operation of the church, but also with education and community fellowship. It has an administrative staff consisting of the senior pastor, an executive assistant pastor, and assistant pastors in charge of special ministries, educational ministries, and youth ministries. There are the traditional deacon, trustee, and usher boards as well as a library committee and a group that runs a precollege seminar for church members who are going off to college. The focus on education reflects one of the priorities of the minister, who promotes the value of higher education in his sermons.

In addition, this church has numerous organizations that promote fellowship among the congregation such as the singles' ministry, the widows' and widowers' club, the bowling league, and the softball team. There is also a church-run marriage counseling program. These organizations and programs show how many diverse groups the church tries to serve. It also emphasizes the church as the center of not only religious activities and political activities but social activities as well.

The Sermon As a Literacy Event: "The Ties That Bind"

One of the more well-known facts about African American sermons is that they are characterized by a call and response pattern, in which the congregation provides feedback to the minister throughout the sermon. This audience participation pattern is always prevalent in the minds of the ministers in this study. It is this pattern that prompts each minister to characterize the sermon as a dialogue, and because of this characterization, to distinguish African American sermons from most other American protestant sermons (there are some exceptions) that more closely resemble a monologue. This dialogic pattern is the rhetorical device which acts as the foundation for the other three devices I focus on in this section of the chapter.

In the ministers' discussions of their sermon preparation, each seems acutely aware of the role of the congregation in the construction of a successful sermon. Even the manuscript minister who writes practically all of his sermons beforehand speaks of making room for the congregation to participate in the sermon. What these ministers do in their "texts" is invite audience participation by using the sermon to create and maintain a community. In a sense, viewing the sermon as a dialogue between minister and congregation makes the sermon a community text written (or created) through collaboration between minister and congregation. What I examine in the remainder of this chapter are the features used by the ministers in the sermons that contribute to this sense of community and create space for the dialogue.

Much of the success and effectiveness of these ministers depend on their creation of a bond between themselves and their congregations. Also, because part of people's identities is linked with the communities in which they hold memberships, when these preachers use sermons to construct communities, they are also constructing not only their identities, but also the identities of the members of the congregation.

Why is it important to create this sense of community? According to the ministers, placing themselves in the congregation, seeing themselves as part of the group, helps them keep their sermons relevant to the congregation, helps build trust between the minister and the congregation, and therefore, makes it easier for the congregation to hear and accept the message that the minister is preaching. Ultimately, these ministers try to eliminate distance between themselves and the congregation through the sermon. Yet, they must maintain the "proper" distance because of their leadership positions. Already, we can see the multiple functions of this literacy event as well as its multidimensional nature.

The rhetorical strategies that the ministers use to construct and maintain community range from the seemingly simple reliance on first person plural pronouns ("we") to the more complex reliance on personal narratives and shared information. Although various rhetorical devices are used by these ministers to construct community, it is also important to note that the theme of community also pervades the sermons as a mechanism for emphasis.

"We, the People." One of the most obvious strategies that each minister consistently uses to help establish a sense of community is to employ the collective pronouns we, our, and us. This strategy is a favorite of these ministers, and although this strategy is not unique to African American sermons (Jellema, 1988), it is a feature that they use effectively. When the ministers use this strategy, they are tapping into the multiple levels of community represented in their churches and establishing their relationships with those communities. Consider the following examples from two different sermons in which the manuscript minister invokes at least three communities: his specific church community, the community of Christians, and society at large. As he taps into these three communities, his membership in these communities is also emphasized:

> Manuscript minister:
> Some of the meanest most miserable ungodly people I know got more degrees behind they names and make more money than most of *us* will ever see in a lifetime.
>
> We not at the pinnacle and we not in the pits. We just in between. Nothing to complain about and nothing to write home about either. We're not on a constant high no matter what kind of rhetoric we spout. And we not continuously in the dumps. Oh we have our moments like everybody else. But for the most part we find ourselves hanging around that gray area called in between.

In the first example, the pronoun "us" is so subtly used that we almost miss it. Based on its linguistic context, we can reasonably deduce that the community that this "us" indexes (Hanks, 1996; Silverstein, 1976) is the specific church community.[5] More interesting than the community that he indexes is that he includes himself in this community with the rest of the congregation. He is constructing his identity as a "regular guy" out there in the pew with little money just like everyone else in the church. Yet he has a B.A., two M.A.'s, and is working toward a doctorate (which he has obtained since the study). He drives an expensive car, makes a most respectable if not enviable salary, and lives in an upper middle-class Chicago neighborhood (in the church parsonage). But he constructs an identity that downplays his credentials and status.

It is important to this minister that he not separate himself from the congregation on the basis of socioeconomic issues. That is seen even more clearly in the second example taken from the first few minutes of one of the manuscript minister's sermons. In this example, "we" can have at least three referents: the church community, the Christian community, and the community of people in general. The primary audience seems to be the church community. However, there are no cues that signal a specific community. Again, the minister establishes himself as a member of all of these communities, constructing his identity and contributing to the construction of their identities as a group. The congregation's apparent acceptance of their identities as shaped in this example (through nods of the head, amens, and other comments) marks their contribution to the dialogue that constructs their identities.

Another prominent community to which the ministers refer consistently is the African American community. This is no surprise given the philosophies of these two ministers. They constantly emphasize their identities as African Americans and try to get their congregations to do so as well. Therefore, many times, the collective pronouns refer to the larger African American community to which the ministers and their congregations belong. Consider the following example from the manuscript minister and a later example from the non-manuscript minister:

Manuscript minister:
The God of Harriet Tubman is an us God—Community.
The God of Martin Delaney is an us God—Community.
The God of Ida B. Wells is an us God—Community.

These names refer to famous African Americans from the past. One reading of this passage is that the God of these noteworthy African Americans who struggled yet accomplished much is a God of the people—a God who embraces African Americans. He is not a them God—a God for the rich and powerful only, or a God for Whites only. African Americans are part of the community too. Here, the theme of community is intertwined with rhetorical devices that construct the community. This passage is also one of those examples, which I will address later, of using an assumed shared knowledge between minister and congregation to construct and maintain community.

An example of the nonmanuscript minister using collective pronouns to emphasize the African American community occurs in statements such as the following:

Nonmanuscript minister:
We can no longer stand in this world as second class in the economic world, but we got to think big.

Previous statements in the sermon signal that "we" refers to African Americans. The nonmanuscript minister implies that he, along with his other sisters and brothers, needs to "think big." Of course, after being in this church for only a couple of weeks, it is clear to the observer that this minister thinks big consistently, and that he is really trying to get African Americans in general, and his African American congregation in particular, to think big. In this case, the minister is trying to change the perceived identity of the community. Yet he has chosen not to place himself apart from the community he is addressing.

"I Can Witness."   This strategy of using collective pronouns to bind the ministers with their congregations seems obvious and simple, but its functions, as shown in the preceding section, are subtle and complex. A less obvious strategy for creating and maintaining a community in the sermon is to use personal narratives and testimonial-like statements. Again, this pattern is prevalent in both the manuscript and nonmanuscript ministers' sermons. These ministers' references to themselves as individuals in the sermons most often take the form of personal stories, testimonies, and testimonial-like statements. In these churches, there appears to be an implied distinction between testimonies and what I refer to as testimonial-like statements. A person who testifies usually gives a detailed account of some tragedy or down time in his or her life. The account ends with how God brought him or her through this bad time. The testimony is usually quite specific. A testimonial-like statement is a more general version of "testifyin'": for example, "God has lifted me up when I was down." However, we do not know what the down period was. My field notes contain several entries concerning how excited and vocal the congregations became in the midst of these ministers' stories or testimonies.

During interviews, each minister commented on how African American churches value personal stories from the ministers. Another minister explained this value most succinctly: "In Black churches, the people want to know what God has done for you [the minister]. What can you testify to?" The ministers gain more credibility and authority when they can show their congregations that they know what they are preaching about because they have been down and survived, they have been scared and conquered the fear, they have had experiences paralleling those of the people in the pew, but they have persevered and prospered. These personal stories provide the congregation with a more intimate view of the minister.

In sharing something personal, be it poignant or funny, these ministers forge even stronger bonds between themselves and their congregations.

Hence, they are strengthening community ties. The following example is a personal narrative that the nonmanuscript minister uses as an illustration in his sermon about Abraham:

> I was in the Marine Corps. I was training in Parris Island. I learned something at Parris Island. It was back in those days in 1954 when they was killing marines down there. Marines died on forced marches. I went down there right after six marines were drowned. When I got there, the first thing I heard when I got off the bus, somebody said "move." Then he called me a name that just hurt me to my heart. When he called me, he said, "Move it you [blank]," and I went to him and said, "Sir, just a minute." I said, "I'm ——. " Then he called me another name. "I don't care who the [blank] you are." It took me a whole week. My heart just lay bare. I was hurt to the core. But every time in the morning they would get up early; when you are tired they would come in and say "move it." We just got in bed. "Move it." My friend and I were put in swimming. I never swam in my life. I didn't know how to swim. They took us into the pool. One day there we were. I thought we were going in there to learn how to doggy paddle. Stand on the side, put your feet up and down, learn how to swim the normal and intelligent way. There we all were there buck naked standing over the side of the pool. I remember all of us lined up. DIs [drill instructors] standing on the side over there. There was a young brother named Logan standing next to me. I said "Logan guess we're going to learn to swim in a minute. They going to teach us how to do this." Logan said, "Yes I've been waiting for this." Then they told us I want you to bend over just like that (demonstrates to congregation). All of us bent over; then I heard this loud crack, "Move it!" I turned and looked back and said, "Do you mean?" "Yes, move it." I looked at Logan and said, "We're on this island out here. We're not going to get out of here. I better move." Logan said, "Are you sure?" I said, "Yes." I jumped in. I took a risk. When I jumped in, I went down. There I was swallowing the whole pool. I went up and down again. I started down the third time. They threw something out and pulled me out. … Brothers and sisters, God is often saying to us, and you know something, I moved at least four times, almost drowned at least four times. But the fifth time I got out there. I found a way of swimming like nobody has ever seen before. I got out that pool. I was not going to drown out there anymore. Brothers and sisters, what I'm saying to you. God said it to Abraham, "Move it."

This lengthy example is actually two smaller stories within one longer one, and it highlights this preacher's skills as a storyteller. Storytelling, be it personal or biblical, is a dominant rhetorical device that this minister uses throughout his sermons. The preceding one is among his most successful, as measured by the large amount and loud volume of feedback he receives from the congregation. In this example, this minister shows himself as a naive, sometimes frightened young man who overcomes these drawbacks by taking a risk, by moving forward. This characterization of him as naive and frightened is in direct conflict with the person that he seemingly is now. He has a confident, self-assured presence. One might view him more as a drill instructor than as a naive marine private. Therefore, sharing this story with the congregation about himself shows the congregation a different, more vulnerable side of him.

This minister also uses the testimonial-like examples in his sermons with similar effect:

Nonmanuscript minister:
A Jesus that I know lives. He is not a dead Jesus. This Jesus that I serve, this Jesus that I know is alive. The Jesus is at this table right now [inaudible] Jesus, he's alive. He lives. How do I know he lives? Because he walks with me and he talks with me. He tells me I am his own. Jesus is the life of the world. Jesus puts joy in my life. Jesus gives me peace when I'm sorrow …

Well what do I get from it? You see these degrees that I've got? Well I see. They're not there just for me. But one is for my father, one is for my grandfather, one is for my great-grandfather, one is for those generations yet unborn. I've come a long way. And don't stop me now. I am what I am Thank God. I am so glad to be [inaudible]. Thank you Jesus. I am what I am. Don't mess with me. Don't mess with me.

The latter example is fascinating because it relates to the earlier example from this nonmanuscript minister of thinking big, and it contributes a new dimension to this issue of constructing an identity through the sermon. While the manuscript minister emphasizes how he is just like everybody else, he also emphasizes how he is not like everybody else. The latter example emphasizes his degrees. The earlier narrative emphasizes how he takes risks. He is constructing an identity for himself as a strong-willed, aggressive, upwardly mobile person. He wants his congregation to reach his heights and not accept being "just plain ole folks." He wants them, particularly his African American congregation, to construct an identity different from that which society has given them, and the implicit message is that he should be the role model for this reconstruction of identity.

Although the nonmanuscript minister appears to distance himself from his congregation by emphasizing his successes, he, in fact, is trying to decrease the gap by appealing to them to rise to his heights and by showing them that his successes were for those who had come before him and for "generations yet unborn." He emphasizes his dedication to his people and, implicitly, his faith that his risks will pay off. The evidence of the value of his strategy is the positive response of the congregation. Their level of feedback increases. They respond vocally, and they applaud with a great deal of energy. Through this focus on himself, this minister skillfully manages to maintain community ties, and he skillfully yet subtly establishes some standards for community behavior: taking risks, thinking big and so on.

The final example that follows fits into two categories. It is another example of the testimonial-like statement, and it is an example that introduces the strategy of using shared information between minister and congregation to emphasize community ties.

> Manuscript minister:
> I don't sing ... because of thunderous ovations and grand audiences. I don't sing ... because I've got a voice like James Cleveland, Dave Peaceton, or Teddy Pendergrass. I don't sing ... because I think I got a solo voice, and I might get discovered by some record company. I sing to praise him. I sing to my little light shine. I sing ... because God has been good to me. I sing because I'm happy and I praise him and I say thank you Lord. I sing because I'm free. And I praise him. I sing because I know he watches over me.

As the manuscript minister delivers this part of his sermon, much of the congregation stands and applauds, waving their hands, and responding with encouragements such as, "preach," "yes," "amen," "thank you, Jesus," and other phrases. While they are responding to the minister's words about himself and his relationship with God, there also seems to be a kind of transformation that takes place. The congregation is moved by the witnessing of the minister, but they also identify with him. That is, the "I," in the example becomes a collective "I" which refers not only to the minister, but also to the community of believers in that congregation. The minister is no longer speaking for himself, but for the community as well. This takes the personal testimony to a new dimension in which the minister's story becomes the people's story.

The manuscript minister says that one of his goals when he prepares his sermons is to seek this collective voice. He views himself as part of the congregation and asks himself "What do I need to hear today?" He is successful only if he is so much a part of the congregation that he sees himself in them and they see themselves in him. Hence, the "I" becomes representational. When the minister and congregation identify with each other so strongly, the community ties are more deeply embedded; the minister is more firmly entrenched as a role model; and his or her use of language and literacy is more influential.

The Knowledge We Share. The previous example provides a segue into the final feature of this literacy event on which this essay will focus: relying on shared knowledge. These ministers rely on shared knowledge between themselves and their congregations to signal community identification. That is, the ministers assume that their congregations, by virtue of their membership in various communities, have a body of knowledge about certain topics, and that this knowledge is part of their culture. Therefore, these ministers assume that they do not need to explain certain references that come under the auspices of these topics. Many of the examples in the sermons point to an assumed shared knowledge of popular culture, of the Bible, and most often, of African American culture and history. The example highlighted in the previous section emphasizes a knowledge of African American music, both secular and gospel. James Cleveland was a well-known African American contemporary gospel singer. David Peaceton is most recently known as a rhythm and blues singer, and Teddy Pendergrass is also noted for being an R&B singer. All of these singers are popular in the African American community and noted for their great voices. The manuscript minister assumes that this information is knowledge that the community shares. Therefore, there is no need to explain his references to them.

In addition to the three references that rely on shared or given information, this example also taps into the community knowledge of music in a different way. Included in the minister's example are lyrics from the popular gospel song "His eye is on the sparrow." Although this song is not unique to the African American community, it is a very popular song in this community. "I sing because I'm happy/I sing because I'm free/I know that he watches over me" are lyrics found in this song. Never in the sermon does the minister make mention of the song title. Again, he assumes that the congregation knows the song. Using song lyrics as examples, either gospel or secular, is a common device for both the manuscript and nonmanuscript ministers. In interviews, each minister emphasized how important music is in the African American community, particularly in the African American worship tradition. Music is so important that it becomes part of the text and, therefore, part of the literacy event. Hinson (2000) suggested that "the tangled world of social experience thus drives us from the particular to the collective, connecting song to sermon, prayer, testimony, holy dancing, and the silent witness of tears" (p. 5). This interaction between musical texts, the spoken word, and the written word is a prime example of intertextuality, a dominant feature of many African American sermons (Bloome & Bailey, 1992; Moss, 2002). One final note: Neither of these ministers makes clear distinctions between secular and sacred music. In deemphasizing the distinctions, they emphasize the broad cultural landscape from which this shared knowledge emerges.

As I mentioned earlier, the ministers also assume a shared knowledge of African American history. Earlier in this essay, I discussed an example from the manuscript minister that used collective pronouns and focused thematically on community: "the God of Harriet Tubman is an us God–community/the God of Martin Delaney is an us God–community/the God of Ida B. Wells is an *us* God–community." The minister went on to mention other famous African American historical figures in the same sermon. Again, he offered no explanation of who these people he named were. His assumption was that the people in the community knew these people, and if they did not, they should. That is, they had better find out about their history and culture, or risk not being considered part of the community. Being in the community and not having such shared knowledge becomes, for some, a motivation to learn. Thus, the minister's strategy is a subtle teaching device like many of the strategies discussed earlier. Using examples from the culture of his congregation not only emphasizes the value of the culture, but also signals that the minister knows the music, history, literature, and ways of the community. He understands and is part of the community. When we assume memberships in the same communities, then we feel comfortable assuming that other members of that community are familiar with much of the same information. Tapping into that familiarity, that common ground, through the text is a major function of the sermon. Tapping into that familiarity also allows the ministers to move their congregations from the familiar to the unfamiliar, by beginning with what people know—a sound pedagogical strategy.

CONCLUSION

This description of the features of the sermon shows its uniqueness both as a literacy event—an ongoing process—and as a literate text. The textual features of the sermon that I have focused on in this essay are (a) the use of collective pronouns in the sermon, (b) the use of personal narratives and testimony, (c) reliance on shared cultural knowledge, and (d) the dialogic quality of African American sermons. Because of its foundational role, the fourth feature—the dialogic quality—could not be treated separately. Instead, it is shown to be an integral part of each textual feature. The ministers use these prominent sermon-associated features to create a community in their churches. The text—the sermon—becomes the major instrument by which to construct and maintain community ties and identities.

As the analysis in this chapter has shown, the first three features are rhetorical devices that the ministers use in their sermons to draw them closer together with their congregation. The ministers use collective pronouns and personal narratives to show their congregations that they are no different from the people sitting in the pews, that they [the ministers] can identify with their congregations. The third device calls for the ministers to display their understanding of cultural knowledge, thus establishing community insider status. These all are devices that encourage the congregation to involve themselves in the making of the text. Seeing themselves as part of the text, as being able to provide feedback, to respond to the minister as part of the sermon is a traditional characteristic of African American sermons, and it is this process that is the essence of the fourth device—the emphasis on dialogue.

This study suggests that because of the dialogic quality of African American sermons and the focus on constructing community identities through the sermon, no fixed boundary between speaker and audience exists. Actually, participant roles constantly switch back and forth during the sermon. Even when a minister writes his sermon beforehand, as the manuscript minister does, he understands, allows, and, in fact, needs audience participation to complete the text. Audience participation in performance events, such as the sermon, is an Afrocentric concept characteristic of many African American communities' performance-oriented events (Thompson, 1983).

The dialogic nature of the text also suggests, because of the lack of fixed boundaries, that the sermon can be viewed realistically as a community text. Although he conceives of the sermon and shapes it, the minister has no real ownership of the text. The ministers in this study argue that once a sermon is preached, it is no longer their own sermon. Thus, there appears to be no concept such as ownership of text or intellectual property in this context. Yet academic literacy, as promoted in U.S. schools and universities, holds as one of its most sacred principles the ownership of words (Moss, 2003). These ministers also suggest that even if they preach the same sermon twice, it really is not the same sermon. Once the audience changes, the dialogue changes, and therefore the sermon changes. In other words, the sermon can never be decontextualized. Much of its meaning is determined by the participants. As the boundaries are blurred between speaker and audience, so too are the boundaries blurred between oral and written patterns in the sermons. Although the sermon is an orally performed event, it also represents a literate text, one that uses varying amounts of writing and speech. This integration of speech and writing is part of the text of the sermon and once more points to the blurred boundaries and seamlessness that characterize this event. This seamlessness can be found not only within the sermons, but also within the service that surrounds the sermon (Mountford, 1991). That is, neither the sermon nor the service can be easily segmented into discrete sections.

The blurred boundaries between speech and writing are most evident when one considers how many devices the manuscript and nonmanuscript ministers' texts have in common, although one minister wrote everything down and preached verbatim from his written text whereas the other wrote nothing. Because the sermon is an orally performed event, one is inclined to think of it as only an oral text, but the sermons are generally rooted in biblical scriptures—a modern-day written text. However, some recent editions of the Bible print long verses in lines or "chunk" lines and verses in ways that most likely point to an oral tradition (Hymes, 2002). In addition, these ministers are highly literate men, as defined by the academy, whose lives are deeply influenced by written words. Yet, clearly, they do not view writing and speaking as an either/or dichotomy. In their communities, writing and speaking are intertwined and interdependent. The boundaries blur.

The nonfixed and blurred boundaries that characterize these ministers' sermons point toward a model of a literate text far different from the model that most quickly comes to mind when one thinks of the kind of literate text that dominates in school, particularly the composition classroom—the academic essay. The academic essay, as traditionally taught to school students in English classes across levels, is ideally characterized by its fixed boundaries between media and genres, a monologic voice, and an emphasis on decontextualized meaning. These are features of the "plain style" essayist literacy tradition (Farr, 1993). That tradition, though, has been challenged on a number of fronts. Within anthropology, Clifford (1988), Clifford and Marcus (1986), Geertz (1988), and others have argued that a written ethnography is inevitably an interpretive creation of the writer rather than an objective description of a particular cultural group, as was assumed until recent decades. Within literacy studies, the tradition has been challenged by the rapid emergence of new technology and thus, new media, resulting in electronic and hypertextual forms of literacy. This study likewise suggests that the academy must broaden its definition of literacy and, in addition, its conceptualization of the literate text and of the "writer" as the "owner" of that text.

ENDNOTES

1. The original version of this essay, "Creating a Community: Literacy events in African American churches," appears in Beverly J. Moss (Ed.), *Literacy across communities*. Cresskill, NJ: Hampton Press, 1994.
2. The original study included three churches in Chicago. For a more detailed discussion of literacy in all three churches, see the full version of this article, "Creating a community: Literacy events in African American churches" in *Literacy across communities,* by B. J. Moss (Ed.), (Hampton Press, 1994) or *A community text arises* (Hampton Press, 2003), the book-length discussion of this study.

3. Regrettably, it was not unusual for many religion scholars before the 1980s and 1990s, to use the masculine pronoun in reference to the clergy.

4. Augustine's original *De Doctrina Christiana* was published circa A.D. 397 to A.D. 427.

5. Hanks (1996) discussed the ways that language points to items beyond the language, in a cultural context. Hanks built on the work of Charles S. Peirce (1955).

REFERENCES

Bloome, D., & Bailey, F. M., (1992). Studying language and literacy through events. In R. Beach, J. Green, M. L. Kamil, & T. Shanahan (Eds.), *Multidisciplinary perspectives on literacy research* (pp. 181–210). Urbana, IL: NCTE and NCRE.

Clifford, J. (1988). *The predicament of culture: Twentieth-century ethnography, literature, and art.* Cambridge, MA: Harvard University Press.

Clifford, J., & Marcus, G. (Eds.). (1986). *Writing culture: The poetics and politics of ethnography.* Berkeley, CA: University of California Press.

Davis, G. (1985). *I got the word in me, and I can sing it, you know.* Philadelphia: University of Pennsylvania Press.

Farr, M. (1993). Essayist literacy and other verbal performances. *Written Communication, 10,* 4–38.

Farr, M. (1994a). *En Los Dos Idiomas*: Literacy practices among Chicago *Mexicanos*. In B. J. Moss (Ed.), *Literacy across communities* (pp. 9–47). Cresskill, NJ: Hampton Press.

Farr, M. (1994b). Biliteracy in the home: Practices among *mexicano* families in Chicago. In D. Spener (Ed.) *Adult Biliteracy in the United States.* (pp. 89–110) McHenry, IL and Washington, DC: Delta Systems and Center for Applied Linguistics.

Farr, M. (2000). Literacy and religion: Reading, writing, and gender among Mexican women in Chicago. In P. Griffin, J. K. Peyton, & W. Wolfram (Eds.) *Language in Society: New Studies of Language in Society* (pp. 139–154). Cresskill, NJ: Hampton Press.

Fishman, A. (1988). *Amish literacy: What and how it means.* Portsmouth, NH: Heinemann.

Geertz, C. (1988). *Works and lives: The anthropologist as author.* Stanford, CA: Stanford University Press.

Gumperz, J. J., & Hymes, D. (Eds.). (1964). *The ethnography of communication, American anthropologist, 66*(6), Part 2. Washington DC: American Anthropological Association. Special Publication.

Hanks, W. (1996). *Language and communicative practices.* Boulder, CO: Westview Press.

Heath, S. (1982). Protean shapes in literacy events: Evershifting oral and literate traditions. In D. Tannen (Ed.), *Spoken and written language: Exploring orality and literacy* (pp. 91–117). Norwood, NJ: Ablex.

Heath, S. (1983). *Ways with words.* Cambridge, UK: Cambridge University Press.

Hinson, G. (2000). *Fire in my bones: transcendence and the holy spirit in African American gospel.* Philadelphia, PA: University of Pennsylvania Press.

Hymes, D. (1962). The ethnography of speaking. In T. Gladwin & W. C. Sturtevant (Eds.), *Anthropology and human behavior* (pp. 13–35). Washington, DC: Anthropological Society of Washington.

Hymes, D. (1972). Models of the interaction of language and social life. In J. J. Gumperz & D. Hymes (Eds.), *Directions in sociolinguistics: The ethnography of communication* (pp. 35–71). New York: Holt, Rinehart and Winston.

Hymes, D. (1974). *Foundations in sociolinguistics: An ethnographic approach.* Philadelphia: University of Pennsylvania Press.

Hymes, D. (2002). Translation of oral narratives. *Anthropology News,* p. 23.

Jellema, L. (1988). *Rhetoric and economics in television evangelism: What evangelists say and do to bring in money.* Unpublished dissertation, University of Illinois at Chicago.

Keeping the Faith. (1987, February). *Frontline* [television program]. Chicago: PBS, WTTW.

Lincoln, C. E. (1974). *The black experience in religion.* Garden City, NY: Doubleday.

Mays, B., & Nicholson, J. (1933). *The Negro's church.* New York: Negro Universities Press.

Mitchell, H. (1970). *Black preaching.* Philadelphia: Lippincott.

Moss, B. J. (1988). *The black sermon as a literacy event.* Unpublished dissertation, University of Illinois at Chicago.

Moss, B. J. (1994). Creating a community: Literacy events in African American churches. In B. J. Moss (Ed.), *Literacy across communities* (pp. 147–178). Cresskill: NJ: Hampton Press.

Moss, B. J. (2003). *A community text arises: A literate text and literacy traditions in African-American churches.* Cresskill, NJ: Hampton Press.

Mountford, R. (1991). *The feminization of the* Ars Praedicandi. Unpublished dissertation. The Ohio State University, Columbus, Ohio.

Peirce, C. S. (1955). *Philosophical writings.* J. Buchler (Ed.), New York: Dover Publications.

Philips, S. (1972). Participant structures and communicative competence: Warm Springs children in community and classroom. In C. Cazden, V. John, & D. Hymes (Eds.), *Functions of language in the classroom* (pp. 370–394).

Saint Augustine. (1958). *On Christian doctrine.* (D. W. Robertson, Translator). New York: Bobbs-Merrill Company.

Scollon, R., & Scollon, S. (1981). *Narrative, literacy, and face in interethnic communication.* Norwood, NJ: Ablex.

Scribner, S., & Cole, M. (1981). *The psychology of literacy.* Cambridge, MA: Harvard University Press.

Silverstein, M. (1976). Shifters, linguistic categories, and cultural description. In K. Basso & H. A. Selby (Eds.), *Meaning in anthropology* (pp. 11–55). Albuquerque: University of New Mexico Press.

Smitherman, G. (1977). *Talkin' and testifyin'.* Boston: Houghton-Mifflin.

Spradley, J. P. (1979). *The ethnographic interview.* New York: Holt, Rinehart and Winston.

Spradley, J. P. (1980). *Participant observation.* New York: Holt, Rinehart and Winston.

Street, B. V. (1984). *Literacy in theory and practice.* Cambridge, UK: Cambridge University Press.

Szwed, J. F. (1981). The ethnography of literacy. In M. Farr (Ed.), *Writing: The nature, development, and teaching of written communication* (pp. 13–23). Hillsdale, NJ: Lawrence Erlbaum Associates.

Taylor, D., & Dorsey-Gaines, C. (1988). *Growing up literate.* Portsmouth, NH: Heinemann.

Thompson, R. F. (1983). *Flash of the spirit.* New York: Random House.

Weinstein-Shr, G. (1986). *From mountaintops to city streets: An ethnographic investigation of literacy and social process among the Hmong of Philadelphia.* Unpublished dissertation, University of Pennsylvania, Philadelphia.

BIKO ND'IGBO

WERE ASUSU IGBO GWA IGBO OKWU, MGBE NILE, EBE NILE, NNE NA NNA, EZI NA ỤLỌ, NWOKE NA NWANYỊ, IKWU NA IBE, NZE NA ỌZỌ, ỌHA NA EZE, TAA NA ECHI, WEE RUE MGBE EBIGHI EBI. ỌFỌ! ISE! YA GAZIE! AMỊM!

A pre-launching plea from
CHICAGO ASSOCIATION FOR THE PROMOTION OF IGBO
LANGUAGE AND CULTURE (CAPILAC)

"Bless this little time we stayed here": Prayers of Invocation As Mediation of Immigrant Experience Among Nigerians in Chicago

Rachel Reynolds
Drexel University

INTRODUCTION: PRAYERS OF INVOCATION AND TRANSNATIONAL CONTEXTS

Prayers of invocation are a form of "verbal art" that most, or all, of us recognize (Bauman, 1977). No matter who we are or where we come from, we will hear them. If not before religious services and funeral services, then often we (over)hear them at the beginning of a workday, or they may be the inauguration of a special event, a sports match, or any other propitious occasion in which getting things off to the right start is embodied by the weightiness of prayer (Baquedano-Lopez, 1999). Although the prayer of invocation is a widespread practice, it will be used in differing contexts and among differing peoples to signify various things.[1] This chapter looks at how prayers invoke the shared identity of a particular ethnic group in Chicago as they meet formally every other month to share recent events and news in their lives, speak their language(s), and plan culture-specific events within their community. The group are Nigerians, more specifically, Igbo people.

These group meetings are "key sites" (Philips, 2000) in which transnational identity is worked out through language, joining together this group of Nigerian people who share similar backgrounds, interests and hopes for the future. One way the group accomplishes this act of community building is through prayers that referentially construct the group in such a way that everyone present is encompassed and conjoined by three common concerns: family, carving out of a special sense of time and space, and faith in the value of the choice to immigrate. The prayer of invocation is a verbal act that places them, with words, in a mentally inhabitable space. These expressions are an act of collective imagination, expressing the meaning of Igbo immigration vis-à-vis the immigrants' group. In other words, prayers of invocation that begin group meetings bind the group by verbally reiterating the patterns of meaningful interdependence and common experience around which group membership revolves. Ultimately, I aim to describe the new forms of community that Igbo speaking people produce for themselves abroad, specifically through talk, specifying the details that can help us conceptualize of Igbo transnational identity in the present historical moment.

To conduct an ethnography of communication, one must collect as much natural data on human communication as possible. To do this, I obtained permission to tape-record public meetings of the ONI group, a not-for-profit immigrant association in Chicago. I joined the group in the 1990s in order to conduct a study in the ethnography of communication (Hymes & Gumperz, 1972; Saville-Troike, 1989). The data in text form in the second half of this chapter reflects some of the oral data I collected. In addition to making tape recordings and field notes based on my attendance at ONI meetings and parties, I also studied the Igbo language. Additionally, I conducted one-on-one interviews with members. Those interviews investigate educational background, immigration and job searches, and literacy and orality practices.[2]

THE NDI IGBO FROM NIGERIA TO ILLINOIS

The people whose talk is described here are Igbo immigrants. Igbo is a term reflecting both an ethnic group and a language. The Ndi Igbo (or "Igbo people") speak one of a dozen dialects of the Igbo language and they identify themselves ethnically as Igbo.[3] They hail from southeastern Nigeria, the most populous country in Africa and a former colony within British West Africa. Nigeria achieved its independence in 1960. In Nigeria, by conservative estimate, there are approximately 10 to 15 million native speakers of Igbo. In Chicago, there are about 5,000 Igbos in a widespread community across the city and suburbs, although many Igbos occupy Chicago's north side Uptown Community Area, and another group are clustered in the southern suburb of Calumet City, Illinois.[4] Most of the people discussed in this chapter came to the United States in their late teens or early twenties to attend American colleges and universities (Reynolds, 2002).

Almost immediately, as I began my fieldwork, I realized that my group members did not always fit the paradigms of transnational network studies conducted by other researchers (Wasserman & Galaskiewicz, 1994). This difference is because the Nigerian Igbo people I know resemble middle-class, professional Euro-, Asian, and African Americans in far more ways than other easily visible and coherent immigrant groups such as Filipino domestic workers in the United States and Saudi Arabia, Greek fishermen in the United States, Turkish Gastarbeiterin in Germany, and Rancheros from Mexico in the U.S. (Basch, Glick-Schiller, Szanton-Blanc, 1994; Farr, forthcoming; Moskos, 1999; Van Hear, 1998).

These Igbo immigrants' educational achievements are immense, with all group members having completed postsecondary education (or they are in the process of doing so). Moreover, even although Igbo people arrive from a poorer and less developed area of the world, they are in many senses the professional elite of Nigeria. For example, many group members grew up in good-sized cities in Igboland in Nigeria with a wide variety of social contacts across ethnic and class groups. Often, they come from families with professional migratory backgrounds instead of land-bound farming economies. Many are the children of physicians, headmasters, teachers, writers, businessmen, and traders, who like Americans of their age, grew up following their families who, in this case, moved across Nigeria and Ghana in response to professional opportunity. Finally, Igbo people inhabit Chicago urban and suburban neighborhoods, with group members ranging up to 150 miles from the center of the network on South Michigan Avenue in Chicago.

This is not to say that there are not poor and undereducated African immigrants and refugees in Chicago. Rather, I have set out to examine the particular group that I entered three years ago to find out how and why they stick together. They are interesting because they constitute a Nigerian transnational middle class, and in many ways, group members are part of the "brain drain," a trend in which educated professionals depart from a country of origin in sufficient numbers to alter significantly the economy and social life of the homeland.

As the evidence presented in this chapter suggests, the lives of these brain-drain immigrants are a complex set of obligations to families here in the United States (Chicago) and there in Nigeria (Igboland), who cope with the guilt and sorrow of having left a homeland behind, even as they are working to sustain that homeland and the people in it. In this sense, they are like most other immigrant groups who share these commonalities: They support lives and life ways back home by regularly remitting cash and gifts to far-off friends and relatives.

But their being highly educated and financially better off than other immigrants adds a different dimension to the network, one in which smart business practice and global professionalization, for example, are primary topics for discussion and primary, if sometimes nebulous, goals for the community. They are well aware that they are part of a transnational class of professional Africans, and they are deeply engaged in notions of how to sustain ties to the homeland that will result in meaningful development of Igbo life in Africa and abroad. They are also aware that they are better off than other ethnic and class groups, here and abroad, even though, of course, racism has been a factor in how they have chosen to live in America.[5] They know that their choices to establish financial and social relationships across the globe, despite being an act of self-preservation of an Igbo middle class, constitute a deep threat to holding Igbo communities together. Finally, they are overarchingly concerned with finding the best ways to sustain Igbo ethnicity, or as they say, "the richness of the culture." Sustaining their heritage here in the United States becomes paramount as Nigeria continues to change very rapidly through economic domination by the West and through the brain drain. In other words, Igbo people abroad have a heightened awarness that Igbo culture is under threat of assimilation on two fronts: There is the process of assimilation to the global order within Nigeria, and then there is the assimilation of their families in the United States into the African American and the Euro-American mainstream.[6]

THE ONI GROUP: A "KEY SITE" FOR PRAYER AND THE PRODUCTION OF A GLOBAL IGBO COMMUNITY

The ONI immigrant group, which stands for Organization for *Ndi Igbo* (a pseudonym), is only one of about 40 such groups in Chicago that are associated with regions and ethnic groups from all over East and West Africa.

Typical of Nigerians, group membership is based on town of origin (Trager, 2001). The ONI group has about 450 members, who come from families affiliated with towns within the same 50 square mile region of Igboland. That they adhere to such a small area is due to the fact that they speak roughly the same dialect of Igbo, and that they have intermarried, endogamously within the region and exogamously between towns within the region.

The ONI group arose out of a chain migration from a specific town in Igboland, in which a few initial or "primary" immigrants chose to settle in Chicago. One primary immigrant of this group arrived in the 1960s for education and stayed when he married an American. After this man and a group of his friends, additional immigrants arrived in the area until a critical mass had formed a network. This network is formalized through ONI, a not-for-profit cultural group, which encompasses a board of directors, a centralized fiscal account, more than 100 member families, and a regular schedule of activities, including meetings for members, picnics, Christmas parties, and an *Ili-Ji* or "New Yam" festival of masquerade, drumming, and dance.[7]

The ONI organization also provides mailing services for members. For example, in 1 year these services entailed mailing to all members invitations to five weddings, three christenings, and three wakes. The members of ONI are predominantly Catholic and Episcopalian (Anglican) because of the long-term presence of English missionaries in Igboland. Igbo social events include a period during which the host collects cash donations, and these events make up a central part of the economy of exchange and support among group members. Generally speaking, the funeral or wake is the most crucial to support, because short-notice air tickets to Nigeria and ceremonial expenses for burials are a heavy financial burden to a grieving family. There are also various emergencies. When I first joined the network, a member had been hit with debris from a dump truck while driving on the highway. During the time this man was in intensive care, members joined together to support his wife and children, while advising them on legal and workmans' compensation issues.

Besides these formal functions of ONI, the network informally provides members with a bimonthly chance to meet together to exchange information, argue, and joke with each other, often using the Igbo language and Nigerian Pidgin mixed with other varieties of English.[8] The organization also provides an updated list of members, with addresses and contact numbers, essentially helping to facilitate constant contact between members.

Thus far, I have described the organization's explicit purposes, but actual gatherings of the ONI group are also something called a "key site" for transnational identity formation. Key sites are not necessarily places, although they can be, but rather conceptual moments and locations in which community is imagined (Philips, 2000, pp. 232–333, summarizing Stuart Hall). The ONI group meetings are a place for the avant garde, a place in which a new group of immigrants is beginning to form a new sense of community. Furthermore, these meetings are one of only a few "key sites" where the group can come together and profess Igbo identity, and that identity is often even something new for these immigrants, many of whom for the first time are developing a sense of the self as an "African" abroad.

Unlike older and larger ethnic groups such as Mexicans or Italians in Chicago (see Nardini, this volume, or the upcoming volume 2 of *Ethnolinguistic Chicago*), Igbo people do not (yet?) have a large number of neighborhood hangouts, businesses, city-funded parades, and other key sites in which to practice identity. Moreover, ONI group members also do not have that identity ratified by others. When one has ethnic spaces recognized by outsiders, one's own ethnicity in a sense becomes ratified and celebrated by other groups in the city. For example, this occurs with the Saint Patrick's Day Parade, or even with the celebratory "Puerto Rico" gateway arch that marks the drive into the Humboldt Park neighborhood or the Little Village archways in the South Side Mexican immigrant and Mexican American neighborhood. It remains to be seen whether the Igbo diaspora will continue to establish larger and better recognized ethnic communities across the globe. Now, however, during a time of great change in Africa and immigration centers across the world, the "key site" of ONI group meetings is an interesting point of entry for understanding how these immigrants have begun to initiate and express membership in a community that is both global and local, both African and Chicagoan.

THE PRAYERS

The prayers I discuss in this chapter happen to occur at the very beginning of a meeting agenda in which the topic of discussion is explicitly concerned with cultural and personal preservation through group effort. The prayers, therefore, are a worthy first look at how ONI members are beginning to construe their sense of selves as an emerging transnational group, as a Chicago ethnic group. These prayer performances are notably about establishing the authority of the ONI group to call together members. They are also about expressing common concerns, reiterated under the following affective topics: family ties, carving out significant increments of time and space, and the notion of faith that immigration has produced something of value for the community.

The following prayers, recorded in 1998–1999, are typical prayers of invocation given at the beginning of every general membership meeting. By contrast, smaller board committee meetings or special planning meetings take place in someone's home, with only four or five ONI members. In these instances, the prayers are said by the host of the meeting, and they are much more tailor made for the particular occasion. At each ONI meeting, the prayer is listed in print directly on the formal meeting agenda for the immigrants' association as agenda item "1." Meeting agenda: 1. Opening Prayer; 2. Introduction of Members; 3. Opening Remarks; 4. Committee Reports; 5. Other Matters; 6. Adjourn. Acting through this agenda, the organization loosely follows Robert's Rules of Order. Figure 7.1. shows a transcript of the contextualization and instatement of a typical prayer speech event, followed by a summary of how the meetings usually open.[9] The event occurs in English.

Prayers of invocation are about putting official ceremonies or gatherings into effect, in this case, a formal meeting. However, like other speech events, the prayers themselves are focal events that can come about only in a wider context, like that of a gathering of Igbo immigrants (Goodwin & Duranti, 1992, p. 3). We notice the prayers because they are a splashy and familiar formulaic speech event and a centerpiece of the beginning of the meeting. But observation of the formation of a meeting shows that the ONI group meetings begin well before the actual inaugural prayer. In the case of ONI group meetings, about 20 to 40 people will have trickled in for at least an hour before the meeting to gossip, share letters and newspaper clippings from or about home, show off their children, and discuss business and politics. This hour or two is itself an African practice, part of the effect of "African time" or the tendency to operate under a pretense of beginning something at an official time but arriving according to convenience, traffic patterns, level of personal interest, or the like.[10] African time is a very special and necessary indulgence for members of the ONI group. Often, the monthly ONI meeting is their only contact with other Igbo people outside family for a few weeks, and people have much to share individually before meetings.

Item A: Example of a prayer of invocation as inauguration of immigrants' meeting.

Everyone present: (talking loudly among themselves in small groups)

President: First thing ... (2 seconds) it looks like (we have a quorum?). And uh, it would be proper for us to start because usually we have a little bit to discuss. And together we start to develop our roll so we can get to go through our agenda and see what we can do and what we have here on the agenda. Um, um, the first item on the agenda is um, opening prayer. And um, I'm calling on ah, Mr. O. to please lead us in prayer.

Mr. O.: No! Lord! (followed by some multiple hushed laughter)

(Everyone stands up as Mr. O extends hands and scoops them upward in the air indicating that it is time to stand.)

Mr. O.: Oh Lord, we call upon you to send among your kids, that we can seek care together and to break bread (on our table?). We thank you for having gotten us over here, and we thank you for having led us through all our activities throughout the year 1998. We want you to bless all our activities for 1999 as we sit here, and then what is on this agenda. All this we ask you in the name of our lord, Jesus Christ.

Everyone present: Amen. (everyone sits down)

President : The second item on the agenda is the approval of minutes... .

Item B: A summary of the form of the typical context for the prayer speech event.

President wrests attention of the people present in room (can take up to 5 min).

President calls upon prayer maker, who then makes some sign of recognition that he or she has been called upon (in the preceding example, a joke about surprise at being called).

Audience rises at a verbal prompt by prayer maker or in response to a gestural prompt by prayer maker (as in the preceding example).

The prayer
    Call to God/completion of the call (contextualizes the prayer within the confines of the meeting situation),
    plus
    "Thank you" portion,
    plus
    Next portion of prayer; which may bea request for blessing, a demand that wisdom be conferred or an implication that what is obscured about God's will is to be realized in the course of the meeting,
    plus
    Closing line, invoking the name of the Lord.

Unison amen.

Audience sits.

FIG. 7.1 Typical prayer speech event.

Because these meetings are sites in which the meaning of Igbo transnationalism is discussed, contested, and shaped by group members,
prayers of invocation are nearly an ideal means by which a usually talk-
ative and bustling group is brought together in immediate silence and
concentration. An interesting way that prayers gain order is by invoking
God's authority, and the authority of the president and the prayer makers, as community leaders, to stipulate group silence and call the meeting to order.[11]

As with many other highly formulaic speech events, the prayers include
some contextualization cues, such as the "I call upon" statements by the
president, or the "call to God" and the unison "Amen." Sometimes, these
contextualization cues include a head nodded and hands curved, palms
upward, through the air to indicate to the audience to rise. All these cues
can be designated as "performance keys" (Bauman, 1992, summarizing
Goffman), and they are the specific, formulaic means by which the people
recognize that a particular type of speech event is occurring. When they
see them, they know it is time to snap to, recognizing the weightiness of
this very formal speech event (for more on this topic, see Gumperz, 1982).
The official meeting begins only when the president must raise his voice to
gain people's attention. Although the people sitting in front of the president
eventually notice him, it takes a few minutes for him to silence enough
people and gain eye contact with enough audience members to know that
everyone is ready to begin the official portion of the meeting. Interestingly,
through personal eye contact, shushing, and gesticulation directed at individuals, the president uses one-on-one forms of communication to form
individual attention into a bona fide audience.

Also, the president, a man who himself has authority to call and conduct the meeting, boosts his own authority by transferring it to a prayer
maker, a man or woman of high social regard because of his or her continuing contributions to the Igbo communities in Chicago. That transfer
of authority from the president to the prayer maker comes through the
president's utterance "I call upon," and it is so integral a part of the prayer
formula that it appears in every prayer transcript in my corpus, more than
two dozen. "I call upon" is also something a bit more than a request by
the president. It is rather an obligation and an honor. By obligation, one
must perform services to the community, especially at the behest of the
president and the group. By honor, the president having chosen that
speaker, does confer (or reiterate) the high status of the prayer marker.
Prayer makers do not, for instance, turn down this request to make the

prayer of invocation. In fact, they always acknowledge that the honor has been received or that the obligation must be fulfilled. In the specific case example presented earlier, the prayer maker uses a joking statement of modesty to acknowledge the call to make the prayer.[12] Conferring honor by asking someone to lead a prayer is one of the ways that ONI group ratifies Igbo leadership in diaspora and formalizes interdependence among group members, by providing ways by which these immigrants can formally, and publicly, serve their community.[13] Furthermore, the ONI group president in Chicago is not necessarily the same person who would be understood unequivocally to be a leader in Nigeria. This is because systems of community governance and representation do not quite apply in the United States. The people who garner the most respect in the United States are respected for transnational success criteria, especially success in American business, and less so for criteria defining success from back home, which involves political and financial success both in the village and in Nigerian regional and national contexts. Likewise, ONI leaders are often those best adjusted to life in America and able through these prayers to provide inspirational and poetic commentary on the nature and meaning of Igbo culture abroad for their homesick audiences.

The audience also rises en masse at the inauguration of the prayer. By dropping their respective conversations to concentrate on the physical act of standing up, and by redirecting their personal attention by facing front and center, the audience is quickly and effectively conjoined for the inception of the meeting. During the prayer itself, audience members also gaze downward, thereby focusing attention and avoiding the distractions inherent in making eye contact. At the end of the prayer, the group responds in unison with "Amen," and then group members sit down. The audience members do not return to their preprayer conversations, and the room is utterly quiet and focused upon the completion of the prayer. The length and topic of the prayer probably also serve to aid forgetting of personal conversational topics with which individuals were engaged at an earlier moment. This entire speech event involves formulaic strategies for group cohesion, creating a corporate body by controlling actions of individual distraction. It is a concentrated effort to prepare an audience to participate as a group, subsuming individual talk. This corporatization is also important considering that this is a body of people who if they were back in the homeland would probably not come together in this form and in this place (an American church basement or meeting hall). It can be seen as a practice that ritually brings the group together, a small first step in the formation of an Igbo ethnic mass in Chicago, as the group accustomizes itself to and negotiates its own group relations in new surroundings.

Now that I have described aspects of how the prayers themselves arise as key events within a larger group gathering, I turn to the main body of the chapter. I walk the reader through the formula of the prayers, explaining how they function to unite and give coherence to group relationships. I begin by looking at the formulas by which the prayers are composed, and then turn in a final section of the chapter to analyze how the prayers address three special immigrant topics: family, carving out a special sense of time and space, and faith. Figure 7.2 shows a transcription of three typical prayers. Prayer 4, by the way, diverges from the first three, because it was a more tailor-made, purposive prayer beginning a special emergency meeting.

THE CALL TO GOD

Although the signal to the audience to rise from their seats begins the prayer process, the opening linguistic part is in the form of the "call to God." At this juncture, the Lord is hailed. This is a complex and powerful moment in any prayer, and a point at which the secular and religious, the cultural and the social are merged. That is, the call to God establishes an umbrella over the group, an abstract reiteration that they are unified under a grand purpose, under the care of one God, a congregation of sorts.

THE THANK YOU

"Thank you for the chance of getting us together here once more" highlights to the Lord that there is a reason why he has been hailed. But the thankful explanation to the Lord also overlaps with other functions of the "thank you" function of the prayer. In these thank you's, we see the first hints of how the ONI network members hold together the group, and with it, an Igbo sense of belonging. That is, through the thank you section, the prayers begin to map out how the volunteers within the network provide an organizational (and with it, a conceptual) structure for understanding immigrant identity. That the ONI group meetings provide "the chance of getting us together" is clearly necessary for members to actually practice Igbo identity as an expatriot group, again, especially because they are spread out all over Chicago, and because they lack the critical mass to oc-

Item C: A comparison of the texts of the prayers.

Prayer 1
1 M.O.: Oh Lord, we call upon you to send among your kids, that we can seek care
2 together and to break bread (on our table?). We thank you for having gotten us over
3 here, and we thank you for having led us through all our activities and trials in 1998.
4 We want you to bless all our activities for 1999 as we sit here, and then what is on
5 this agenda. All this we ask you in the name of our lord, Jesus Christ.

Prayer 2
1 N.D.: Bless us heavenly father, our god; we thank you for this gathering. We thank
2 you for our brothers and sisters, who are here and away. Fada, we thank you for
3 everything you have done for us. Bless this little time we stayed here, now that we
4 have provided the meeting father, the way you want it, in the name of Jesus Christ our
5 Lord.

Prayer 3
1 V.U.: Oh God, our heavenly father. Thank you for the chance of getting us together
2 here once more. We thank you for the blessings we know and that are known to us.
3 Lord, as we gather give us the wisdom to conduct this business successfully. Give us
4 the wisdom to understand that what we are doing belongs to our children, our
5 children's children. Give us the wisdom to know that we have the where and the
6 withal to do it all, if we believe, so we are asking in Jesus' name to give us that daily
7 bread.

Prayer 4
1 S.: Our heavenly father, we pray that however our discussion will go today it will be
2 held in the spirit of oneness and brotherhood. And that we don't tell anything to (pass
3 along our?) struggle but that on the other hand that whatever we do, it will be clear to
4 us what you are wishing about what we represent, which is ONI, that is easy for us
5 to have our tempers, and that we must curb them so that all our operations will be
6 very positive and directed towards our goals. All this we ask; allow us to do our best.
7 Amen.

FIG. 7.2. Transcription of these typical prayers.

cupy neighborhoods, restaurants, community centers, and so forth. The chance of getting everyone together would indeed be slim if the ONI group volunteers did not rent a hall, keep a roster, mail out meeting announcements, organize group picnics and children's activities, and the like.

Furthermore, these thank you's are both public and indirect. This method of thanks involves indirection in which a thank you to God is also a thank you to the organizers of the meeting. It is very much in keeping with Igbo feelings about scrutiny for good deeds and a general prohibition against too much public praise outside proper ritual contexts (Okolo, 1990; Nwoye, 1992). As one informant put it when I asked him who is most talented at directing ONI group members through talk, "Our pride don't let us identify any speaker." When I pressed him to name names, he said, "You've seen it, you saw it, you felt it" and then he left the discussion at that. This indirect form of thanks within the prayers is an example of how group members can "see" and "feel" in some way a public sense of what group leaders do to cohere these immigrants so far from home. In this way, the entire raison d'etre of the immigrants' group is celebrated as members see it and feel it happening before them during each meeting.

Now that I have discussed how the prayers have been contextualized, and how they are initiated in such a way as to establish a sense of authority behind the meeting and express thanks for those who have arranged for that meeting, I turn to three paramount topics for immigrant concerns that appear in the prayers. Earlier, I contended that the meetings are a key site of negotiation for immigrant identity and the meanings of immigrant life. Prayer makers directly address these negotiations by playing with and placing down words that generate group conceptions and self-conceptions out of the vicissitudes of immigration. The first involves the need creatively to segment or carve up a special sense of time and space through the poesy of the prayers. This is done to minimize temporal and physical distance from the homeland, as well as to share this common concern with each other.

IMMIGRANTS AND TIME AND SPACE

In prayers 1 and 2, the conflation of large spans of time and space is a central topic, as evidenced by "We thank you for having gotten us over here" and thanks for those "who are here and away" as well as "bless this little time we stayed here." The second part of the thanks section of the first two prayers involves an immediate invocation of immigrant status by discussing the "here and there" of immigrant lives, and paradoxically, the notion of thanking the Lord for his help in facilitating this painful divide across the Atlantic Ocean. This is a topic for emphasis through poetic devices. In the samples reproduced in Fig. 7.2, for example, people use lexical couplets such as "here and away," a type of code switching, and understatements to express the pain of separation from the homeland in time and space. But notably, in doing so, they are also calling attention to the temporal and spatial disjunctures that immigration causes. These are foremost things in immigrant lives, and they are explicitly a program that ONI group members share with each other and something with which the group helps them to deal. It is something that makes them something new, transnationals.

The ability to immigrate and the act of doing so are both a bane and a blessing, a complex tearing apart and reconstruction of one's whole society, at home and abroad. Particularly in West African contexts, the brain drain among young professionals is acute, accelerating a process by which local industry and state structures continue to break down. First of all, economic crises force the most talented and energetic young members of a society to go abroad for education, and for meaningful employment. Due to the loss of this talent, even less economic value is generated in local economies. Meanwhile, state and local structures undergo de-development as the universities and secondary schools crumble and professionals and technologists abandon industrial development programs in Nigeria. From abroad, these same immigrants are partially or wholly supporting large numbers of family members by remittances home, who increasingly come to rely on these remittances, and who increasingly "export" their children abroad for education and job training (for a contrast case about Senegalese transnational immigrants, see Buggenhagen, 2002). Additionally, most group members use any extra income to hedge their bets by real estate purchases and other investments in the United States, England, and Nigeria to ensure that they will be able to retire comfortably on a family homestead in Igboland. At this point in time, though, ONI group members do not really get to retire and return to Igboland. Many die in America. Funerals make up a large part of community relations abroad, and there is always talk about the best insurance policies that will transport a body home to be buried, or how to support widows and children abroad.

The peculiar place of the African immigrant abroad is one in which he or she becomes a backbone for the homeland, even while spending the most productive and robust years of adult life in a foreign land. This paradox is expressed continuously in public discourse among the Igbo immigrants of the ONI group, and it appears in the prayers in a number of places. Collapsing time and space, conjoining it or unifying it, I contend, is an important emotive balm for ONI group members. It momentarily closes the spatial disjunctures that are the center of such intense paradoxes in immigrant lives. "Here and away" does just this, placing a conceptual umbrella over two disparate places and joining them, momentarily, at a unitary and imagined Igbo location.

"BLESS THIS LITTLE TIME WE STAYED HERE"

In the second prayer, a subtle code switch as well as an understatement is creatively and poetically applied to express the spaces in which immigrant life is lived, when the prayer maker says, "Bless this little time we stayed here." The code switch involves a usage of what these Igbo people call "broken English," and in this case, "stayed," a simplified tense from Nigerian Pidgin, is used to express perfect indicative. This same speaker, N.D., in other contexts does indeed use the perfect indicative "bless this little time we've stayed here" that we know from codified, high-prestige, standardized English dialects. What is happening is that N.D. is using elements of Nigerian Pidgin to express solidarity or a deeper connection with his people, taking them back home, in a sense, through the sounds of a familiar dialect. Often, N. D. does this sort of code switching, in three languages; English, Nigerian Pidgin, and Igbo. But it is the understatement that is most noticeable. I now turn to examine "this little time" that N.D. is creatively carving out as the time–space that these immigrants inhabit.

N.D. immigrated to the Chicago area in the early 1980s when he was 20 years old. He spent the subsequent decades working to sustain himself and a family in Illinois, as well as his other family members abroad and at home (with an older brother's help). Firmly middle class, with an M.B.A., a college-educated professional wife, a house in the suburbs, and four college-bound children, N.D. has told me that he feels very ambivalent about his success here. When I asked when he might return to Nigeria permanently, he said that he would go in a heartbeat. So when I asked why he remained here, he simply said, "I honestly don't know." He said it slowly, in a deep but muted voice, and became quiet and introspective. Like most ONI members with whom I talked, he is buoyed by an intention to return to the homeland, but he also does not really anticipate being able to make this happen until he is much older, if at all.

"Bless this little time" types of understatement convert two or three dozen years of a bustling lifestyle among the American professional class to a provisional and measurable unit of time. "This little time here" certainly does not express a long time (e.g., 20 plus years!), nor the dreaded "forever." For example, that only a "little time" is spent "here" implies, presumably, that the homeland is where one gets to spend the forever. Likewise, N.D. reinforces the provisional notion of life abroad by using the word "staying" instead of "settling." The way N.D. carves out time here is specifically a kind of act of imagination.

Compare N.D.'s statement with a statement by one of the professional immigrants cited in Basch et al. (1994):

> In a world configured into nation-states, each claiming that its population maintains a unique history, culture, and identity, those who must live their lives across borders may come to see themselves as potentially unauthentic, feeling at home in neither their "home country" nor the United States. "My life," we heard Dr. Paul confide to his hometown association, "has no meaning." *Imaginings* of the deterritorialized nation build on these yearnings for belonging and acceptance. (p. 242) [italics mine]

Ironically, the notion of a "life with no meaning" expresses the very importance of immigrant groups, as institutions, in providing a means by which one can "imagine" the significance of one's community abroad and find "belonging and acceptance." In this case, the "territory" of the deterritorialized nation appears as an imagined and definite unit of time and space, despite the fact that these immigrants' economic and professional status is by no means subject to a definite time span. N.D. pointedly underimagines, evading the threat of meaninglessness by using prayer words to make the United States somewhere one visits and Nigeria one's home. In other words, the ONI immigrant group meetings are key sites for the expression of immigrant despondency, and through that expression, creative modes of dealing with the despondency are publicly imagined and made into acts of group unification.

N.D. is one of the most popular speakers in the group precisely because of his imagination and ability to express it. People are willing to hear him telescope 20 years abroad into a profound expressive understatement that ends up stressing how little time matters and how much sustaining one's people does. In that sense, being (transnational or diasporic) Igbo for these people means the very act of sacrifice in order to sustain the homeland. In another sense, the sacrifice also entails or is manifested by a public yearning for the homeland that everyone comes together to share, a space in which the nebulous emotion of longing is made meaningful because it becomes a shared belonging.

RECONSTITUTING FAMILIAL RELATIONSHIPS: "WE THANK YOU FOR OUR BROTHERS AND SISTERS WHO ARE HERE AND AWAY"

Another means by which the immigrant community is fused involves reconstituting familial relationships so that their meaning is understood within a transnational system. Every person in the room is there among relatives or people related to them by intermarriage. As mentioned earlier, the organization membership is based on towns of origin in Igboland, and people tend to marry exogamously from town to town, but endogamously within the region. Additionally, in the Igbo language, one's age-mates among both patrilineages and matrilineages are referred to as "brother" or "sister" (see Agbasiere, 1998, for more on the linguistic and social significance of kinship relationships in Igboland). In this instance, the notion of interdependence in the group network also indicates obligations at home. One is not only supporting one's immediate family at home economically, but also is responsible for one's behavior toward others abroad on the basis of sanctions and social interests that will inevitably catch up to one from the homeland. Following the conduit of letters, phone calls, and visitors who move through the network, it is apparent that Igbo people in Chicago must avoid social transgression abroad so that such shame will not return home and cause strife there, and news does travel fast. Furthermore, both abominable and good behavior back in Igboland will be heard about, and will have repercussions and effects in the United States.

To return to a question that is culture specific about family economics and remittances, biological siblings, and particularly in ONI group *dede* and *dada*, older brothers and sisters, respectively, are embedded in a system of support that keeps the elderly of the family in Igboland safe and healthy. Furthermore, uncles in many cases are obligated to support their nephews (and sometimes nieces) abroad. Indeed, studies of Igbo communities in Nigeria have concluded that a cardinal reason for Igbo success in business and education is the strength of the Igbo extended family system (Silverstein, 1984). A particularly noticeable example from my field notes is that members of the ONI group also refer to themselves as the "Jews of Nigeria," alluding to the stereotype that Jewish people succeed because they protect their own business and family interests in diaspora. All these Igbo networks of obligation are tightly reproduced and broadly represented in an abbreviated form through one simple sentence: "We thank you for our brothers and sisters who are here and away."

This obligation to support extended family also extends into the future. As V.U. says, "Give us the wisdom to understand that what we are doing belongs to our children, our children's children." Again, the notion of the Igbo family abroad is given a new imaginative scope through the locus of the prayer. In this case, we know that the "we" who is providing for children is this specific generation of immigrants who bear the pains of divorce from the homeland to sustain its present and future generations. I again reiterate that the system of close family and regional ties among Igbo people is very important. It must be maintained and reproduced abroad by ONI group members in such a way that members can find Igbo spouses for their children as well as cultural and business contacts abroad for the future of the Igbo people in general. Without this immigrants' group, the second generation would have greatly reduced chances of maintaining ties to the homeland, and people in the homeland would have fewer opportunities for education and economic development.[14]

But V.U.'s statement is even further charged with pathos, because it also acknowledges that there is possibly an even greater price to pay for immigration: the loss of one's own culture among one's children if one does not actually have the "where and the withal" to earn enough to reproduce and sustain Igbo practices in the transnational milieu. The task of preserving a culture by having immigrated is seemingly impossible, especially while one's children are undergoing (at least partly) the assimilation that American culture encourages. This implausible state of affairs is acutely expressed in this portion of V.U.'s prayer. It is a curious moment of doubt, and I tentatively wonder if it might be a way to catharsize the clear possibility that the perceived meaninglessness of immigrant lives is indeed a real factor for them, something to be faced or acknowledged. The possibility of meaninglessness is indirectly confronted here. V.U. does this when he expresses immigrant life as a gambit in which one must have the "where and the withal" or face the dissolution of one's home culture. But this possibility of meaninglessness is also countered immediately, through faith, "if we believe."

FAITH

V.U. is a spiritually and emotionally strong individual, often chosen as spokesperson for the community, in part because of his great skill at expressing the mechanism of faith in immigrant lives. In the third prayer, V.U. develops a map of how that faith works, beginning with "the blessings we know and that are known to us" and the practical wisdom that the group needs "to conduct this business successfully." Then he calls for "wisdom to understand" that the Igbo immigrant's raison d'etre is preserving a life for the children, and knowing the strength, the "where and the withal" to do it (note also that V.U. has creatively adapted the phrase "wherewithal" into the poetic device of a lexical couplet "where and withal"). Finally, when V.U. asks that god "Give us the wisdom to know that we have the where and the withal to do it all, if we believe ..." he shares with his cohorts the fact that as immigrants, they all have had rough times and times of doubt in which getting by on faith has seemed to be all there is. Sometimes meaning is possible and meaninglessness avoided only, "if we believe."

Through prayer, the notion of shared faith is part of an affective maneuver in speech, an aspect of group coherence that is constituted through talk. In other words, the notions of faith expressed creatively in these prayers are part of an individual experience that can be made an affective statement for the group. They may be believing somewhat different things individually, but certainly they all are believing together, experiencing faith collectively.

But the tropes of faith in these prayers go beyond the simple present, again, to invoke the similar past experiences these immigrants have with "faith," and to evoke their future. As V.U.'s statement earlier implies, one needs faith that what will happen in the future is a good thing (although a poor outcome is also possible), and that the Igbo immigrant project will turn out well for everyone. I also note here that when V.U. acknowledges what sort of culture loss may be at stake, he is also reminding and inspiring group members to carry on in their duties to sustain Igbo culture abroad.

This discussion would be incomplete, however, if I did not also address the role that faith plays in the quotidian problems of immigrant life, particularly as the immigrants initially struggle to succeed in a new land. A common thread among all the ONI immigrants is an immigration narrative, an arrival story, in which each and every informant discusses how shocking the American experience is. Members of ONI have said to me that before coming to America, as young Nigerians, they did not realize how hard immigration is. Each one talks about being surprised to find that the United States is not paved with streets of gold, like a Hollywood movie, and other statements of that ilk.[15] Group members also say that racism, American stereotypes about Nigerians and Africans in general, and the complex web of problems associated with the Immigration and Naturalization Service (INS) are also confounding, strenuous, and poorly understood problems. The initial experiences of arrival and learning to navigate through a foreign culture and its state systems are like flying blind, waiting for the inscrutable and Kafkaesque decisions of the INS to come through, trusting total strangers such as landlords for the first time in their lives, having no choice but to take employment from people who prey upon immigrant labor, handing over one's life savings to an immigration lawyer who tells one that a visa may still not be forthcoming, coping with the random quality of state department services in the Nigerian embassy, and even finding one's way across the country and enrolling in college without knowing a soul for hundreds of miles in any direction. Through any single one of these experiences, one has to believe one's life will turn out for the better or one simply will not make it. Here, again time is also provisional, and it becomes important to minimize spans of time in which life is painful and mysterious, having faith that a better day will come. In other words, having faith is a explicit immigrant habit, developed through the vicissitudes of the experience. And faith will often do during the moments in which immigrant life, again, appears to have no readily apparent meaning.

Likewise, N.D. also attests that the challenges of immigrant life are an obscure but livable aspect of God's will that must be played out in faith, in which we trust that what we are doing is what God wants: "Now that we have provided the meeting father, the way you want it, in the name of Jesus...." Indeed, this is a powerful message considering that once one has committed to immigrate for education and jobs, there is not often a means of turning back. This is especially so as a brain drain accelerates the inability of the homeland to develop and use the talents of its people, in a vicious downward spiral, and although the outlook is presently not good for the future of Nigeria, vis-à-vis the brain drain, there is a historical inevitability here that none of us can yet see. The Igbo community is joined around this possibility by the phrase "the way you want it." God's will is sometimes obscure, and that this is so frequently is made an expression of hope that there is a central purpose to striving through life that will, we hope, be manifest. Furthermore, perhaps it is a matter of faith, when one has no other choice, to keep on keeping on in the hopes that a better time will come and Nigerians can live well and peaceably at home.

CONCLUSION

I have tried to show how prayers of invocation help to form community at key sites of transnational identity expression. They play a special function in developing an umbrella of concerns for whatever group they are serving to bind. The prayers of invocation discussed in this chapter serve to create a corporate body of Igbo people who can share each other's intimate concerns as immigrants, noting that the immigrants' group itself is a means by which immigrant concern abroad is made preeminent and a purposive expression of Igbo transnational identity. The specific prayers are in many ways ideal forms for unifying a group in that they are about imaginative ways of expressing what immigration is about, mapping out the meaningful ways that immigrants' lives are embedded with each other abroad. Moreover, the prayers provide a means to imagine how their lives remain part of the home community in Nigeria. Because immigrants are often so despondent over the time and space disjunctures that immigration incurs, these prayers derive affective power by the poetic ways they segment off or carve up time and space, an act that ameliorates the pain of the immigrant paradox in which one works and lives for a homeland from which one has been so long and so distantly divided. Family relationships are also mapped out abroad, with the system of these relationships reconstituted momentarily during immigrant meetings to remind people exactly where they are nested in a latticework of transnational obligations and social sanctions. The family is also mentioned as something that will carry on if today's predecessors have the faith and the will to see these family through to the future, especially with the high hopes that children and grandchildren will continue to carry forward a connection to the homeland or sustain an Igbo community abroad. Finally, I bring up the way that faith appears in the prayers as a meaning substitute. That is, if one cannot imagine what will happen, and can give no immediately relevant meaning to what goes on in one's life, a common occurrence among immigrants, one can bank on faith to get by. Time and again, Igbo immigrants say they are strengthened by that faith. These prayers of invocation unify the group abroad by providing a poetic moment in which the members can experience the notions of that faith can be experienced collectively as transnational immigrants.

ENDNOTES

1. Not all culture groups will specifically call inaugural prayers "invocational." I am using the term here to refer to a specific function of these types of speech events occurring at the beginning of a meeting or ceremony, and marking that ceremony as having begun: "to call on (a deity, use, etc.) as in prayer or supplication; to declare to be binding or in effect; to appeal to, as for confirmation; to petition or call on for help or aid; to cause, call forth, or bring about" (*Random House Dictionary of the English Language,* 1966).

2. One important note on the data in this chapter: The evidence I present here reflects the experiences of middle-aged Igbo people. Although I have limited evidence from older and younger generations, I have concentrated mostly on this group because I know the most about them and they constitute the central core of the ONI group. This group shares the following commonalities. To begin with, they all are currently in their 40's, and they lived a childhood through the Biafran–Nigerian war. Another commonality is that they came of age for higher education schooling around the time that the U.S. government completed a 1981 treaty with Nigeria admitting 240 Nigerians per year for professional training in the American higher education system (U.S. Secretary of State, 1987). This is a fortunate coincidence in that it encouraged a type of Igbo chain migration that centered around migration for higher education. All of the people in ONI group I interviewed or otherwise know about came to the United States on student visas to pursue professional higher education. This makes them different from those immigrant groups in which members arrive as undocumented aliens, or from the tiny minority of immigrants with refugee visas. Those types of immigrants tend to remain outside the realm of legitimacy conferred by obtaining baccalaureate or graduate training in the United States. It is also less strenuous, for example, to convert a student visa into a professional visa and later on, a green card, than it is for undocumented African immigrants to find legal documentation as unskilled workers. That ONI group members are mainly middle class, professional, and suburbanite reflects this trend in Igbo migration patterns.

3. As mentioned in the introductory chapter of this volume, it is problematic to define ideas such as "ethnic group." My criteria for understanding Igbo as a coherent ethnic group is that the Ndi Igbo call themselves such, and their neighbors—Yoruba, Ogoni, Ibibio—also understand that Igbos are a distinct ethnic subgroup of Nigerian citizenry. Additionally, Igbo ethnic affiliations vis-à-vis national politics were entrenched in a new way after the Biafran–Nigerian war of 1966–1970. This civil war was a war of succession in which Igbos all over Nigeria had to return to the traditional Igbo homeland in the southeast to escape ethnic persecution by other Nigerian ethnic groups. The war did not go well for the Igbo Biafrans, and millions were killed or died from disease. To this day, Igbo identity is marked in Nigeria by stories of the war and its threat of genocide. See Doug Anthony (2002) for studies on war, genocide and identity formation. See also Van den Bersselaar (1998) for prewar studies.

4. This is my own estimate, based on census figures for numbers of Africans in the Chicago area (a little more than 4,000 Nigerians in 1990). It is also based on my own personal count of Igbo network members in the three large Igbo immigrant associations in Chicago (taken over the course of fieldwork between 1997 and 2001). Census figures, INS figures, and others are highly unreliable for a number of reasons, and at a number of levels. Igbo ethnicity is not counted in any way, probably because the census is concerned merely with "race" and "nationality" as a category, and the ethnic group itself is not as large as Asian or Mexican groups who through sheer numbers warrant their own census category. Also, census forms often conflate African American and African by category. Other potentially reliable ways to reconstruct ethnic diversity among Africans in Chicago could include researching school records for bilingual classrooms and court translation contracts (skillfully done by Garcia, 1997, for New York City). However, because Igbos abroad usually speak English with native or nearly native competence, they usually do not appear in the paper record as requiring translators. In other words, nothing presently available is as reliable as my old-fashioned head count. If anything, my count is a low estimate. My count includes children, considering them to be Igbo even if many (probably about 75%) are American born. This is because they are automatically eligible for Nigerian citizenship and because their parents consciously raise them to be familiar with the culture, customs, and language "back home."

5. All the network members with when I have spoken mentioned that U.S. race relations affect their lives deeply. But having grown up

without it, Nigerians often do not deal with it the same way that Americans do, either inwardly or outwardly. It should be noted that by and large, group members' networks of family and friends abroad include many African Americans, probably predominantly African Americans. Some (about half) of my informants say they prefer to live in African American neighborhoods in order to evade racism, both the overt and the semiconscious acts that may occur in everyday life in White, Asian, or Latino neighborhoods. Of course, in any neighborhood or workplace, they experience xenophobia.

6. Interestingly, one way these immigrants resist assimilation is through the Church. There are North Side Catholic churches in Chicago that offer services tailored for Nigerian immigrants, for example. This is also facilitated by the fact that the Catholic Church often recruits priests from abroad, and that many young celebrated priests are from Igboland or nearby Yorubaland in Nigeria, another by-product of the brain drain.

7. There are many analogs to this type of club; they are a widespread immigrant phenomenon. Italian and Polish and Puerto Rican immigrants to Chicago also establish social clubs, although they tend to purchase and maintain actual clubhouses, whereas Africans tend to rent halls or meet in private homes (see for example, Nardini 1999 and Nardini, this volume, on Italian American social clubs). Besides these highly organized immigrant associations, which are legally registered with the state and maintain not-for-profit status, there are also informal immigrant "hangouts." Several local commercial establishments that happen to be owned by Igbos or Nigerians often serve this function. In Chicago, for example, one finds the Equator Club on North Broadway, a Nigerian nightclub, or the African restaurant Toham on Devon Street.

8. Most Igbos in this network grew up speaking Igbo in the home and Nigerian pidgin (which despite its label is technically Creole) among neighborhood children. This pidgin is not really standardized across Nigeria, and speakers tend to mix various pidgin words and phrases and syntax with Nigerian English, another not-yet-standardized variety, but one nonetheless that is very similar to British English. In other words, Igbos, and Nigerians in general, are heteroglossic in many varieties of English. This is illustrated by the following two samples of Nigerian pidgin taken from Jibril (1997). They run the gamut between one closer to a pure pidgin and one closer to standard English. Sample 1: "If to se una de Lagos en, una fo enjoi taya bikos no bi onli chop una fo chop plenti, una fo drink to nonsens sef." [If you had been in Lagos, you would have enjoyed yourself thoroughly because it would not have been just good food that you

would have found in abundance; there were drinks in superabundance too.] Sample 2: (a radio announcer's explanation of the field of biochemistry): "Dis subject dem day call biochemistry, na him be de one wey day study about the chemical wey day de body of every living ting, weder na animal or plant." (Jibril, 1997, pp. 234–237). See Bamgbose, Banjo, & Thomas *New Englishes: A West African perspective* (1997) and Elugbe and Omamor, *Nigerian Pidgin* (1991) for fascinating collections of papers on this topic.

9. A note about transcription: These prayers are transcribed in blocked paragraphs in an attempt to make them appear as "texts." At points where the transcriber had to surmise the words of the speaker, the unclear utterances are put in parentheses with a question mark at the end. Pauses in discourse are indicated in number of seconds. Other parenthesized items are descriptions of movements or other paralinguistic features.

10. The basic rules of African time among my informants are as follows: (a) The event or appointment will always begin at least 30 min late. (b) The lateness is subject to the level of interest that the community has in the event. If it involves a sensational trial or a celebrity appearance, everyone will be there sooner rather than later, but if it is a routine appointment, sometimes people will take an extra day or two to get there. (c) If you have nothing better to do, then come a bit early (but still late) and socialize. African time is subject to a reduction ratio of approximately one fourth in the United States. That is, for every 4 hours or days late one may be in an African country, one is only 1 hour or day late in the United States.

11. See Hill and Irvine 1992, p. 6. on the idea of making a "doubled voice" as Mikhail Bakhtin calls it. This involves speaking one's own words while invoking the authority to speak those words through another instrumentation. In this case, the prayer maker is the instrument through which talk with God is conducted.

12. "I call upon" also functions to cede the floor publicly to another speaker, formalizing turn taking in a strict manner.

13. Although I have two recordings of women as prayer makers, they are of poor quality and I elected not to use them as exemplary tokens in this paper. Interestingly, the same woman was called upon in both instances to give a prayer. She was on the management team of the organization, so she was a key player and well known to all the members of the organization. Other male prayer makers were on both the management team and the board of directors, but some prayer makers were simply of high standing in the community. That standing generally pertained to the person's commitment to and participation in the organization. That is, peo-

ple who came to every meeting and expressed their opinion frequently, but politely, in public were most likely to be called upon to give a prayer or invocation.

14. The two members of the second generation who have gotten married so far—admittedly this is only a few, but most are still too young—have married Igbo people. When possible, Igbo folks in the ONI group send their children to Nigeria for a few years of primary schooling as well, to ensure that they learn the Igbo language and customs, as well, probably to allay fears that their children in the U.S. will join gangs or have children too young. Sometimes Igbo mothers will send their children to live with relatives back home while they pursue advanced degrees. This practice appears to be not only acceptable, but laudable.

15. There is a literary tradition of the Igbo immigrant novel that painstakingly examines the psychological stress to immigrants shocked at how hard the experience really is, and shocked at how different the United States, or United Kingdom, really is compared with expectations. Two fine exemplars: Buchi Emecheta's autobiography *Head Above Water* describes the "miracles" of her having survived immigration to London and Ike Oguine's novel *A Squatter's Tale* describes two generations of immigrants an overeducated, underemployed young Igbo man and his alcoholic uncle,struggling for survival in the Bay Area. Finally, the ONI network itself has a writer who has outlined the immigrant struggle in his nonfiction novel, *The Good and the Bad: Only in America. The Route from Nigeria to America* (Bno, 1999).

REFERENCES

Agbasiere, J. T. (2000). *Women in Igbo life and thought.* New York: Routledge.

Anthony, D. (2002). *Poison and medicine: Ethnicity, power, and violence in a Nigerian city 1966–1986.* London: Heinneman.

Bamgbose, A., Banjo, A., & Thomas, A. (Eds.). (1997). *New Englishes: A West African perspective.* Trenton, NJ: Africa World Press.

Baquedano-Lopez, P. (1999). Prayer.*Journal of Linguistic Anthropology,9*(1–2), 197–200.

Basch, L., Glick-Schiller, N., & Szanton-Blanc, J. (Eds.). (1994). *Nations unbound: Transnational projects, postcolonial predicaments, and deterritorialized nation-states.* Langhorne, PA: Gordon & Breach Science Publishers.

Bauman, R. (1977). *Verbal art as performance.* Prospect Heights, IL: Waveland.

Bauman, R. (1992). Disclaimers of performance. In J. Hill & J. Irvine (Eds.), *Responsibility and evidence in oral discourse* (pp. 182–196). New York: Cambridge University Press.

Bno, B. (1999). The good and the bad: Only in America: The route from Nigeria to America. [On-line]. Available: www.bdic99.com Accessed: 2/15/00.

Buggenhagen, B. A. (2002). Prophets and profits: The family politics of remittances, bridewealth and homemaking in Senegalese murid communities. *Journal of Religion in Africa, 31*(4), 367–395.

Elugbe, B. O., & Omamor, A. P. (Eds.). (1991). *Nigerian pidgin: Background and prospects*. Ibadan, Nigeria: Heinemann Educational Books.

Emecheta, B. (1986). *Head above water*. Oxford: Heinemann.

Farr, M. (forthcoming). Rancheros in Chicagoacán: Ways of speaking and identity in a Mexican transnational community.

Garcia, O. (1997). New York's multilingualism: World languages and their role in a U.S. city. In O. Garcia & J. Fishman (Eds.), *The multilingual apple: Languages in New York City*. Berlin: Mouton de Gruyter.

Goodwin, C., & Duranti, A. (1992). Introduction. In A. Duranti & C. Goodwin, (Eds.), *Rethinking context: Language as an interactive phenomenon* (pp. 1–42). Cambridge, UK: Cambridge University Press.

Gumperz, J. (1982). Contextualization conventions (chap. 6). In *Discourse strategies*. Cambridge, UK: Cambridge University Press.

Hill, J. H., & Irvine, J. T. (Eds.). (1992). *Responsibility and evidence in oral discourse* [Introduction]. New York: Cambridge University Press.

Hymes, D., & Gumperz, J. (Eds.). (1972). *Directions in sociolinguistics: The ethnography of communication*. New York: Holt, Rinehart and Winston.

Jibril, M. (1997). The elaborations of the functions of Nigerian pidgin. In A. Bamgbose & A. Thomas (Eds.), *New Englishes: A West African perspective*. (pp. 232–247). Trenton, NJ: Africa World Press.

Moskos, C. (1999). The Greeks in the United States. In R. Clogg (Ed.), *The Greek diaspora in the twentieth century*. New York: St. Martin's Press.

Nardini, G. (1999). *Che bella figura: The power of performance in an Italian ladies' club in Chicago*. Binghamton: State University of New York Press.

Nwoye, O. G. (1992). Linguistic politeness and sociocultural variations of the notion of face. *Journal of Pragmatics*, *18*(4), 309–328.

Oguine, I. (2000). *A squatter's tale*. Oxford, UK: Heinemann.

Okolo, B. A. (1990). Indirectness in discourse: A study in paradoxical communication among the Igbos. *Language and Style*, *23*(4), 495–505.

Philips, S. (2000). Constructing a Tongan nation-state through language ideology in a courtroom. In P. Kroskrity (Ed.), *Regimes of language: Ideologies, politics, and identities* (pp. 229–257). Santa Fe, NM: School of American Research Press.

Random House dictionary of the English language. (1966). J. Stein (Ed.). New York: Random House.

Reynolds, R. (2002). An African brain drain: Igbo decisions to immigrate to the U.S. *Review of African Political Economy*, *92*.

Saville-Troike, M. (1989). *The ethnography of communication*. London: Basil Blackwell.

Silverstein, S. (1984). Igbo kinship and modern entrepreneurial organization: The transportation and spare parts business. *Studies in Third World Societies*, *28*, 191–209.

Trager, L. (2001). *Yoruba Hometowns: Community, identity, and development in Nigeria*. Boulder: Lynne-Rienner.

U.S. Secretary of State, Department of State. (1987). *U.S. treaties and other international agreements*. (Vol. 33, Pt. 3, 1979–1981, Treaty No. 10261). Washington, DC: U.S. Government Printing Office.

Van den Bersselaar, D. (1998). *In search of Igbo identity: Language, culture, and politics in Nigeria, 1900–1966*. Leiden, Netherlands: Leiden University Dissertation Service.

Van Hear, N. (1998). *New diasporas: The mass exodus, dispersal and regrouping of migrant communities*. Seattle: University of Washington Press.

Wasserman, S., & Galaskiewicz, J. (1994). *Advances in social network analysis* [Introduction]. Thousand Oaks, CA: Sage.

Photograph by Michael Maltz

8

The Arab Accountant
As Language Mediator

Sharon Radloff
University of Illinois at Chicago

AMIN, AL-MUHASIB

It is 6:30 on a Monday morning and Amin, al-muhasib (Amin the accountant), as his clients know him, is already in his office, pouring his first cup of sweetened Arabic coffee, having just finished a breakfast of Quaker instant oatmeal. Amin is not merely an accountant. President of Maalik Accounting, Inc. (both Amin and Maalik Accounting, Inc. are pseudonyms, as are all personal and business names in this chapter), he is an accountant with a master of business administration degree and a master of science degree in accounting. He is also an Internal Revenue Service (IRS)-enrolled agent, an accountant certified to represent clients before the IRS. More important, Amin's position as an accountant to a largely Arab immigrant clientele has cast him in the role of language mediator, a linguistic and cultural liaison between his Arab immigrant clientele and the various layers of government in the United States.

Amin is a Palestinian Arab Muslim originally from a small village south of Jerusalem on the West Bank of the Jordan River, an area that was originally Jordanian territory, but since 1967 has been under the governance of Israel. Amin is a naturalized American citizen. In 1970, at the age of 24 years, and having secured a visa to study in the United States, he arrived in Chicago directly from a job in an Arab state in the Persian Gulf to which he had fled after the 1967 war between Arab countries and Israel.

Amin subsequently married an American-born European American woman, obtained his bachelor of science degree, became an American citizen, and worked his way up from hospital janitor to company financial analyst for one of the better-known institutional management companies in the United States. He was joined during this period (1970–1975) by his brother and many other Jordanian and Palestinian males. They were encouraged by the informal communication network of Arab students that had evolved in Chicago and other United States' cities, and that had cast its net across the Atlantic to the Middle East and the Arabian Peninsula. After receiving his master of business administration in 1979, Amin returned to work as an accountant for an Arab company in the Persian Gulf where he remained until 1987.

On his return to Chicago, and chafing under the rule of others, his entrepreneurial spirit led him to partner with a few other Arab Americans in a small accounting and tax firm while obtaining both his Master's degree in accounting and his certification as an IRS-enrolled agent. By this time, he was fluent in English, as well as in his native Arabic. He was typical of a group of young, single Arab males, who having come to Chicago to study in the early 1970s, settled in the far West Side Austin neighborhood of Chicago. By and large they married American-born women of non-Arab descent, and most had children. All became successful businessmen or skilled laborers, working either on their own or for well-established companies and settling into a reasonably comfortable, if not always happy, middle-class life in northwest Chicago or Chicago's western and northern suburbs.

PURPOSE AND METHODOLOGY OF THE ESSAY

Unlike the many Arab immigrants who preceded this group or the many who followed it, this group of young men were atypical, but not unique, in their residence patterns, marriage partners, education, jobs, and perhaps even in luck and personality. They found community support not among an established Arab community, but among themselves as brothers, cousins, or friends. They looked, at least at first, not toward their past in the Arab world but toward a future in the United States. They married women from the United States instead of reaching back home for a suitable partner, limited their family size to two or three children, and achieved some degree of higher education in U.S. schools. They enjoyed an environment of support from like-minded companions rather than from their families back home (and thereby were in some degree free from the Arab cultural obligation that such family support entails, which will be explained below) and worked for well-established businesses or in well-paying industrial jobs rather than in small, family-owned Arab-oriented businesses. Consequently, Amin and his peers assimilated into the mainstream of the dominant social, political, and civic culture of the United States. But like millions of immigrants before them, their ties to their homelands remained strong, in great part because of the unbreakable bonds to both the family and the land they had left behind.

It is this constellation of atypical characteristics that has thrust the Maalik Accounting firm into its special position as a language mediator. It is the purpose of this chapter to describe that position. I illustrate how Arabs confront the need to deal with the various government agencies and people that regulate their lives. In doing so, I hope to illuminate an aspect of immigrant life that native U.S. citizens rarely see.

The research for this essay was gathered primarily through a participatory action approach, a method pioneered by sociologist William F. Whyte in his of study Boston's Italian American youth gangs in 1943. The research for this chapter involved observation of the day-to-day functioning of Maalik Accounting over a 3-year period, interviews with the accountants, and participation in the workings of the firm as a part-time employee during those 3 years. Specific demographic data on the Arab community and Maalik's clientele were gathered from published sources, as well as from the files of the firm itself. The "whys and wherefores" of many of the phenomena observed have been interpreted as expressions of specific cultural ideologies or as the result of them.

To recapitulate then, this chapter is a result of observing the workings of a small Arab American accounting office located on the northwest side of Chicago. It shows that Maalik's accountants, all naturalized U.S. citizens of Palestinian Arab extraction, act as language brokers between their clients and the various government agencies at the federal, state, and local levels.

It describes how language is used in the office between the accountants and their clients, who have varying levels of English and Arabic linguistic skills, and who possess varying connections to both U.S. culture and their native Arabic cultures. This chapter also describes how language is used to translate the clients' business and personal transactions with government bodies into more effective and efficacious interactions. This chapter does not suggest that the experience of all Arab immigrants in the United States can be characterized similarly (Aswad, 1974; Hagopian & Paden, 1969; McCarus, 1994; Suleiman, 1999). What it does propose to demonstrate is that there are sources, such as Maalik Accounting, in the Arab immigrant community itself that are and can be developed into rich resources for the language requirements of Chicago Arab immigrants in their communications with government agencies and the other non-Arab establishments of Chicago. Because the overwhelming majority of Maalik Accounting's clients are male, the pronoun "he" will be used, except in those contexts wherein gender differentiation must be made.

CULTURE AND LANGUAGE

Definition of Culture

This study is about language. But language is itself a cultural product and process. It is, therefore, imperative that what is meant by culture be explained. Duranti (1997) proffered a comprehensive description of culture that recognizes it as a fluid and dynamic nexus of social, communicative, and symbolic practices and tools that are useful in describing the "similarities and differences in the ways in which people around the world constitute themselves in aggregates of various sorts" (p. 23) at any given time, past or present.

Accordingly, culture is a social system of practices, knowledge, and ways of interpreting reality, the origins and changes of which are based in historical and ecological circumstances. These practices and worldviews are transmitted across time, space, and generation both by formal cultural institutions of learning and by the multifarious interactions of everyday life. Although it is convenient, and to some degree valid, to talk of American culture as referring to North Americans living in the United States and Arab culture as that culture encompassing that part of the world where Arabic is the dominant language and Islam the dominant way of life, it would be wrong to characterize each of these cultures as monolithic and invariant.

For instance, in the United States, there are subcultures found in various immigrant communities that differ radically from the "dominant" culture. Similarly, Palestinian Arab culture differs in many details from other Arab cultures defined by political names such as Yemeni, Egyptian, or Jordanian. Even American nonimmigrant subcultures flourish in opposition to each other: rural versus urban culture, Southern versus Western culture, Midwestern versus Eastern seaboard culture, and so forth. Likewise, in the Muslim Arab world, each country has a Christian subculture, a Bedouin subculture, and cultural divisions between various Muslim sects such as the Shi'ites and the Sunnis, as well as non-Arab ethnic minorities. The operative words here are dominant and subculture. The dominant culture is that nexus of behavior most predictable of a particular aggregate of people, in this case, people residing in the United States and people residing in the Arab-speaking areas of the Middle East, respectively. Subculture is the term used to describe those people who, while participating in the dominant culture because of living patterns, socialization, or history, maintain distinct cultural features not shared by the dominant culture.

Language Issues

Arabic and English differ not only in terms of vocabulary, syntax and pronunciation, but also in writing systems. Therefore, the problems that Arab speakers of English as a second language encounter in oral discourse are not only repeated in written discourse, but also are compounded by the requirement that they must read and write in a second orthographic system. Briefly, Arabic is a Semitic language that shares little in structure and morphology with English, a Germanic language of the Indo-European group of languages. Unlike the vocabulary of English, 40% of which is Latin and shared with the Romance branch of the Indo-European family of languages, very few words in the basic everyday vocabularies of English and Arabic are shared.

Further complicating the Arabic–English language divide is the different orthographic systems. The English alphabet, derived immediately from the Roman alphabet, is made up of consonants and vowels and is written and read from left to right. Arabic uses a triconsonantal system (i.e., the root word is made of three consonants; vowels, not usually written, are assumed from the context) and is read and written from right to left. Moreover, many sounds in English and Arabic are not shared. As a result, many Arabic phonemes are written in multiple ways in the English alphabet, especially if they affect surrounding sounds or are themselves affected by surrounding sounds. A further complication is that many phonemes of the written language are pronounced differently by different Arabic speakers. For instance, the Arabic sound written in Arabic script as ق may be pronounced "g" by Egyptians, but as "q" by Palestinians. Moreover, because vowels are not written and are subject to being colored by the surrounding consonants, pronunciation, as well as local convention, may determine how the vowel is written in English. These linguistic phenomena create a very peculiar and frustrating transliteration problem that Maalik Accounting must solve when dealing with personal names on government documents.

The most common problem, and most troublesome by any measure, involves the spelling of Arabic names in English. An Arabic name may be spelled in English in many different ways. For instance, the common Arabic name Mohammed, written in Arabic as محمد and pronounced "mohʌmmɪd," can be written variously in English as Mohammed, Mohammad, Mohamed, Muhammed, Mohemed, and so on. On the other hand, different Arabic names may be spelled exactly the same in English because the phonemes that distinguish them in Arabic may be written by the same letter in English. For instance, distinct Arabic names such as فتحي, (fat-hi) and فادى, (faa-di) both can be written in English as *Fadi* (fad-i). As discussed earlier, how these names are written in English is dependent on factors such as the Arab to English transliteration conventions of the Arab immigrant's country of origin, the phonemic system of that country's particular Arabic dialect, and the knowledge that the person filling out the document (whether Arab, American, or yet some other nationality) has of both English and Arabic orthographic conventions.

Often, an individual will have a number of documents such as a birth certificate, marriage certificate, school grade report, or social security card, on which his name is variously spelled because each document was completed at a different time, in a different place, and by a different government official. This is a particularly vexing problem when these documents must be matched to the name on the social security card. Even a one-letter change in spelling will render a tax return invalid or cause problems with immigration documents and other legal papers.

THE ARAB IMMIGRANTS IN CHICAGO

According to the Arab–American Action Network (AAAN) (1998), there were three distinct waves of Arab immigration to the United States before 1989. The Arab community first took root in Chicago on the near South Side around Michigan Avenue more than 90 years ago with the settlement of Syrian Lebanese Christian families, a smaller number of Palestinian Muslims (mostly male), and even fewer Palestinian Christians (again, mostly male). This wave subsided in 1924 when the United States adopted quotas that limited immigration from the Middle East, Southern Europe, and Eastern Europe.

A second wave of immigration from the Middle East occurred just after the end of World War II (AAAN, 1998). This wave, abetted in 1948 by the creation of Israel on land the Palestinian Arabs claimed as their own, comprised mostly Palestinians and lesser numbers of Assyrians, Iraqis, and Jordanians. The Palestinians and the Jordanian immigrants joined the older South Side Arab community, which by then extended to the Gage Park and Chicago Lawn areas (see map in Introduction), whereas the Assyrians and Iraqis settled on Chicago's North Side. Palestinian women were a substantial part of this second wave, either joining husbands already in the United States or immigrating along with their husbands.

A 1965 change in U.S. immigration policy, which now emphasized family reunification, propelled yet a third wave of Arab immigration, mostly from the Palestinian West Bank and from Jordan, to Chicago (AAAN, 1998). After peaking in 1969, this wave remained fairly consistent until 1989, when a fourth influx of Palestinian immigration, caused by the increasingly difficult economic conditions in the West Bank, began, which continues into the early years of the 21st century.

Today, the center of Chicago's Arab community is still located in Gage Park and Chicago Lawn (see map in the Introduction) and is primarily Palestinian Muslim (AAAN, 1998). Many southwest Chicago suburbs such as Oak Lawn, Tinley Park, and Bridgeview (see map) have experienced increases in the number of Arab residents, as many Palestinian and Jordanian Arabs who prospered moved out of the city. The AAAN reports that the Chicago Commission on Human Relations Advisory Council on Arab Affairs estimates the non-Assyrian Arab (Assyrians are a separate Middle Eastern ethnic group) population in Chicago to be approximately 150,000, 57% of whom are Palestinian and 20%, Jordanian. The remaining 23%, according to the Advisory Council's report cited by the AAAN study, comprise 7% Egyptians, 4% Iraqis, 3% Syrians, 2.6% Lebanese, 2% Yemenis, and 2.4%

from other Arab countries. Many of these Arab immigrants arrived in Chicago on family reunification immigrant visas. The great majority are Muslim. No such demographic data are available for any other areas of Chicago or Illinois outside of Chicago, although research to gather such data is planned by the AAAN.

The economic and social conditions of this multinational Arab community range, according to the AAAN (1998), from that of the Egyptians, who tend to be highly educated (and presumably well off), to the mostly middle-class entrepreneurial Jordanians, to the Palestinians who vary from middle-class and educated to impoverished and undereducated. Among a representative sampling of the adults of this community studied by the AAAN, 75% were either permanent resident aliens or naturalized citizens. These adults represented families in which both parents were Arab immigrants, many of whom had American-born children. Of the Arab families sampled, 60% were impoverished. Whether economically comfortable or not, the adult males in the community owned stores or worked in stores located either in the community or in African American communities. The wives in this Arab community were almost exclusively homemakers. It is a general Arab cultural belief that the "early child training on the development and structure of a man's later character" (Hamady, 1960, p. 220) is of utmost importance, and it is the mother's job to ensure that the child is nurtured correctly (AAAN, 1998). Consequently, Arab households generally have just one adult breadwinner.

What strikes one most forcefully in the 1998 AAAN study is the emphasis not only on the Arab community's sense of identity, (ethnic, cultural, and religious), but also on its members' insistence that adult, as well as children, must develop English language skills in order to gain entry into American society, be it in relation to employment, education, health, or citizenship benefits, or in dealing with myriad government agencies. Because English language skills require time to develop, it is not surprising that the community also sees a need for ready access to fluent Arabic and English bilinguals.

MAALIK ACCOUNTING, INC.

Maalik's Personnel

It is now nearly 9:30 a.m., and the four other daytime employees of Maalik Accounting have joined Amin. As is often the case in small Arab immigrant businesses, Maalik's employees are related either by blood or marriage or through common ties to their Palestinian homeland. Maalik Accounting is located on the northwest side of Chicago in the Mayfair neighborhood (see location on map in the Introduction). The business district is predominantly Korean and Chinese, but is also home to a mixture of other ethnic enterprises: Hispanic, East Indian, Arabic, Eastern European, and Western European.

Sherif, Amin's nephew, his brother's son, is a newly married 30-year-old who entered the United States on an immigrant visa at the age of 19 years. He holds a master's degree in accounting from an Illinois university. Fluent in English and Arabic, he has a small share in closely held Maalik Accounting, Inc., and serves as Maalik's chief ambassador to its clients, and also seconds Amin's command in the office. Sherif is also responsible for most of the Arabic-to-English translation of documents, and for obtaining from the clients the information needed to complete their various government and legal documents. His wife's family is from his West Bank village, but she spent her formative years in an Arab state in the Persian Gulf before entering a university on the West Bank to study computer science. She is currently completing her bachelor of art's degree in Chicago and learning English.

Samir, a 20-year-old college student majoring in accounting, has worked part-time at Maalik since high school. His family is originally from the same village as that of Amin and Sherif, but wended their way to Chicago after spending many years in the American Virgin Islands. Samir is the youngest of the family's many children, who were born in various parts of the world. His older brothers were born and partially schooled in the West Bank, thus learning and using Arabic extensively as a first language. His two oldest sisters were born in the West Bank, but were schooled in the Virgin Islands and the United States, so were exposed only to Arabic until starting school, and thereafter to both Arabic and English equally. However, the two youngest sisters were born and schooled first in the Virgin Islands and then in the United States. Samir was born and entirely schooled in the United States. Consequently, the family's bilingualism runs the gamut from the parent's complete facility in speaking Arabic but continual struggle in English to the three oldest children's fairly good but accented English to the middle children's balanced bilingualism to Samir's complete facility in English now time sharing with a newly rediscovered but fluent Arabic. Whereas the parents can write Arabic but not English, all their children can write English but not Arabic. Samir had almost completely abandoned Arabic for English from the age of 5 years, when he started school, until he began working at Maalik. Samir's command of both oral English and Arabic and his understanding of both Arabic and American customs make him a perfect candidate for sharing Sherif's duties and helping Sherif in his accounting and ambassadorial functions.

Khadija, or Um-Mohammed, as she is respectfully called in the office, according to the Arabic tradition of addressing a mother and father after their first son, is Maalik's secretary. A middle-aged Muslim woman who does not dress in Hagib style (consisting of a head covering and long dress coat with long sleeves), she is originally from a village on the West Bank and is married to an African Muslim. She came to work for Maalik Accounting after her children had reached adulthood. She performs bookkeeping and computer data entry, tasks she learned years earlier when she worked for a global company overseas.

The author manages Maalik's computer system, performs English-to-Arabic, French-to-English, and Spanish-to-English-translation, and writes all the business correspondence for both Maalik and its clients. Born in a western suburb of Chicago to ethnic White Europeans, her family over the years has grown to include Mexican, Palestinian Arab, and East Indian ethnic groups. She came to work part-time for Maalik through persons acquainted with one of Maalik's employees.

Talal works at night, and like Amin, is an accountant and officer of Maalik Accounting. It was Talal who gave Amin his start in the independent accounting business. He is also Maalik's Spanish language expert, being trilingual in Spanish, Arabic, and English. Talal's father was born in a village near that of Amin's in Palestine and subsequently immigrated to Latin America. Talal's mother is Hispanic, and he spent his boyhood in both the country of his father and that of his mother. However, holding to the Arab–Muslim custom of the child belonging to the father's family, Talal was brought up to identify himself as an Arab and calls Palestine his home, although he still maintains his ties to his Spanish-speaking heritage.

It is Maalik's unusual blend of both cosmopolitanism and traditional ethnic identity that positioned the firm as a language broker. Given the relative catholicity of their backgrounds, their multilingualism, and their bonds to other cultures, as well as inherent personality traits, Maalik has built a reputation not only for providing good accounting and tax services, but also for providing a liaison to the English-speaking world. What then is Maalik Accounting's business and what is its customer base?

Maalik Accounting's Core Business

It is nearing 9:30 a.m. and it is the 5th of the month. Both state and federal payroll taxes are due on the 15th of the month. State sales taxes on revenue earned for the month and the Chicago city tax on sales of soft drinks are due by the 20th. Maalik's office is therefore a beehive of activity. Khadija and Samir are busy finishing up the clients' monthly payroll, keying data into the computer programs that produce state and federal forms that subsequently will be mailed or taken to the clients, who then will make out checks to be sent to the government or their banks to cover the payments due. The author is keying in sales from the clients' business documents, data used by both Amin and Sherif as input to their sales tax programs. Khadija, and Samir when he is in the office, also will be doing this work. Any time after 11:30 a.m. or so, Sherif and Samir will leave to visit the clients, to give them their completed sales tax papers so they can write out checks to the state and/or city, to collect the documents from them to prepare their monthly sales taxes, or to collect monies owed to Maalik for past services. Most regular clients, and there are approximately 450 of them, are visited sometime during the month in person by Sherif and Samir. If they are new, they will certainly be visited by Amin or Sherif for the first few months. When the tax deadline is near, Amin also will visit clients to pick up needed tax-related documents. Talal then will handle any overflow work from the day when he comes at 6 o'clock in the evening.

Normally, however, Amin will remain in the office to work on sales taxes yet to be done, prepare corporate income taxes due on the 15th of the month for those businesses whose fiscal year ends that month, take calls, and see office visitors for any number of reasons, from interpreting a letter from the city water bureau to filing new corporation papers with the state to translating documents to be sent with immigrant visa applications that Maalik will also prepare. Sherif will bring back to the office many similar requests gathered during his client visits. Upon his return to the office, there will usually be two or three clients waiting to see him on matters that require his immediate attention. Frequently, a client will show up days after a scheduled appointment. Although during these busy times, which last from the 5th through the 20th of the month from May through December and every day during the January-through-April income tax season, this failure to keep appointments on time is frustrating; showing up at the scheduled time is something Maalik hopes its clients will do, but does not expect. Maalik's accountants exist in a cross-cultural time warp that forces them to hold appointment times on one hand as a promise according to North American norms, and on the other hand, as a possibility according to Middle Eastern, East Indian, and Hispanic cultural norms. Once the 20th has passed, or in the case of income tax season April 15, the workload eases up somewhat, so that the deferred clerical and noncritical client requests can be handled.

Maalik Accounting's Clientele

Represented in the 450 businesses that one of Maalik's accountants will personally visit, or at least telephone, during the month are Arab Muslims from most of the countries of the Middle East and North Africa: Iraqis, Syrians, Algerians, Moroccans, Sudanese, Egyptians, Palestinians from both Israel and the West Bank, Jordanians, and Yemenis. Also represented are a very small number of Christians from Lebanon and Palestine, Mexicans, Cubans, Pakistani Muslims, Indian Christians and Hindus, African Americans, and a very few European Americans. Among Maalik's clients, 74% are Palestinian Muslim, 10% are Yemeni Muslim, and 7% are Jordanian Muslim. These same 450 regular clients make up 40% of Maalik's personal income tax customers.

The remaining 60% of Maalik's clients are individuals who file their personal income taxes once a year. On the basis of the last names by which they filed in 1999, or in the case of the accountants' personal knowledge of repeat customers, their ethnic extractions (citizenship and birthplace are unknown), are in the following descending numerical order: Arab, Hispanic, Pakistani, Indian, European American, African American, and others (including Korean and Chinese from the neighborhood and those that could not be classified by name or personal knowledge). Although the 450 businesses represent only 40% of Maalik's clientele, they represent 80% of the source of Maalik's income. Furthermore, because of the shared language and Arab identity, it is because of the special demands of its Arab clientele that Maalik has become a language broker and cultural liaison to American culture and government agencies and services.

In terms of location, 52% of Maalik's Arab business clientele live on the northwest side of Chicago, many in the ward where Maalik is located; 14% in the South suburbs; 11% on the south, southwest, or southeast side of Chicago; 11% in the north and northwest suburbs; 8% in the western suburbs; and 3% on Chicago's West Side. The remaining 1% live in Indiana. The business locations of these Arab clients have a distribution that differs from that of where they live: 29% on Chicago's north or northwest side; 29% on Chicago's west side; 27% on Chicago's south, southwest, or southeast side; 3% in the Chicago's downtown area; 6% in the south suburbs; 4% in the western suburbs; 2% in the north or northwest suburbs; and 2% in Indiana.

Maalik Accounting provides basic services such as bookkeeping, payroll record-keeping, and financial, sales, and income tax reporting to a clientele base of mainly small, local, Arab-owned businesses. Its raison d'être, however, has been and remains filing sales and income tax reports to various government bodies at all levels of government on behalf of its clients. Although Maalik has targeted a mainly Arab immigrant business clientele, the firm's large signage, business cards, and new office announcements (sent out when their space requirements expanded and they moved to their own building 4 years ago) have all been in English. For a short time after the move to the new building, flyers in Arabic describing Maalik's services decorated prominent places in the office. There is also a 3´ x 2´ sign in the window announcing their services in Arabic. Income tax time in the early months of the year, at least until April 15, brings in additional clients, mainly Arabs, but also walk-ins of assorted ethnicities and ethnic blends from the surrounding commercial and residential neighborhood and those drawn in by word-of-mouth from existing clients. The heavy emphasis on English in announcing their services was a conscious attempt to broaden the client base beyond the Arab community.

The initial decision, however, to concentrate on serving small Arab immigrant businesses, especially on Chicago's northwest side, was a deliberate move to take advantage of a ready and needy client base to which, through their multilingualism, they had advantageous access. They are not without competitors in a market that is labor intensive but commands low fees, and one that provides a necessary but begrudged service, tax accounting. Observation of the work that goes on daily at Maalik Accounting and the human interactions that take place in accomplishing that work demonstrate how a number of cultural features have both shaped and constrained Maalik's market: in-group and out-group loyalties (Triandis 1972), reciprocity expectations (Mauss, 1925/1990), the position that bargaining plays in the marketplace (Hamady, 1960), and shame and honor versus guilt and self-respect as a motivator of moral action (Abu-Lughod, 1986; Barakat, 1993).

Before discussing these features, it must be emphasized that in keeping with the definition of culture assumed herein and defined previously, the discussion focuses on general cultural ideologies, or the broad tendencies that define the culture of a particular population even as that culture undergoes inevitable and constant transformation (Barakat, 1993). Any one culture or any one individual of that culture may hold to such beliefs in varying degrees and may or may not act on these beliefs consistently, if at all. On the other hand, multiple cultures may share multiple beliefs and may act on them in relatively the same way and to the same degree. Thus, it is fairly justifiable to speak of the multiculturalism of the United States and yet claim that there is a dominant culture based on Western European values that are imposed and propagated (in principle at least) by American institutions of power, law, and education. One may ask, however, how one can justify treating the many Arab cultures that have developed across different Middle Eastern political entities in modern history as one Arab culture.

The justification is in the observation that the many different nationalities of the Middle East and North Africa, recognized as Arab by Western scholars, and who make up the majority of Maalik's customer base, show remarkably similar behaviors and attitudes in the four aforementioned cultural features. Moreover, these different nationalities all consider themselves to be Arab. Barakat (1993) attributes this common identity to a constellation of cultural features composed of a shared but heavily diglossic language (Arabic) (Altoma, 1969), a predominantly shared religion (Islam) for which a knowledge of a common literary Arabic is essential (Shouby, 1970), and, importantly, to shared historical memories (Barakat, 1993), genealogies (formed from tribal and familial traditions passed down from generation to generation) (Abu-Lughod, 1986), and political institutions (no matter how secular) based largely on Koranic tradition (Bakarat, 1993). Said (1979) thus characterized a continuum of Arab cultures from pre-1975-civil-war Lebanon, the most Westernized of Arab cultures, to Saudi Arabia, the most traditional.

The In-Group. The Arab immigrant, not unlike any other immigrant or native U.S. citizen, finds paying taxes troublesome and onerous. Like some other immigrant groups, but unlike native-born U.S. citizens and the dominant culture of the United States, Arab immigrants generally come from cultures operating in a political environment that has solidified the family as the sole in-group to which an individual readily claims allegiance. It is from this in-group that the Arab citizen primarily derives rights, and it is to this in-group that he/she owes obligations (Barakat, 1993; Hamady, 1960; Laffin, 1975). It is also the case that the good of the family takes precedence over the good of the individual (Abu-Laban & Abu-Laban, 1999), and for that matter, the good of the state. In return for subsuming his or her own individual desires, the individual derives from the family self-worth, security, and identity (Abu-Lughod, 1986; Bakarat,

1993). Islam has served to buttress this ideology, according to Hamady (1960), by focusing on the family and religious community at the expense of the individual and the secular state.

One must however make, a qualification to this collectivist view of Arab familial relationships and not misinterpret it as a suppression of all individuality. Farr (2000) described how the ranchero culture of Mexican immigrants in Chicago is much more family oriented than that of the "dominant Anglo "individualistic" culture (p. 70), but allows for individualistic expression through achievement. Arab cultures share with Mexican ranchero culture this deep commitment to family while allowing leeway for the individual to achieve that at which he or she excels, albeit within the bounds of a strict family honor code.

Shame and Honor.   Arab cultures emphasize the external restraint of shame. Openly breaching the community's behavioral code brings condemnation not only upon oneself for not obeying, but also upon one's family, which is held as the responsible entity for this disobedience (Laffin, 1975). In a culture wherein nonpolitical justice is still largely a matter of family or local community enforcement rather than state regulation, public shame is a powerful form of control, far outweighing being pure of heart (Barakat, 1993; Hamady, 1960).

Intertwined with shame is honor. In the Arab world, honor is the other side of the coin of shame. Honor in the context of Arab cultures is the authority earned by maintaining and practicing the group-oriented values of "generosity, honesty, sincerity, loyalty to friends, and keeping one's word" (Abu-Lughod, 1986, p. 87). Shame brings dishonor to the family (Abu-Lughod, 1986) because it reflects a loss of the moral worthiness of that family

Reciprocity.   The fragility of the social contract in most Arab states (Choueiri, 2000; Viorst, 1994) and the hold that loyalty to the family has on the individual have created the system of reciprocity in the Arab countries. Mauss (1925/1990) characterized reciprocity as a basic economic transaction of a society. However, it is one so intermingled with the social and cultural life of a people that its manifestation varies from culture to culture. One of the ways that reciprocity manifests itself in Arab cultures is to make business transactions a highly personal matter, a tradition that endures because most business in Arab countries is still dominated more by the spirit of the small entrepreneur than by the ethos of corporate culture (see Barakat, 1993, for a discussion of modern economic challenges facing the Arab countries).

Bargaining. The most direct route to such personalization of business is bargaining over the price of goods and services. That is, until a personal relationship is established, Arabs do not give because they cannot hope to get anything in return. To transact business in a face-to-face situation is to expect that the price first quoted is only an opening foray into personally establishing what will be paid in the end. A price is agreed on that the buyer is willing to give and the merchant is willing to receive through the reciprocal give and take of a personal face-to-face interaction.

To return to the point of this discussion of ideology, it is this confluence of beliefs about family shame and honor, reciprocity, bargaining, and in-group inclusion that keeps competition fierce, fees low, and work loads large for Maalik. Most of Maalik's Arab immigrant clients come from countries in which there is little or no tradition of accountable taxation by governments that will be returned in services to the people. Ajami (1992) characterized governments in Arab countries in one way or another to be *sulta,* and "to refer to authority as sulta and to today's ruler as the sultan is to underline how little has changed between the rule and ruled" (Ajami, 1992, p. xvi) over the centuries. Consequently, paying taxes on money earned with one's hard work to a distant impersonal government, with no perceived reciprocity from that body, is not only for these immigrants largely onerous but senseless and immoral. But because the various U.S. governmental bodies have numerous checks in place to collect such monies and to punish if they are not collected, compliance is necessarily high. Therefore, the Arab immigrant businessman has little incentive to spend much time systematically organizing his records by sales type, putting the burden for doing so on the accountant. He, therefore, resists the idea that the accountant's single piece of paper showing his tax due to the government each month can possibly cost more than a trifle. Consequently, he generally tries to use this as a bargaining chip to get the lowest price he can for the work. It must be said that Maalik's accountants belong to both regional and national accounting societies and attend a number of accredited seminars and classes a year to keep their enrolled agent status and, more important to keep abreast of changes in the tax laws. In talking to accountants who deal mainly or only with nonimmigrant American clients at these gatherings, they have become aware of how easy a life these other accountants have. This latter clientele, in contrast to Maalik's, generally keep good records, have grown up with a cultural tradition, although not a liking, for paying taxes, and do not seem to flinch at paying accounting fees two to three times what Maalik, Inc. receives in its market.

Added to this is the constant haggling over price. Because Maalik keeps its own operation on a cash flow basis, it sets fixed prices. But invariably the clients try to bargain down the price, believing Maalik has set it intentionally high for the purpose of initiating a bargaining session, which is invariably done in very personal rather than in economic terms. According to Hamady (1960), the "Arab conducts his business, social duty, and pleasure at the same time" (p. 73). Paying the accountant for services rendered, then, becomes reciprocation for a gift given rather than a purely impersonal economic transaction (Mauss, 1925/1990).

Finally, given the Arab immigrant's experience with an often more distant and ineffective government (Ajami, 1992), it is difficult for him to develop loyalty to the government. Rather, his loyalty is tied to his family or extended family here and back home. His identity is defined by how well he does in the family's eyes, not how good he is in paying taxes to the government. Therefore, his income and what it can provide are a measure of his self-worth and his worth in the eyes of his family. To pay too much to the government is senseless when he could very well be using that money to help his family. Therefore, the shame of failing to provide well enough for his family in their eyes and in the eyes of others is an immorality that makes paying taxes all the more troublesome for the immigrant. Maalik's accountants, from a combination of profit motive, an acquired American attitude toward paying taxes, and an Arab's more personal approach to business, ease the Arab immigrant business owner 's transition to viewing taxes as just a routine cost of doing business in the United States.

It is, then, the bilingual and bicultural accountant who understands the political and economic realities of owning a business in the United States, and specifically in Chicago, who can help the immigrant business person maneuver through the minefields of business regulations, taxes, and immigration laws while maintaining his client's dignity and self-worth. Such is the service that Maalik performs for its clientele, no matter their ethnicity. But because their clients are overwhelmingly Arab and the accountants all are fluent in both English and Arabic, it is the Arab clientele who take most advantage of Maalik's acumen. Thus, Maalik's operation affords an opportunity to study how an unrecognized and unofficial source of language brokering, in this case an accountant's office, can work to provide access for Arab immigrants to U.S. institutions and eventual acculturation into U.S. society.

MAALIK ACCOUNTING, INC.—LANGUAGE MEDIATORS

Arabic Spoken Here

Although Arabic takes a secondary role in the exterior signage of Maalik's office, once inside, the customer or visitor finds Western poster art mixes with Koranic suura (verses) and Palestinian village pictures and maps as wall decorations. Sales brochures and an occasional free Arabic-language newspaper take their place on the small foyer table top along with the *Chicago Sun Times,* the *National Geographic,* and the *Smithsonian* magazine. Plants, as is customary throughout the Arab Middle East, are situated in corners and desks throughout the office. Prominently displayed is a large bulletin board, which not only provides customer service numbers for the IRS and other government agencies, but also serves as an ad hoc advertising board where both Arab clients and nonclients have tacked up their business cards, 90% of which are entirely in English. The other 10% vary in the ratio of English to Arabic, but all have at least the business name and telephone number in English.

A new or unfamiliar customer walking in is addressed in English. If his response is in English, the conversation will continue in English unless or until the customer replies in Arabic. Once a customer is seen by an accountant, conversations may be in Arabic or English, which usually is the choice of the younger clients who have been in America since their preteens. Whether an Arab client chooses to speak in English or Arabic, code switching between the two languages will invariably take place. Government agency names, telephone numbers, addresses, and terms heard only in English in America, such as "sales tax," "income taxes," "Illinois Secretary of State" are rendered in English by all parties. During hectic sales tax times or when April 15 is looming near, one hears English, Spanish, Arabic, Hindi, and other languages being spoken. English, Arabic, and Spanish are used by the accountants, as well as by the clients, whereas the other languages are spoken among the clients of like language backgrounds.

Even when political storms may be gathering in the United States or in the Middle East, the conversations in the office very rarely deviate for long from the business at hand. Matters are too pressing and time is critical, given the client work load. Even so, relationships between the accountants and their clients tend, of course, to be more personal, as befits a small firm such as Maalik. Furthermore, within the Arab community, business relationships are always personal relationships. Whether in person or over the phone, rarely is any name but one's first name used. Moreover, the Arab client as a rule expects regular personal visits from the accountants, often at their places of business, something expected in the United States for salesmen, but not for accountants. Good manners also play a part in this personalization. If a client knows that Amin has made the pilgrimage to Mecca, he is addressed by the honorific Haj rather than by Amin. A person with a son is addressed as father or mother of his or her son's name rather than by a first name. Humor also is prominent in this relationship, although its loud tones are often mistaken by native-born Americans for arguing. When things go amiss between accountant and client, such problems cannot be judged as just business. They must most often be excused, explained, and if necessary to avoid hurt feelings, not directly stated. In cultures that prize interpersonal relationships and the avoidance of shame over the blunt truth, the immorality is clearly on the side of telling the truth (Hamady, 1960). It is the Western concept of fibbing done to avoid hurt, only more generalized and done without guilt.

The typical Arab client of Maalik Accounting is a male in his early 30's who has been in the United States for an average of 10 to 15 years. He will be married just a few years and may have at least one preschool child born here in America. At the extremes, there are business owners who carry underage Illinois driver's licenses and others who have lived in the States since the 1960s who are in their 60's, whose children are first-generation Americans, and whose grandchildren are second-generation Americans. Often these immigrants have come to the United States as single males in their late teens following other family members, as current U.S. immigration policy favors family reunification (Cainkar, 1999). They then generally marry women from their extended family or village and bring them to the United States. The wives generally stay at home to raise the children. The few Arab women clients of Maalik are hair stylists who are Christian and from larger urban areas in the Middle East. Ajrouch (1999) explained this tendency for Arab immigrant women in America to stay home as a result of Islam's insistence on man's honor lying in his ability to support his family (Aswad, 1999) and women's honor as a sine qua non in a family's identity. Thus her role is in raising the children and maintaining her distance from those forces outside the home that might corrupt her and, thus, her family's honor.

On the other hand, Seikaly (1999) explained that middle-class Arab women, Christians in particular, who also share the patrilineal concern of Muslim society with women's honor, tend to be more flexible and better able to accept a more worldly lifestyle than the majority of immigrant men and women who come from lower economic strata. Aswad (1999) emphasized the difference between patrilineality and patriarchy, a distinction that many Westerners do not understand. In patrilineal societies, men and women trace their lines through the father. It has nothing to do with control of power by the male over the female, which defines patriarchy. Patrilineal descent means that when a woman marries, the children of that union belong to the father's line. However, the power of the women's patrilineal line is not thereby diminished. In fact, Aswad made the point that when patrilineal families live near each other, both sides of the parental lines are continually in contact and in cooperation with one another, and also are made aware of the male children the female has produced in her marriage. The bride price is an explicit recognition of the woman's contribution to her husband's family, and the female can exert power through her family's lineage. As a result, there is generally not the tentativeness and self-consciousness in Arab women that one sees in many young American women over their roles, their worth, and their bodies.

Of course, economic necessity may force the woman into the world, where her subtle strength comes to bear. For instance, when one of Maalik's Arab–Muslim clients was killed, his widow took over his business in the inner city as a matter of survival for her and her family. She even applied for loans, sold the business, and started a new one. She did this through the intercession and help of Maalik, who provided her the language expertise to document in English her business and financial situation for creditors.

The Road to Language Services

It is 2 o'clock in the afternoon. Sherif and Samir are back from their rounds visiting customers, delivering their sales tax and payroll papers, and collecting fees. Amin has stayed in the office to take sales and payroll figures over the telephone from his clients. Khadija and the author are busy with paperwork. Sherif and Samir have visited Arab customers in a wide variety of businesses. The neighborhood grocery or combined grocery and liquor store in the inner-city African American neighbor-hoods had once been the traditional source of ownership for the Arab immigrant, just as the Southwest Side has had the reputation as the home of the traditional Arab community. But Maalik's Arab clients have over the past decade, especially during the boom economy in the 1990s, become more and more diverse in their business ventures, their demographics, and in the services they ask of their accountants. A greater variety of Arab businesses are being established in the African American inner city, in the Latino neighborhoods of Pilsen and Humboldt Park, in the non-Arab northern, southern, and western sub-urbs, and even in downtown Chicago: dollar stores are replacing gro-cery and liquor stores as are gas stations/food marts, fast food restaurants (both franchises and independents), and stores that spe-cialize in tobacco, clothing, electronics, communication, furniture, and business fixtures.

This diversification and dispersion has been accelerated by inroads made by the Chicago city regulation allowing wards to vote themselves dry or to shut down liquor stores too near schools or churches. Although Maalik has provided the literacy power to help particular liquor store own-ers remain open, others have seen the handwriting on the wall and have changed businesses rather than take the tremendous time, money, and resources required to fight the action. The city of Chicago has also been particularly aggressive in the inspection of grocery stores in areas consid-ered for regentrification or in the process of such. The constant disruption in business has caused the owners to sell out and reestablish themselves in less vulnerable businesses.

Maalik also counts among its clients craftsman and skilled laborers such as auto repair mechanics, hair stylists (both men and women), car-penters, plumbers, and engineering consultants. Two of the fastest grow-ing business areas are limousine services and freight hauling. Many Arabs, to take the advantage of the house-buying boom in Chicago and the near suburbs, have gone into real estate and mortgage businesses with the most well-known firms in the country, their business cards tacked up on Maalik's bulletin board.

Where once a growing base of Palestinian Muslims and a few Jorda-nian Muslims comprised all of Maalik's Arab client base, an increasing number of Yemeni Muslims are becoming business entrepreneurs, joined by Arabs from various other countries (see earlier discussion). With this increased prosperity as well as business and demographic diversification comes an increase in regulations and laws to be understood, business acumen to be acquired, and immigration forms to be filled out, as well as vital documents to be translated so more family members can be brought over sooner. Especially with increased prosperity, the young Arab male can marry much sooner than before, accumulating faster the wealth required to bring properly a bride from back home to the States. Yet, Maalik is also turned to when a client fails or recommends someone to the firm who has not been able to partake of the new American economy, and for whom Maalik must supply affidavits for various public assistance programs.

Thus what had started out for Maalik as a small, relatively uniform client base with few language needs has burgeoned into a relatively large and multifaceted clientele with consequently greatly increased needs for language-related services. The increasing time spent on language matters was one of the factors in Maalik's decision to automate as much of the business as possible. Investments were made in computer networking and access to the Internet, in more powerful computers and printers, and in various tax calculation, word processing, form creation, and desktop publishing software.

Brokering Language: The Role of Language Mediator in an Arab Community

The Arab immigrant community that Maalik serves is not a geographic whole, but an economic entity brought together primarily by a common need for accounting expertise to file sales, income, and payroll taxes with federal, state, and local governments for its businesses. Unlike the situation in the mainly rural and small village areas in the Arab countries where most of Maalik's clients have their roots, deciding to go into business in America is not just a matter of finding a small vacant enclosure on the main route to and from one's village or nearby village, getting supplies, and beginning to sell goods. It is clear, after observation of Maalik's business operations and the exchanges between accountants and their clients, that the entrepreneurial Arab immigrant going into business in the United States, specifically in a large city like Chicago, will initially fill out papers that will give him the right to fill out even more papers so that he can remain in business and be subjected to current rules and regulations that will and do change sometimes literally overnight. He will learn more about how government really works than most native-born Americans ever will.

When it is time for this new entrepreneur to bring his family or new wife to the United States from back home, he will be confronted with the U.S. Immigration and Naturalization Service, which again will require many forms to be filled out and documents to be translated into English from Arabic, or often in the case of Morocco and Algeria, from French into English. Certain immigration forms require accompanying income tax returns, letters verifying certain vital statistics, credit standings, or the like. Frequently letters or affidavits must be written and sent to American embassies in the homeland to verify or explain certain situations such as employment and living arrangements.

As in the case of the widow who sold her deceased husband's business and started her own, an Arab immigrant might at some time need to apply to a bank for credit, so he or she will need a financial statement. At other times, he or she will need letters verifying an employee's salary in order for the employee to begin or continue getting public aid benefits. Distributorships may want to sell a certain line of products, so letters must be written to wholesalers requesting catalogs and price information. Finally, just as an individual's income tax might fall into an auditable category for one of many reasons, so does that of a business, and it is Maalik to whom the Arab immigrant business client will turn when either the state or federal government decides to conduct an audit of his or her business, be it a payroll, sales, or income tax audit.

The Business of Going Into Business

Amin is sitting with a client, patiently explaining to him in Arabic the benefits of incorporating his proposed business. Code switching is constant. Sentences first used by the accountant in discussing the steps required to set up a business legally are peppered with words and phrases in English that pertain to notions first encountered in the United States. These English words and phrases will become part of the code-switching repertoire of the Arab client. A few of these more common terms are incorporation, state sales tax, federal sales tax, payroll, FICA, IRS, withholding, and all U.S. addresses and telephone numbers.

This first-time entrepreneur is working on a shoestring budget. Amin explains to him the benefits of incorporating and protecting his personal assets and sways the new owner to incorporate, despite the higher initial outlay of cash to the state. Only six of Maalik's clients are partnerships or sole proprietorships. Amin will take the corporate name the neophyte businessman has chosen (in this case it is Q & R Foods & Liquor, Inc.) and check with the Secretary of State's office over the telephone or via the Internet to determine whether this name is available or not. If so, the next step can be taken. If not, then a new name must be chosen and verification repeated. Amin will then fill out the incorporation form and prepare the forms to obtain both state and federal identification numbers for the corporation. These numbers are required on all documents and correspondence submitted to the respective government bodies. Amin has the client sign all the forms, which he then sends off with the client's checks to the state in payment for the processing of these forms. Fees will also have to be paid for state and city business licenses.

Because Q & R Foods & Liquor, Inc. will be located in Chicago and will be selling liquor, Amin asks the client if he has investigated whether the ward (a political entity in Chicago presided over by an alderman who represents people of the entity in the City Council) in which the store is to be located has been voted dry (liquor cannot be sold) or is still wet (sale of liquor is permitted), and if wet, whether the store is near a church or school. Opening a store in a dry ward or too near a church or school will disqualify the owner from obtaining a liquor license. This particular store-owner does not know these facts, so Amin gives Sherif the assignment of finding these things out. The owner will also be investigated by the Chicago Police and must be cleared by them before the Chicago Liquor Commission will grant him a license. It will be Sherif who will act as the owner's liaison with the police. A state liquor license must also be obtained, but obtaining it is contingent on having a city liquor license. The client by this time is likely to be so overwhelmed that the protests he initially raised at all this have subsided, and the client quite literally puts his future in the hands of Maalik. Given that, Amin emphasizes to the new corporate president that it is the corporation president's responsibility to supply Maalik with accurate sales and payroll data to minimize the chances of being audited by the state or federal government. The new owner will become aware also of the very aggressive, although seemingly uneven, program of health and building inspections that the city of Chicago maintains, especially in gentrifying neighborhoods or in areas that for one reason or another are politically sensitive.

From the preceding description, it is undeniable that in dealing with government representatives, either in person or on paper, a good and quick command of English is essential, in addition to an understanding of both U.S. and Arab cultural patterns. When to use humor, when to be firm, and when to be conciliatory, as well as how one expresses these attitudes, are necessary aspects of this understanding. Although one cannot argue against a law, one may be able to argue debatable points of law successfully. Maalik did such a thing for a client who was having trouble obtaining a liquor license after having bought a store in a Chicago neighborhood whose residents firmly controlled who could and could not sell liquor in their ward. Maalik used sophisticated business practices to send out letters under the client's signature to the ward's alderman and church and community leaders detailing the store owner's character and commitment to the neighborhood, and conducted a mass petition mailing to area residents. The client won his case for a liquor license. The point is that here was a good and responsible man who needed the language brokering services of Maalik to achieve a goal that was eluding him for no other reason than he did not have the language and cultural resources to contend with a challenge mounted against him.

The work Maalik is doing over and above what accountants usually do results from the Arab immigrant's deficiency or perceived deficiency in English. Even if he speaks English well enough, it is often the case that he does not read it or does not read it well enough, having not had English in school but having picked it up in daily living. Frequently, having learned English this way, he has picked up the vernacular of the people he is most around. This may have a detrimental affect on him when dealing with government agencies. African Americans who use Black English vernacular (BEV) have a hard enough time in standard English environments (Fogel & Ehri, 2000). It is even worse for the Arab American who speaks BEV. It is not just that it is surprising coming from an Arab, but that it cultivates an air of distrust as to why he would be speaking a nonstandard English dialect that African Americans themselves often would not use in situations calling for standard English.

There is yet another stumbling block to effective communication for the Arab immigrant. The Arab immigrant is often reticent about divulging personal details to people not known to him, such as government agents or representatives. Amin, Sherif, and Talal, being Arab, invoke a more immediate trust. Being a professional who can help them yet understand the need for personalization in Arab business transactions fosters a trust that makes the giving of personal information a more natural chore for the Arab immigrant client.

Buying and Selling in the Economic and Linguistic Marketplace

While Amin is handling his new client, Sherif is with two other clients: an Arab client selling his dollar store to an enterprising Mexican American man. Cheaper than a lawyer and more trusted, Sherif draws up a bill of sale that will be typed on the computer to the formal and exact template that Maalik has created for just such a purpose: Mohammed (Mike) A. Ismael is selling to Felix (Sandy) Sandoval 100% of the shares of his dollar store, No Mas que Dollar, which is located in the Mexican Pilsen neighborhood. The three converse in English only because Sherif does not know Spanish. Mohammed, a Palestinian immigrant who has been in business in this Mexican neighborhood since coming to the United States a few years ago, speaks Spanish more fluently than English. Felix speaks both English and Spanish well, having immigrated to the United States as a preteen.

During the selling negotiations, Sherif answers Felix's questions about the legalities and tax obligations that govern Illinois businesses in Chicago. It is likely that if Felix has no accountant, he will keep the store with Maalik. This is actually the way most of the non-Arab clients of Maalik became Maalik's customers. Once all questions are answered and the bill of sale is signed by both parties, the buyer and seller shake hands with Sherif. *"Ma?a Salaama"* (Arabic for good-bye) is exchanged between Sherif and Mohammed and some English variant of good-bye between Sherif and Felix.

Awaiting Sherif is a Yemeni store owner, Naji, president of two different corporations: one a tavern located on the near North Side and the other a retail merchandise store located much further north in the city. Naji is an American citizen who has decided it is time now to bring his wife and six children, whom he sees in regular visits to his home in Yemen, to the United States as immigrants. Sherif pulls from his files of various immigration and naturalization forms downloaded from the INS site on the Internet in PDF format an I-864 affidavit of support, takes down current economic as well as biographic data from Naji, and hands the information to one of the clerical employees to type. Sherif will also translate or have one of the other Arabic speakers in the office translate Naji's marriage certificate and the birth certificates of his wife and six children from Arabic into English.

Maalik has created computerized forms for both birth and marriage certificates of most Arab countries. All preprinted information on the original

Arabic certificate is included and translated into English on the form so that it is just a simple matter of filling in the relevant names, places, and dates of the various parties involved in the birth or the marriage. Furthermore, because governments change their certificate formats over time and governments themselves change or are changed, there are multiple forms for most of the Middle East entities that must be translated. Within Israel, all certificates for Israel's Arab citizens are in Hebrew. In the West Bank, under Jordanian rule between 1948 and 1967, all certificates were issued in Arabic, whereas under Israeli rule between 1967 and 1994, both Israel and Jordan issued birth certificates: Jordanian certificates were in Arabic and matched whatever format was used in Jordan proper, and Israeli certificates were in Arabic and Hebrew, formatted especially for the West Bank Arabs. Before the 1994 formal establishment of the Palestinian National Authority on the West Bank, only Jordan issued marriage certificates and passports to West Bank Arab residents and, of course, these are in Arabic. The Palestinian National Authority now issues in Arabic its own documents for births, marriages, and travel. Morocco and Algeria, depending on the era, may have issued documents in French, Arabic, or both French and Arabic. Yemen's documents may be from either South Yemen or North Yemen before 1990, or from the united Yemen after that date. Naji requires for his wife and children three different formats for their birth certificates given the different times and government entities in which they happened to be born. However, his marriage certificate is from North Yemen because his marriage took place before the 1990 unification.

Maalik can turn around INS applications very quickly because of the availability of the forms on the Internet and the convenience of their computerized templates of the various certificates that need to be translated, which are saved and can be retrieved quickly if needed for some other purpose later. This form completion service by Maalik not only unburdens the petitioner from filling out forms in English, which he may not quite understand or fears he does not understand, but also relieves him of the onerous chore of trying to understand instructions on the forms, which are confusing enough for a native English speaker.

Naji must rush back to his store, so he will come back the next morning to go over the finished forms with Sherif to ensure that all the data are correct before he signs them and gives Sherif the fee for the work. Sherif will then mail the forms for Naji using the latest INS addresses downloaded from the Internet.

When Things Break, Call the Accountant

Both Sherif and Amin are now free of clients, at least for the time being. Amin continues to work on those corporate income taxes that are due on the 15th of the next month, and Sherif takes to sorting through a small laundry basket filled to overflowing with correspondence to Maalik's clients from the federal, state, and local governments. These envelopes and forms were given to Sherif or Samir during their visits to the clients. Many are as yet unopened. It will be Sherif's job to go through each piece of this correspondence and determine what action should be taken, if any. Although Maalik does the tax calculations, it is the client who is responsible for paying his taxes, and it is the client to whom the state sends all forms and correspondence. Sherif has Samir or Khadija file the forms for later reference.

The other correspondence may require a variety of actions, which the clients expect Maalik to handle. This may be a response to the state regarding a late tax payment or to a notice from the federal government that the client's personal income tax is incorrect for one reason or another and a deduction is being disallowed. Sherif finds a letter from City Hall informing business owners of a new city of Chicago litter tax on businesses. Sherif had heard rumors about this from other clients, so he will now need to call City Hall to inquire about the exact regulations of the new tax that the city has just instituted and then explain personally to each affected client what this means.

If the correspondence concerns a late tax payment, Sherif will check Maalik's file for the client to verify that the information there is correct and then contact the client and explain what the state is requesting. The client's response will determine whether Sherif will compose a letter for the client detailing why he should not be penalized in interest or fees for a late payment or write a letter making arrangements for payment of the tax and the penalties.

If the correspondence is a federal tax matter, it is most likely regarding a seemingly unwarranted deduction because of a problem with a discrepancy in the name of the taxpayer or a dependent and the social security number filed with that name. The IRS automatically matches social security numbers and names filed on tax returns with the social security numbers and names on file with the Social Security Administration database. Occasionally, it turns out to be no more than a one-digit mistake in the social security number entered on the tax form. More often than not, however, the problem arises either because of inconsistent transliteration of the name from the Arabic writing system to the Roman alphabet and/or because the difference in naming standards between Arab cultures and the U.S. government.

As detailed earlier in this chapter, there are multiple ways of writing an Arabic sound using the English alphabet. Consequently, depending on who is writing out his name, the immigrant may have his name written as Faisil on his social security card but as Feysul on his driver's license, which he gives to the accountant to copy on his (Faisil) income tax form. The IRS in cross-checking names and social security numbers on tax forms against those on the SSA database will then reject the name and social security number as invalid.

The problems caused by these spelling differences are compounded by the differences between how any Arab refers to himself by name and how a U.S. native refers to himself. Ask an Arab immigrant his name, and he will reply with only his first name. To clarify the name, he may add his second name, which is his father's given name, and his third name, which is his grandfather's given name. The family name is not regularly used in naming oneself. Therefore, children will be listed on the social security cards with their first, second, and possibly third names without a family name, but then be listed on the tax forms by their first and family names. A fiancee, although legally married on paper back home in a private ceremony, does not take the husband's name until after she has arrived in the States and has been formally married in a public celebration. This may take place after she has applied for her social security number in her maiden name. At tax time, the accountant dutifully fills out the tax return in her married name. The IRS will then write the taxpayer indicating that the return is being processed without one or more deductions because of the name and social security card discrepancy. Letters then must be written by Maalik to the IRS explaining the situation and usually including copies of the social security cards of the affected dependent to prove that an error was made and that the deduction is legitimate.

Maalik's accountants also act as liaisons between the client and the IRS when it is necessary to telephone the agency. The IRS will take calls only from the taxpayer involved, so the taxpayer will come to Maalik's office to call and then have Sherif or Amin form the proper English question to ask the IRS. The taxpayer will then repeat the response aloud so that Sherif or Amin can interpret the answer in Arabic for him. If an audit is performed on a federal corporate income tax return, it is Amin, an IRS-enrolled agent, who will personally represent his client before the IRS.

The most exacting function that Maalik performs for a client is to represent him to Illinois state sales and payroll tax auditors who, in attempting to increase state revenues, review the sales and payroll records of selected businesses in the hope of finding unrecorded, and therefore untaxed, sales or wages. A payroll audit is fairly insignificant and involves a short visit of an auditor to Maalik's office to review a client's payroll records. This usually involves, on the average, a small number of standardized forms for each two or three employees (no Maalik client has more than 15 employees).

The sales tax audit is much more complicated and involved. The auditors may spend 5 days reconciling the sales tax forms calculated by Maalik from the documents or numbers submitted to the accountants by the client with boxes of original invoices, bank statements, and register tapes that the client must bring to Maalik's office in order to justify the sales figures given to Maalik. Sherif or Amin will answer questions about these records in the stead of their client, who will be kept advised of the proceedings. When the auditor has completed the review, the auditor will make a judgment as to whether additional taxes are owed or not, and if so, how much. If the auditor determines that additional sales taxes are owed, he or she will allow the client, through Maalik, to accept or reject the judgment. If the client rejects it, he is brought in to present his appeal to the auditor's superiors. Amin and Sherif will fight aggressively but fairly to save their client every penny possible. They have thus earned the respect of the state auditors, as well as the trust of their clients. If a compromise cannot be reached or if the state is unwilling to compromise and the amount asked for is large enough, Maalik will suggest that the client hire a lawyer and appeal the judgment through the court system. If the client does so, Maalik will then work with the lawyer in preparing the case for the client.

THE ROAD TO THE FUTURE

It is 6:00 p.m. quitting time, and Amin has been in the office nearly 12 hours. Sherif has been working nearly 10 hours, either at clients' places of business or in Maalik's offices. Neither Amin nor Sherif bother to clear their desks before leaving because they will pick up immediately in the morning where they left off the night before. Just as Amin and Sherif leave, Talal arrives for the "second shift," which usually consists of doing translations of documents and filling out immigration forms for his Spanish- and

Arabic-speaking clients. Amin and Sherif give instructions to Talal to take business license renewals for clients downtown the next day to be processed by the state or the city.

While Amin will come directly to the office the next day to work on more corporate income taxes and manage the office, Sherif will be accompanying Yafai, a Yemeni immigrant, to a far western town outside Chicago to conduct business. As the Arab business community matures, especially in times of relative economic prosperity and opportunity, it will be drawn to ever more frequent and deeper contact with mainstream U.S. society, as it struggles at the same time to reconcile the various mores and norms of the United States. with the mores and norms of the various Arab cultures that comprise its background. One way this will be played out is seen in the experience that Sherif and his client Yafai will encounter in looking for business opportunities increasingly distant from the Chicago metropolitan area. Sherif and Yafai will meet with small-town officials considerably less sophisticated and less cosmopolitan than officials in Chicago or its suburbs to ask them to grant Yafai a license to run a liquor store in that town. Sherif, with his command of English, characterized by an Arab accent mitigated by a Midwestern U.S. English accent and his knowledge of both American and Arabic ways of speaking, will try to smooth Yafai's dealings with town officials, who have had little or no personal contact with minorities, let alone Arabs, and have previously been suspicious and wary of Yafai's request. Sherif has done this type of liaison duty before and realizes how even a humorous remark in Arabic, literally translated into English and used to break the ice by bringing a more personal aspect into the conversation, can backfire with Americans and result in an enmity that is difficult to overcome. Thus, Sherif's consul will be helpful in two ways. It will instruct Yafai in U.S. ways of speaking and ensure a greater chance of obtaining his goal.

A successful outcome in any one of Maalik's efforts, of course, is not ensured. The small town council may deny a liquor license. An auditor may refuse to compromise. The city inspector may refuse to renew a business license because the owner of the building in which the store is located did not pay his water bill, despite the pleadings of Sherif on behalf of the store that the business rents only from the owner and is not responsible for the water payments. The client nevertheless knows that the issue of a language barrier has been minimized, and that his request, if not successful, has at least been fully understood.

The 1998 AAAN Needs Assessment Report recognizes the need for informal community support, as well as formal institutional support for the language and cultural needs of Arab immigrants in Chicago. It also recognizes that this must reach outside the extended family if the members of the Arab immigrant community are to thrive and work successfully with non-Arab Americans. Through Maalik, the Arab immigrant business community that comprises Maalik's client base is provided with an unofficial support mechanism for its language and cultural needs while its primary economic requirements are also being met. The traditional Arab support system made up of the extended family in-group has in Maalik's small business community been replaced by a wider in-group that is bound not by blood, but by a common language and culture in a shared drive for economic prosperity.

REFERENCES

Abu-Laban, B., & Abu-Laban, S. (1999). Arab–Canadian youth in immigrant family life. In M. Suleiman (Ed.), *Arabs in America: Building a new future* (pp. 140–153). Philadelphia,PA: Temple University Press.

Abu-Lughod, L. (1986). *Veiled sentiments: Honor and poetry in a Bedouin society.* Berkeley, CA: University of California Press.

Ajami, F. (1992). *The Arab predicament.* Cambridge, UK: Cambridge University Press.

Ajrouch, K. (1999). Family and ethnic identity in an Arab American community. In M. Suleiman (Ed.), *Arabs in America: Building a new future* (pp. 129–139). Philadelphia, PA: Temple University Press.

Altoma, S. J. (1969). *The problem of diglossia in Arabic: A comparative study of classical and Iraqi Arabic.* Cambridge, MA: Center for Middle Eastern Studies, Harvard University Press.

Arab American Action Network. (1998). *Needs assessment report.* Chicago: AAAN.

Aswad, B. (1974). *Arabic-speaking communities in American cities.* New York: Center for Migration Studies of New York and the Association of Arab–American University Graduates.

Aswad, B. (1999). Attitudes of Arab immigrants toward welfare. In M. Suleiman (Ed.), *Arabs in America: Building a new future* (pp. 177–191). Philadelphia, PA: Temple University Press.

Barakat, H. (1993). *The Arab world: Society, culture, and state.* Berkeley, CA: University of California Press.

Cainkar, L. (1999). Ethnic safety net among Arab immigrants in Chicago. In M. Suleiman (Ed.), *Arabs in America: Building a new future* (pp. 192–206). Philadelphia, PA: Temple University Press.

Choueiri, Y. (2000). *Arab nationalism: A history.* Oxford, UK: Blackwell Publishers.

Duranti, A. (1997). *Linguistic anthropology.* Cambridge, UK: Cambridge University Press.

Farr, M. (2000). "A mi no me manda nadie." Individualism and identity in Mexican ranchero speech. *Pragmatics, 10,* 61–85.

Fogel, H., & Ehri, L. C. (2000). Teaching elementary school students who speak Black English vernacular to write in standard English: The effects of dialect transformation practice. *Contemporary Educational Psychology, 25,* 212–235.

Hagopian, E. C., & Paden, A. (1969). *The Arab–Americans: Studies in assimilation*. Wilmette, IL: Median University Press International.

Hamady, S. (1960). *Temperament and character of the Arabs*. New York: Twayne Publishers.

Laffin, J. (1975). *The Arab mind considered: A need for understanding*. New York: Taplinger.

Mauss, M. (1925/1990). *The gift* (W. D. Halls, Trans.). New York: Norton.

McCarus, E. (1994). Introduction. In E. McCarus (Ed.), *The development of Arab American identity* (pp. 1–7), Ann Arbor, MI: University of Michigan Press.

Said, E. (1979). *Orientalism*. New York: Vintage Books.

Seikaly, M. (1999). Attachment and identity. In M. Suleiman (Ed.), *Arabs in America: Building a new future* (pp. 25–38). Philadelphia, PA: Temple University Press.

Shouby, E. (1970). The influence of the Arabic language on the psychology of the Arabs. In A. Lutfiyya & C. Churchill (Eds.), *Readings in Arab Middle Eastern societies and cultures.* (pp. 688–703). The Hague, the Netherlands: Mouton.

Suleiman, M. (1999). Introduction: The Arab immigrant experience. In M. Suleiman (Ed.) *Arabs in America: Building a new future* (pp. 1–21). Philadelphia, PA: Temple University Press.

Triandis, H. C. (1972). *The analysis of subjective culture*. New York: Wiley-Interscience.

Viorst, M. (1994). *Sandcastles: The Arabs in search of the modern world*. New York: Alfred A. Knopf.

Coleson landstiger i Göteborg.

9

They Did Not Forget Their Swedish: Class Markers in the Swedish American Community

Carl Isaacson
Sterling College

Between 1870 and 1910, Chicago became the second largest Swedish city in the world. Several neighborhoods were dominated by Swedes, and the Swedish language was the language of the streets and commerce in large parts of "Swedetown" centered around Chicago and Wells, to the south in Englewood, further north in Lakeview, in Albany Park, and in Andersonville near Clark and Foster (Department of Development and Planning, City of Chicago, 1976, p. 28). The language of these American city streets, however, was not the pure Swedish of the Royal Academy, nor the provincial dialects of the immigrants' home villages. It was a blended speech, mixing provincial or regional dialects, "proper" Swedish and American English, which came to be known as American Swedish.

As a spoken language, American Swedish transcended class boundaries. Both educated and uneducated Swedish Americans used it. One example of the speech was cited by Arthur Landfors, in a 1974 study of the phenomenon. In that article he used the American Swedish phrase *i storet och bajat en svetter*, [in the store and bought a sweater] as an example of a poor use of the dialect. A more educated Swede, Landfors (1974) explained, would have used the Swedish Americanism *storet* instead of the proper Swedish *handel* and the American sounded *svetter* (roughly pronounced the same as "sweater") instead of the proper *ylletröja*. But using *bajat* (which sounds much like "buy it") clearly marked the speaker as uneducated (p. 4).

This little phrase is typical of the type of blends used by the Swedish Americans. It substitutes English words, "store," "buy," and "sweater," continues to use Swedish conjunctions and articles (*en*, [a], *i*, [in], and *och*, [and]), but pronounces and inflects the English in Swedish (*storet*, definite of store, replaces the proper Swedish words *handel* or *affär; bajat*, the past perfect of *baj*, pronounced "buy," replaces *handlade* or *köpte*; and *svetter* pronounced "sweater," replaces the Swedish *tröja*). However, in addition to blending English and Swedish, these immigrants came speaking provincial dialects, which were also blended into American Swedish until the distinctions among dialects began to disappear on the American soil.

Although as noted, American Swedish was a "common" language of the immigrant, it was nevertheless used as a class distinction. Landfors (1974), for example, asserted that he spoke "cultivated" American Swedish, implying that there were many whose American Swedish was not. The woman who spoke of going to the store and buying a svetter was judged by others as being of lower class origins. The negative judgment, argued Landfors (1974), could be accounted for by cultural and educational differences. "[T]he lady with the more cultivated Swedish-American [sic] had arrived in 1908 and had had a better education than most Swedes. The other lady had arrived here at the beginning of the 1890s and her schooling was very limited" (p. 7). The way in which American Swedish was spoken was seen as a class and culture marker in the living community.

Even more so, American Swedish was used as a literary device to portray the lower classes, the uneducated and uncultured. Swedes educated through our high school level in Sweden may indeed have used American Swedish as their daily language, but they saw it as an inferior means of expression,as compared with the culturally rich and ennobling language of the motherland. This meant that it rarely saw use in the "serious" literature of the Swedish American community. Although much of what this public read was either imported or devotional in nature, a large number of Swedes in America wrote for a Swedish-speaking audience. Almost all of that literary production, which included poems, essays, novellas and the like, was written in "proper" Swedish.

The association of American Swedish with the "lower" classes also meant that the intellectual elite of the community battled, unsuccessfully, against the use of this blended speech and for the preservation of "proper" Swedish. This battle should be seen in the context of a larger attempt to improve the cultural life of their countrymen in America. From the 1890s through the 1920s, Swedish language publications emanating from Chicago included a large portion of "fine" literature, books of etiquette, cookbooks, "letter forms," high-minded poetry from both Sweden and America, and essays asserting that the blended speech was "gibberish," marking the speaker as an uneducated servant.[1]

The blended speech had few advocates willing to write in the language or speak on its behalf. Among them was Kansas colorist and painter Gustav Malm. In his novel *Charli Johnson Svensk Amerikan* [Charlie Johnson Swedish American] (1909) and his play *Här Ute* [Out Here] (1919), he argued for common sense in "the language question." Malm understood that "proper" Swedish was not the mother tongue of the majority of the immigrants. His characters demonstrate with a sad realism that Swedish could never become the "language of the heart" for the American-born generation.

Yet, even without advocates, the habit of using blended speech as the language of daily commerce persisted well past midcentury. It was still in common use when Folke Hedblom in the 1960s and Lennart and Lilly Setterdahl in the 1970s conducted their interviews of Swedish-born Americans. Glimpses of the language can be found in some correspondence between America and Sweden, just as dialectal Swedish was common in the correspondence from Sweden to America. Today, the language has disappeared. Whereas today's Swedish, even in Sweden, is filled with English loan words, many of which are parallel to the blended American Swedish, Swedish Americans are largely just English speakers.

This study of the literary expressions of blended speech and the battles to preserve proper Swedish in America hopes to show that this particular ethnic community, now solidly middle class, was as richly divided as American society itself. Its language, more than geographic location, club affiliation, or economic status, provides the researcher with clues as to how the classes in Swedish America saw themselves, experienced the new world, and rose from peasant origins to middle class success in America.

LITERARY EXPRESSIONS OF AMERICAN SWEDISH

There were few Swedish Americans who dared write the language they spoke. Because it was considered by journalists and educators, the cultured newcomers, and the occasional visitor to be "*rotvälska*" or gibberish, an ugly language fit only for the servant class, it was avoided in print. Anna Olsson of Lindsborg, Kansas, and her contemporary, Gustaf Malm, also of Lindsborg, knew the blended speech well and attempted to reproduce it faithfully in their novels and plays. Swedish writer Henning Berger, after a brief Chicago residence in the 1890s, used few examples of it in his novels and short stories. By and large, Berger's characters speak a literary Swedish, including the Irish cops and the African American servants (Berger, 1901, 1906). Only drunks or barkeepers use blended speech, occasionally blending not only English but also German with Swedish. The broadest use of American Swedish, and according to the estimate of journalist Ernst Skarstedt (1930), one of the most faithful reproductions of the speech, is in Frithiof Colling's two short comic novels.[2] (Collings also wrote under the pseudonym G. Carlson.)

To tell the tale of a Swedish American returning home to Sweden after 13 years in Minnesota, *Mister Colesons Sverigeresa* [Mister Coleson's Trip to Sweden], Colling needed a comic language. He chose American Swedish. The daily speech of most of his countrymen in America worked well to create the sense of linguistic misunderstanding that is the heart of this short novel. The opening of the story sets the tone for the whole book. In American Swedish it sounds like this:

> *Jag filade illa. Tiderna voro dåliga. Vintern hade varit kall och min flicka hade också blivit kall och jag började längta hem till Sveriget. Pengar hade jag plenty, ty jag hade arbetat och sävat här i tretton år ....*(p. 1)[3]

A literal translation of the passage runs as follows:

> I felt ill. The times were bad. The winter had been cold and my girl had also become cold and I began to long to go home to Sweden. I had plenty of money since I had worked and saved here for thirteen years ....

But, if we want to preserve the comic flavor of Colling's work, we would have to translate it into "Swinglish," the exaggerated comic dialect of Jorgy Jorgesson or Minnesota's Boone and Ericson:

> I vas feelin' pretty blue. Da times dey vas mighty bad. Da vinter vas kolt and my girl she vas gettin' kolt too. So I vas lookin' pretty hard at goin' back te Sveden. I had me plenty money 'cause I'd been savin' it up fer da last terteen years I been verkin here, yah.

Incorporating elements from the primary language into the secondary language, as Colling did, using *filade* for "feel" instead of the proper Swedish *mådde,* and *sävat* for "saved" instead of the Swedish *sparade,* then code switching to English with "plenty," created the same kind of comic misunderstanding that one gets in any linguistically based joke. But it also provoked a laughter of recognition. The Swedish American would hear him- herself making the transition from the "mother tongue" to English.

Colling was not content to generate all of his comedy through linguistic misunderstanding. His is also a social comedy of class misunderstanding. Two episodes in the novel portray the class structure of Sweden at the turn of the century: Coleson's experience returning home and his trip to Stockholm.

Shortly after leaving the steamship in Gothenburg, Coleson and his Swedish American traveling companion, Miss Peterson, travel inland by train. On the journey, tiring of the slow train travel, the pair step off at the station in Torskerum to get some *exersejs* [exercise]. Not heeding the station inspector's call, they nearly miss the train, but hop onto the rear platform on the last car. Unable to enter the car, they ride to Snäsesjö (a fictional town name) on the platform, where they are told that they have broken the rules and cannot continue on this train. They are forced to stay the night in this little town. The hotel "clerk," actually a maid, asks if "the gentleman" and "the lady," will have a room with one bed or two. Coleson upbraids her for assuming that they are married, or that they are living together without marriage, and insists: "You don't need to insult the lady, for she is a decent girl and we are not married." The maid breaks into tears, not because she has been scolded, but because Coleson has resorted to the second person familiar "du" in his direct address:

> "What has me upset is that you've called me 'du,' when all the best gentlemen call me 'Miss,'" she said, and began to pout.

> I was silent, since I was in a bad humor, but I thought, "This is some mischief. Have all the serving girls become 'Miss' while I've been away?" (Carlson, G. 1908, p. 16)

Coleson looks like a gentleman, a member of at least the middle class. His peasant origins are made clear to the reader when he finally arrives at his home. He uses his apparent social status and his fine American-made clothing to enter the home unrecognized by his father. Asking to rent a room, even naming the room he wants—the little attic room above the family space—he is met with rejection. That room, his father tells him, smells of tanning sheepskin and sauerkraut. His offered of payment of five crowns does not move his father, who is angered at the perceived arrogance of this "fine gentleman" who "thinks he's too good to take off his hat when he comes into a stranger's cottage." Unable to bear the shame any longer, Coleson reveals his true identity: "Don't you recognize me, I'm your son Jonas, come home from America" (p. 21). Father will agree that this is his son only if he is shown the sign of peasant life: a missing toe lost as the boy was learning to chop firewood. When Coleson reveals that he lacks that toe, the prodigal is welcomed home.

Again, Colling uses class issues, particularly the clearly defined manner in which the overclass would show respect for the underclass, as a source of comedy. Because Coleson looks like a member of the overclass, but is in fact a member of the underclass, his true identity can be shown only via a hidden sign. In the scenes with his family Coleson's new "class" is a source of pride, and Jonas is seen in a positive light. With the rest of the village, Coleson is exposed as one who does not understand the responsibilities of wealth.

At a party celebrating the engagement of two members of the peasantry who have attained some class status, the "juryman's" daughter and the "squire shop keeper" (*handlesmanpatron*, indicates one of substance, worth, and status), Coleson is feted more than the bride and groom to be. Twice during the party he is approached for a small loan. The first time, approached by a young student, Coleson responds:

> "Don't try with me," as Anna Stina says. "First of all, I never do business [*bissniss*] with those who treat me [*tritar*]. Second, I never loan money without security. Third, I never loan money to any single person.

> "That is a miserable religion you have. You must have learnt that in America," said the student.

> "I sure have, and that's why I don't loan money to young dudes [*herradudar*] and other loafers [*låfare*], even though I now have several thousand in the pocketbook." (p. 24)

Coleson meets the onslaught of beggars with Yankee ingenuity, no sense of the obligations of wealth, and a healthy dose of American Swedish. (*Bissniss, tritar, herradudar,* and *låfer* will not be found in any Swedish lexicon. They are examples of American words inflected as Swedish verbs and nouns.) Coleson remains a part of the Swedish American peasant class, marked by both his habits and his language. If the confusion of his class status is apparent in his hometown, it becomes even more evident when he arrives at Stockholm.

There he checks into a big and, he presumes, expensive hotel. He is a bit disconcerted by the fact that his hotel room has no lock on the door. He has heard that there are many bad characters in Stockholm:

> So I did what I usually do in American hotels in the poorer quarters: I stuffed my pocketbook and gold watch and revolver under my pillow and then went to sleep. (p. 35)

Coleson awakens early in the morning, the sun streaming through the hotel windows. He recalls that sunrise in Stockholm is considerably earlier than in Minnesota, and just as he is about to fall back asleep, hears "someone who carefully turned the door handle." He feigns sleep, watching as the intruder enters, rummages through his pockets, removes a tobacco plug and corn cob pipe, and then proceeds to make off with his clothing and shoes. Coleson sits upright in the bed, aims the pistol at the supposed "thief" and shouts out, "Up with your hands! Otherwise I'll kill [*killar*] you, you son-of-a-gun [*sönnaförgunn*]!" (p. 35).

The "thief" quickly escapes, but returns a few minutes later with two police, who want to arrest Coleson. The comedy becomes both class and language oriented. Coleson has mistaken a concierge for a thief. When asked to surrender his pistol, he responds in English, "What for," which becomes a pun on the Swedish word *får*, meaning "sheep." The police threaten to arrest him for attempting to shoot the hotel employee. Discovering that Coleson is simply confused by the common practice of better hotels, one of the policemen asks, "Haven't you ever stayed in a better hotel before?" (p. 36). America's wealth has moved Coleson out of the economic "underclass," but has not taught him how to behave in the social "overclass."

Coleson's experience with class issues was not uncommon among Swedish Americans. They were by and large of peasant origins, and had little use for matters of hygiene and manners. To help raise the lower classes, the guardians of the community published a number of helpful manuals. One favorite genre was the cookbook. Another included books of household advice on "scientific" and "enlightened" methods of child rearing and housekeeping. A third was the *Brefställare* or "Letter Writer," which instructed the new immigrant in the proper forms of address, and in particular types of letters and correspondence, in both Swedish and English.

The 1883 Engberg and Holmberg's *Fullständigaste Engelsk-Svenska Brefställaren för Svenska Folket i Amerika* [Most Complete English Swedish Letter Writer for the Swedish People in America], published in Chicago, offered a short course in English weights and measures, bookkeeping, proper English pronunciation, and proper Swedish spelling, in addition to its letter forms.

The forms themselves are given in English and Swedish on facing pages. They are remarkable for their formality. A letter from a suitor to a woman whom he has recently met, and now wishes to ask to marry him, reads like something out of Oscar Wilde's upper class London society:

1. A respectable citizen asks the hand of a young lady

Dear Miss M_____:

Scarcely had I the pleasure of becoming acquainted with you when I felt the most ardent desire of being united to you for life. Should your heart be still disengaged, and you feel that you can return the affection that I entertain for you, you would make me the happiest man on earth. In thus asking for your hand I consider it my duty to inform you of my circumstances. I have a complete establishment, and my fortune is such that I can offer you a life free from the usual cares of existence. (p. 94)

The Swedish is an exact translation of the English, punctuated as the English version. This is not the sort of letter one reads passing among the Swedish Americans. Those letters tended to be much less formal, and were punctuated quite eccentrically, if at all. Moreover, Swedish syntax is far different from that of English, and far more regular than English.[4] The advocacy of an Americanized style in letter writing should be seen as another step in the process of moving the peasant-class Swede into "respectable" society. The old writing habits and styles, the crude run-on sentence, and the inelegant expression of circumstances including commentary on the weather was to be replaced by a refined American style, the style of the "upper crust" of Chicago society.

In addition to offering "letter forms," the elite also attempted to raise their countrymen through the teaching of etiquette. In 1911 the Swedish newspaper *Hemlandet* [The Homeland] gave the *Praktisk Handbook för Svenskarne i Amerika* [A Practical Handbook for the Swedes in America] as its annual premium to subscribers. Included in this book was a short course in the rules of etiquette. This section begins, "Courtesy is natural for elevated sensibilities ..." (p. 352). Coleson's sensibilities are not elevated. They are the common sensibilities of the rising middle class, driven by money and uncorrected by "higher" mores and customs. Coleson, with his American Swedish language and peasant manners is the epitome of the Chicago Swedish American at the apex of that community's existence.

Coleson remains little better than a clown. Colling's good natured fun with his title character does not disguise the fact that he judges Coleson and those like him fairly harshly. A much gentler treatment of the Swedish American and his American Swedish is found in the two works of Gustav Malm: his novel *Charli Johnson, Svensk-Amerikan* and his play *Där Ute*. In both books, the speaker of American Swedish is portrayed as somewhat naive, but good-hearted and hardworking. In Malm's characterization, one has the sense of the Jeffersonian nobility of the farmer statesman. The settlers on the plains of Kansas and Nebraska may speak an odd blend of Swedish and English, and there are the venial among them, but the country is also capable of bringing out the best in the newcomer.

The hero of Malm's novel, Charli Johnson, is a newcomer from Sweden. He finds a home, working as a hired hand, on the Månson farm in Nebraska. Whereas Charli speaks a proper Swedish, the family speaks blended American Swedish. Malm develops a love interest between Charli and the farmer's daughter, Änni. Wanting to be more Swedish, Änni attempts to improve her command of the language. While on a visit with relatives in Iowa, she writes a letter home to Charli to demonstrate her new language skills. Charli reads the letter, and listens to Mother Lina's commentary on her daughter's ability. In Lina's speech we see a representation of Swedish dialect writing, as well as the American Swedish blend.

> *Väl, ho va allti den bäste i klassen i den svenske skolen, å dä kan en se, ho skrifver ju some en präst, tösa, om ja nu ska säjat, fast ja ä mor åt na. Dä va många på våra trakter där hemma som inte skref ett dugg bätter, ja många skref inte hällta så bra, och ho kan engelska möe bätter. Väl, dä som ja säjer, detta ä ett välsignadt köntri, för en kan få bå edikäsjen och annat här. Skrif nu å ge na en fin änser, och säj åt na att ho behöfvericke skämmas för ho ä soid.*

> [Well, she was always the best in the class in the Swedish school, and that anyone can see. She writes like a clergyman, the dear girl, if I can say that even though I'm her mother. There were many in our part of the country back home who didn't write one whit better; yes, and many didn't write half as well, and she knows English much better. Well, it's like I say, this is a blessed country where one can get an education and anything else. Write her now and give a fine answer, and tell her that she doesn't need to be ashamed of being a Swede.] (Malm, 1909, p. 122)

Mother Lina inserts a number of English loan words, such as country, (*köntri*, approximately our pronunciation of "country") and education (*edikäsjen*, pronounced "edication") into her speech. She also substitutes the English *bätter* (which approximates the English pronunciation "better") for closely related Swedish *bättre*. These are all representations of American Swedish. But just as interesting is Malm's use of the conventions of representation of Swedish dialects. For example, the Swedish verb "to be" [*är*] is consistently represented in a common spoken form "ä"; the definite article *det* becomes *dä;* whereas the conjunction "and", [*och*] is represented by "å".

By the time Malm wrote this book (published in Chicago in 1909), the conventions of peasant dialect in Swedish literature were already 60 years old. Those conventions begin with F. A. Dahlgren's folk play *Värmländingarna* [The People of Värmland], premiering in Stockholm in 1846. Common peasant speech throughout Sweden tended to drop final consonants, to exchange a short "e" (pronounced as in the American slang for ate, "et") for the closely related *ä* sound (as in the English "set"), and generally to elide articulations thought proper by the Swedish Academy. Mother Lina's speech, even when it approaches "proper" Swedish, marks her therefore as a member of the Swedish peasant class. In America, she has become a solid middle-class farmer's wife, but she has never changed the speech habits of her childhood.

Charli, looking at the same letter from Änni, is not nearly as sure of Änni's brilliance in Swedish as her mother. Although he does not comment on it for Lina, his thoughts issue in a judgment of the girl's linguistic ability. He reads the letter several times and then comes to the conclusion: "The spelling went well enough, but the form …. It was clear that she thought in English and translated the thought to Swedish. Yes, English was her mother tongue, the language of her heart, and who could reproach her for that" (p. 122).

That phrase, "the language of the heart," or *hjärtespråket* recurs as a theme in Malm's novel, as well as in Swedish American arguments for preserving the linguistic peculiarities of the community.

In the novel, this concept receives two clarifications from Malm's mouthpiece, Mr. Wård.[5] Wård, considered by many in the community to be a bit eccentric, if not mad, keeps himself apart from most of his fellow Swedish Americans. He is something of an intellectual, a widower, and a lover of literature, art, and most important, conversation. Malm's puts Charli into Wård's small circle of friends. Charli takes his concerns about the preservation of Swedish in America, his longing for culture, and his desire to return home to Wård. From Wård he receives sage advice, and most important for Charli, the intellectual stimulation he needs to mature. It is Wård who clarifies the concept of "the language of the heart." After Charli shows Änni's letter to him, Wård advises, "Every human being has his own dear mother tongue, and one loves it as one loves parents and as one loves his native land" (p. 125).

Later in the novel Wård adds further clarification. Reviewing Charli's Swedish Christmas program with the church's youth Wård remarks:

> The songs went remarkably, and you have succeeded well, Charli, but you have expected too much of your singers. How can you, for example, want them to sing with feeling "hear the wind sighing in the forest" who've never seen a Swedish forest, much less heard it sigh? Or how do you think that they would be able to sing about Sweden as freedom's birthplace on earth when they have learned from their childhood that America is the only free land in the world? (p. 171)

The language of the heart, in other words, is the language in which the deepest thoughts, feelings, and aspirations of a life are expressed. It is a language of prayer and piety. It is a language loved as one loves parents. It is not simply a matter of the words one knows, but the culture in which one has learned to know those things. This linkage between language and culture was common among the Swedish language preservationists as well. A Swedish born Swede was assumed to have a special feeling for the Swedish natural environment. That Swede believed that no other forest sighs quite the way a Swedish forest sighs.

The experience of nature, of course, is quite different for the peasant and farming class than for the intellectual and leisure class. Malm's Mr. Wård, with his feeling for nature, does illuminate a facet of Swedish self-consciousness. From the classic period onward, the poets have long sung the glories of the Swedish landscape. For the farmers, American Swedish, a practical language, probably better expresses their relationship to the land.

This is not to say that the speakers of American Swedish were without culture and the desire to understand the finer points of literature and music. Contrary to Colling's view of the Swedish American, Malm makes it his point to demonstrate that culture and intelligence remain alive in the new world. Charli makes that discovery while in Lindsborg, Kansas, for the annual performance of Handel's *Messiah* at Bethany College.

In the Anderson home, (Mrs. Månson's relatives), Charli is schooled on the finer points of the oratorio by an American Swedish–speaking farmer. For three pages, using very little American Swedish, Malm allows this farmer to explain the sensibilities needed to properly hear *Messiah* sung. When Anderson discusses farm or family life, he falls back into the blended speech. But here he is as one inspired, who can express the longings of his heart and mind only in the language of the heart.

Malm uses a postperformance episode to underscore his point that many Swedes have a mistaken impression of Swedish Americans. The picture painted in *Mister Coleson* of the rich but boorish American cousin worked as a literary device because the image had already assumed mythic proportions in Sweden. On the train back to Nebraska, Charli is given opportunity to critique the existing Swedish image of the Swedish American.

Seated behind Charli and Änni on the train are two Swedish visitors. One is a short, Swedish gentleman scholar who has come to America to study the life of the Swedish American. Next to him is a "fat, red-faced gentleman, whose whole exterior spread the rumor that he was a bit of a broken down Swede." These two Swedish critics fall into a conversation, which exhibits their general low regard for the cultural achievements of the Swedish Americans. In America, culture has become so debased that the fat, broken-down Swede has been denied work, thought of as a beggar, and treated despicably by his social inferiors. The scholar asks, "Why not write home?"

> "Write home! Oh yes! ... No thank you, but it feels good now and again to meet a real Swede and speak the pure language."
>
> "But why not write a long, realistic description of these experiences, that could of course warn others."
>
> "Only a few of the better class of Swedes have come here, though it would feel a little less tedious to have another poor devil. The others no power in the world can stop, and as long as compulsory defense service becomes heavier every year, no newspaper article is going to help. The rest who come here, they look as if they can endure anything. They've been cut and polished into Philistines." (p. 229)

Charli can stand no more. He lashes out at the two critics, informing them that the Swedes they so lightly dismiss have made a garden out of a land recently teeming with buffalo. They are not, he says, stableboys and housemaids, but heroes. What's more, the art these two dismiss so lightly is of the finest quality, and freely available to the sons of Sweden's lowest peasant class.

You forget, my good gentlemen, that there were on that platform last night those who studied their art, not only in Stockholm but also in Berlin and Paris, and you forget that that art which you and yours ought to have a boundless respect for, is free—free even for these sons of peasants and farmers. I had the honor, my fine gentlemen, the night before last, to be enlightened by an unschooled farmer whose deep learning one finds only among specialists, and the question concerned nothing more or less than just this subject: music. (p. 233)

Malm's Charli Johnson is on his way to becoming an apologist for the Swedish American community, and likely a speaker of American Swedish. At the novel's end, he has married Änni, settled on his own farm, and become a respected member of the immigrant community. Within the context of the novel, however, we do not encounter the major shift in language habit represented by Malm as dialectal speech.

The Scandinavian languages are particularly suitable for literary representations of dialect, because they are almost entirely phonetic. Nearly every consonant and vowel is meant to be vocalized. The conventions Malm used to portray both American Swedish and dialect speech were already well established by the turn of the 20th century.

These conventions found popular voice in the work of Dahlgren, and poets such as Gustav Fröding (1860–1911) and Nils Ferlin, (1898–1960). Yet, among the Swedish Americans the most influential of the Swedish writers to give literary voice to the peasant must be Albert Engström. Although Dahlgren's play was performed more often in Chicago than any other Swedish language play, and although Fröding remains a favorite of the Swedish poetry-reading populace, it was Engström who was best known. Much of that exposure came through reproductions of his work in the annual almanacs of the Dalkullan Company.

Steered by Andrew Löfström, the North Clark Street concern produced these annual volumes from 1898 well into the 1940s. These almanacs included a generous helping of jokes, many of which were stolen from Engström. Engström's representations of peasant life, in both word and drawing, also filled many pages in Dalkullan's popular joke books, *Bland Kolingar och Kogubbar* [Among the Charcoalers and Cowherds] (Löfström, 1908). Issued in two volumes, the 1908 first volume was still on sale through Dalkullan's store and by mail order at the Captain's death in 1935.

Typical of the joke/drawing combination is *Han kände till krutet.* [He knew where the gunpowder was]. Confronted by a beggar calling at her door, a lone wife attempts to chase him away, threatening him with her husband's power if he does not leave. The punchline, delivered by the bum, reads, "Ja, när en karlstackare ä' gift me' en så'n som frun, så ä' han aldri' hemma" [When a poor guy's got a wife like you, he's never home]. Again, we see the elided final consonant of peasant speech, and this time we also note missing median consonants in "så'n," an abbreviation of "sådan." In case we have not already understood that this is peasant speech, Engström includes a drawing of the encounter. On the right we see a properly dressed, stern, and rather plump middle-aged Swedish housewife. As a sign of her class status she has a Pekinese pup at her side. To the left of the lady and the dog stands the bum, his chest thrust forward, a battered hat tilted indifferently on his head, and a drunken grin on his lips. The class distinction is carried by both the words and the images. He looks and sounds like a peasant (Löfström, 1908, p. 152).

American Swedish as a literary language resembled the literary expressions of peasant life in Sweden. In both places nonstandard Swedish was given a phonetic spelling. For example, the spelling *seja* (to say) was substituted for the correct *säga*, making the spelling fit the pronunciation. Other common words spelled the way the peasant class used them include such things as *mej* for *mig* [me], *te* for *till* [to], and so forth. The change in spelling was dictated in both the dialect writers of Sweden and the American Swedish representation of speech habits by the phonetics of Swedish spelling. Unlike English, Swedish sounds out every letter, although particular consonant and vowel combinations will change the value of the sounds.

The point is that there were by the 1890s well-established conventions for the representation of regional variations in pronunciation. It was these conventions that allowed authors such as Malm to spell education "edikäsjen" with a reasonable certainty that a Swedish reader either in America or Sweden would be able to understand exactly how the Swedish American actually spoke. Because in the literature of the time, these regional variations were always put into the mouths of peasants, a reader would always connect nonstandard pronunciation with peasant life.

Even in sympathetic portrayals such as Malm's, all of the characters represented as speaking nonstandard Swedish are drawn from the lower strata of society. In most Swedish American literature, they are comic figures, just as most of literary peasants were in Sweden. They are a joke at home in America and at home in Sweden. It is no wonder that the more educated members of the community sought to remove this habit of speaking "ugly gibberish."

The battle between the preservers of proper Swedish and the speakers of American Swedish raged almost as long as the existence of the language in America. Ultimately, the correctors of the common folks lost in their efforts to preserve proper Swedish in America, in fact to preserve any Swedish as the language of daily life.

THE PROTECTORS OF PROPER SPEECH

The attempt to convince Swedish Americans to speak "proper" Swedish rather than American Swedish must be seen in the context of the attempt to preserve the use of the Swedish language in America, and to raise the cultural tastes of the population generally. In this struggle the newspapers, church schools, and annual literary collections were the primary written tools. In addition, the children's club movement, begun with the founding of Vårblomman, [Spring Flowers] promoted the Swedish language and culture through teaching the second-generation children.

These attempts to raise the culture of the working-class Swedish American reveal the depth of division in this supposed homogeneous ethnic group. There was a clearly identifiable, educated "elite," who decided what would be good for the "working class" and attempted to give the workers what they ought to have. Early attempts to raise cultural aspirations include the literary periodical, *När och Fjärran* [Near and Far], published from 1871 to 1872 by Johan Enander, editor of the Swedish language weekly, *Hemlandet* [The Home Land]. More successful were the annuals, the *Kalender*, annual anthologies of poetry, prose, fiction, and nonfiction, much of it religious and patriotic. The authors were both Swedish Americans and Swedes in Sweden. All the literature was of the finest, most proper Swedish.

Perhaps most successful in disseminating a love of fine literature and modeling the correct use of the mother tongue were the premiums given to subscribers by the Swedish language press. These often substantial books were really an accident of history, an attempt by publisher Alexander K. Johnson to increase subscribers to his Chicago-based newspaper, *Kuriren* [The Courier]. By the turn of the century each of the major papers offered subscribers an annual volume, including histories of the United States and Sweden and the Spanish American War, a view of the 1898 Swedish exposition, biographies of Sweden's King Oscar II and William

McKinley, and literary works from both Sweden and America. Among the popular literary volumes were a Swedish translation of *Uncle Tom's Cabin*, August Strindberg's quasi-historical study of *The Swedish People*, stories by Sigurd (Alfred Hedenstierna [1852–1906]), Esias Tegnér's *Frithiofs Saga*, and Zacharias Topelius' popular stories *Fältskärns Berättelser* [The Army Surgeon's Stories]. This multivolumed work was reissued several times during the peak years of Swedish publishing in Chicago.

These works of national romanticism gave a sense of importance to the homeland of Swedes, for which many continued to long, as manifested in their striving to retain their culture. Tegnér and Topelius especially, with their sense of national destiny, were the perfect vehicles to lift the Swedish worker in America to new cultural heights.

Cultural enrichment of the Swedes in America was, in the opinion of many, a lost cause if the Swedish language were lost. Language was not simply utilitarian, a way of conducting business, but it was also the vehicle for identity. The Swedish language was the vehicle by which *svenskhet*, [Swedishness], was carried from generation to generation.[6] That central thesis is echoed through three generations of immigrants, from the time of the Chicago fire up to the imposition of immigration quotas in 1929. By the late 1920s and into the 1930s and 1940s, the Swedish American institutions that had fought hard to preserve and use Swedish in their life recognized the inevitable and began to shift toward English. Most notable among those institutions was the Augustana Synod Lutheran Church. Between 1919 and 1931, the Synod gradually moved from Swedish to English as its official language (Lindmark, 1972, p. 88).

Despite its failure, the attempt to preserve Swedish in an English-speaking culture deserves attention. The tactics used by leaders of the Swedish American community provide an informative lesson in the dynamics of immigrant assimilation.

Two elements are particularly worthy of examination: church school efforts and advocacy for "proper" Swedish. In part, both efforts failed because they took a hectoring tone, informing the lower classes of the "ugliness" of their speech and the valuelessness of their culture. In part, they failed because it was not possible for these immigrants to be residents of two cultures, to blend American virtues with Nordic ideals.

Foremost among the church efforts to preserve the Swedish language were the school books. The *Församlingsskolans Läseboken* [Congregational school readers] published by the Augustana Synod, attempted to meet the need for instruction in the Swedish language for children of the immigrants.[7] The second edition (Bersell, 1890), explains the purpose of this volume as an all encompassing introduction to the Swedish language, Swedish rules of grammar and spelling, Swedish American culture, and what we would see today as Evangelical Christian piety.

> In the choice of readings the greatest care has been exercised to use those which, in content, are suitable for our Swedish America situation, and which yet have running through them a pure, pious impression, wherever such could naturally occur, and which allows the positive Christian message enter into the story. (p. 1)

Because the reader was meant to be used with all grades, it begins with the simplest A-B-C book materials, teaches the peculiar sounds of the Swedish language to nonnative Swedish speakers,[8] and the reading of Germanic Gothic print, a print style still common at the turn of the century.

The book, as promised, inculcates piety throughout. In the first readings, these are strictly Christian piety. However, later materials, meant for older students, also teach social and civic American piety. By the time students have finished a congregation's course of study, they will have been exposed to basic scientific knowledge, the history of the Augustana Synod, bits of general European history, and a very brief sketch of the history and virtues of both Sweden and America, all, of course, in Swedish.

The reader gave those who stayed through the course a lesson on the beauty of the Swedish language. A relatively accurate, although somewhat simplified, version of the rise of Swedish as a language distinct from the others in the Germanic language group precedes propaganda for the Swedish language. Swedish is described as an "expressive and beautiful-sounding" language that today "stands among the foremost" in the world.

> The Swedish language is manly and powerful. It rings like steel on the mountain. Sung by the great poets, it has become proud and lustrous as few other languages. This language deserves also our love and care. It is our mother tongue. It is the language which has been spoken by our ancestors since ancient days. It ought to be holy to us, since it reminds us Swedes in this country that we are brothers and derive from one and the same sublime and powerful people. He makes himself into a fool who is embarrassed by this, his mother tongue, for it is a noble language and honored among the wise people of the world. We should only blush if we use it in swear words and other low and discourteous talk. The Swedish language is a holy inheritance from our forbears, and we may not neglect it, but ought to use and improve that inheritance. For if we lose it, we lose at the same

time all the best that we have inherited and perhaps become orphans without a heritage lost in the mass of humanity from other nations. (p. 379)

Even while praising Sweden, her language, people, and leaders, the
reader also contains a healthy dose of American filiopiety. The biography
of Washington repeats Parson Weems' story of the axed cherry tree and
young George's inability to tell a lie. Franklin and Lincoln are hailed as
great heroes of freedom. The North American continent is singled out as
"beautiful and richly blessed by God." "For such a land as our home we
ought to properly thank God. And that thanks is best shown thusly, that we
allow ourselves to be formed into good and useful citizens ..." (p. 184).
Sweden is holy, the land of our fathers. Swedish is holy, the language of our
forbears. But America is holy and the land in which we are privileged to
live. Therefore, America is owed our willingness to become good citizens.
The implication that good citizenship would require the use of English, implying that one would eventually leave Swedish behind is inescapable, but
seems not to have occurred to the editors.

Despite the implications of their own educational materials, the
"elite" continued to believe that Swedish could and ought to be preserved in America throughout the period of the great migration. The
need for and possibility of preserving the language forms the heart of P.
M. Magnusson's article *Två Kulturer* [Two Cultures], in *Godjul* [Merry
Christmas, undated, probably 1917], the Augustana Synod's replace-
ment for its annual reader, *Prairieblomman* [The Prairie Flowers].
Magnusson's defense of the Swedish language is a common one. The
Swedish language equals Swedishness, and loss of the one equals loss
of the other. Culture, a sense of national pride and identity, and language are inseparably mixed.[9] This is the other side of the "language of
the heart" issue we saw in Malm's novel. Where Malm admitted that the
"heart's speech" was English for the second generation, Magnusson argues for a continuation of Swedish language institutions as a continuation of the Swedish American culture.

Magnusson's article was likely written during World War I. With that
war came powerful restrictions on the use of all non-English languages. In
1915, the country embarked on a campaign of "antihyphenationism." In
May of that year, President Wilson called upon a gathering of newly naturalized citizens to lay aside their native lands and become fully Americanized. "A man who thinks of himself as belonging to a particular national

group in America has not yet become an American ...." In October of that same year, expresident Theodore Roosevelt spoke in more strident tones of the need to lay aside the mother tongues:

> The one absolutely certain way of bringing this nation to ruin ... would be to permit it to become a tangle of squabbling nationalities, an intricate knot of German Americans, Irish Americans, English Americans, French Americans, Scandinavian Americans or Italian Americans, each preserving its separate nationality, each at heart feeling more sympathy with Europeans of that nationality than with other citizens of the American Republic. The men who do not become Americans and nothing else are hyphenated Americans, and there ought to be no room for them in this country. (Lovoll, 1977, p. 25)

The battle of antihyphenationism is reflected in Magnusson's 1916 article, which begins "The immigrant was no hyphenated individual." The push for a pure, unhyphenated American was certainly most severely felt during the war years, but its effect continued after, as did the attempts to persuade the Swede to retain Swedish as the mother tongue. The battle was not only a political one, but also a matter of popular culture. Israel Zangwill's four-act drama *The Melting Pot* appeared on Broadway in 1908, and from it we take both the concept and the phrase "melting pot" to describe the ideal relationship of the individual immigrant to the whole American society.

Scandinavian American intellectuals resisted the idea of blending in. Norwegian journalist and novelist Waldemar Ager maintained that "there are hardly any immigrated races that do not lose some of their best qualities by coming into the melting pot" (Lovall, 1977, p. 80). Among the Swedes, the resistance to the antihyphenation campaign reached its zenith with John Carlson's 1923 tract, *Hvarför böra vi bibehålla och bevara, vårda och bruka svenska språket i Amerika?* [Why ought we preserve and protect, care for and use the Swedish language in America?]. Carlson addressed himself first of all to the Swedes in America, scolding them for their stupidity in letting go of their language and culture. "Some say that it shows humility and politeness [to let go of our Swedishness]. Yes, it certainly does, and great *stupidity* as well" (p. 5). His argument is that each nationality adds something unique to the American society. The Swedish contribution to that unique mix is lost when, instead of maintaining the Swedish language and culture, the immigrants adopt the English language, and with it the customs and culture of England. To be true Americans, Carlson argued, Swedes need to value their own culture. For they have come from a free land to a free land. Materially, they have arrived impoverished, but culturally, they are a people with a rich heritage.

Moreover, is it not an irony that Americans place such a high value on their children learning Latin, a dead language, whereas the Swedes speak a rich and noble living language? He who knows two languages must be more valuable to the country and to himself than he who speaks only one. Therefore, retention of the Swedish language is not simply an option, but a necessity. Refusal to speak only English is not stubborn clinging to the past, but the duty of the present. Culture and language are preserved together, and Swedes have the duty to preserve and pass on that which they have inherited.

The problem with Carlson's argument is first that the process of Americanization was already eroding Swedish language usage among the Swedish Americans. Second, the culture Carlson wished to uphold through the use of Swedish was the high culture of the Swedish Academy and the universities, a culture foreign to most of the immigrants. A more realistic view of the language and culture preservation question is presented in Gustav Malm's play *Här Ute* [Out Here].

> Despite the fact that you priests harp early and late on the need to preserve the language, you have not gotten to the bottom with the question, none of you. Yes, I'm telling it as it is. Phrases are phrases, but facts continue to be the facts. None of us has reckoned with all of emigration's circumstances and outcomes. But one of the heaviest and most painful of these is the continuation of our mother tongue amidst this country's language. If you take the pains to attempt to preserve proper Swedish here among our people, you're building on air. How is one to demand that others hold onto that which they never owned? The emigrant has as much to do with "proper" Swedish as with Strindberg's books and Lindblad's songs. The emigrant's language is the dialect of Vestgöta, Värmland, Skåne, Småland, Dalarna and so forth. Out here they blend together and they each speak each other's dialects. After having been out here for a while one blends in a mass of English words, in part because there is no word like these in their restrictive village language, in part because the words blended in are easier. (Malm, 1919, p. 28)

That the newly arrived Swede spoke a regional dialect rather than "proper" Swedish was a well-recognized phenomenon. That did not stop insistence on "proper" Swedish from becoming an important subordinate argument for the attempt to preserve Swedish language and culture in America, and to raise the Swedish American "underclass" to the same social status as the "overclass," which in America meant the bourgeoisie.

One of the chief "educators" in the need to speak "proper" rather than "American" Swedish was novelist, essayist, editor, and poet Johan Person.

Person's insistence was slightly ironic. He was himself the child of a peasant family, had stopped formal education in the seventh class, and was largely self-educated beyond that elementary school level. He emigrated in 1887, worked at occasional labor until 1895, when he began his career as a newspaperman. For the next 2 years, he was on the staff of Chicago's *Svenska Tribunen*, leaving that post to become editor of the East Coast paper *Svea* in 1897. The next year he took over as editor of *Skandinavia*, another East Coast paper, moving to Minneapolis and *Svenska Folkets Tidning* in 1901. From Minneapolis, he returned to Chicago, and the *Kuriren*, then to *Vestkusten* in San Francisco, back to Minneapolis and *Posten*, and finally, after a period of unemployment, back to *Kuriren* in 1914, remaining editor until his death in 1921 (Skarstedt, 1930, p. 149).

In his newspaper career, then, Person was able to study the whole of the Swedish American community in the United States. He declared that he was unable to speak well in any of the three languages he had learned: Swedish, American, and American Swedish (Skarstedt, 1930, p. 149). Yet he became one of the spokespersons for the movement to restore "proper" Swedish as the common language of the Swedish Americans through his *Svensk-Amerikanska Studier* [Person, 1912]. Written during the period of unemployment and published by Augustana Book Concern, this little volume covers the whole of the Swedish American experience, including where Swedes live in America, the Swedish American desire to buy a lot and build a house as quickly as possible, the happy and the unhappy Swedes in America, and why they are that way. For our purposes, Person's essay "Språket" [The Language] with its insights into the use of American Swedish is crucial to an understanding of the problem.

Person noted in this essay that the blended language had become quite common throughout the Swedish American community. In his experience the reasons for use of the blended speech were several. One was an attempt at social climbing. Those who regularly spoke and even thought in English may have found it difficult to revert to Swedish, even though it was their mother tongue. They also included a large number of English loan words in their Swedish, although they had no difficulty keeping Swedish out of their English. That seemed to Person a sort of snobbery, a kind of social climbing, by which Person meant that the new immigrant considered the American, English-speaking culture "higher" than the Swedish-speaking culture.

There are those, he admitted, whose use of American Swedish was a result of poor education back home, and distance from the fatherland. Then there was a third group of Swedish Americans, those who used English more than either Swedish or the "gibberish" of American Swedish. Foremost among these were the servant girls. They had learned their English from their American employers, and had also learned the class status that English afforded them, as English "is spoken rather the same by all social classes (in the sense that one can speak of classes in this country)" (p. 133). On the other hand, their Swedish marked them as members of the peasant class. "It is an old Swedish prejudice, which hasn't been blown away in the trip over the Atlantic, that it is shameful to be 'from the country'" (p. 133). It was, of course, not only socially better for these girls to speak English, but it also sounded better than their dialect, maintained Person, for the commonest dialects among the Swedes who have emigrated, the Skånsk, Smålandsk, and Värmlandsk "certainly aren't beautiful" (p. 134).

These dialects each represent forms of blended speech in themselves. Skåne and Småland, both once provinces of Denmark, retained a solid Dano-Norwegian substratum. Värmland, on the border with Norway, contained elements of the provincial Norwegian, which was canonized as Nynorsk in the 19th century. These, maintained Person, sounded "less than beautiful," as did the blended speech of American Swedish. They all sounded as if one had forgotten one's Swedish, and as if one "came from the country" (i.e., was an unsophisticated hick). That was precisely the image the rising middle class wished to avoid. They might become Americanized, but they were not hicks. What the critics of American Swedish could not see was that this new "dialect" was developing and may well have become a living language had the insistence upon "not being a hick" given way to a true egalitarianism, such as we saw in Charli Johnson.

CLASS AND THE STORY OF THE SWEDISH AMERICAN COMMUNITY

When the story of the Swedish American community in Chicago is recounted, it is most often told as the stories of the community's "great" men, such as editor Johan Enander, Episcopal Priest Gustavus Unonius, poet Jacob Bonggren, or even socialists like Aksel Josephson or Henry Bengston. These "proper" Swedish-speaking Swedes, whatever their income, belonged to the "overclass," the educated elite. Their politics, their writings, and their culture are taken to be indicative of the life of this part of Chicago's ethnic mix. This is the culture, drawn from both Sweden and Swedish America, that the campaign to preserve and use "proper" Swedish sought to advance.

But, there is another view of this ethnic community's life, a view from below. That culture is not as accessible to the historical researcher as the life of journalists, publishers, social propagandists, intellectuals, and school teachers, for those who lived that life left little documentary evidence. Few members of the "hard working class," and even fewer of the "undeserving poor" produced literature.

While we do not have literary works from the bulk of Chicago's Swedish Americans, we do have clues to how they spoke, what they thought of themselves, and what they were becoming in this new land. These clues are mostly indirect. What they show us is a people passing through a linguistic "stage" of blended speech, longing to rise in class status and often unsure how to be what they were becoming, a "voluntary" ethnic group in America's sea of ethnicity.

The blended speech of American Swedish, along with "proper" Swedish as the language of everyday commerce, social life, and religious life eventually disappeared from Chicago, even as the drive to raise cultural awareness succeeded. The Swedish American of the second and third generation often expresses regret that they do not speak more than *en lite grann* [a little bit] of Swedish. When American Swedish and "proper" Swedish gave way to English, the organizations to which these immigrants belonged ceased to perform the rites and rituals in the language of the old country. When Swedish gave way to English as primary speech, the entertainments in which listening was more important than reading (primarily theater, but also radio programming) came to an end. Although Swedish-language singing remains an active part of the community's life, it is carried on in a greatly diminished fashion by groups who will not survive another generation, and even they do not perform exclusively in Swedish.

In this chapter, we looked at the use of blended speech as a class marker. Swedish Americans were acutely aware of class differences. The class distinctions of the New World were like those known in the old country, where being "from the country" was considered a source of shame, and being a peasant a source of comedy. If the class distinctions in America never led to the kind of workers movement that eventuated in the Social Democrats' rise to power in Sweden, it was perhaps because the "working-class" Swede in America always saw himself as capable of becoming a material success, becoming *bas* [boss]. It was a dream to be realized through hard work, ethnic connection, and the use of English.

A few years ago I was asked to translate a series of letters from a Swedish American private to his family. The private, a Minnesota boy, was serving on the front lines in France at the time of the writing. The letters revealed little about army life during World War I that is unknown from other historical narratives. What they revealed was a thorough immersion in American Swedish. That dialect was so complete that the family's Swedish relatives, who had been asked to take on the project, had given up hope of translating these brief letters correctly. One cousin wrote, "He has forgotten his Swedish." Private Lindstrom never forgot his Swedish. He simply spoke another regional dialect version of the language, a version in keeping with his status as a farmer, an American peasant, on his way to becoming comfortably middle class. Unfortunately, Private Lindstrom never returned to complete his "edjikasion" in English. Just weeks before he was due to leave France, a transport he was driving blew up, leaving him dead on the battlefield after the battle had ceased. His fate is like that of the speakers of American Swedish. Never able to reach maturity as a language, it has now largely ceased to have any influence on the life of the community that calls itself Swedish American.

ENDNOTES

1. Einar Haugen's definitive study of American Norwegian demonstrates that the habits of the American Swedes were quite similar to those of the Norwegians. The major difference, however, came with the politicization of Nynorsk, both at home in Norway and in America. Because speaking one of the dialects was a political issue, it did not have the same use as a class marker (Haugen, 1953, p. 154ff).

2. Colling was born in Bubbetorp, Blekinge. He was one of the many Swedish Carlsons. Upon emigration in 1878, he took the name

Colling, after his family home in Kollinge, Småland. He was active for a time in the Minneapolis Swedish community, moving to San Francisco in 1883. His second short novel was *Där igen, genuint svensk-amerkinska, humoristiska skildringar, försedda med teckningar av författaren själv* [There again, genuine Swedish American sketchs, complete with drawings by the author himself] (Skarstedt, 1930, p. 47).

3. The work had originally been published in 1896 in Minneapolis.
4. Gösta Bergman, in his *A Short History of the Swedish Language* noted the increase of regularization in a number of areas during the 19th and 20th centuries. (p. 34) Regularities in the syntax of the language include placement of the verb, always in the second place in a sentence, the formula determining placement of modifying clauses. One feature of the language that gives nonnative speakers the most difficulty are the so-called "wandering adverbs," whose place in any sentence varies with regularity. (Bergman, 1947). English grammar, by contrast, admits far more irregularities.
5. The name "Wård" means to take care of, a function that Wård performs for both the Swedish language and Charli's intellectual development and social maturation.
6. To a certain extent, one must admit that the "preservers" were correct. Much of Swedish high culture was lost in the shift from Swedish to English. The greatest writers of Sweden, Carl Michael Bellman, Tegnér, Gustav Fröding, Hjälmar Bergman and even Nobel laureate Ivar Lo Johansson are known to Swedish Americans only as names, if at all. Few Swedish Americans have read these works in their original language, although translations of their works remain popular among the second and third generation seeking to reclaim something of the high culture of the old country.
7. The Common School Reader as a genre began appearing in 1868. After the institution of universal compulsory schooling in 1842, authorities in Sweden felt the need to improve reading, the general level of education, and the taste for fine literature through these readers. In look, feel, and price, the Common Readers of the Augustana Synod bore a striking resemblance to those of the motherland.
8. The "sj" sound and the "tj" sound, are particularly difficult for English speakers. They approximate the "sh" in "shucks" and the ch in "check," but the likeness is only approximate.
9. Even while working at an apology for the Swedish language and culture, author P. M. Magnusson felt the need to translate

"proper" Swedish nouns into their American Swedish equiva-
lents. Thus "handelsboden," a store, is clarified by the parentheti-
cal translation into American Swedish "ståret"; "tingshuset" by
"kårthuset"; "skolstämman" by "skolmiting"; and "skogslägret"
by "lumberkampen" (10). By the end of the 1910's, "proper"
Swedish had become at least strange enough to many readers
that American Swedish was needed.

REFERENCES

Berger, H. (1901). *Där Ute, skisser.* [Out there, sketches]. Stockholm: C. & E.
     Gernandts Förlags AB.
Berger, H. (1906). *Ysaïl, en berättelse från Chicago* [Ysail, a story from Chicago].
     Stockholm: Bonniers Förlag.
Bergman, G. (1947). *A short history of the Swedish language.* Translated by Francis
     P. Magoun, Jr. & Helge Kökeritz. Stockholm: The Swedish Institute for Cultural
     Relations.
Bersell, A. O. (Ed.). (1890). *Församlingsskolans Läseboken* [The congregation
     schools' reader]. Rock Island, IL: Augustana Book Concern. 1890.
Carlson, G. (1908). *Mister Colesons Sverigeresa: Svensk-Amerikansk Humoresk*
     [Mister Colesons trip to Sweden: A Swedish American humoresque]. Chicago:
     And. L. Löfströms Förlag.
Carlson, J. S. (1923). *Hvarför böra vi bibehålla och bevara, vårda och bruka
     svenska språket i Amerika?* [Why ought we preserve and protect, care for, and
     use the Swedish language in America?]. Publisher unknown.
Department of Development and Planning, City of Chicago. (1976). *The people of
     Chicago: Who we are and who we have been.* City of Chicago: Department of
     Development and Planning.
Fullständigaste Engelsk-Svenska Brefställaren för Svenska Folket i Amerika [The
     most complete English Swedish letter writer for the Swedish people in Amer-
     ica]. (1883). Chicago: Engberg & Holmbergs Förlag.
Haugen, E. (1953). *The Norwegian language in America: A study in bilingual behav-
     ior.* The Bilingual Community. Philadelphia: University of Pennsylvania Press.
Landfors, A. (January 1974). On the Swedish-American Language. *Swedish-Ameri-
     can Pioneer Historical Quarterly, 25,* 3–12.
Lindmark, S. (April 1972). The language question and its resolution. *Swedish-
     American Pioneer Historical Quarterly, 23,* 71–95.
Löfström, A. (Ed.). (1908). *Bland Kolingar och Kogubbar: Samling af Illustrerade
     Skämtbitar på Vers och Prosa. Första Samlingen* [Among charcoalers and cow
     herders: A collection of illustrated comic material in verse and prose: The first
     collection]. Chicago: Andrew L. Löfströms Förlag.
Lovoll, O. (Ed.). (1977). *Cultural pluralism versus assimilation.* Topical Studies 2.
     Northfield, MN: The Norwegian-American Historical Association.
Lovoll, O. (1998). *The promise fulfilled: A portrait of Norwegian Americans today.*
     Minneapolis: University of Minnesota Press.

Magnusson, P. M. (1917/December). *"Två Kulturer" God jul*. Rock Island, IL: Augustana Book Concern.

Malm, G. (1909). *Charli Johnson, Svensk-Amerikan* [Charli Johnson, Swedish-American]. Chicago: The Engberg-Holmberg Publishing Company.

Malm, G. (1919). *Härute; Verklighetsbild ur svensk-amerikanarnes havrdagslif i fyra akter* [Out here: Pictures from reality out of the everyday life of Swedish Americans in four acts]. Lindsborg, KS: Bethany Printing Company.

Person, J. (1912). *Svensk-Amerikanska Studier* [Swedish-American studies]. Rock Island, IL: Augustana Book Concern.

Praktisk Handbook för Svenskarne i Amerika [A practical handbook for Swedes in America]. (1911). Chicago: Hemlandet Publishing.

Skarstedt, E. (1930). *Pennfäktare: Svensk-Amerikansk Författare och Tidningsmän* ["Pen swordsmen": Swedish-American authors and journalists]. Stockholm: Åhlen & Akerlunds Förlag.

Photograph by Michael Maltz

10

Italian Patterns in the American Collandia Ladies' Club: How Do Women Make *Bella Figura?*

Gloria Nardini
University of Illinois at Chicago

Italians have immigrated to Chicago since about 1850. The greatest numbers came between 1880 and 1914, with additional peaks in the 1920s and in the period from 1946 to the 1980s, when Italian immigration ended.

According to Rudolph Vecoli, early immigrant colonies consisted of the Assumption Church neighborhood, early Chinatown, the Taylor Street area, the Northwest Side Santa Maria Addolorata parish, the North Side 22nd ward known as "Little Sicily," the Tuscan settlement on 24th and Oakley, and assorted South Side communities. Suburbs included Blue Island, Chicago Heights, Melrose Park, and Highwood (Candeloro, 1995, pp. 229–234).[1]

World War II saw the end of a geographic base for the Italian community as people moved out of their Little Italies. What survived was "a community of interest based almost entirely on voluntary associations and self-conscious identification with Italian-ness" (Candeloro, 1995, p. 245).

The Collandia Ladies' Club[2] was founded in Chicago in the 1950s as an auxiliary to the Collandia Men's Club, started in the 1930s by immigrants from Lucca.[3] It consists of American-born Italian women and Italian-born post–World War II immigrant women.[4] Entitled to membership because they have husbands in the Men's Club, these women have as their purpose "to help the men."[5]

The Collandia Club is recreational, its heart simple. Lifetime friendships are formed and fostered here where members come to play cards, to place *bocce*, and to speak Italian. Everyone knows about everyone else's troubles and pleasures. People get married, raise children, and grow old together. In some ways the Collandia represents the *caffe* and the *piazza* of the *paese* left behind.

At the Collandia, I engaged in 2½ years of long-term participant observation (Hymes, 1974) to reach an emic interpretation of the culture. I came to realize the importance of being not just bilingual, but also bicultural.[6] That is, I came to understand the extent to which language and culture are inextricably bound at the Collandia Club. Despite 30 to 40 years of living in Chicago, a familiarity with English, and incorporation of American holidays, the underlying mores of this club are Italian.

Of these underlying mores, the most important phenomenon is the Italian cultural construction known as *fare bella figura,* literally "to make a beautiful figure." Figuratively, the phrase means "to engage in appropriate visual display, to look good, to show off, to put on the dog"—in short, "to perform." Its opposite is *fare brutta figura*, literally, "to make an ugly figure," which means to engage in behavior lacking in appropriate style, flair, or *sprezzatura*. This last term, coined in 1528 by Baldassarre Castiglione in *The Book of the Courtier*, purports to be the key to explain correct "gentlemanly" behavior. Castiglione (1528) urged his courtier to

> steer away from affectation at all costs, as if it were a rough and dangerous reef, and (to use perhaps a novel word for it) to practise in all things a certain *sprezzatura* which conceals all artistry and makes whatever one says or does seem uncontrived and effortless. ... So we can truthfully say that true art is what does not seem to be art; and the most important thing is to conceal it, because if it is revealed this discredits a man completely and ruins his reputation. (p. 67)

At the Collandia Club, a *bella figura* performance is always expected, encouraged, and constituted.[7]

Analysis of a partial transcript of a Collandia Ladies' Club financial meeting shows that within this bilingual, bicultural community, the concept of *bella figura* is transferred into speech in English, too. That is, whether speaking Italian or English, one must *fare bella figura*.

This analysis answers the following questions:

What is the social context of this interaction? That is, how do these women "present" themselves? How are they members of the same speech community?

What are the communicative strategies at work here? How do the women create "conversational involvement"?

Where does "performance" occur? How is this an example of a communally constituted performance?

What role does indirection and the view of women as "powerless" users of language play in this discourse?

The overarching question of this analysis remains: How are language and culture inextricably bound? I maintain that in this transcript[8] the Collandia Ladies claim social power for themselves through their linguistic use of *bella figura*. Thus, interpretation of their ways of speaking, both gendered and culture rich, is dependent on the social context of the Collandia Club for its full meaning.

To use Hymesean terms, in this communicative situation, otherwise known as the end-of-the-year Collandia Ladies' Club officers' financial meeting, a communicative event takes place: The women ask the Men's Club president for a reduction in Ladies' Club debt as they attend to finalizing their books. Within this event occur discrete communicative acts, specifically, a series of performances, one defined as a "starring moment." This dazzling act is a definitive performance of *bella figura* by the Ladies' Club treasurer.

Analyzing a communicative event requires that attention be paid to its salient components. Adapting Hymes' (1974) framework, Saville-Troike (1982) treated scene as composed of genre, topic, purpose/function, and setting (pp. 137–150).

In this case, the genre is persuasive discourse. Rina, the treasurer, wants the ladies to help her convince Ciro, the Men's Club president, that less money is owed to the men than is actually shown in their books. First, the Ladies' Club paid for expenses that, by rights, do not belong to them, and for which the Men's Club should reimburse them. Second, they were not reimbursed even for bills, such as for the stamps used on New Year's

Eve mailings, for which the Men's Club does accept responsibility. There-fore, instead of paying the total, which they owe to the Collandia Men's Club for the Ladies' Christmas Party, Rina wants Ciro to acknowledge the Men's Club's expenses so she can deduct them. Thus, her topic and func-tion are straightening out who is responsible for what so that efficient pay-ment can be made.

The setting for this meeting is the banquet room of the clubhouse. At this point, having clarified their finances for themselves, the women are waiting for the Men's Club president. When Ciro enters, he participates from a standing position next to the seated ladies.

The participants are nine women,[9] only two of whom do not speak and understand Italian. Six women are members of 15 or 20 years' standing.[10] They have held myriad offices, chaired important events, played *bocce*, decorated, cleaned, and performed the thousands of functions that the Collandia Ladies' Club yearly takes upon itself. They present themselves, therefore, as a formidable force of actors whose current routine is to verify that money has been appropriately allocated so that the yearly books can be closed to everyone's satisfaction. This routine is not new, for there is a tradition that the Ladies' Club meets with the Men's Club president at the beginning of each fiscal year to finalize expenses. Not new, either, is the tension located in gender, which always arises about what, specifically, the women owe the men.

The message form is colloquial English, with occasional code switching to Italian. Much of the nitty-gritty of the exchange, the message content about who owes what, occurs between Rina and Ciro so that they fall into an act sequence of rhythmic exchange that moves to a quicker, louder pace, ultimately leading to a temporary "rupture" of sudden silence. Much overlapping, some unintelligible, goes on throughout except during these "ruptures." Sometimes side conversations can also be heard.

The components called "rules for interaction" are defined by Saville-Troike (1982) as "prescriptive statements of behavior, of how peo-ple 'should' act, which are tied to the shared values of the speech commu-nity" (p. 147). In this instance, they define what topics the women are allowed to discuss publicly. Namely, there are to be no complaints about whether it is correct to follow the bylaws, which prescribe that only $1,000 may be kept in the Ladies' Club treasury. What should be discussed is how the bylaws are being followed. The burden of explaining is put upon trea-surer Rina, who should do most of the talking to Ciro. Any public entreaty she makes to lessen the financial responsibility of the Ladies' Club can be

accepted or denied by him, because he is in full agreement that the Ladies' Club exists to "help the men." In the midst of refurbishing the banquet room and the kitchen, he is eager for money.[11] As president of the
dominant male club, Ciro can say pretty much anything he wants.

The norms of interpretation concern following the "real rules" of the
Collandia Club. These involve working hard to make money, being frugal,
accepting what one is entitled to and nothing more, and following tradition.[12] Because these "real rules" rely upon oral tradition, their reconstruction depends on the memories of long-time members. Therefore, much of
the conversation between the women specifies who has always done or
paid for what. Much discussion also seeks to enculturate newcomers into
these long-standing traditions.

According to Stubbs (1983), "transcribing conversation into the visual
medium is a useful estrangement device, which can show up complex aspects of conversational coherence which pass us by as real-time conver-
sationalists or observers" (p. 20). I use the "estrangement device" of
discourse analysis to look at gendered notions of power and powerlessness as encoded in language. Here I use a feminist frame of reference that
takes as (historically) important the things men do. In it, men operate as
the default category and women operate as "other." I show how in their
discourse these Collandia women recreate the man-as-powerful and
woman-as-powerless themes with which they are societally familiar.
"Power" in this case has to do with who controls the purse strings of their
auxiliary. I also show how the women's language is imbedded in a micro-
cosm of strategies, mostly of indirection, which historically have been
used by the powerless against the powerful. Actually, this is my point, that
the participants in this discourse are not fully aware of the deeper implications of gender roles and *bella figura*, the cultural code, which constrain
them to act in the ways that they do. This transcript shows them
seamlessly bringing the two together. For, as Goffman (1959) said, "We all
act better than we know how" (p. 74). This meeting is ostensibly about
money, but money is really a moot point because profits beyond $1,000 go
to the men anyway.

What then is the meeting really about? I think it concerns the tensions
involved in maintaining *bella figura* in the handling of this money. That is,
the Collandia Ladies' Club accepts that the dominant club is the Collandia
Men's Club, but they want acknowledgment for themselves, not just for
their part in making this club work, but for their organized, rule-bound, tra-
dition-following part in making this club work. Scott (1990) called this kind

of discourse a hidden transcript of resistance, a "creation of autonomous social space for assertion of dignity" (p. 198). In other words, the Collandia Ladies' Club wants acknowledgement of their *bella figura*, as is evident in the following transcript.

TRANSCRIPT OF FINANCIAL MEETING

Lines represent breath groups; CAPS imply that the tone is louder and the pitch higher; bold-faced italicized comments (to right and left of dialogue) are explained later in the text of the chapter; and English translations are in brackets after the Italian.

The Prologue (no man present)

1 Rina: Pretty soon Ciro's going to come—*#2 powerless*
2   you're all here. You're all officers.
3   Ask him to deduct this $826.95.
4   It's all their expenses.
5   Easter, Mother's Day, Xmas decorations …
                    {overlapping comments}
6 Jeanne: But wait, you owe them for the dinner yet.
#1 direct
7   Deduct that 800 …
8 Rina: You, you deduct.
#2 powerless
9 Frida: That's right.
Echo #1 direct with no man present
10 Rina: You deduct.
#2 powerless
11   See if they're willing to do it.
12   If they're willing to deduct, you do it.
13 Jeanne: That's right.
#1 direct
14 Sofia: Why not?
Echo #1 direct with no man present
15 Jeanne: It comes down to a matter of

#1 direct

16   you guys are letting them do it to you.

17 Sofia: That's right.

Echo #1 direct with no man present

18 Jeanne:They're going to get it anyway,

#1 direct

19   but to me it's the principle.

20   If they want to put these women down,

21   I mean let's …

Act One: The Show

{"Hi, Ciro" from many as Men's President walks in.}

22 Rina: Whenever you have a moment, eh …

23 Sofia: Sit down, Cirino.

24   *Metteti al tavolo, Ciro.* (in baby voice)
                 [Sit at the table, little Ciro.]

25 Rina: Whenever you have a moment, we're ready.

26   We want to show you our books.

27   We want to pay the bills.

{Some comments unintelligible. Ciro briefly goes elsewhere.}

Prologue (continued)

28 Nora: *Questa roba che l'hai scritta te,*

Language of power with no man present

29   *l'hai fatti te i soldi di quelle li?*

30   *Allora perché devi paga'?*

[This stuff that you wrote down,
did you make the money from it?
Then why do you have to pay?]

31 Rina: Well, we gotta.

#2 powerless

32   That's why we're here.

33 Sofia: That's because they find the women so soft.

Echo language of power with no man present

Act One (continued)
{Ciro returns.}

34	Sofia:	Sit down, Ciro.	
35	Dora:	Did you hear how nice Sofia's saying,	
36		"Sit down, Honey?"	

{overlapping comments—much back channel "uhhm"
as approval throughout following section}

37	Rina:	Of all the money that was passed to us from last year,	
		song	
38		all the ... everything that we collected ...	
39		all the profits that we made ...	***entreaty***
40	Ciro:	(Yeah)...	
41	Rina:	The money that we have outstanding ...	***and***
42		it	
43		or how it all was spent...	
44	Ciro:	(Yeah,) where's my money?	
45	Rina:	Wait.	

{general laughter}

46	Rina:	*Ora questi qui, questi qui,* ***dance***	
		[now these here, these here]	
47		they were spent like at Easter,	
48		Easter eggs ...	***incantation***
49	Ciro:	(Yeah)...	
50	Rina:	Easter bunny	
51		and then for Mother's Day	
52		and the presidential banquet ... so the ladies feel that this ...	

{many unintelligible comments}

53	Rina:	They want to take it off the money	

#1 direct (first time)

54		that we owe you for the Xmas party.	
55	Ciro:	*Porca Miseria!* (walks off)	***temporary rupture***
		[For crying out loud!]	

{confusion}

56	Sofia:	Come over here, Ciro, Ciro ...	***rupture commented on***

57 Rina: See, I mean—why do we want to get aggravated?
                   {many comments}
58 Gloria: No, he's coming back.
59   He's going to go to the bathroom.
60 Rina: No, he's going to go …

Act Two
{Ciro returns.}

61 Jeanne: No, the men—it comes down to a matter of
#1 direct
62   principle …
63 Ciro: Okay.
64 Jeanne: We have to give it up anyway,
#1 direct
65   but we want to be reimbursed by you
66   so that our books reflect what we've really done.
67   Do you know what I'm saying?
68   When we send out your cenettas,
69   you should be paying for those stamps.
70   Normally they do.
                   {Nora chimes in approval.}
71 Ciro: We do. We pay for those cenettas.
72 Rina: But like—I sent out New Year's Eve.   *song*
73   I sent out New Year's Eve.   *and*
74   Nobody reimbursed us for that.   *dance*
75 Ciro: If you sent out New Year's Eve,
76   you got the bill,
77   we pay you for New Year's Eve.
78 Jeanne: There—see?
#1 direct
79 Rina: Oh, well,   *final performance*
80   I don't HAAAVE the BILLLL.   *re-starts argument*
                   (Louder tone, higher pitch)
81 Ciro: (continuing) because everybody come with the bill
82   They say here

83		so many stamps for that	
		{overlapping unintelligible comments}	
84	Rina:	Okay here, you know how many members we have;	
85		one to every member—	
86		We have a hundred and sixty seven.	
87	Ciro:	(overlapping) But you gotta …	
88	Nora:	But they have to have a voucher	
89		to put in their books.	
90	Jeanne:	Eighty-seven dollars is …	
91	Rina:	Well, who <u>bought the stamps</u>?	*entrapment/indirect*
92	Frida:	Excuse me … I know that Norma … (unintelligible)	
93	Rina:	(overlap) Whoever <u>bought the stamps</u> …	*song*
94	Ciro:	Well, who <u>bought the stamps</u>?	*and*
95		Maybe we <u>bought the stamps</u>!	*dance*
96	Rina:	No, no, no!	
97	Ciro:	How do you know?	
98		If we don't know who <u>bought the stamps</u> …	*song*
99	Rina:	Because I have them all in here	*and*
100		from the—	*dance*
101		<u>They were bought</u>—	*(cont.)*
102		<u>they were bought</u> from the E. Postmaster—	
103		E.P. postmaster.	
104		I have the check!	*invoking authority*
105	Ciro:	(continuing and overlapping) because …	
106	Gloria:	(overlapping and correcting) E.P. she's saying	
107	Rina:	E.P. …	
108	Dora:	Oh, Matilda!	
		{several voices: Matilda B!}	
109	Ciro:	Matilda—	
110		Maybe we give her the money;	*song and*
111		we are giving the money …	*dance*
112	Rina:	(overlapping) III gave her the CHECK—	
113		how could you—	*powerful starring moment*
114		WHAT YOU SAYING—	
115		THAT SHE GETS THE MONEY TWICE?	
116	Ciro:	I don't know. (very softly)	*temporary rupture*

Different women see this issue differently. Jeanne, not Italian at all—only married to a second-generation Italian American—adopts the most direct method of negotiating with Ciro, the Men's Club president. (On the transcript I have marked her comments "#1 direct.") For her, the issue is clear-cut: "They're going to get it, anyway" (line 18), but it has to do with the "principle" in "our books" (lines 19, 62, 66). Jeanne expects that saying what she means will accomplish what she wants—that Ciro will reimburse her for expenses that are rightly his, that monies used by the women will be shown by the women as their expenses, and that the logic and "justice" of her method will be recognized by all. As an American-born feminist, for her the most important issue has to do with equality of representation. She is involved in establishing her role in the discourse of power, but she fails to understand *bella figura*. So when she says "There—see?" (line 78) to the others to indicate Ciro's compliance and fairness, she is the only one to view the matter as closed.

Rina, an Italian who migrated to Chicago at age 12, engages in almost total indirection. (I mark her comments "#2 powerless." They form part of the prologue.) She looks for solidarity: "Pretty soon he's going to come—you're all here. You're all officers. Ask him to deduct ...." (lines 1–3). In lines 28–30 when Nora code switches to Italian to ask why the Ladies' Club has to pay for events wherein they did not take in the profits, she answers, "Well, we gotta. That's why we're here" (lines 31–32). Rina speaks the quintessential language of the powerless: We are here to fulfill an agenda that we do not really control. While establishing this conflict, she seems to be reciting lines to a script. (I mark this "entreaty.") Note especially the rhythmically balanced way she sets up her initial exchange of appositives with Ciro. Twice she speaks in breath groups of threes, repeating "all" four times. I have underlined the lines:

37	Rina:	Of <u>all the money that was passed to us</u>
		from last year,
38		<u>all the</u> ... <u>everything that we collected</u>....
39		<u>all the profits</u> that we made.....
40	Ciro:	Yeah ...
41	Rina:	<u>The money that we have</u> outstanding....
42		<u>it</u>
43		or <u>how it all was spent</u>....

The language and prosody here are similar to classical dramatic exposition, in which the conflict is briefly encapsulated for the audience at the beginning of Act One. It seems fair to say that there is more (unconsciously?) going on in Rina's discourse than meets the eye.

In fact, The Prologue can be regarded as a contest between the language of the powerless and the "direct" language of power,[13] all spoken with no man present. None of this is performative language, for it is private and not meant to impress —the women are simply discussing what they should do before their dialogue with the Men's Club president.

When Ciro, an Italian who immigrated at 17 years of age, appears, the action becomes almost like a play, with the women as the chorus and Ciro as the main actor. (This section is marked "Act One, the Show.") Here is the Don with his handmaidens metaphorically kissing his hand. In the opening lines, Rina has set the stage for her entreaty. Her words are graceful, almost poetic:

25 Rina: Whenever you have a moment, we're ready.
26   We want to show you our books.
27   We want to pay the bills.

She now takes the main role opposite Ciro, and the rest of the women, unconsciously perhaps, drift back and forth between being performers and audience, but all—except Jeanne—are privy to the fact that this is a "show."

Sofia too has entered into the play by code switching into diminuitives. "Cirino" she calls him in line 23, perhaps to mimic a sort of tongue-in-cheek playfulness appropriate to the unfolding drama in which he must be cajoled. This mood contrasts with her "why not?/that's right" refrain in lines 14 and 17, dead serious throughout the earlier transcript, where in line 33 she also called the women "so soft." However, that was the discourse of power, appropriate, she seems to think, when only the ladies are present. That this language is a public departure for Sofia is evidenced by the fact that President Dora remarks on her sweetness in lines 35–36, "Did you hear how nice Sofia's saying, 'Sit down, Honey?'"

Throughout "The Show, Act One," a rhythm is established as if for the performance of a metaphorical song and dance. For example, Ciro reiterates "yeah" three times as Rina dances around him with a recitation of the financial items to be discussed.

40 Ciro: (Yeah)...
41 Rina: The money that we have outstanding....
42   it

43   or how it all was spent....

44 Ciro: ◯Yeah◯ where's my money?

45 Rina: Wait.

           {general laughter}

46 Rina: *Ora questi qui, questi qui,*

           [now these here, these here]

47   they were spent like at Easter,

48   Easter eggs.... ***incantation***

49 Ciro: ◯Yeah◯...

My circling of "yeah" in lines 40, 44, and 49 indicates that Ciro, too, is circling, waiting for the request he knows is about to come, for in lines 37–43 Rina had used seven synonyms as a sort of introductory refrain: "money," "everything," "collected," "profits," "money," "outstanding," "spent." In line 44 the first comment Ciro makes before walking off—"where's my money?"—reiterates the "money" of Rina's refrain.

"Wait," she says in line 45, postponing an answer to his question. It is as if he has disturbed her rhythmic, repetitive incantation of what he owes her. These are her "lines," so to speak:

46 Rina: *Ora <u>questi qui, questi qui,</u>*

           [now these here, these here]

47   they were <u>spent like at Easter,</u>

48   <u>Easter eggs</u> ...

49 Ciro: Yeah ...

50 Rina: <u>Easter bunny</u>

51   and then for <u>Mother's Day</u>

52   and <u>the presidential banquet</u> ... so the ladies

       feel that this ...

My underlining shows how she repeats herself with every breath, five times in all, always in breath groups of three, as if chanting a mantra designed to change Ciro's mind.

Finally, she gets to the point in lines 52–54, which is that "the ladies feel" that they have been shortchanged.[14] "They want to take it off the money that we owe you for the Xmas party," she states bluntly. It is her first direct statement. Hearing her request, Ciro becomes angry. In line 55 he cries, *"Porca Miseria"*—glossed to "for crying out loud"—an expression of annoyance, and intentionally walks off. So this act comes to an abrupt and dramatic close, marked "temporary rupture."

52   and the presidential banquet ... so the ladies
            feel that this ...
                {many unintelligible comments}
53 Rina: They want to take it off the money
  #1 direct (first time)
54   that we owe you for the Xmas party.
55 Ciro: *Porca Miseria!* (walks off) ***temporary rupture***
            [For crying out loud!]
                {confusion}
            The attention is clearly on Ciro now. In fact, his perfor-
            mance is so terribly important that we all comment on it.
56 Sofia: Come over here, Ciro, Ciro ... ***rupture commented on***
57 Rina: See, I mean—why do we want to get aggravated?
                {many comments}
58 Gloria: No, he's coming back.
59   He's going to go to the bathroom.
60 Rina: No, he's going to go ...

In this interlude, the women become audience to Ciro, for his departure has brought the song and dance to a close. Rina, who had briefly tried a somewhat direct approach to set up her plea, drops this rhetorical strategy in line 57: "See, I mean, why do we want to get aggravated?" Thus she replicates the age-old powerlessness of women theme, the role of accepting subservience. Italian-born Sofia drops her former playfulness to speak directly in line 56, "Come over here, Ciro." I attempt a Jeanne-like logic, which does not fail to take into account the drama Ciro has invoked. "He's coming back," I say in line 58, implying that we get another chance at the dialogue. Is this an aside? Do I sense that we have not yet finished the play? Only Jeanne remains silent. Has she not perceived Ciro's leaving as an "exit" in the play?

When Ciro returns, Act Two begins. Jeanne again approaches him (lines 61–70) with the direct, logical discourse of the American feminist. She acknowledges that "we have to give it [the money] up anyway," but she is still concerned with the "principle" she mentioned earlier. "Normally," she says, the men pay for the stamps used on their mailings.

She implies that his response will not be anything other than "normal," almost as if she has not seen him yell, "*Porca Miseria*" (line 55) and run off. Notice how Jeanne's dialogue in lines 61–70, which I have marked "#1 direct," sounds more like written prose than oral discourse.

It could be written like this:

> We have to give it up anyway, but we want to be reimbursed by you so that our books reflect what we've really done. Do you know what I'm saying? When we send out your cenettas, you should be paying for those stamps. Normally they do.

Only "Do you know what I'm saying?" sounds like real talk. In the rest of her lines, there are no repetitions, no incomplete phrases, none of the emotional sense of the previous responses to Ciro's leave-taking. When Ciro says in line 71, "We do. We pay for those cenettas," Jeanne seems content that they have reached consensus about the New Year's Eve mailing. So she says in line 78, "There—see?," meaning that everything is now settled.

Rina, however, is unwilling to "settle," so she begins another song and dance.

72 Rina: But like—<u>I sent out New Year's Eve</u>. **song**
73   <u>I sent out New Year's Eve</u>. **and**
74   Nobody reimbursed us for that. **dance**
75 Ciro: If <u>you sent out New Year's Eve</u>,
76   you got the bill
77   <u>we pay you for New Year's Eve</u>.

The phrase "New Year's Eve," which I have underlined along with its pronoun subjects, is rhythmically invoked twice by both Rina and Ciro, but for different purposes. She means it as an example of how the Men's Club has overlooked her; he means it as an example of their willingness to be equitable. These lines repeat the song and dance of lines 37–51 in Act One, which Ciro had brought to an abrupt close with *Porca Miseria!*)

Now when Jeanne says, "There-see?" (line 78), Rina launches her final—and most important—performance. She says, "Oh, well, I don't HAAAVE the BILLLL," (lines 79–80) with great emphasis on both "HAAAVE" and "BILLLL," thereby contesting Jeanne's direct "settling" of the account. Ciro, too, has been involved by agreeing to the "bill" as proof of sale. We can look at this indignant comment of Rina's two ways. Either she is implying that "having the bill" is not necessary for someone of her moral fiber, the treasurer who would never attempt to get reimbursed for any illegitimate expense. Or, because she knows that she has the canceled check from the E.P. post office, which is better than having the "bill," she is setting Ciro up for a fall. Whatever she means—and I suggest that she is (subconsciously) out to ensnare Ciro—she effectively re-starts the argument.

Next, in line 91 she asks a (seemingly) innocent question, "Who bought the stamps?" to which she already has the answer. (I have marked it "entrapment/indirect.") Ciro speaks from a position of power. "Maybe we bought the stamps," he says in line 95. Again, they engage in a song and dance in which each takes a turn repeating the significant words of the other. (I have underlined their seven repetitions of "bought the stamps.") It is a prelude leading up to Rina's invoking of authority in lines 102–104. When she mentions the "E.P. postmaster" and the "check," she has won, at least directly, the battle for financial credibility.

91	Rina:	Well, who <u>bought the stamps</u>? ***entrapment/indirect***
92	Frida:	Excuse me … I know that Norma … (unintelligible)
93	Rina:	(overlap) Whoever <u>bought the stamps</u> … ***song***
94	Ciro:	Well, who <u>bought the stamps</u>? ***and***
95		Maybe we <u>bought the stamps</u>! ***dance***
96	Rina:	No, no, no!
97	Ciro:	How do you know?
98		If we don't know who <u>bought the stamps</u> … ***song***
99	Rina:	Because I have them all in here and
100		from the— ***dance***
101		<u>They were bought</u>— ***(cont.)***
102		<u>they were bought</u> from the E. Postmaster—
103		E.P. postmaster.
104		I have the check! ***invoking authority***

But Ciro is not quite ready to give up, despite everyone's realization that "Matilda" in line 108 "bought the stamps" from the "E.P. postmaster." So another song and dance scene occurs in which he and Rina repeat "money" and "check." It is almost a reprise. Notice how the lines are parallel in structure: first the subject pronoun—he says "we" twice, but she corrects him with "III"—then the verb "give" and then "money." Her line 112 is said at the same time as his line 111, thus leading to the finale.

110	Ciro:	Maybe we give her the money;	***song and***
111		we are giving the money ...	***dance***
112	Rina:	Ill gave her the CHECK— (overlapping)	

It is interesting that ostensible powerlessness (indirection) seems to be the position with which Rina is most comfortable, because she reacts against Ciro in a wonderfully dramatic scene.

112	Rina:	(overlapping) Ill gave her the CHECK—	
113		how could you—	***powerful starring moment***
114		WHAT YOU SAYING—	
115		THAT SHE GETS THE MONEY TWICE?	
116	Ciro:	I don't know. (very softly) ***temporary rupture***	

She shouts in indignation. It is her starring moment. In it she upstages Ciro.

Another temporary rupture occurs. Ciro's ending comment of "I don't know" is spoken softly, no longer a part of the tempo previously established. Unlike his parallelism in lines 110–111 "Maybe we give her the money/we are giving the money," it is now clear that Rina has outperformed him. He knows it, she knows it, and so do all the women who have been part of the chorus. Only Jeanne, perhaps, oblivious to the subtleties of the discourse, does not.

According to Tannen (1989), "Cultural patterns .... provide a range from which individuals choose strategies that they habitually use in expressing their individual styles" (*Talking Voices,* p. 80). My explanation of Rina's style is that she has created the strategy of *sprezzatura* or "studied carelessness," as recommended by Castiglione (1528) in *The Courtier.* Her repetitions of "You—you deduct" (line 8) and "I sent out New Year's Eve" (lines 72–73) and "who bought the stamps?" (line 91) imply a lack of entitlement for the Ladies' Club, even though she knows better. Despite the fact that she is legitimately in the right, she chooses not to make her claims outright to Ciro. After all, she could have said, "I don't have the bill. I have the canceled check for the stamps." But she deliberately withholds this information until later. When she finally does tell him, she invokes the authority of "postmaster" and "check" two times (lines 102–104, 112)—Ciro never mentions these words.

Perhaps she senses that she needs a moment of highly emotional display, a *figura* of sorts, in order to have him realize the legitimacy of what she has to say, for whenever the argument appears to be settled, she brings it up again. The first temporary rupture—his yelling out of "*Porca Miseria*" in line

55—occurs because Ciro is in control; the second temporary rupture—when he almost whispers "I don't know"—occurs because he is not. At the end, if Ciro answers "no" to "What you saying ... that she gets the money twice?" he admits Rina was right; if he says "yes," he makes himself look stupid. So he has no viable answer. Therefore, Rina's performance, embedded in the context of (seemingly) powerless female discourse, has invoked the all important cultural construct of *bella figura* by putting Ciro in the position of making a *brutta figura* no matter what answer he gives. By saying "I don't know," he admits that she has won the challenge. The power of the performance is hers—there are no words left for him.

All of us, except possibly Jeanne, are, in some sense, engaged in performing a role in this play. Nora, in describing the unresolved gender tensions at the Collandia, is initiating me into the discourse. Sofia is pretending to believe in male dominance with Ciro, yet acting directly powerful with the women. Ciro himself is acting like the Men's Club president. The other women provide the choral backdrop. Rina's role is the most directly performed of all because in her attempt to impose her views upon Ciro, she is most in need of the performative persuasion drama affords (Goffman, 1959). Thus, she chooses to perform *bella figura*, a juxtapositioning of cultural forms, which she is able to invoke because she is both bilingual and bicultural.

But Ciro is bilingual and bicultural, too. He knows exactly what she is doing, and—perhaps—even admires and approves of it. So he acquiesces in applauding her performance, and they are able to move on to the business at hand. Ciro's quiet "I don't know" of line 116, his second "temporary rupture" which might seem almost a defeat, in actuality simply marks a shift in his behavior. The play is finished. "Come on, Ciro," Rina says when it's all over, "we've gotta take care of this." She sits down. He sits down. The bills get paid with very little drama. Rina has "won," so to speak, her right to deduct.

By the end of my analysis of this transcript, we can understand the culturally-specific drama captured within it. So we return to the questions posed at the beginning.

What is the social context of this interaction? That is, how do these women "present" themselves? How are they members of the same speech community?

The social context is that all the women are members of the Collandia Ladies' Club who know the "real rules" and are familiar with the issue of entitlement—namely, who has the right to do what?—the topic of almost all their overt discussions. This entitlement obtains both among the women themselves and between the women and the men. Moreover, their familiarity with the code of *bella figura* gives them a shared knowledge of rules both for their own conduct—for how they "present" themselves—and for interpreting each other's speech.

The women show this knowledge by attempting to get Ciro to return after the first "rupture," after he has shown the necessary pizzazz to win the first round. They need to engage with him again to make their entreaty work. At the second "rupture," however, they realize that the *tour de force* has been Rina's, and they say nothing, knowing that there is nothing to say. She has won.

What are the communicative strategies at work here? How do they create "conversational involvement"?

The overlapping, the frequently poetic-like repetition, the pace of what could be called a "high-involvement" style are what Tannen (1991) considered "ethnic style," as are Rina's (and Sofia's) strategies of indirection. "Conversational involvement" in the drama comes from all the participants' realization that a *bella figura* performance has occurred. Thus, except for Jeanne, they are speaking in English but "performing" in Italian. As "insiders," they are able to weave for themselves an emotional and philosophical involvement that operates throughout their conversation with Ciro.

Where does "performance" occur? How is it communally constituted and recognized?

"Performance" occurs twice, both times co-constructed by Rina and Ciro as they battle for control of the finances. Both performances end in a temporary "rupture." In the first case, we know that Rina is starting a performance (line 37) because she begins a list of synonyms, items for which the Men's Club bears responsibility. She speaks in breath groups of threes four different times (lines 37–39, 41–43, 46–48, and 50–52), frequently repeating herself, using repetition as "the central linguistic meaning-making strategy" (Tannen [1989], *Talking Voices*, p. 97) of poetics. Except for the one time she directly asks Ciro for what she wants, Rina engages in indirect language, also a poetic strategy. But her performance does not work because Ciro abruptly walks off without giving her an answer.

The second time, Rina signals her performance with a change in stress, pitch, and duration. Again, she speaks in breath groups of three lines (lines

72–74); again she uses repetition to create a poetic parallelism that becomes more and more authoritative as it escalates. The words she chooses invoke an official financial authority: "stamps," "postmaster," "check." At the end, her voice becomes the loudest it ever has been on the tape. She also uses a pause right before the *coup de grace* in line 115, "THAT SHE GETS THE MONEY TWICE?," as a signal to pay attention. This time her performance works because she has cowed Ciro. All he can do is mumble softly, "I don't know."

We know when the performances have ended because, in both cases, the normal give and take of conversation ends. The first time (line 55) entails a confusion of overlapping comments in which all the women become an audience to Ciro's dramatic exit; the second time (line 116), the silence signals Ciro's and the audience's acknowledgment of his defeat. According to Bauman (1977), "A not insignificant part of the capacity of performance to transform social structure … resides in the power that the performer derives from the control over his audience afforded him by the formal appeal of his performance" (p. 16). In this case, "control" means the power to stop what had been proceeding conversationally. In other words, Rina achieves power because her audience is stopped in its tracks by her cleverness.

The ladies have helped constitute this "performance" by their willingness to let Rina speak for them; their willingness to be the audience is heard in back-channel hums of approval throughout. Rina, too, is clearly considering and speaking for them as she states in her entreaty: "You're all here, you're all officers, ask him to deduct." During her second performance, their mention of "Matilda" as the woman "who bought the stamps" lends credibility to her outrage at Ciro for implying that he gave her the money.

What role does indirection and the view of women as "powerless" users of language play in this discourse?

Stubbs (1983) maintained that much of language use is indirect, and that "a central problem for analysis is therefore the depth of indirection involved" (p. 147). This insight allows us to view much of this discourse as meaning other than what it literally says. For example, Rina's lines 26–27 "We want to show you our books. We want to pay the bills," probably really means "We want you to acknowledge that some of what we have paid was not really our responsibility." But because her meaning is expressed indirectly, if she happens to be wrong, she can save face later by claiming that she really wanted simply to "show our books." This is the power of indirection: Paradoxically, it can claim powerlessness for itself and so not be left without any way to repair a *brutta figura*.

How are language and culture inextricably bound?

Discourse analysis serves as an important tool in describing this bond, because it shows us how one creates and, at the same time, is created by the other. That is, to examine the language of this transcript without acknowledging the primacy of the cultural construct of *bella figura* as a frame is virtually impossible. Otherwise, much of what goes on becomes unclear, or worse—nonsensical. But we also cannot understand *bella figura* as a cultural construct unless it is played out as a specific linguistic performance. Otherwise, there is no meaning in what occurs. They are two sides of the same coin. That is, if we do not understand the intense importance of display and spectacle in this speech community, we also fail to realize how Rina's artful performance operates in the claiming of power. And if we do not understand how Rina's artful performance operates in the claiming of power, we also fail to realize the intense importance of display and spectacle in this speech community.

In conclusion, these women's ways of speaking, both gendered and cultured, are dependent on the context of the Collandia Ladies' Club for their full meaning. This transcript, a wonderfully rich and woven tapestry, allows us to understand that *bella figura* operates in language as well as in nonverbal behavior. Rina's performance, a dazzling display of verbal art, validates yet again the cultural code in which it is embedded.

ENDNOTES

1. Generally speaking, these neighborhoods were formed by chain migration patterns, with immigrants coming to live alongside others from their same town or region.
2. The name is a pseudonym, as are all the women's names except mine.
3. Lucca is a province located in Tuscany in north central Italy, where the dialect spoken is very close to standard Italian. By contrast, most Italian immigration to Chicago was from southern Italy.
4. The conditions they encountered, although challenging, were not the *miseria* attributed to the illiterate waves of the early 1900s.

Generally, these *lucchesi* arrived equipped with literacy, job skills, and contacts already in place.

5. These words were told to me over and over again by different members.

6. I, too, am bicultural and bilingual, for my father was born in Lucca; I was born in Chicago, as was my mother, whose parents came from Liguria and Tuscany.

7. It goes without saying that to encourage *bella figura* means to avoid *brutta figura*. The latter may be even more important.

8. It is a transcribed audiotape.

9. Five of the Italian speakers were born in Italy, four in Lucca. The other two, American-born, come from *Lucchesi* parents. The non-Italian speakers are married to bilingual *Lucchese* men and identify strongly with the Italian community.

10. Newcomers are monolingual president Dora, monolingual Jeanne, and bilingual Gloria (me).

11. The Collandia Club has owned its own clubhouse since the early 1970s. Expenses for the building are constant.

12. See Nardini (1999) *Che Bella Figura! The Power of Performance in an Italian Ladies' Club in Chicago*, State University of New York Press for a full explanation of the "real rules" of the club.

13. Farr's (2000) Mexican ranchero franqueza seems to be a similar phenomenon.

14. Note Rina's use of "feel," which implies a sort of weblike intuition. Jeanne had said, "Do you know what I'm saying?," which is more of an intellectualization

REFERENCES

Bauman, R. (1977). *Verbal art as performance.* Prospect Heights, IL: Waveland Press.

Candeloro, D. (1995). Chicago's Italians: A survey of the ethnic factor 1850–1985. In M. G. Holli & P. d'A. Jones (Eds.), *Ethnic Chicago: A multicultural portrait* (pp. 229–259). Grand Rapids, MI: Eerdmans.

Castiglione, B. (1528). *The book of the courtier.* (Trans. Sir Thomas Hoby, 1994). London: J.M. Dent and Sons.

Farr, M. (2000). *A Mi No Me Manda Nadie!* Individualism and identity in mexican ranchero speech. *Pragmatics, 10,* 61–85.

Goffman, E. (1959). *The presentation of self in everyday life.* New York: Anchor Books.

Hymes, D. (1974). *Foundations in sociolinguistics: An ethnographic approach.* Philadelphia: University of Pennsylvania Press.

Nardini, G. (1999). *Che bella figura! The power of performance in an Italian ladies' club in chicago.* Albany: State University of New York Press.

Saville-Troike, M. (1982). *The ethnography of communication.* Oxford: Basil Blackwell.

Scott, J. (1990). *Domination and the arts of resistance: Hidden transcripts.* New York, London: Yale University Press.

Stubbs, M. (1983). *Discourse analysis: The sociolinguistic analysis of natural language.* Chicago: The University of Chicago Press.

Tannen, D. (1989). *Talking voices: Repetition, dialogue, and imagery in conversational discourse.* Cambridge, UK: Cambridge University Press.

Tannen, D. (1991). Indirectness in discourse: Ethnicity as conversational style. *Discourse Processes, 4,* 221–238.

Photograph by Michael Maltz

11

Lithuanian and English Language Use Among Early Twentieth Century Lithuanian Immigrants in Chicago

Daiva Markelis

Eastern Illinois State University

It wasn't that you sent your children to Lithuanian school to BECOME Lithuanian. You sent your children to Lithuanian school because you WERE Lithuanian.

—Father Edward Stockus

Driving through the South Side Chicago neighborhood known as Back of the Yards, so named because of its proximity to the famous Stockyards, a newcomer might well notice the number of churches: It seems as if there is one on every block. Surely one of the most striking is Holy Cross Church on 46th and Wood—Sv. Kryziaus Baznycia, the cornerstone reads—an orange brick baroque-style building with a white concrete rim of frosting. It is the church where Jurgis Rudkus, the Lithuanian immigrant hero of Upton Sinclair's *The Jungle*, would have gone to Sunday Mass, if he had been the kind of man to go to church.

A hundred years ago one would have heard mostly Lithuanian spoken in this neighborhood. Today, Spanish fills the streets. Some of the individuals I

275

have interviewed for my research, the children or grandchildren of Lithuanian immigrants, complain about the influx of immigrants from Mexico, ruing the fact that the Masses at Holy Cross are now in Spanish. Misguided beliefs about the language use of their own predecessors are at least partly the cause of their discontent. "Why can't they speak English?" one woman exclaimed. "My hardworking grandfather learned English in a snap."

My research belies this simplistic notion of language acquisition and presents a different historical picture. The first generation of Lithuanian immigrants in Chicago held on to their native tongue, often fiercely. Although these immigrants spoke Lithuanian because it was practical to do so—they lived in close proximity to other Lithuanians—emotional and political reasons played a part in Lithuanian language maintenance as well: In many cases, a conscious effort was made to keep Lithuanian alive. In contrast, learning English was a process motivated by the day to day exigencies of life and often varied according to individual motivation and talent. Most first-generation Lithuanian immigrants learned at least some English, but it was rarely through formal settings such as government-sponsored classes, but on the job, through union activities, or otherwise in the give and take of everyday life. My goal in this chapter is to present a portrait of Lithuanian immigrant life that focuses on these two important aspects: Lithuanian language maintenance and English language learning.

For this study I have used historical documents such as letters and newspapers, as well as ethnographic interviews with the children of Lithuanian immigrants. I have conducted more than 25 interviews, each lasting approximately 2 hours. Among my most important participants were the sisters of the Order of St. Casimir, a Lithuanian congregation founded in Pennsylvania in 1907. I spent an entire day at the Motherhouse on Chicago's South Side talking to the sisters, most of whom are older than 80 years, about their families, all of whom had emigrated from Lithuania around the turn of the century, as well as their own early childhood experiences with reading, writing, and speaking, whether in English or Lithuanian.[1]

BACKGROUND

Lithuanians were among the over 23 million people who entered the United States from 1881 to 1920, during the so-called Great Wave of Immigration (Daniels, 1990, pp. 123–124). Although actual immigration figures are problematic—there was no separate U.S. census category for Lithuanians until 1910—an estimated 300,000 Lithuanians left their homes in search of economic opportunity[2] (Fainhauz, 1977, p. 42). Unemployment in Lithuanian was high, caused in part by the disintegration of feudalism in the mid-19th century and the growth of new industries that could not accommodate the number of untrained farm workers (Fainhauz, 1991, p. 16). Young Lithuanian men of agrarian background, and fewer women, left for the United States, spurred on by stories of fellow countrymen amassing enough wealth to return home and buy land.[3]

Whereas the earliest Lithuanian immigrants settled in the coal mining regions of Pennsylvania, where the intense development of the coal industry provided many job opportunities, by 1910 Chicago had begun to replace Pennsylvania as the center of Lithuanian immigration. Chicago's rapid industrialization and the prospect of readily available work in the meatpacking industry began to lure Lithuanians in ever greater numbers (Fainhauz, 1977, pp. 35–36). Sister Cordia Vaisvilas, whose father worked in the Stockyards for many years, estimated that about one third of all Lithuanians in Chicago found work there in the early years of immigration. Cordia remembers watching the workers coming home with their feet wrapped in bandages: "It was the lowest kind of work you could get." The only advantage to working in the Yards, according to Cordia, was that it was relatively easy for an immigrant to find a job there because a knowledge of English was not a requirement (personal communication, October 24, 1995).

Most Lithuanian laborers lived in the vicinity of the actual yards, the area known today as Back of the Yards, bordered by Halsted Street on the east, Western Avenue on the west, Pershing Road and Garfield Boulevard on the south and north. Others settled in neighboring Bridgeport, located to the east of Halsted. A defining feature of both Back of the Yards and Bridgeport was diversity, one that reflected the ethnic makeup of the Stockyards themselves. Lithuanians lived and worked among Germans, Irish, Poles, Slovaks, Russians, and Czechs.

LANGUAGE MAINTENANCE: SPEAKING ONLY LITHUANIAN

Although Back of the Yards and Bridgeport were polyglot neighborhoods in which no one language dominated, the different ethnicities tended to congregate with members of their own group. Sister Cordia remembers growing up in the heavily Lithuanian atmosphere of Union Avenue in Bridgeport: "There were Lithuanian stores. We had a Lithuanian dairy. On the corner was a Lithuanian butcher shop. We were able to make a living, knowing only our own language." Father Edward Stockus recalls the diversity of Bridgeport, where other groups were grudgingly acknowledged, but one kept firmly to one's own:

> There were four churches within walking distance of where we lived. One Polish, St. Mary's. Then there was the Italian and the Irish church. So why did I go to St. George's, which was further from the Irish church, St. David's? St. David's was across the street, but I walked to church four, five blocks,away, to go to St. George. Because that was my church, you see. That was the Lithuanian church.

Stockus stresses that, even as late as the 1930s, one was able to get along in Bridgeport knowing only Lithuanian: "The butcher, the baker, and the candlestick maker were all Lithuanian. When my grandmother sent me to the store, I spoke Lithuanian to the shopkeeper. When I came home, we spoke Lithuanian" (personal communication, May 26, 1995).

Not only were practical, day-to-day transactions conducted in Lithuanian, but larger, more complex needs for affiliation were met in fellowships and clubs wherein only Lithuanian was spoken. In 1900 there were 39 Lithuanian organizations in Chicago alone. Many were mutual aid societies, others were political or religious in nature, and still others were specialized groups—theater lovers, musicians, doctors (Kucas, 1971, p. 72). Sister Cordia's father belonged to the Simano Daukanto Fellowship, a national club for men whose initial purpose was to raise funds for the education of poor Lithuanian students, but which, like many other organizations, served a social purpose as well, holding carnivals, bazaars, and dances.

Most of these events were advertised in Lithuanian newspapers, which were found in almost every Lithuanian household according to the participants in this study. Although it is difficult to ascertain how many Lithuanian immigrants read newspapers, and with what fluency, it remains a fact that from the beginning of mass immigration to 1955, about 220 Lithuanian newspapers and other periodicals appeared in the United States (Fainhauz, 1977, p. 32). Many of these had a limited life span or served a circumscribed geographical area, but several ran for decades and had nationwide circulations. *Draugas* [The Friend], a Catholic daily newspaper based in Chicago since 1913, is still widely read today. The socialist-oriented *Naujienos* [The News], founded in Chicago in 1914, stopped publication only in the late 1970s. The first major Lithuanian paper published in Chicago was the popular *Lietuva* [Lithuania], whose first issue came out in 1896.

In addition to providing news of local events as well as important stories happening across the country, many of the papers served as a means of connection to Lithuania. Readers wanting to know of the problems their countrymen were facing, especially in their slow walk towards independence from Russia, had this news made readily available. Conversely, inhabitants of Lithuania often had access to U.S. based Lithuanian publications. Readers there would thus have been aware of the opportunities and struggles facing their compatriots in the United States, such as the communities that were forming and the schools and churches that were being established.

That many early Lithuanian newspapers survived, even flourished, says something about the need for ethnic identification, given the fact that the first steps toward establishing a Lithuanian press in the United States were so difficult. Because the center of publishing in Lithuania during the press ban had been Eastern Prussia, the first Lithuanian publishers had few actual models of how newspapers and books were produced. In addition, there had been no uniform grammar for Lithuanian, as there had been for Polish. A greater problem was the general lack of formal education on the part of Lithuanian immigrants. In 19th century Lithuania, economic motivations for learning to read and write were few. Fainhauz (1977) contends that between 1899 and 1914 the rate of illiteracy among Lithuanian immigrants in the United States was 53% (p. 21).[4]

We see another strong indication of the conscious maintenance and fostering of Lithuanian language and culture in the popularity of Lithuanian parochial schools in Chicago during the second decade of the past century.[5] Although it is difficult to calculate how many Lithuanian children attended parochial schools as opposed to public schools (the latter did not keep statistics of the ethnic backgrounds of students), the parochial schools were more numerous. The first Lithuanian school in Chicago, St. George's, was founded in 1894. Other parish schools soon followed, among them Holy Cross in Back of the Yards, Providence of God on 18th Street, Our Lady of Vilna on the near west side, Immaculate Conception in Brighton Park, All Saints in Roseland, and St. Anthony in the suburb of Cicero. Although enrollments in Chicago-area Lithuanian parochial schools were initially low, they rose steadily over the years. The following figures represent Holy Cross.

1904—80	1912—410
1905—160	1913—414
1906—180	1914—434
1907—200	1915—515
1908—215	1916—554
1909—240	1917—682
1910—310	1918—831
1911—340	

(*Golden Jubilee Book of the Holy Cross Lithuanian Roman Catholic Parish Chicago, 1904–1954*, 1954, p. 108)

The year 1911 was an especially important one for Lithuanian parochial education in Chicago. Mother Maria Kaupas, the cofounder of the Sisters of St. Casimir and its first mother superior, celebrated the dedication of the order's convent, which guaranteed an educational base in Chicago and a future supply of teachers. Katherine Burton [1958] writes that at the dedication, "Huge crowds wandered through the building and the grounds. It was clear from their words that many felt that this was indeed a new era in Lithuanian education" (p. 93).

Lithuanian grammar, reading, and history were part of the curriculum in Lithuanian parochial schools, as were Bible history and catechism, both taught in Lithuanian. English reading and grammar were also required, as were geography, mathematics, and penmanship, all in English. Although the subjects taught in Lithuanian schools were similar to those of other parochial schools in the Chicago area, the atmosphere, according to Sister Agnesine Dering, was overwhelmingly Lithuanian:

Our prayers were in Lithuanian. We went to confession in Lithuanian. We had catechism in Lithuanian. We had a beautiful reading book in Lithuanian for each of the different grades. All the external prayers were in Lithuanian. We used to address the sisters in Lithuanian. (personal communication, October 24, 1995)

The Lithuanian used in school was often reinforced in after school activities. Poetry readings, plays, and reading contests were popular. Christine Konstant remembers having to memorize lines for plays in her parochial school in the south side neighborhood of West Pullman. Konstant was a good student, but never won any prizes because her Lithu-

anian pronunciation "wasn't as good as the others'." When the priests organized events such as parish anniversaries that involved the talents of the
school's students, Konstant participated, but in her own words, "wasn't a
star" (personal communication, April 7, 1997). Dering, on the other hand,
was known as "a good reader," and was often asked to read prayers and
participate in school programs. Her Lithuanian pronunciation was considered "excellent," which she attributes to having read out loud to her grandmother as a girl.

Of course, not all parents could afford private schooling for their children. Economic considerations played a large role in why Jean Janula and
her sister Viktorija Leberes went to Seward School on 46th and Hermitage,
the public school that Lithuanian children in the Stockyards district attended (personal communication, January 30, 1996). Sometimes other
factors influenced parents to send their children to public schools. Vyto
Grigas' father was a staunch socialist who distrusted the clergy. Grigas Sr.
believed that his children could engage in Lithuanian activities outside of
school hours (personal communication, September 15, 1998).

In spite of having missed out on the heavily Lithuanian parochial school
experience, Janula, Leberes, and Grigas all belong to Lithuanian organizations and subscribe to Lithuanian newspapers. What undoubtedly helped
them maintain a strong sense of ethnic identity was that their parents, like
many first-generation Lithuanian parents, encouraged the use of Lithuanian in the home. Some parents went beyond simple encouragement. Sister Angela Balciunas recalls: "My mother was so afraid that I would forget
Lithuanian, so we *always* had to talk it at home" (personal communication, October 24, 1995). Sister Cordia's parents would raise their voices every time she or her siblings uttered a word in English. Her father would turn
to her mother, shake his head, and say, "As nezinau kas bus su tais vaikais.
Mes nesusisnekesim su jais" [I don't know what's going to happen to
those kids. We won't be able to communicate with them].

This last statement—we won't be able to communicate with
them—gets to the core of the emotional reasons that guide language
maintenance. Although "emotional" may seem too imprecise and un-
scholarly a term to use to explain the issue at hand, the assimilation of the
second generation into the mainstream through the increasing use of English is an emotional issue, one that most immigrant groups in the United
States have faced. The literature of U.S. immigration is replete with examples of the conflicts that surface in families when children acquire English
and look askance at the native tongue of their parents. Hilda Satt

Polacheck (1991), writing about the immigrant children in her West Side Chicago neighborhood, observed that as soon as they learned to speak English, they began to look down on those who could not, especially parents (p. 65). Louise Montgomery, in her 1913 study of the Stockyards, contended that dress and speech were "the visible signs of the distance between parents and child" (pp. 59–60).

The remembrances of an older Lithuanian immigrant poignantly convey the situation of parents faced with the disjunction of their families because of the cultural "advancement" of their children through their American education and their native knowledge of English.

> My children have grown up. They are educated, and the education given them by America has taken them from me. I speak English only as an untaught alien can speak it. But my children know all the slang phrases. They speak differently, they act differently, and when they come to visit me, they come alone. They do not explain why they do not bring their friends, but I instinctively sense the reason. (Roucek, 1952, p. 189)

For Lithuanians in the diaspora, there was another strong motivation for consciously maintaining their native tongue, this one political in nature. Concerns about the possibility of linguistic annihilation were widespread among Lithuanian immigrants, who had experienced suppression of their language during the 42 years of the czarist press ban. Having secretly fought to maintain that language under czarist oppression, most Lithuanians were unwilling to give it up now that they had the opportunity to speak and publish it freely. In the Lithuanian American community, we find pro-Lithuanian language sentiments as early as 1896, when the newspaper *Tevyne* [The Homeland] published an article stating that one day Lithuanians in the United States would become completely "anglicized," an opinion many readers of *Tevyne* did not want to accept. The Simano Daukanto Fellowship in Chicago wrote a letter to the newspaper, which read, in part:

> We felt very sad and hurt reading your story. Shivers ran up and down our spines to think that one day we will become anglicized. We hope that one day Lithuania will have its freedom. Until then, we urge all Lithuanians to use only Lithuanian. (Eidintas, 1993, p. 122)

Priests in their sermons urged the use of Lithuanian in the home partly for nationalistic reasons (Wolkovich-Valkavicius, personal communication, March 21, 1997). Visitors from Lithuania, such as the politically minded writer Zemaite, made fun of those Lithuanians who had become Americanized. Zemaite (1917), in a short story published in the Chicago-based *Naujienos,* presents us with a scathing portrayal of a Lithuanian American landlady who speaks a hybrid kind of Lithuanian, in which Lithuanian suffixes are appended to English words. She is depicted as obese and vulgar, with ragged, dirty, and, worst of all, completely English-speaking children.

It is difficult, of course, to determine to what extent the maintenance of Lithuanian among Chicago immigrants was a deeply held political belief, encouraged by the clergy and press, to what extent it was a result of the parental desire for family cohesion, to what extent it was a practical decision made on a daily basis. Most likely a combination of factors was present. A kind of momentum effect may have been at work, with parents, for example, sending their children to Lithuanian schools because this was what was done in a particular neighborhood. As Father Edward Stockus explained, "It wasn't that you sent your children to Lithuanian school to BECOME Lithuanian. You sent your children to Lithuanian school because you WERE Lithuanian."

A GRADUAL MOVE TOWARD ENGLISH

Despite the often insular nature of life and the focus on the maintenance of the native tongue, it was inevitable that first-generation Lithuanians in Chicago learned at least some English. Given the right circumstances, some even became more or less fluent speakers. Those immigrants who lived in communities with fewer Lithuanians, for example, acquired English more readily than those residing in neighborhoods such as Back of the Yards. Sister Anita Petrosius, whose parents came to the United States in 1890, grew up in an area where there were only two other Lithuanian families. Her mother had to speak English to buy food at the local grocery store. She began by pointing out items she wanted to buy. Her first English words were "I want this." Eventually, she was able to converse with her neighbors, although, according to Anita, it was in a very "broken" English (personal communication, October 24, 1995).

It was also necessity that motivated Sister Cyril Krasauskas' father to learn English. He acquired a job as a janitor in a heavily Jewish neighborhood on the West Side where most of the residents spoke English and Yiddish. He was eventually fluent enough to acquire a reputation as a jokester, and was especially popular with the older Jewish ladies (personal communication, October 24, 1995).

Many of the participants in this study cited work as a locus of English language learning for their parents, especially in the meatpacking industry. The workers in the Stockyards came from many different ethnic groups at various stages of assimilation and levels of English language knowledge. Lithuanians worked with Poles, Irish, Czechs, Russians, Mexicans, and African Americans. Although knowledge of English was not necessary to obtain a job (management looked for "a good pair of hands," according to Sister Cordia), the desire and need to communicate with workers of many nationalities was a strong motivating force in the learning of English.

We get a sense of how this interethnic communication might have worked in the following conversation from Upton Sinclair's (1985) *The Jungle*. In this passage, Jurgis is applying for a job. The manager asks him:

"Speak English?"

"No; Lit-uanian." (Jurgis had studied this word carefully.)

"Job?"

"Je." (A nod)

"Worked here before?"

"No 'stand."

(Signals and gesticulations on the part of the boss. Vigorous shakes of the head by Jurgis.)

"Shovel guts?"

"No 'stand." (More shakes of the head.)

"Zarnos. Pagaiksztis. Szluota!" (Imitative motions.)

"Je."

"See door. *Durys*?" (Pointing.)

"Je."

"Tomorrow, 7 o'clock. Understand? *Rytoj! Prieszpietys! Septyni!"* (p. 39)

Sinclair uses italics to signify Lithuanian words, with *zarnos, pagaiksztis,* and *slzuota* signifying "guts," "end of a broomstick," and "broom," with *durys* meaning "door," and *rytoj, priespietys,* and *septyni,* the words for "tomorrow," "before noon," "seven." That the supervisor had learned these difficult words implies that those in management positions absorbed at least some of the vocabulary of the foreigners, and by the end of *The Jungle*, of course, Jurgis speaks and reads English freely.

A dynamic similar to the one found in the multicultural atmosphere of the Stockyards occurred in activities centered around union involvement. Antanas Kaztauskis, a young Lithuanian laborer on the cattle-killing floor, who told his story in 1904 to a writer for *The Independent*, related the following:

> The night I joined the Cattle Butchers' Union I was led into the room by a negro member. With me were Bohemians, Germans, and Poles, and Mike Donnelly, the President, is an Irishman. He spoke to us in English, and then three interpreters told us what he said. Since then, I have gone there every two weeks, and I help the movement by being an interpreter for the other Lithuanians who come in. That is why I have learned to speak and write good English. (1990, p. 20)

For Upton Sinclair's (1985) hero, Jurgis Rudkus, joining the union also provided the motivation needed to learn to speak English, as well as to read and write it:

> One of the first consequences of the discovery of the union was that Jurgis became desirous of learning English. He wanted to know what was going on at the meetings, and to be able to take part in them. (p. 111)

Curiosity about what was going on in the world sometimes manifested itself in smaller ways. Kaztauskis mentions that in the boarding house during the evenings, those men who did not play cards would read aloud from newspapers. In this way, Kaztauskis picked up the meanings of many new words, sometimes words of a political nature such as "graft" and "trust."

Such communal reading practices were common among Lithuanian immigrants. William Wolkovich-Valkavicius remembers newspapers being passed around at various gatherings, such as socialist meetings: "People would sometimes linger afterwards and somebody might read an article and explain a word or two that *he* knew, that maybe the others didn't."[6]

Individuals were made aware of the usefulness of English through both Lithuanian and English newspapers. Although the former spearheaded the cause of Lithuanian nationalism, they often encouraged their readers to familiarize themselves with the American way. Some newspapers, such as *Keleivis* [The Traveler], published weekly English lessons in the early

1900s. Most facilitated the immigrants' adaptation to their new surroundings through news stories about current political events in the United States, articles on health and hygiene, and advertisements touting new products and services. The first written manifestations of hybrid American Lithuanian words occurred in such advertisements. An ad for insurance in *Lietuva* (1909) reads "Mes Apdraudziame" and then, in parentheses, "Insuriname" (p. 5.)

It is likely that as Lithuanian Americans moved up the economic ladder and had more money to spend on luxury items, their awareness of advertisements for such items increased, and, in a sense, so did their exposure to English. Even in the Communist paper *Vilnis* [The Surge] (1926) published in Chicago, amid articles extolling the virtues of collective ownership, we find advertisements for Milda Auto Sales, "featuring the wonderful Studebaker," for Baldwin pianos, for Woolworths, and for real estate—"we buy and sell homes, farms, and businesses" (p. 11). The same advertisements frequently appeared in newspapers with completely different political ideologies.

Writers and editors of Lithuanian newspapers often walked a fine line between wanting to expose their readers to the benefits of American culture and believing it was their duty to admonish them not to forget that they were, first and foremost, Lithuanians. *Naujienos*, for example, often urged its readers to join Lithuanian organizations and be active in Lithuanian political groups. At the same time, the editors advocated an appreciation of American cultural values. A writer for *Naujienos* reviewed a play called *Experience* running at the Garrick Theater in Chicago:

> Everyone should see this production. It would pay our young people to take a greater interest in real art, which furnishes more food for the spirit than our own theater. It is not necessary to know the English language well to understand these productions, because they are acted so realistically that they can be understood even without words. (Naujienos)

Lithuanian newspapers also promoted the reading of books by publishing excerpts from works of literature as well as by listing books that were available for sale through the mail in their back pages. Whereas most of these books were in Lithuanian, many were translations of American and English authors such as Mark Twain, Henry Wadsworth Longfellow, Daniel DeFoe, and Charles Dickens. The April 6, 1906 *Keleivis* advertised an "intelligent" English grammar book that could be ordered for $1.25 (p. 6).

Advertisements for *Kaip Rasyti Laiskus Lietuviskoje ir Angliskoje Kalbose* [How to Write Letters in Lithuanian and English] appeared in successive issues of *Lietuva* in 1910. The book was touted as part of a package deal promising an easy method of learning English. Lithuanian–English dictionaries were popular, although expensive. A listing in the January 1, 1909 issue of *Lietuva* [Lithuania] offered a leatherbound Lithuanian–English dictionary for four dollars (p. 9). Many of the participants in this study remember such volumes. Vyto Grigas showed me his late father's dictionary, a huge 1911 leatherbound edition in excellent condition of Antanas Lalis' Lithuanian–English and English–Lithuanian dictionary. Lalis, who emigrated to the United States in 1895, published 10,000 copies, in four editions, of his popular dictionary (Fainhauz, 1977, p. 170).

At this point, the reader might wonder about formal or "book" learning: How many Lithuanian immigrants availed themselves of English language classes, for example, especially those free classes offered by the government? The period of great immigration was one that spawned concern about the growing number of potential citizens unable to speak English. In government-sponsored adult education programs, the teaching of English was thus considered to be of primary importance. The singleness of purpose of the earlier Americanizers was often expressed through hyperbolic language, with the teaching of English to immigrants seen as akin to going to battle. A 1909 article in the *Chicago Record Herald* on Mary McDowell's work teaching Back of the Yards immigrants begins with this sentence: "Making good American citizens of the conglomerate colony of Lithuanians, Croations, Bohemians, Poles and Slavonians ... is the *herculean task* to which Miss Mary E. McDowell and her co-workers ... have set themselves during the coming winter" (Medwedeff, 1909, p. 15, emphasis mine). Ernest Talbert (1912), in discussing the marked dropout rate of immigrant children in Back of the Yards, writes that "the faulty knowledge of our language and institutions, and the precarious family incomes all conspire to defeat the most *heroic attempts* to 'hold' the pupils after the fifth grade" (p. 9, emphasis mine).

A few of the individuals I have interviewed do remember their parents taking advantage of classes offered by the government. Ben Norbut related how his mother, who a came to this country in 1910 as an 18-year old, had attended classes at St. George's parish in Bridgeport to learn English, but remained for only a short period of time. Other concerns, such as work and family, were more pressing (personal communication, November 5, 1993). Sister Dilecta Kriauciunas' father attended classes in Chicago— again, for only a couple of months. Sister Dilecta had asked her father about the brevity of his stay: "Pa, why didn't you finish?" He answered, "I was ashamed. The *tycerka* [woman teacher] was younger than me" (personal communication, October 24, 1995)

Algirdas Margeris (1956) also had a *tycerka*, one on whom he developed a crush. Although she was older than Margeris, and, in his words, "plump," and "a spinster," he enjoyed the way she would sometimes sit down next to him on a bench meant for one. Margeris remembers her teaching him how to pronounce the word "Washington": "You have to pronounce it Uosinkton, not Vasington" (p. 18).

Perhaps as a response to American schools that were not meeting their needs, Lithuanians started their own evening schools. One well-known institution, founded in 1908, was the Ausra school and bookstore in Bridgeport, on 33rd, between Halsted and Morgan (Margeris, 1956, p. 106). The Lithuanian Socialist Alliance held classes there whose purpose was to teach both spoken and written English. However, a teacher at the school began to realize how difficult it was to teach English grammar to students who did not know *Lithuanian* grammar. He thus changed tactics, and began his course with an introduction to Lithuanian grammar, then slowly moved on to English: "In this way I taught them both languages, one might say, at the same time" (p. 107).

A fairly unusual educational venue was a correspondence school founded in Chicago in 1913, allowing those who had difficulty attending regular classes a chance at formal education. To attract students, a fancy catalog listing the subjects was published. It was interspersed with inspirational maxims dealing with education, such as "The words *I can't* are found only in the dictionaries of stupid people" (Margeris, 1956, p. 111), revealing the growing American cultural influence of the cult of "positive thinking."

It is important to note that in both of these schools, English was only one of many subjects. The correspondence school, for example, offered classes in history, mathematics, foreign languages, and art. In general, however, such classes were luxuries that most workers could not afford.

Whereas some Lithuanians learned English through formal schooling, many more acquired it in the give and take of everyday life, learning from friends, neighbors, and coworkers, piecing together words here and there. Newspapers and street signs were often more effective texts than schoolbooks, children more successful instructors than experienced teachers.

This last scenario—older individuals learning from children—was a common one, occurring in a wide range of situations, from those in which several words and phrases are learned to those in which learning of a more extensive kind takes place. Sister Dilecta's parents listened to their children talk, and in this way picked up words and phrases. Sister Dilecta clearly remembers her mother's first words in English:

> One time we were eating. Mama was making pancakes. She was in the kitchen, and we heard her say something. We couldn't hear her. "Ka mama? Ka mama?" She said, "I don't chew my cabbage twice." Her first English words. "Jus manot kad as durna, kad as nemoku kalbeti angliskai!" [You think I'm stupid, that I don't know how to speak English]. "I don't chew my cabbage twice." She heard us say that. And she learned from us.

Christine Konstant's father, who was highly literate and often wrote articles for the Lithuanian papers, often asked his children the meaning of English words: "If he ran across an English word he didn't know, he didn't hesitate to ask us what it meant. If he had to write something, he'd say 'Now, how would you say this in good English?'"

Upton Sinclair perceived the acquisition of literacy in a similar way, as a social, rather than individual practice, with parents learning from children, and husbands learning from wives. In a scene from *The Jungle (1985)*, the family gathers around a flyer advertising a house for sale in three different languages: German, Polish, and English. The family pores over the brochure. Ona, Jurgis' wife, the most literate family member, attempts to "spell out its contents" (1985, p. 56). Later, when Jurgis begins to realize the importance of knowing English, he is helped in his quest by friends and family members: "The children, who were at school, and learning fast, would teach him a few, and a friend loaned him a little book that had some in it, and Ona would read to him" (p. 111).

Those unacquainted with communities in which several languages co-exist may view this kind of situation—adults learning a language from children—as an aberration. In fact, it was (and is) a common scenario. Algirdas Margeris first learned English from the children of his landlord. The Czech immigrant Louis Adamic (1932) learned how to read English by observing others read, especially the children of the Zemlar's, a family with whom he boarded for some time. He asked them questions about what they were reading, focusing both on individual words and broader meanings (p. 75).

As parents learned English from their children, these children were furthering their own English language education, whether at school or through contact with other children. It was inevitable that these children would grow up to acquire full fluency in English. For the participants in this study, even those who were raised in the most Lithuanian of families, as were the Sisters of St. Casimir, English become the dominant language at some point in their adult lives. Although Lithuanian had been the first lan-

guage of all of the sisters, and many of them went on to teach in the Lithua-
nian parochial schools in Chicago, most preferred talking to me in English.
Other participants in this study, such as Christine Konstant, speak very little
Lithuanian today. Her children do not speak it at all.

CONCLUSION

The editors of the 1896 *Tevyne* were thus correct in their assessment that
one day Lithuanians living in the United States would become "anglicized."
That the "anglicization" took longer to accomplish than the editors of
Tevyne had expected says something about the persistence of Lithuanian
ethnic identity. What the Simano Daukanto Society urged in response to
Tevyne's 1896 prophecy—that Lithuanian immigrants speak only their native tongue until Lithuania gains its independence from Russia—was, in reality, a fairly accurate prediction of what happened. Lithuania achieved
independence in 1918, and the postwar years saw a marked decline in the
use of Lithuanian in the home (Fainhauz, 1977, p. 29). Political reasons for
the conscious maintenance of Lithuanian were removed. At the same time,
a certain percentage of Lithuanian immigrants returned to Lithuania.

There was, however, another, even greater, factor that contributed to
the decline of Lithuanian language use in the United States. The 1920s saw
a huge standstill in emigration to the United States. Congressional debates
on immigration restriction in 1920–1921 led to stopgap measures and
eventually a law that limited immigration according to quotas based on already existing numbers of immigrants (Daniels, 1990, pp. 236–237). By the
end of the 1920s, the number of European immigrants had dropped to an
all-time low of 150,000 (p. 239). The efforts needed to sustain a first language in the wake of ever-increasing exposure to the dominant language
and in the absence of practical, emotional, or political reasons for doing so
are enormous. With some exceptions, so-called "minority" languages are
usually maintained only as long as steady immigration or other contact
with the "homeland" continues.

For Lithuanian immigrants, issues of ethnic identity, language maintenance,
and assimilation dominated the 1920s. An increase in mixed marriages among
Lithuanians after the war accelerated the use of English, especially when
non–Lithuanian-speaking spouses began attending traditionally Lithuanian
churches. St. George's Church in Bridgeport, following the lead of other
churches, introduced sermons in English in 1924 to accommodate these
spouses, although not without some protest (Wolkovich-Valkavicius, 1988, p.

112). Lithuanian newspapers began to grapple with an increasingly bilingual readership, as well as with the question of how to engage the interest of young people increasingly reluctant consciously to maintain the native language of their parents. In 1923, the journal *Vytis* [The Knight], the official organ of the Knights of Lithuania, began publishing a column in English, "Our American Friend" (p. 112). The student magazine *Giedra* [Clarity] posed the following question in 1924: "How can one who speaks Lithuanian instill national love in those who understand very little or are totally ignorant of the Lithuanian language?" (Fainhauz, 1977, p. 28).

The writer of the *Giedra* article acknowledged the inevitability of Americanization, a destiny that did not escape other immigrant groups of the time as well. The Immigrant Commission, the joint House–Senate group created in 1907 to study issues relating to immigration, and often highly critical of immigrants, discovered that more than 95% of children born in the United States during the first decade of the 20th century to foreign parents eventually learned English. The Commission also found that the longer immigrants lived in the United States, the more likely they were to learn English (Immigrant Commission, 1911, 1:474–485). The situation is not so different in the United States today. Studies show that most immigrants from Mexico and other Spanish-speaking countries do learn English (Baron, 1990, p. 23).

Whereas the local fruterias and mercados in the Back of the Yards will most likely survive, given the growing Mexican and Mexican American population in Chicago, the problems that Lithuanian immigrants faced almost a hundred years ago are not so different from those that other groups, including Mexicans, grapple with today. Although each immigrant group arrives with its own distinct culture, all share similar concerns—finding a job, a decent place to live, and a school to educate one's children. Each engages in similar balancing acts—learning English while maintaining and promoting the language of their forefathers and mothers, a language that helps to foster an emotional bond with their children, a language from which they acquire such an important part of their identity.

ENDNOTES

1. All of the participants in this study agreed to having their real names used. Translations of conversations that took place in Lithuanian are mine, as are translations from Lithuanian printed sources.
2. Before 1910, Lithuanians were grouped with the Russians, whose subjects they had been for more that a century.

3. The immigrants that are the focus of this article were Roman
   Catholic. Many Lithuanian Jews emigrated during this period as
   well. Their patterns of employment were different from those of
   non-Jewish Lithuanians, and their educational and linguistic
   backgrounds also differed.

4. Publishers of newspapers helped to promote literacy by urging
   Lithuanians living in the United States to read more. The
   Lietuviska Gazieta [Lithuanian Gazette], for example, encouraged its readers to follow the example of other immigrant groups,
   especially the Jews, in "uplifting" the race (Prunskis, 1957, p. 303).
   It is important to note that literacy was viewed in terms of learning
   to read and write in *Lithuanian*, at least initially. Newspapers also
   urged readers to join Lithuanian organizations and to teach their
   children the Lithuanian language.

5. Parochial schools were popular among other recent immigrant
   groups as well. Ethnic-community mother-tongue schools, as
   Joshua Fishman (1985) termed them, were extremely common
   among immigrants until the World War I (p. 364). The editor of
   the Chicago-based *Greek Star* wrote that "the Greek school will
   train children to be Greeks so that they will not be digested in the
   vastness of America" (Kopan, 1981, p. 80). The record book of
   1913 for St. Joseph's, a Polish school in the Back of the Yards, reveals in its list of subjects not only history, grammar, and geography, but also Polish reading, Polish grammar, and the history of
   Poland (Slayton, 1986, p. 51).

6. We find such collaborative reading among other immigrant
   groups of the time. A young Croatian immigrant, talking about the
   influence of the paper of the National Croation Society, the
   Zajednicar, stated that even nonliterate Croatians received the
   paper: "There is always some man in the lodging house who
   reads the Croatian and American papers aloud, and so everyone
   hears the news" (Park, 1922, p. 139).

REFERENCES

Adamic, L. (1932). *Laughing in the jungle: The autobiography of an immigrant in
America*. New York: Harper and Brothers.
Baron, D. (1990). *The English-only question: An official language for Americans?*
New Haven: Yale University Press.
Burton, K. (1958). *Lily and sword and crown*. Milwaukee: Bruce Press.
Daniels, R. (1990). *Coming to America: A history of immigration and ethnicity in
American life*. New York: Harper Perennial.
Eidintas, A. (1993). *Lietuviu Kolumbai* [Lithuanian Columbuses] Vilnius: Mintis.

Fainhauz, D. (1991). Lithuanians in the USA: Aspects of Ethnic Identity, Chicago: Litthuanian Library Press.

Fainhauz, D. (1977). *Lithuanians in multiethnic Chicago*. Chicago: Lithuanian Library Press.

Fishman, J. (1985). The significance of the ethnic community mother-tongue school. *The rise and fall of the ethnic revival: Perspectives on language and ethnicity*, Mouton: Berlin.

Golden Jubilee of the Holy Cross Lithuanian Roman Catholic Parish, Chicago, 1904–1954 (1954). Chicago.

Immigrant Commission. (1911). *Report of the Immigration Commission, 1911*. Washington, DC: Government Printing Office.

Kaztauskis, A. (1990). The life story of a Lithuanian. In H. Holt (Ed.), *The life stories of undistinguished Americans* (pp. 6–20). New York: Routledge.

Keleivis [The Traveler]. p. 6. Grammar book (Advertisement, April 6, 1906).

Kopan, A. (1981). Greek survival in Chicago: The role of ethnic education, 1890–1980. In P. d'A. Jones & M. Holli (Eds.), *Ethnic Chicago* (pp. 80–139). Grand Rapids: William B. Eerdmans.

Kucas, A. (1971). *Amerikos lietuviu istorija*. [A history of Lithuanians in the United States]. Boston: Lietuviu Enciplopedijos Leidykla.

Lietuva [Lithuania]. Kaip rasyti laiskus lietuviskoje ir angliskoje kalbose (Advertisement, March and April issues, 1910).

Lietuva [Lithuania], p. 9. Lithuanian-English dictionary. (Advertisement, January 1, 1909).

Margeris, A. (1956). *Amerikos lietuviai ir angliskuju skoliniu zodynas* [The Lithuanians of America and a Dictionary of English Loan Words: 1872–1949]. Chicago: Naujienos.

Medwedeff, S. (October 10, 1909). American citizens in Chicago. *Chicago Record Herald*, 5–9.

Lietuva [Lithuania] Mes apdraudziame. (Advertisement for insurance, March 12, 1909). p. 5.

Vilnis [The Surge]. p. 11. Milda auto sales. (Advertisement, August 6, 1927).

Montgomery, L. (1913). *A study of Chicago's Stockyards community: The American girl in the Stockyards district*. Chicago: University of Chicago Press.

Naujienos [The News.] Experience. (Review of play, April 14, 1916). Foreign Language Press Survey, Reel IIA, Sec. 3D (1). Microfilm Department, Daley Library, University of Illinois at Chicago.

Park, R. (1922). *The immigrant press and its control*. New York: Harper and Brothers.

Polacheck, H. (1991). *I came a stranger: The story of a Hull-House girl*. Chicago: University of Illinois Press.

Prunskis, J. (1957). Amerikiniai lietuviu laikrasciai [Lithuanian-American newspapers]. In V. Bagdanavicius (Ed.), *Kovos metai del savosios spaudos* [Lithuania's fight for a free press] (pp. 299–314). Chicago: Lithuanian Community of Chicago.

Roucek, J. (1952). Lithuanian Americans. *One America: The history, contributions, and present problems of our racial and national minorities* (pp. 184–194). F. Brown & J. Roucek, (Eds.). New York: Prentice-Hall.

Sinclair, U. (1985). *The jungle*. New York: Penguin. [Original work published 1906.)

Slayton, R. (1986). *Back of the Yards: The making of a local democracy*. Chicago: University of Chicago Press.

Talbert, E. (1912). *Opportunities in school and industry for children of the Stockyards District*. Chicago: University of Chicago Press.

Wolkovich-Valkavicius. (1988). *Lithuanian Fraternalism: 75 years of U.S. Knights of Lithuania*. Brooklyn: Knights of Lithuania.

Zemaite. (December 7–11, 1917). Svetur tarp savuju [A stranger amongst my own]. *Naujienos* [The news], 291–292, 294.

12

Class Identity and the Politics of Dissent: The Culture of Argument in a Chicago Neighborhood Bar

Julie Lindquist
Michigan State University

"Let's get somebody in that can run this country like a *business!*" Jack is once again singing the praises of Ross Perot, Texas billionaire and independent candidate in the 1992 presidential election. Jack stands at his usual place at the corner of the bar, his ashtray full and beer mug empty in front of him. He never sits, but as the hours drag on, he is beginning to lean more heavily on the bar. Lately, he has been looking all of his 52 years, but now the prospect of a good argument has rejuvenated him. From my position behind the bar there is no place to hide; I will have to respond to Jack's gambit. But Jack knows what I will say just as well as I know his routine. The challenge in this game is to deliver oratory, not to fashion the perfect syllogism. A newcomer looks on in alarm, having mistaken this ritual fabrication of a cultural text for a rupture in the social fabric. I know that before my shift is over we will have strenuously debated virtues of the presidential candidates, and that we will have managed to persuade each other only to commit even more enthusiastically to our original positions. I brace myself and light another cigarette: This play is hard work, and the night is young.

At the Smokehouse Inn, a restaurant-lounge in a working-class suburb south of Chicago, working men and women gather daily to invent a space for sociable leisure, to seek respite from the quotidian realities of their working lives.[1] The Smokehouse is a place of fierce community, of imagined history and garrulous sociability. Yet this space, although safe from the demands of work and everyday responsibility, is a scene of controlled antagonisms and managed contradictions. A stranger to the scene might conclude, from the voices raised in hot dispute all around her, that the arguers there had nothing in common. But after returning to the same scene time and again to find the same arguers in the same positions and engaged in debate on the same topics, she might begin to understand that the noisy confrontations she hears are in fact structured and consensual, and that the arguers do in fact share lives, histories, and strategies for making sense of both. She might even be tempted to conclude that those at the Smokehouse are participating in an important (if not exactly sacred) ritual.

The idea of "class culture" presents interesting problems for scholars across disciplines, pointing as it does to the place where social structures and material conditions meet the particulars of local practice, in the politics of the everyday. What I am attempting here is, in a sense, tautological: I begin from the premise that there is such a phenomenon as "class culture"—a meaning-making, historical social organism whose collective experience arises out of a particular relation to the larger political economy—and end by implicitly affirming the existence of a distinctive working-class culture.[2] Like such ethnographers of working-class life and language as Douglas Foley (1990) and Aaron Fox (1994), I see class culture as a local problem, and would likewise contend that local institutions are good places to witness the microdynamics of social production.[3] My aim is to show "class culture," in this case working-class culture, to be a localized rhetorical invention. I hasten to add, here, that this does not mean that it has no basis in structural or material relations. Rather, I mean that it is produced and reproduced discursively, that it is constituted by the particulars of the relationship between ideology and practice.[4] I am especially concerned with the social uses of argument as a speech genre, the performance of which is significant to the formation and maintenance of group identity. For this reason, I give interpretive priority to *rhetoric*, an emphasis that foregrounds what is strategic, hortatory, and conflictual in acts of communication.[5] At the Smokehouse Inn, *argument* is a locally controlled rhetorical production and the principle modality through which Smokehousers express class identity in practice while disclaiming the viability of "class" as a theory of social relations. In the routinized practice of argument, people both assert a collective identity and resist its homogenizing effects.

In what follows, I first establish the Smokehouse as an institutional site for the production of distinctive cultural forms and class ideology. Next, I frame class identity as a problem of rhetoric. Finally, I offer an interpretation of an exemplary verbal performance to show how argument not only serves as the occasion for performance of local thematics, but also expresses tensions in ideologies of class identity.

THE SMOKEHOUSE AS WORKING-CLASS INSTITUTION

The Smokehouse Inn is both a distinctively local institution and a place like a thousand other such places in the Midwest. My claim that barroom culture is metonymically related to "working-class" culture rests on the assumption that barrooms are institutional microcosms of social organization, sites where culture is produced through expressive practice.[6] Historians and anthropologists of working-class social life have shown that bars have traditionally functioned as spaces mediating between home and public spheres; also, that this role has remained intact even as industrial bases and patterns of labor have changed and neighborhood demographics have shifted. Others have suggested that working-class bars are places where the social order is inverted, and where local values of reciprocity, sociability, and vernacular speech forms are asserted over their bourgeois counterparts of competitive consumption, social mobility, and standards of linguistic propriety.[7] Roy Rosenweig, for example, links bars to the historical predicament of the worker, and suggests that bars as sites of sociability came to be associated with resistance to bourgeois values of individualism and acquisitiveness. At the bar, explains Rosenweig, workers "affirmed communal over individualistic and privatistic values" (1993, p. 247). Many Chicago communities, particularly those with large populations of industrial workers, have dense concentrations of neighborhood bars. Historians such as Slayton (1986) and Duis (1983) have documented the important role taverns have played in the cultural life and social organization of working-class communities in Chicago.[8]

With Rosenwieg and and others, I hold that local bars can function as contexts for expressions of working-class resistance to mainstream middle-class values, and as such offer opportunities to observe how people in working-class communities experience themselves in relation to dominant social codes.[9] The suburban site of the Smokehouse, Greendale, has an attenuated, rural geography that presents a marked contrast to the multiplex urban density of traditional working-class enclaves such as Cicero or Bridgeport, yet it does not suffer from lack of drinking establishments from which local workers can choose to spend leisure time. Of the four genres of barroom in the area—corner bar, dance club, strip joint, and restaurant lounge—the Smokehouse is the latter. It nonetheless functions as a *neighborhood* tavern, perhaps all the more so for its potential to locate the willfully dislocated.[10] It occupies a building with a family-style restaurant famous for steak and barbecued ribs; its proximity to the attached dining room enforces a level of decorum to which the patrons of a corner would never be subjected (men drinking at the bar during restaurant hours are admonished to "watch the language" so as not to offend women and other diners not privy to the codes and rituals of male sociability).[11] Yet it attracts a regular clientele of working men and women who spend much of their leisure time at the bar, although these same clients rarely, or never, patronize the restaurant.

Depending on your point of view (or your place in the scene), the bar itself is either invitingly cozy or darkly claustrophobic. There are no windows; this public space guards its privacy fiercely. This insular, smoke-suffused room serves its blue-collar population—machinists, builders, Teamsters, and service workers—as a public forum, as a place to seek out a stable society of friends and coworkers and to engage these others in conversation and debate about current issues and political events. In fact, one might conclude that the Smokehouse serves the same function that neighborhood yards and porches once served before working-class Whites moved out from urban centers. That is, it is a physical and symbolic agent of the local, a repository of folk histories and originary tales.

For many people from Greendale and its adjacent suburbs, the Smokehouse is the nexus of leisure, truly a home-away-from-home. Many of its regulars spend several hours a day, several days a week, drinking beer and *shooting the shit* at the Smokehouse.[12] The bar is both a space apart from the routinized space of work and a compressed, concentrated space of leisure where the textures of sociality are pressed into relief. As a site of leisure, the Smokehouse barroom represents the institutionalization of challenges to institutional authority. The marking of leisure time with the ritual celebration of vice suspends the constraints of normal social arrangements, such that the local sheriff bellies up to the bar next to the neighborhood drug dealer, the immigrant octogenarian bends elbows with the young single mother. Like the butter-saturated popcorn set in front of you by the bartender upon your arrival, talk is plentiful, flavorful, and cheap. People come to the Smokehouse because they know they will find someone "at home" there, someone to listen to their stories of getting by, getting over, and getting even.

THE PRACTICE OF IDENTITY

For the Smokehouse cohort, "class" is experienced phenomenologically, not philosophically. The cultural logic about class is that it is irrelevant to social experience—at least as a theory, an interpretive language, a way to locate oneself in social space. Smokehousers voice common political interests—lower taxes, less unemployment, more pay, better working conditions—and they generally see politicians as working against their interests as working whites. At the same time, Smokehousers do not claim membership in a "working class" as explicitly defined by a history of disenfranchisement from dominant discourses or institutions. Unlike other clearly identifiable cultural themes such as work, education, race, or politics, class remains implicit, unnamable. "Class" has no place in the cultural lexicon, is not present in everyday discourse as an organizing metaphor for social phenomena. If an explicit theory of class is absent, however, its practice is everywhere. Precisely because so little is spoken about class per se, much is said. As a phenomenology of identity relations, its unnamability makes it highly narratizable.[13] Class ideologies are encoded in themes of ethnicity, education, and politics; such themes structure narratives and animate public discussions. Yet even as *class* is sublimated into other social alignments and rhetorical domains, the identification with *working* is explicit. Whether or not Smokehousers will tell you they are "working class," they want you to know that they are *people who work*. Talk of work encodes dominant values of productivity, practical knowledge, proximity to and control over products of labor, sharing of social and economic resources.

Such themes and tensions in Smokehouse logics of identity are yet more effectively illustrated by the terms of my own position in Smokehouse society. As an ethnographer, I spent over a year behind the bar as a participant and observer, distributing drinks and collecting data on everyday speech.[14] My post behind the bar was the ideal ethnographic position: Like the paradoxical position of the participant–observer, a bartender is simultaneously central to, and at a remove from, social action.[15] This ambiguous identity as academic and worker put me at the center of another kind of social dilemma as well: As one with enduring connections to the neighborhood, I was an insider (I grew up in the surrounding community, and got the Smokehouse job through a friend of a friend from a prior bartending job). As an academic, my investment in a rhetorical economy in which theory is perceived to operate as currency apart from practice—where ideas circulate as commodities, and where "saying" also counts as "doing"—meant that I would always be set apart from Smokehousers, for whom doing and saying, or producing and philosophizing, earn very different kinds of social and economic rewards.

Yet my status as insider in practice, outsider in theory was what earned me a secure—if not always comfortable—place among others at the Smokehouse. In fact, one might say that my position as insider depended on my willingness to perform the role of outsider, to present a challenge to cultural logics. As an egghead with middle-class aspirations, I became a catalyst for public performance, and in particular, for performances in arguments about politics.[16] This was a role I was not entirely unwilling to play, as unsettling as it often was, for at least it gave me a way to have a place among others (and, I should confess, to affirm my own upwardly mobile status). Apart from my participation in particular argumentative events, however, I was generally constructed as a symbol of supercilious bourgeois intellectualism.[17]

One particularly vexing occasion should serve to illustrate. I was working behind the bar one busy Friday afternoon after the news had just broken about an exhibit set up at Chicago's Art Institute by art student Dred Scott Tyler. Tyler, it seems, had created an art exhibit that involved his placing an American flag on the floor in such a manner as to invite museum-goers to step on it. Imagining that such an issue would be too volatile to contain, I carefully (and no doubt conspicuously, given my usual willingness to participate in arguments) avoided interjecting my own judgments about the morality of Tyler's action, or taking up any of the disgusted excoriations of him voiced by some of the bar regulars. Before long, however, one regular, Wendell, jerked a thumb in my direction and said, "Now take Julie here. She's one of those that thinks it's okay to walk on the flag!" In that moment I was constructed as the embodiment of an oppositional position and imputed with the predictably self-interested and naïve motives that emerge from class privilege. In the next, I found myself struggling, and failing, to communicate my position (that although I did not condone the artist's actions I would defend his right to them) against a roiling storm of invective. [18]

My role as symbolic opposition to prevailing cultural logics—and in particular, to the logic of identification with *work*—is neither incidental to what has emerged as data, nor to my interpretation of it. I not only recorded, but also helped to constitute, the rhetorical situations in which arguments happened. That I functioned as antagonist, as well as bartender and ethnographer, will be important in considering the circumstances and meaning of argument as a performed genre.

A CLASS ACT: JACK DOES PEROT

Local bars, although purportedly public (as the moniker "pub" would affirm), can be fiercely private domains, as Gerry Philipsen discovered in his ethnographic adventures in a Chicago neighborhood he calls "Teamsterville." Upon arriving on the scene of the barroom-cum-research site, Philipsen (1992) recalls noting that "this was not merely a public place open to anyone, but an enclave in which some but not other personae were welcome," and that "there was no sign outside the tavern, because 'everybody' knew who belonged there" (p. 3). At the Smokehouse, whatever cultural boundaries can't be enforced with brick and mortar are concretized in the practice of conventional speech genres. The social network at the bar is defined not only by its location in the real space of the barroom, but also by how its members locate themselves with respect to these forms of talk. Smokehousers participate in routinized expressive genres such as *shooting the shit* (unmarked conversation), *giving shit* (joking), and *telling it like it is* (narration), and *arguing*. Skillful participation in and metacommentary on the terms of any given genre are a way to communicate one's solidarity with the group's interests and practices, but argument, foregrounding as it does instabilities and tensions in class ideologies, is the genre that invites performance.

The idea that performance is an index, or at least an expression, of social arrangements is a central assumption of folklore and sociolinguistics (Bauman 1977, 1986, 1991; Briggs 1988; Hymes 1975, 1996; Tannen 1989), but has long enjoyed currency across fields and disciplinary methods from the interactional sociology of Erving Goffman to the ordinary-language philosophy of J. L. Austin (1975) and the rhetorical theory of Kenneth Burke. (1969) Studies of communicative behavior across communities have shown various ways verbal performances affirm cultural values (Bauman 1986; Briggs 1988; Farr 1993, 1994; Kirshenblatt-Gimblett 1984; Shuman 1986). The issue of how speech becomes performative in particular domains is significant to the relevance of verbal performance as an index of relations between social relationships and ideology (Bauman 1977, p. 25). Although Smokehousers render verbal performances in telling jokes, relating stories, and so on, by far the genre of talk most closely aligned with performance is argument. Here, it becomes the expression of male sociality, of antibourgeois garrulousness and contentious play.[19] Arguments are a significant site of cultural production inasmuch as they instantiate episodes of verbal art—a practice that functions, as working-class ethnographer Aaron Fox (1994) explains, "to reflexively examine the ideological structure of the 'ordinary' events and discourses it takes as both its raw materials and as objects of scrutiny," thereby working as "a challenge to and a celebration of a particular social order" (p. 2).[20]

The following dramatic episode stars Jack, a prominent Smokehouse regular. It illustrates not only how arguments occasion performances, but also how performances do both social and epistemic work and how these functions are part of the same processes of identification. In this scenario, the argument that occasions Jack's performance becomes a framing device for sustained artful narrative. This argument is exemplary in its rhetorical style, framing and progression, and is typical of the kinds of performances that are often staged in arguments with me. As is so often the case, I am pitted against a powerful male and am constructed as someone who speaks out against the interests of, or at least doesn't take seriously, the predicaments of workers.

Because verbal performances are enacted by powerful members of the group (usually men, but always people who can speak from an ethos of experiential wisdom and productivity), it is not surprising that Jack is so often at the center of them. Jack is one of the most visible—and audible—regulars at the Smokehouse. He is a 52 year-old former steelworker who now owns a music store where local rock musicians come to buy guitars, give lessons, and rent equipment.[21] Jack comes in to drink beer and socialize every night; his absence at the bar inevitably invites speculation on his whereabouts. He is typically the center of sociability, and, although he has his own cohort of close friends, transcends the boundaries of smaller barroom cliques. When Jack is at the Smokehouse, he stands at

his corner, the prestigious spot at the bend of the horseshoe-shaped bar. At
this geographic and discursive fulcrum, Jack commands a place of high
visibility: His position at the bar is analogous to that of patriarch at the head
of a dinner table (or, perhaps more appropriately, a speaker at a podium).
In case anyone has missed the point about his stature, Jack does not sit on
a stool, but remains standing, all the better to assume a stentorian posture
should the occasion arise. Jack's claims to territory are honored by his cohorts, as well: I have seen others who had been occupying Jack's spot va-
cate it apologetically upon his arrival. For Jack to take another place, or for
someone else to claim it, would be a heresy against the social order of the
bar. It would be just as unlikely for Jack to change places as it would be for
him to remove the Greek fisherman's cap he always wears, or—for that
matter—for a woman to enter the bar and persuade the men to switch the
television from a football game to a talk show. Jack's presence, as well as
his position at the bar, constitute one of the many predictable facts of the
heavily routinized quotidian culture of the Smokehouse. Jack's elevation
above other seated bar clients, as well as his position at the bar's "head,"
symbolically assert his standing among Smokehousers: When Jack
speaks, he commands an audience.

The argument in the following transcript takes place late on a Monday
evening in September of 1992.[22] The bar is empty, save for Jack; Arlen, the
bar manager; Maggie and Roberta, waitresses who have finished their
work in the dining room and are now relaxing at the bar after their shifts
are over; and me, the late-shift bartender. The discussion has turned, following a news report covering the campaigning efforts of candidates in
the 1992 presidential election, to a debate about the merits of candidates
Bill Clinton, George Bush, and Ross Perot. In what follows, Jack delivers a
thematic oration that comprises a series of highly stylized narratives. During most of Jack's monologue, the others are, like any well-behaved audience, silent and attentive. But after listening to Jack praise Perot for his
"business sense," I move to challenge Jack's assertion that "running the
country like a business" would be a good thing, that it would offer solutions for everybody, and press for particulars. I attempt to get Jack to offer
specific features of what he believes to be the benefits of Perot's plan, a
move that he eludes in favor of escalating proclamations of my own
shortsightedness and naivete. As Jack moves into full performance, I try
repeatedly and unsuccessfully to claim the floor to get Jack to elaborate
his assertions, but finally cede the floor to Jack as he takes center stage to
demonstrate his right, through the sheer force of his rhetorical artistry, to

speak for others—Smokehousers, and working people in general—who
share his interests:

 1 Jack: ... LET'S get SOMEbody
                who UNderstands
                MONEY!

    Julie: But he understands it from a point of view that—
 5   Now, what is Perot's plan for
                welfare reform?

    Roberta: The people would be WORKING!
    Jack: The point is, hon, we're going like this—
    Julie: How? Is he going to—is he going to advocate child care for
                women—

10 Jack: Jul, we're going like this—! (makes a masturbatory gesture)
                People are bein' taxed, taxed, TAXED!

    Julie: —who want to go back to work?

    Jack: Do you understand what's HAPP'NIN'?

    Roberta: They already GET child care care free!

15 Julie: No, no, but I mean if they want to get OFF welfare,
                and go get a job at minimum wage—
                How are they going to get ahead?

    Jack: You didn't even understand what we just said.
                He is the only one talkin' about jobs,
20   and neither candidate TALKED about jobs,
                until Perot got in, and was thirty-six percent!
                He said, *I don't wanna talk about nothin'—jobs!* They said,
                Well, what about the gay issue? He said,
                Bitch, I said, JOBS! And they said,
25   *What about this issue?*
                He said—

    Roberta: If everybody in America pulls together and everybody was
                working,
                then *maybe*—

    Jack: —the country needs JOBS! Don't worry about the tax
                system;
30   if we have jobs there'll be taxes; all the programs'll stay
                intact.

And they kept askin' him questions. *I don't wanna know about that—JOBS!*

He's the ONLY man that talked, If you don't get this country working,

then you're gonna have NO money—

Julie: How's he gonna DO that? How is he gonna do that?

35   How is he gonna make it so that people have jobs—?

Jack: (more loudly): I would rather have him than Bush or Clinton,

that don't know NOTHIN' about a job,

other than suckin' government money all their life,

they don't know a THING about a job,

40   they don't know a thing about PEOPLE in here,

who are workin'; they NEVER have.

Here's some sonofabitch at least had a company that PAID people!

Julie: Well, you ac—

Jack: (still more loudly): He knows something about jobs,

45   what he was talkin' about. The other two know nothing!

They been SUCKIN' off the government!

They know NOTHIN' about jobs.

Perot has got a big company—you're right!

And I—I don't know—I will STILL lean toward him,

50   because he wants to get people—he underSTANDS;

I have a business, and I know there's kids come in every day,

and there's one thing they lack,

that I didn't have twenty years ago.

Donny (Jack's business partner) and I went—

55   thirty years ago—we went in the mill; you had a JOB.

I had a CREdit union, I could buy a CAR,

I could buy a HOUSE;

There ain't a FUCKIN' kid today that could ever buy a car or a house today—

He got NOTHIN'!

60   He—I mean, he's a SCAB!

He's makin' five bucks a—you know, an hour, or less—I got a daughter—!

Ah, five bucks?! *I* was makin' SEVEN, in frickin' SIXTY!

I was—you know, one thing this country needs, is jobs!
I don't care about Germany, Russia, NOTHIN'!
65 And Perot is the only man that talked that shit
—he's the ONLY one!
I don't care about insurance,
I don't care about this,
I don't care about Europe, Mexico;
70 *I don't care about NOBODY!*
Get the kids in my country jobs! They can't buy nothin'.
And! The more they TAX, for the system they're in,
less and LESS people have business.
Here's a good example—right here! There's less money;
75 the man is makin' less money,
he's FUCKIN' over the employees—
it's less, and it's less, and it's LESS …
I'm no different. For the first time in my life, I laid off two
PEople! You know?
And I mean, I watch Tony's Pizza—NO! It's less, they keep
it up!
80 The real estate taxes went up; insurance is up forty-seven
percent, but—
and—they keep it up!
Whaddaya gonna do? You need someone that got some
frickin' *sense*! NOT,
Oh, we're gonna make the GOVERNMENT—
Maggie: People WANNA work. People don't wanna sit home.
They—want—to—WORK!
85 Jack: … that's bullshit. There's people that WANT to work,
though—
Maggie: That's what I'm SAYIN'—they WANNA work!
Jack: Yeah … but … there's gotta be someone who can direct,
that knows what jobs are all about.
It's—you can't have—Clinton, Gore, Quayle, Bush—you
know, huh,
90 the government'll pay 'em! you know—you know—but,
do THEY have vacations?
They have, you know, I mean, they're paid all the TIME!
If—if Perry don't have the money,

HE don't get a vacation,
NO one gets a vacation!
95   *I* don't get a vacation! This is BULLSHIT!
You should—the government should work ...
and balance their budget; if they don't,
they penalize them, where the government is trillions of
dollars in debt! Bullshit!
Get someone in there, that understands—
100   the JAPS don't do that;
the GERMANS don't do that;
they HELP their people.
And they have—you know, NO. This is ... they only guy,
that—
I don't know anything about
105   —talk for talk, you can TAKE your Clinton;
he's gonna run you under;
Bush is gonna run you under;
I don't know if the other guy's gonna run you under;
he's makin' sense to me: *Get the people in this country
jobs.*
110   I don't wanna talk about GAYS,
I don't wanna talk about ABORTION,
I don't wanna talk about ANY of yer other bullshit ...
once everybody has a JOB in the country, it'll be right.
We-we'll be able to feel good about it
115   —EVERYTHING!

It is clear that Jack intends not only to showcase his own rhetorical expertise, but also to articulate the group's conventional interpretation of its political predicament. In keeping with these general observations, the generic features that most clearly mark Jack's oratory as performative are the poetic strategies it employs, including repeated key phrases (lines 37–40 and 106–108) progressively amplified assertions (lines 67–70 and 100–103) and parallel constructions (lines 67–70 and 110–113). In framing the speech as a performance with these stylistic cues, Jack also marks the speech as a special case by assuming a posture of speaking *for*, rather than *to* or even *at*, his audience. There is a reciprocal cause-and-effect relationship at work here: Jack's position in the Smokehouse community gives him the authority to *speak for*, but it is performances such as these in which Jack displays his distinctive virtuosity, that help to legitimize his position.

Jack's performance draws from rhetorical topoi or thematic resources that articulate the cultural logic of the group: Politics is a bunch of privileged types blowing smoke. The more talk there is, the less action. Work is the life experience that qualifies you to speak and to make decisions about the lives of others. The job situation is getting worse. Unemployment is the most pressing issue in national politics, and is the economic base of—not just another example of—social identifications. In the same way that one accumulates capital through investments, Jack's authority as cultural spokesperson accrues exponentially and recursively: His role at the bar entitles him to speak these cultural logics, and in so doing, he qualifies himself further to do so.

Having assumed the responsibility of speaking *for*, Jack resolutely ignores any efforts at intervention in his oratory: He does not qualify what he says, nor does he acknowledge any of the questions I pose as requests for elaboration. In deflecting possible challenges to the logic for which he speaks, Jack both authorizes that logic as the *common sense,* and legitimates his claim to enact it publicly. He controls the floor by implicitly circumscribing the terms of the argument: Everything follows from the premise that the solution to all other social ills is "jobs," and although Jack does not explain how Perot will actually create them, he prevents me from redefining the terms of the argument by implying that I'm missing the point of the *Perot equals business sense equals jobs equals solutions to all social problems* equation. Instead of qualifying his arguments, Jack instead escalates into a virtuoso performance in which he amplifies his point as he dramatizes a familiar Smokehouse theme, declining opportunities for manufacturing jobs. Roberta attempts to intervene, but Jack will not allow an aperture into his oratory, even for others to voice support.

Jack's poetic technique of "reporting" presidential contender Ross Perot's words give his narrative added momentum (lines 22–24, 67–70, and 109). Rather than removing layers of metacommunication to reveal another's speech in its most unmediated, referential form, the strategy of "reporting" (really, resituating) the words of another amounts to reinventing their words for one's own purposes. As Tannen (1989) explained, reported speech both reinterprets the utterance reported, and produces a constructed dialogue that adds dramatic force and calls upon a fictive collaborator to authorize the utterance (pp. 109–112). Ross Perot, it should be noted, earned the admiration and loyalty of many at the Smokehouse for his "real-world" politics of corporate pragmatism and bootstrap economics. Perot has, in fact, become emblematic of such a political orientation, and he was often invoked in my presence to trigger arguments. Perot's disclaimers of political interests and engagements have earned him the right to speak for working-class interests even though he is corporate billionaire. There is a widely held belief that all politicians are "in somebody's pocket." Hence, the reasoning goes, Perot is rich and therefore free of ties to special interest groups. So Jack is not merely parroting Perot's words—rather, he is dramatically taking on the character of Perot. He *takes on* Perot, in the sense that he takes him on as a character; he speaks "through" him. In so doing, Jack is aligning himself, and by extension, those for whom he speaks, with the ethical stance of Perot. In effect, Jack's own exhortations come together in a duet with Perot's yet more powerful ones. Jack's voice situates Perot's, and Perot's authorizes Jack's. Jack-as-Perot-as-Jack speaks powerfully of the interests of those who must work, if not the "working class."

That the speech emerges in the context of the challenge allows Jack's performance to succeed as a dramatization of Smokehouse cultural logic. Although I become more and more peripheral to Jack's oratory, my presence as obvious dissenter makes the performance possible: Without a contrasting background against which to foreground the cultural logic of the group, Jack's argument would by heard by his audience as "pure show," would be revealed as strategic discourse, and would undermine Jack's authority to speak cultural truths. By rendering these truths publicly and in a style uniquely his own, Jack manages to distinguish himself even as he proclaims solidarity with the group. His rhetoric is attuned to the pathos of his audience, and works by attempting to discredit my own ethical authority as Liberal Democrat Clinton supporter. If the speech seems to be directed as a response to my challenge, it is actually aimed at, and stylized for the appreciation of, his larger audience. By "persuading" the others of what they already believe to be true, Jack constructs an ethos of experiential wisdom. By speaking *to* (really *by way of*, as *against*) me, he disguises his showmanship as an appeal to logic.

It would be tempting to conclude that performances such as this work only to affirm stable and circumscribed ideological structures, yet it is the very *instability* of the conventional belief structure that invites the performance. It is precisely because the Smokehouse "scene" represents a frame in an ongoing historical process of cultural invention that performances become necessary to offer commentary on the "state of the union" from moment to moment. Performances at the Smokehouse appear to supply further evidence for Richard Bauman's (1977, 1986) observation that verbal art generally expresses tensions between tradition and innovation, between conservative and emergent forms. At the Smokehouse, where the conflict between "liberal" and "conservative" political orientations is precisely what is at issue in arguments, this tension is made explicit. In order for arguments to dramatize the script of Smokehouse cultural logic at any given time, contexts for performance must include not only someone who speaks *for* the cultural logic, like Jack, but someone who speaks *against* it, like me. Whether both of these poles are actually given voice in an argument or not, it is the implicit presence of the opposition that makes performance possible. If opposition is not represented in each situation, it will likely be artificially constructed (the bar manager, Arlen, delighted in describing to me how my point of view would be invoked in an argument even when I was not there to argue it). A dissenting voice, in other words, is manufactured in order to reconfigure the rhetorical situation, thereby making dissensus viable and performance possible.

ARGUMENT, PERFORMANCE, AND THE SOLIDARITY OF DISSENT

The central place of political argument in the everyday life of the Smokehouse suggests the extent to which ideologies of class identity participate in local processes of rhetorical invention. Although, of course, the everyday realities of the people who inhabit the Smokehouse are profoundly shaped by material conditions, these conditions are always subject to (and the subject of) interpretation. In performances of agnostic discourse, Smokehousers invent a dynamic class identity and situate it within a larger narrative of cultural logic. Arguments about "politics" serve as occasions for Smokehousers to position themselves rhetorically not only as individuals within the group, but also as a group against the larger social landscape. By participating in arguments, a Smokehouser can both distinguish himself from the guy on the next barstool and from those who would never dream of occupying barstools in places like the Smokehouse. Arguments, inasmuch as they open spaces for (and authorize) narrative performances, allow Smokehousers to experience cultural solidarity in expressions of difference.

My presence as one who dissents from the conventional ideology helps to reconcile the contradiction between consolidating and individuating functions of rhetoric. It both opens possibilities for Smokehousers to claim distinctive positions with respect to the cultural logic, and draws the parameters of that logic. In arguments with me—designated representative of those who do not recognize the material exigencies of the cultural logic—Smokehousers can voice dissent without risking public identification as dissenters. Arguments make room for performances, performances dramatize narratives; narratives announce the place of the group in the social world. By participating in arguments, Smokehousers can narrate the unnamable, theorize cultural practice, and express ideology without sacrificing individual distinctiveness to solidarity. In argument, narratives are made possible (without a structure of contention, performances would be divested of their narrative authority by being exposed *as* performances); narratives articulate the contradictions of working-class identity.

In describing the highly consensual and orchestrated nature of cultural performance, Erving Goffman (1981) observed that in performance, "a tacit agreement is maintained between performers and audiences to act as if a given degree of opposition and accord existed between them. Typically, but not always, agreement is stressed and opposition is underplayed." Here the scales weighing agreement against opposition appear to be tipped the other way: Actors in performed argument agree to "play," but players, once having consented to the rules of the game, foreground dissent. This situation is, I suggest, in part a function of how Smokehousers experience themselves as participants in a unified "working-class" culture even though—and especially because—they are, on the whole, reluctant to define it such.

Because Smokehousers feel that they can claim neither the established political power of the middle class nor the emergent power of groups now recognized as having been historically marginalized, they experience a good deal of ambivalence about their collective political identity. It is as a consequence of this ambivalence that argument—as a discourse of conflict—becomes the genre of speech that invites performance. Because Smokehousers are unable to name themselves as a political body—to do so would to be acknowledge the structural imperatives of class in America—they must find other ways to express social boundaries, to lay claim to distinctive cultural traditions. Ritualized agonistic rhetoric clears a space for individuals to express their shared class experiences safely, in expressions of difference. Only by actively building dissensus in this way can Smokehousers resolve tensions that exist not only between group solidarity and individual difference, but also between lived experience and the claims of the American myth of unfettered social mobility. The absence of a conventional language to allow Smokehousers to articulate a shared political predicament means that every statement of dissent against the cultural logic must also contain the assurance of assent. Performed argument allows people to manage this tension without perceiving it as a strategic contradiction. As agonistic, indecorous, or disruptive as arguments at the Smokehouse may be, they are always, finally, class acts.

ENDNOTES

1. "The Smokehouse Inn" is a pseudonym, chosen both because the bar adjoins a restaurant famous for its smoked barbecued ribs, and because "Smokehouse" suggests the second favorite pastime vice of the bar's clientele.
2. Although it may seem circular to begin and end with the premise that there is such a thing as "class culture," this is no more vexing than the problem that any sociolinguist faces in identifying any given "speech community"—an entity that is at once an a priori heuristic abstraction and a conclusion about the distribution and use of sociolinguistic resources—as a research site.
3. See Fox (1994) for a provocative discussion of the problematics of representation that attend the ethnographic study of class culture. Fox described such a project as "ironic" in its contradictory aims and outcomes: "Oscillating between the challenging cognitive estrangements of otherness and the all-too-familiar, 'class cultures' taunt ethnographers, resist disciplinary containments, and inspire endless sociological head-scratching" (p. 1). Taking up Foley's (1990) discussion of the ambiguous status of class culture as a social organism. Fox observed that class culture is an "epistemological hybrid" constituted by its dual status as a political and an anthropological culture (1994).
4. Woolard (1985) saw questions of hegemony and cultural reproduction—specifically, the nature of "hegemony" and the extent to which local forms can be said to participate in "reproduction"—as the exigency for sociolingusitic research on community practices. On the basis of her own sociolinguistic research in Catalonia, Woolard concluded that "the emphasis by reproduction theorists on formal institutions such as the school is mis-

placed" and that "the structuralist representation of dominant, hegemonic ideologies as impenetrable does not capture the reality of working-class and minority community practices" (p. 738). My own research begins from this premise.

5.   As an ethnography of speaking, this study is deeply rooted in the assumptions about the situated nature of linguistic behavior established by Dell Hymes (1974) and others. Although "rhetoric" is not a term ordinarily associated with anthropological linguistics, I find it useful in emphasizing linkages between performance, ideology, and what linguistic anthropologists might call "rights of participation," and in accounting for ways in which the poetic operates as a function of the hortatory. I see this ethnographic account of Smokehouse rhetoric as a project in "the rhetoric of the everyday," a formulation suggested by Ralph Cintron (1997) to describe critical ethnographic work informed by theories of rhetoric, culture, and social production.

6.   Despite the enormous potential for bars to yield microcosmic views of American social structures and practices, there exist only a handful of studies conducted in such institutions. In a bibliography of ethnographic research on American cultures published in 1992, Michael Moffett counted four studies either situated in bars or including extended discussions of barroom life: those of Read (1980), Bell (1983), Halle (1984), and Weston (1991). In addition to these, I have located three others, those of Cavan (1970), LeMasters (1975), and Spradley and Mann (1975). Only two of these, the Halle and LeMasters studies, take the culture of working-class Whites as an object of inquiry; none was published in the past 15 years.

7.   See, for example, Halle (1984) and Fox (1993, 1995) for discussions of bars as institutional sites for the expression of resistant (or at least, oppositional) working-class identities; see Hoggart (1957) for an early analysis of the role of bars in the production of British working-class ideology.

8.   Following from her extensive study of behavior in 100 bars in the San Francisco area, Sherri Cavan (1970) concluded that bars have predictable codes of conduct that cut across class lines, that they have entirely distinctive institutional rules for social practice. I would argue that these codes of conduct are modulated by the historical status as bars as local, working-class institutions, and that the behavior one finds in bars is not, as Cavan seems to suggest, empty of significance for inferring patterns of social meaning that prevail "outside."

9. Lest it be objected that my claims here are too ambitious, I should make clear that I am not arguing that this oppositional function is unique to White working-class bars—other kinds of bars may well serve analogous (although not necessarily identical) purposes elsewhere. See, for example Michael Bell's (1983) ethnography of speaking in "Brown's Lounge," a Black middle-class bar. Bell noted that what goes on in Brown's can, by virtue of the bar's status as a community institution, be seen as a place to read performances of class and race identity. Bell explained that "the world of Brown's, the environment and complex of human activities that make it up, exists in order to permit the patrons to see themselves and their actions while they are in the bar as consistent with their own definitions of what it means to be Black and middle class" (p. 6).

10. The building that houses the Smokehouse was once a branch of the Underground Railroad. Now, ironically, Greendale (a pseudonym) is a stop on the Southward commute to ever more rural, ever-Whiter, pastures. Yet older people who frequent the bar still strongly identify with the southside urban neighborhoods from which they came. These ex-Roselanders, -Pullmanites, and -Fernwooders speak as if they were forcibly uprooted and displaced from communities in which they once enjoyed a utopian society of camaraderie and mutual support. Still, that many of the bar's patrons who no longer live and work in the Greendale area continue to visit the Smokehouse on weekends speaks to the relative stability of their social networks, and to the significance of the bar as a geographic nexus of these networks.

11. Many ethnographers who have studied barroom cultures (Halle, 1984; LeMasters, 1975; Spradley & Mann, 1975) have noted that bars have traditionally functioned as male territory, as spaces where ritual celebrations of masculinity are given ceremonial treatment. This is generally true of the Smokehouse as well, yet women are—can be—active participants in the life of the bar. They can construct an ethos that allows them to claim a place among the ranks of socially visible men either by actively taking part in male-solidarity rituals (such as drinking shots, telling "dirty jokes" and buying rounds of beer), or by referring to an extrinsic ethos that is conferred upon those who (e.g., bartenders and waitresses) publicly identify with work that is productive by male standards (see Halle 1984 for a discussion, well supported by research in a community of workers at a chemical plant, of the relationship between class identity, masculinity, and productive

labor). That the bar adjoins a restaurant and is therefore inhabited by women at work no doubt modulates male control of social practice.

12. *Shooting the shit* is an emic term that refers to unmarked, highly sociable speech. It is the stream of everyday discourse, the default mode of communication in which other marked genres such as *giving shit* and *arguing* are embedded.

13. In narratives, in other words, Smokehousers both affirm and test the limits of the cultural logics of class. See Stewart (1996) for an extensive overview of definitions of and approaches to narrative in cultural studies, linguistics, anthropology, and folklore (p. 29). After listing several possible functions of narrative, Stewart concludes that "whatever its presumed motives are traceable effects, and whether it takes a relatively authoritative, monologic form or a more open, dialogic form, narrative is first and foremost a mediating form through which 'meaning' must pass." To put it another way, she says, "Stories are productive. They catch up cultural conventions, relations of authority, and fundamental spatiotemporal orientations in the dense sociality of words and images in use and produce a constant mediation of the 'real' in a proliferation of signs" (p. 30).

14. The logistics and ethics of data collection presented special challenges given the status of Smokehousers as a private society within a public institution. My general method for gathering data on natural speech was to switch on a small, handheld tape recorder as episodes of argument (or in some cases, storytelling) happened. Although I did not always remind people of the presence of the tape recorder as I recorded each episode of talk, I did discuss my plan to record data with the owner of the Smokehouse as well as with those regulars who make up the core of the social network under study. So the people who are the participants in this research knew I was working on a project designed to learn "how people talked about politics in the real world," and that I was likely to record conversations (even if I didn't announce my intent to record particular stretches of discourse). Although many at the bar told me that they were supportive of my efforts to write something that might be read by people who didn't know what "life in the real world" was like, my research project was seen as an eccentricity—as yet another indication, no doubt, of the peculiar ways of academic types.

15. As I have said elsewhere, a bartender, who is by definition a participant–observer in/of the social life around her, is a kind of "nat-

urally occurring ethnographer" (Lindquist, 2002). Both dimensions of this in-and-out-of-things role are highlighted by the geography of the bar at the Smokehouse: The bar is shaped like a tight horseshoe so that the bartender is literally at the center of social life, half of which, at any given moment, is going on behind her back.

16. Smokehousers tend to be much more interested in national politics than local or international politics. Most of the arguments that constitute my data corpus are about the candidates and platforms in the 1992 political campaign, although Smokehousers argue about the politics of a range of other social issues (as, for example—to name one hot topic—the trial of the police officers in the assault on Rodney King).

17. Many at the bar have commented on the similarity of Smokehouse society to that dramatized by the long-running sitcom Cheers, and more established regulars have even gone so far as to compare my own persona to one of its characters, intellectual snob Diane Chambers.

18. Although my role as antagonist emerges from my habit of privileging abstraction from local experience over values of productivity and practical knowledge, that role is also a function of my gender. It is of course significant that I am a woman who speaks against local interests. As Sherry Ortner (1991) has noted, "Gender relations for both middle-class and working-class Americans carry an enormous burden of quite antagonistic class meaning" (p. 171). She goes on to explain that "it appears overwhelmingly the case in working-class culture that women are symbolically aligned... with the 'respectable,' 'middle-class side of those oppositions and choices," (p. 173). These cross-significations are certainly operative at the Smokehouse, where real work and productivity are attributes of socially appropriate men.

19. A large and venerable body of sociolinguistic research connects working-class solidarity to highly gendered expressions of sociability controlled by high-status males. Fox (1995), for instance, writes that in high-involvement working-class speech styles, "full performance is metapragmatically associated with powerful males" and that "male discursive power is closely linked to high levels of performativity—assembling caricatured gender-indexical topics and emphasizing emotional intensity, expressive dynamism, emphatic paralinguistic style, invasions of others' physical space, polemical uses of invective and insults in agonistic engagements, sustained narrativity, repetitiveness, and

publicness" (p. 2). The point here is not to show that women have no part in performances, no voice in the invention of culture—indeed, Fox went on to show how working-class women may "reverse" this order of dominance through ironic performance of the same elements—only that Jack's right of participation in arguments of this kind are attributable to his gender and status.

20. Fox's (1995) conclusions about the ideological workings of "artful discourse" echo what folklorists and anthropologists have suggested about the ethnopoetic function of verbal art, and follow from his own research on the culture of a rural working-class bar near Lockhart, Texas. My research at the Smokehouse supports Fox's assertion that verbal performances function poetically to affirm and critique conventional cultural logics simultaneously.

21. Even though Jack has bought into a business and is therefore now a "businessman," he nonetheless retains strong ties to local interests. His financial success notwithstanding, he (unlike Perry, the owner of the Smokehouse) continues to identify with the employment situations and political interests of industrial workers.

22. The following transcript is edited to render the rhythm and flow of natural speech, and therefore does not use special notation to specify such paralinguistic features as pause length, intonation patters, and the like. Emphasis is indicated by capital letters, and reported speech is italicized. Lines are broken to emphasize such artistic features as parallelism, repetition, and progressive amplification.

REFERENCES

Austin, J. L. (1975) *How to do things with words*. J. O. Urmson & M. Sbisa (Eds.). Cambridge, MA: Harvard University Press.

Bell, M. J. (1983). *The world from Brown's lounge: An ethnography of black middle-class play*. Urbana: University of Illinois Press.

Bauman, R. (1992). Disclaimers of performance. In J. H. Hill & J. T. Irvine (Eds.), *Responsibility and evidence in oral discourse* (pp. 182–196). Cambridge: Cambridge University Press.

Bauman, R. (1986). *Story, performance, event*. Cambridge: Cambridge University Press.

Bauman, R. (1977). *Verbal art as performance*. New York: Newbury Press.

Briggs, C. (1988). *Competence in performance: The creativity of tradition in Mexicano verbal art*. Philadelphia: University of Pennsylvania Press.

Briggs, C. (1996). *Disorderly discourse: Narrative, conflict, and inequality*. New York: Oxford University Press.

Burke, K. (1969). *A grammar of motives*. Berkeley: University of California Press.

Cavan, S. (1966). Liquor license: An ethnography of bar behavior. Chicago: Aldine.

Cintron, R. (1997). Angels' Town: Chero ways, gang life, and rhetorics of the every-day. Boston: Beacon Press.

Dius, P. R. (1983). *The saloon: Public drinking in Chicago and Boston 1880–1920.* Urbana: University of Illinois Press.

Farr, M. (1994). Echando relajo: Verbal art and gender among Mexicanos in Chi-cago. *Proceedings of the Berkeley Women and Language Conference.* Berke-ley: Department of Linguistics.

Farr, M. (1993). Essayist literacy and other verbal performances. *Written Commu-nication, 10*(1), 4–38.

Foley, D. (1984). Does the working class have a culture in the anthropological sense? *Cultural Anthropology, 4*(2), 137–163.

Foley, D. (1990). *Learning capitalist culture: Deep in the heart of Tejas.* Philadel-phia: University of Pennsylvania Press.

Fox, A. (1993). The bitch about country music: Split-subjectivity in country music and honky-tonk discourse. In G. Lewis (Ed.), *All that glitters: Country music in America.* (pp. 131–139). Bowling Green, OH: Bowling Green State University Popular Press.

Fox, A. (1994). The poetics of irony and the ethnography of class culture. Special is-sue of *Anthropology and Humanism, 19*(1), 53–72.

Fox, A. (1995). The "redneck reverse": Language and gender in Texas working-class women's verbal art. *Proceedings of the SALSA II conference*, 189–199.

Goffman, E. (1959). *The presentation of self in everyday life.* New York: Doubleday.

Goffman, E. (1981). *Forms of talk.* Philadelphia: University of Pennsylvania Press.

Halle, D. (1984). *America's working man: Work, home, and politics among blue-collar property owners.* Chicago: University of Chicago Press.

Hoggart, R. (1957). *The uses of literacy: Aspects of working-class life, with special reference to publications and entertainments.* New York: Oxford Press.

Hymes, D. (1974). *Foundations in sociolinguistics.* Philadelphia: University of Pennsylvania Press.

Hymes, D. (1975). Breakthrough into performance. In Ben-Amos & K. Goldstein (Eds.), *Folkore: Performance and communication* (pp. 11–74). The Hague: Mouton.

Kirshenblatt-Gimblett, B. (1984). The concept and varieties of narrative perfor-mance in East European Jewish culture. *In R. Bauman & J. Sherzer (Eds.), Ex-plorations in the ethnography of speaking* (pp. 283–308). Cambridge, UK: Cambridge University Press.

LeMasters, E. E. (1975). *Blue-collar aristocrats: Lifestyles at a working-class tavern.* Madison: University of Wisconsin Press.

Lindquist, J. (2002). *A place to stand: Politics and persuasion in a working-class bar.* New York: Oxford University Press.

Moffatt, M. (1992). Ethnographic writing about American culture. *Annual Review of Anthropology, 21,* 205–229.

Ortner, S. (1991). Reading America: Preliminary notes and class and culture. In R. G. Fox (Ed.), *Recapturing anthropology* (pp. 163–191). Santa Fe: School of American Research Press.

Philipsen, G. (1992). *Speaking culturally: Explorations in social communication.* New York: SUNY Press.

Read, K. E. (1980). *Other Voices: The style of a male homosexual tavern.* Novato, CA: Chandler & Sharp.

Rosenwieg, R. (1983). *Eight hours for what we will.* New York: Cambridge Univer-sity Press.

Shuman, A. (1986). *Storytelling rights: The uses of oral and written texts by urban adolescents.* Cambridge, UK: Cambridge University Press.

Slayton, R. A. (1986). *Back of the yards: The making of a local democracy.* Chicago: University of Chicago Press.

Spradley, J., & Mann, B. (1975).*The cocktail waitress: Women's work in a man's world.* New York: Knopf.

Stewart, K. (1996). *A space on the side of the road: Cultural poetics in an "other" America.* Princeton, NJ: Princeton University Press.

Tannen, D. (1989). *Talking voices: Repetition, imagery, and dialogue in conversational discourse.* Cambridge, UK: Cambridge University Press.

Westen, K. (1991). *Families we chose: Lesbians, gays, kinship.* New York: Columbia University Press.

Woolard, K. (1985). Language variation and cultural hegemony: Toward an integration of sociolinguistic and social theory. *American Ethnologist, 12*(4), 738–747.

Photograph by Michael Maltz

13

Chinese Language Use in Chicagoland

John S. Rohsenow

University of Illinois at Chicago

In this chapter[1] I describe contemporary Chinese language use in the Chicago metropolitan area (referred to locally as "Chicagoland"), and show that the linguistic differences between Chicagoland's three different Chinese- speaking communities correlate with both historical and contemporary sociopolitical forces. Although Chinese live throughout the Chicagoland area, they focus their activities on, and in many cases live in or near, one of three areas: the older "(South) Chinatown" centered at Wentworth Avenue and Cermak Road (2200 South), the newer Southeast Asian "North Chinatown" centered along Argyle Avenue between Broadway and Sheridan (5000 North) in the Uptown area, and the newer more dispersed communities of professionals in such surrounding suburbs as Westmont, Naperville, Schaumburg, and Evanston, many of which focus primarily on the Di Ho Supermarket complex in Westmont, or similar communities in and around Arlington Heights, Morton Grove, and Hoffman Estates. I first explain the historical background that accounts for this tripartite division of the Chicagoland Chinese community, and the corresponding linguistic divisions that correlate with them. I also explain the historical and linguistic background of the different language and "dialect" variations in China and Southeast Asia that contribute to the linguistic and cultural diversity of the Chicagoland Chinese communities, briefly describing the nature of the Chinese written language, which both unites and yet sometimes divides them. Having established this historical and linguistic background, I then specifically examine various facets of Chinese language use in these Chinese communities, specifically which Chinese "dialects" are spoken where and why, the Chinese language media in the area, religious and other specialized literacies, and Chinese language education in Chicagoland.

HISTORY OF CHINESE IMMIGRATION TO CHICAGO

The present South Chinatown is an outgrowth of the first Chinese community established in Chicago in the 1880s.[2] As in most Chinatowns in the United States, the majority of the first Chinese in Chicago came from the Toisan (Taishan) area of Guangdong (Kwangtung)[3] province in southern China, and spoke some local variation of the Toisan dialect of Cantonese. The name "Cantonese" popularly refers to the group of related Chinese dialects forming the Yue language subfamily of Chinese because Canton is the English name for Guangzhou (Kuangchow), the capital city, of the southern province of Guangdong (from which the British Crown Colony of Hong Kong was expropriated in 1898) where various dialects of this related subfamily are spoken (Ramsey, 1987, p. 98). Because the city of Canton, and later nearby Hong Kong, were two of the few port cities open to Westerners in the 1800s, Cantonese speakers from this area were among the first to make contact with Americans. Given the chaotic conditions in China at that time—famine, the Taiping Rebellion, and the increasing encroachment of the Western powers on China—Chinese from the Toisan area southwest of Canton began to emigrate to California, first attempting to participate in the 1848 California gold rush, then working on the western section of the transcontinental railroad in 1869, and on farms and in industry in California. Toisan, a tiny rural district 60 miles southwest of Canton, was the district most accessible to the sea when U.S. ships came to recruit cheap labor in the mid 1800s. Thus about 86% of Chinese Americans trace their ancestry to Guangdong province, and most to the Toisan district.

Worsening economic conditions and anti-Chinese sentiment in the western United States at the end of the 19th century caused some Chinese to take the newly completed railroad eastward looking for employment opportunities and less socially prejudicial conditions. As the terminus of the western railroads and as a major industrial center, Chicago was a natural endpoint for some of these Chinese to settle in their search for better economic and social opportunities. Although the original "Chinatown" at Clark and Van Buren Streets no longer exists, the branch neighborhood established in about 1910 on the near south side around the intersection of Wentworth and Cermak (22nd Street) still flourishes, and is now considered to be the city's oldest existing Chinatown and a major residential, shopping, and tourist center. A traditional Chinese memorial arch inscribed with the Chinese characters for the Confucian slogan *Tianxia wei gong* (the community is everyone's responsibility). over South Wentworth at Cermak acts as a gateway to South Chinatown. Not only the store and restaurant signs, but also the street name signs are in both English and Chinese characters. Since the early 1960s, residents of this originally seven-square-block area have expanded into the Bridgeport area just south and west of Chinatown, and more recently into the abandoned railroad and industrial areas just to the north and west. Following the historical pattern of immigration based on clan and family connections with others from the same Toisan-speaking area of Guangzhou, the majority of the residents of this expanded Chinatown community to this day speak some dialect of Cantonese. There are still a large number of Toisan speakers in Chinatown, but as emigration and immigration from China and other areas of Southeast Asia have become increasingly easier in the past 25 years, more recent immigrants from Hong Kong, the city of Canton (Guangzhou), and other dialect-speaking areas have added to the dialect mix, and the Cantonese of the city of Canton has now become the standard, despite the long history of Toisan speakers in the United States. Because Toisan is still a relatively impoverished rural area of China, more recent immigrants from the provincial capital of Canton (Guangzhou) who speak the regional standard will claim that they cannot understand the Toisan dialect. Other recent immigrants from the former British Crown Colony of Hong Kong just to the south, who consider themselves to be much more cosmopolitan, consider their Hong Kong accent and more urbanized slang to be superior to both.

As we shall see, by no means all of the more than 48,000 people who identify themselves as "Chinese" on the census forms in the Chicagoland metropolitan area live in South Chinatown. For the historical reasons just described, however, the South Chinatown area continues to be a point of immigration primarily for recent Cantonese-speaking immigrants from China, Hong Kong, and other communities of "overseas Chinese" residents in Singapore, Malaysia, and other parts of Southeast Asia. In 1970, there were about 3,100 Chinese in South Chinatown, mostly still concentrated in the core area at the north end of the Armour Square district around Wentworth and Cermak, where they constituted 70.9% of the total population in that immediate area. By 1980 the Chinese population had grown to 3,926, comprising 73.8% of the area's population.[4] In both the 1934 and the 1990 censuses, South Chinatown had 41 percent of the City's Chinese population. (Kiang, 1992, pp. 6, 9.) By 1990 the total number of Chinese in the entire Amour Square census area was 5,546, concentrated in the four tracts north of 31st Street, of whom 5,059 stated that they used Chinese at home and 986 stated that they lived in "linguistically isolated households."[5] In the northernmost census tract immediately around Wentworth and Cermak Chinese constituted 100% of the population, whereas they constituted 78%, 53%, and 68% of the other three census tracts immediately to the south down to 31st Street.[6]

South Chinatown has also expanded south and west into the northeastern tip of Bridgeport, "with several Chinese developers buying lots and building townhouses heavily marketed to the Chinese community," with the result that in 1990 "one in six people [was] Asiatic, practically all Chinese," making Bridgeport "the fourth largest Asiatic community in the city."[7] The population in the two census tracts of Bridgeport immediately bordering Chinatown in 1990 were each 66% Chinese, and in the three census tracts bordering them 23%, 31% and 26% respectively.[8] Every census tract in Bridgeport is at least 10% Chinese. In the 1990 census, the total number of those in Bridgeport identifying themselves as Chinese was 4,889, with 4,335 using Chinese at home.[9] (See author's note on p. 354.)

In the late 1990s, land in the old Santa Fe railroad yards along the Chicago River just north of Cermak and Archer Avenue was developed into a new "Chinatown Square" shopping and restaurant complex and the 14-acre new Santa Fe Gardens residential area. In October, 2000 the Chinese American Service League, a social service agency that helps new immigrants, estimated that "about twelve thousand people of Chinese descent live[d] in the Chinatown vicinity."[10] By January, 2002, the Chinese "population in the Chinatown area (which includes part of Bridgeport) [was reported to have] grown to 18,000 from 12,000 in the last five years, according to the 2000 census." (Kennedy, 2002.) Early figures from the 2000 census reported that immigration to the United States is at its highest rate since the 1930s, with the greatest resultant population growth concentrated in the major urban areas such as Chicago. With increasing legal and illegal immigration from the Peoples Republic of China and other Chinese communities in Southeast Asia, and the continuing importance of Chinese speaking communities such as Chicago's Chinatown for many limited English- or non-English-speaking immigrants, one can assume that, when released, the 2000 census will indicate increasing numbers for the present and future population of Chinese in these three areas of South Chinatown.

For the historical reasons described earlier, a majority of immigrants to Chicago's South Chinatown have generally consisted largely of rural or urban working-class Cantonese speakers from southern China, Hong Kong, or Southeast Asia.[11] Because of this, until recently the adult population of the South Chinatown area was relatively undereducated. In 1980, the median years of school completed among those older then 25 years was 10.4 years, as compared with a Cook county average of 12.46 years of schooling. Correspondingly, there is a lack of English skills in South Chinatown. In 1980, of 992 Chinese ages 5 to 17 years, almost 92% indicated that they "spoke a language other than English" (i.e., Chinese, usually Cantonese), and more than 24% of them indicated that they did "not speak English well, if at all." Among the 3,571 who were 18 years of age or older, almost 98% "spoke a language other than English in the home," and more than 50% reported that they or others in their home spoke English poorly, if at all. By 1990, almost 17% of households in South Chinatown were linguistically isolated from the surrounding English-speaking community. More than 60% of the Chinese in the area who were older than 5 years of age "[did] not speak English very well." In the November, 2002 election, for the first time Cook county was required to make ballots and instructions available in Chinese because early results of the 2000 census showed that at least 5% of eligible voters are Chinese "who do not speak English well enough to participate in the electoral process." (Groark, 2002). If international immigration continues to provide a large part of the rising growth rate of the Chinese population in Chicago, then there is little reason to expect that these figures declined in the decade since 1990, or that they will decline in the first decade of the new century. (See author's note on p. 354.)

Racial discrimination and anti-Chinese exclusion laws effectively blocked any significant additional immigration of Chinese to the United States from 1882 through 1943. Laws against the immigration of Chinese women combined with antimiscegenation laws and social prejudices against intermarriage on the part of both Whites and Chinese prevented the development of any significant class of second- and third-generation Chinese Americans more assimilated and integrated into the "mainstream" of American society.[12] Thus, many second- and third-generation Chinese residing in the Chinatown area continued to be functionally bilingual, at least orally, as opposed to the pattern of language loss over the generations usually encountered with European immigrant families during that time period. At the same time, from their very beginnings in Chicago, many Chinese families had dispersed themselves throughout the city, initially in order to maximize the opportunities for their small owner-operated laundry and restaurant businesses, the two service occupations in which they suffered no competition. With the final repeal of the Exclusion Laws in 1943, and with the flood of refugees from the Nationalist—Communist civil war after the end of World War II (1945–1950), the overall Chinese population of Chicago doubled from 3,000 to 6,000, and some Chinese families began to move to the newly developing post-World War II suburban areas in and around the City of Chicago proper (Moy, 1995, p. 383).

This new possibility of immigration to the United States and special provisions in the immigration law for family reunification allowed the existing Chinese community in Chicago to expand and stabilize, whereas the communist "takeover" of the mainland of China in 1949–1950 caused a major influx of new immigrants, not only of rural and working class relatives from the traditional Toisan area of Guangdong province in southern China, but also of a totally other new group of primarily affluent and educated (usually U.S. or European educated), English-speaking immigrants dispossessed by the communist revolution. This latter group came from all over China, speaking a variety of other Chinese languages and dialects, but almost all were literate, educated, and fluent in the national standard language of China, commonly known in English as "Mandarin (Chinese)." These other affluent, educated, English-speaking educated Chinese generally avoided their Cantonese-speaking compatriots in Chinatown, except for occasional forays in from other parts of Chicago or the suburbs to shop for Chinese foodstuffs or to visit more authentic Chinese restaurants.

We should explain here that the family of related languages spoken by Han Chinese all over mainland China, Taiwan, and Hong Kong usually is divided by linguists into eight major subfamilies of mutually unintelligible spoken languages ("regionolects" or "topolects"), which are then subdivided into numerous related "dialects." It must be stressed that the various subfamilies of the Chinese languages, and even some "dialects" of the same language subfamily, are mutually unintelligible, although the shared written Chinese characters are at least in principle intelligible to all who are literate enough to read them. "Mandarin" Chinese is a standard national language ["Guoyu" (Kuo-yü)], created in the 1920s after the "May

Fourth Movement" of 1919. It is based on the dialect of Beijing (Peking), the traditional "northern capital" of China, from which scholar-officials or "Mandarins" ruled all over China in the emperor's name until the fall of the last emperor of the Qing (Ch'ing) dynasty in 1911. Technically speaking, the English term "Cantonese" should be used only to refer to the regional standard dialect of the city of Canton (Guangzhou), and the term "Yue" used for the larger subfamily of dialects (e.g., Toisan dialect, Hong Kong dialect) related to it (Norman, 1988, p. 214).

Although it was not as severely isolated as the Chinatown ghettos on the U.S. West Coast in the late 19th and early 20th centuries, nevertheless limited English skills and a general feeling of racial prejudice combined with a distrust and ignorance of the surrounding White community did serve to keep Chicago's South Chinatown community to a certain extent socially and linguistically isolated at least through the first half of the 20th century. The primarily working-class and small business Chinese population of South Chinatown and the adjacent areas continued to conduct their daily affairs in Cantonese and to read and support Chinese newspapers in Chicago, New York, and California. Community business and social organization in the Chinese Consolidated Benevolent Association and in the local branches of the two major "tongs" or merchants' associations, which until recently dominated all of America's Chinatowns, the On Leong Tong and the Hip Sing Tong, also were conducted entirely in Toisan Cantonese, because many of their leaders did not speak English (McKeown, 2001). The few part-time Chinese classes offered by these associations or by the Protestant and Catholic churches in Chinatown served only to attempt to give minimal literacy in Chinese characters to children and adult illiterate native speakers of Cantonese.

RECENT CHINESE IMMIGRANTS TO CHICAGOLAND

The class of educated, Mandarin-speaking refugees from communism were the vanguard of the second group of Chinese in the Chicagoland area. The majority of these and those who followed them now live scattered throughout the city and in such surrounding suburbs as Naperville, Schaumburg, and Evanston, focusing many of their activities on the DiHo Supermarket complex in the suburb of Westmont, or in other suburbs around Chicago such as Arlington Heights, Morton Grove, and Hoffman Estates, which have developed similar but smaller shopping areas catering to the Asian immigrant community. Initially, many of these refugees dispersed themselves throughout the major urban areas of the United States, usually based on their professional or business opportunities. As they integrated into American society, they spoke their family dialect and/or Mandarin only at home or with Chinese friends, while speaking English at work and elsewhere. Starting in the l950s and 1960s, this more educated and affluent group continued their strong tradition of education for their children by encouraging them to enter U.S. colleges and universities to prepare for careers in medicine, dentistry, engineering, science, or technology. This pattern naturally gave rise to the more commonly encountered American immigrant phenomenon that their children became fluent, literate, and educated in English, with some having a passive knowledge of the oral Mandarin, Shanghainese, or whatever Chinese language was spoken by their parents and grandparents at home, but only as a "kitchen language," in a pattern similar to that of other second-generation children of European immigrants to Chicago.

After 1950, when diplomatic relations between Communist "Red China" and the United States were severed and anticommunism flourished, there was virtually no immigration from the newly established Peoples Republic (PRC) on the mainland of China, and only a little from Hong Kong and Taiwan. From the early 1950s through 1965, the few immigrants from the latter two places consisted primarily of either relatives of Hong Kong Chinese already in the United States, or additional refugees from mainland China who had fled across the southern border to the tiny British Crown Colony (leased from China until 1997) or across the Taiwan Straits with Chiang Kai-shek's retreating Nationalists to the island of Taiwan (Formosa), which had been reclaimed by Nationalist China in 1945 after 50 years of Japanese occupation. These immigrants to the Chicagoland area largely followed the settlement and linguistic patterns just outlined. However, changes in immigration policy passed by Congress in 1965 replaced the quotas that had for more than 80 years severely restricted immigration of Chinese and other Asians to the United States with equal quotas for each country. These new policies also gave preference to Asian immigrants with professional skills and to those wishing to unite with their families. In addition, beginning in the mid-1960s, increasingly large numbers of college graduates from Taiwan and Hong Kong began coming for postgraduate study at American universities, and—under liberalized immigration laws—staying on as immigrants working in the expanding U.S. economy, and later bringing over their relatives to join them in the United States.

After graduating with master's or doctoral level degrees in science and technology, these U.S.-educated Chinese immigrants and other professionally trained immigrants from Taiwan followed the earlier refugees of the 1950s, working and residing either in Chicago itself or in the rapidly expanding belt of technology firms in the surrounding suburbs. Having no social or linguistic affinity with the primarily merchant- or working-class Chinese found in the traditional Cantonese-speaking Chinatown community, this new class of Chinese immigrant professionals dispersed themselves throughout the Chicagoland suburbs in the same manner as other college-educated Americans and immigrants with U.S. postgraduate degrees. The increasingly large numbers of these families began to from social bonds and communities in the suburban areas, but they differed from the traditional patterns found in Chinatown and many of Chicago's other older ethnic enclaves in following a new immigrant pattern of not living in concentrated geographical proximity.

Using English in the workplace and speaking Mandarin or Taiwanese at home, many of these professional families encouraged their children to become fluent and well-educated in English in preparation for college and university study as previously described. Yet, also wanting to preserve their families' Chinese linguistic and cultural heritage, they established Chinese heritage language schools in an attempt to promote their children's education in the Chinese national language, Mandarin, in speaking reading, and writing (Wang, 1996). In the Chicagoland area, as elsewhere in the United States, the majority of "Saturday schools" for these "heritage language learners" are supplied with Chinese language teaching materials by the offices of the government of the Republic of China on Taiwan in downtown Chicago. The schools are usually staffed by volunteer parents with teaching experience in Taiwan, and supported by a local Chinese community or by a Chinese Christian church congregation for the children of their parishioners. The Taiwan government also subsidizes teacher-training workshops and conferences as well as summer language camps in the Midwest and in Taiwan for students in these programs.

The Republic of China relocated to the island of Taiwan in 1949 after the defeat of Chiang Kai-shek's Nationalist party by the Chinese Communists on the Chinese mainland, and superimposed a population of slightly more than 1 million Mandarin- and other dialect-speaking mainland Chinese refugees from all over China onto an existing, population of 10 million ethnic Taiwanese speakers.[13] Taiwanese is a dialect of Fujianese (Fukienese) belonging to the Southern Min (Min Nan) language subfamily of Chinese, also spoken in the adjacent mainland province of Fujian (Fukien), whence Chinese speakers of this dialect had emigrated to Taiwan beginning in the 1600s. During the 50 years of Japan's occupation of the island (1895–1945), all education was in Japanese, and the Chinese national language was not taught. After Taiwan's retrocession to China in 1945, Mandarin Chinese began to be taught in Taiwan's schools, but Taiwanese continues to be spoken at home by the majority of the population, and much scientific work and business continued to be conducted in Japanese by the older generation through the 1970s. In addition, the forced imposition of the exiled Nationalist government onto the ethnic Taiwanese majority compounded tensions between the two ethnic groups to the extent that intermarriage was initially infrequent, and the two groups remained and continue to remain separate (Gates, 1987; pp. 44–46, 54–57). This pattern to some extent continues in the social pattern of the two groups of immigrants from Taiwan in the United States. That is, religious and social groupings tend to be segregated between Taiwanese speakers and Mandarin-speaking descendants of mainland refugees, although both groups are fluent in the national language, Mandarin. Although separate social and religious activities may be conducted in these two different Chinese languages by the two different immigrant groups, nevertheless the Chinese language Saturday schools organized by both groups teach their children only the national language, just as is done in the educational system in Taiwan. With the passage of time and in the immigrant situation, some of the interethnic tensions between the two groups have begun to diminish, and when they interact, they speak either Mandarin or English. (More details on the present status of these Chinese-language Saturday schools are given later.)

THE DEVELOPMENT OF NORTH CHINATOWN

After the fall of Saigon in 1975, many ethnic Chinese, residents in Vietnam for generations, who were mostly business people and thus considered "capitalist," were expelled by the new communist government or fled as "boat people." After their immigration to the United States, many of these Southeast Asian ethnic Chinese refugees from Vietnam or other countries in Indochina were sponsored or assisted by Chinese communities in the United States. The majority of these ethnic Chinese refugees from Indochina were "overseas Chinese" (*huaqiao*) originally from the coastal province of Fujian (just north of Guangdong province, opposite the island of Taiwan), who in addition to their own Chaozhou (Teochew) or "Hokkien" (Fukien) dialects of Fujianese had also learned Cantonese and/or Mandarin in order to conduct their businesses. (Until 1975, the Chinese in Vietnam, especially those in the Cholon section of Saigon, had their own Chinese newspapers and school system in which spoken and written Mandarin were taught as a second language.)

In Chicago in the mid-1970s, these Southeast Asian refugees joined a second smaller Chinese community that had relocated to the Uptown area when the remnants of the original downtown Chicago Chinatown at Clark and Van Buren Streets were cleared to build the new Metropolitan Correctional Center. Argyle Street between Broadway and Sheridan began to be known informally as North Chinatown, as many Southeast Asian Chinese refugees opened Chinese stores and Chinese or Vietnamese restaurants and many purchased homes in that area. Upon first arrival, they were supported by various public and private social service agencies. While the On Leong Tong Merchant's Association at that time remained in South Chinatown, the rival Hip Sing Tong moved its headquarters north to Argyle Street and encouraged development in the Area (Moy, 1995, pp. 386–387). Similarly, whereas the Chinese American Service League opened as a new federal- and state-funded social service agency in South Chinatown, the similarly funded Chinese Mutual Aid Association and other similar agencies for refugees from Vietnam and other Southeast Asian countries located their headquarters in or near this burgeoning new "North Chinatown." The elevated train stop which visually dominates Argyle Street now sports a Chinese-style red and green roof, rivaling the Chinese memorial arch over Wentworth Avenue at Cermak Road in South Chinatown. These social services agencies both serve the immigrant community in their own languages and dialects, and also offer classes in English, citizenship, and other useful topics taught in Chinese and Vietnamese.[14] As in Vietnam and the other Southeast Asian countries whence they had come, these families may speak the Chaozhou or Hokkien dialects of Fujianese at home and in their social groups, but in doing business, they can usually also speak some Mandarin and/or Cantonese, and often the non-Chinese language of their country of origin (e.g., Vietnamese, Cambodian, Laotian, Thai, Burmese, Malay).[15] Like their Cantonese-speaking counterparts in South Chinatown, however, those who are literate in Chinese do read American Chinese newspapers published in Chicago or in New York or California, and watch videos either in Cantonese or Mandarin. In 1990 in the Uptown census area surrounding North Chinatown, 1,678 people identified themselves as Chinese, 1,404 of whom said they used Chinese at home. In the Edgewater area immediately to the north, 1,632 identified themselves as Chinese, with 1,519 using Chinese at home, and in the neighboring Rogers Park and West Ridge census areas just to the north and west of Edgewater, the figures were 788 Chinese, with 722 using Chinese at home, and 1,268 Chinese, with 1,242 using Chinese at home.[16]

Under the 1965 immigration law, each country in the eastern hemisphere with which the United States has diplomatic relations was given a quota of 20 thousand immigrants a year, not including family members of those already in the United States. In 1979, the United States established full diplomatic relations with the Peoples Republic on the mainland of China (PRC) and 3 years later in 1982 the PRC was also given a similar quota. Since that time, the greatest number of arrivals of Chinese in the United States have been from mainland China. Those who were relatives in Toisan and elsewhere in south China of Cantonese speakers from China and Hong Kong already in the United States, as well as other Cantonese- and Fujianese-speaking Chinese from south China, both legal and illegal, have tended to follow the well-beaten path to America's Chinatowns, including Chicago's, for the usual reasons of family connections, linguistic and cultural familiarity, limited English skills, and the like. These new arrivals from "Communist China," not being connected through or schooled in traditional Chinese family ties because of the deliberate destruction of such institutions by the Chinese communist government, do contribute to the swelling of the two Chinatowns' populations, but do not always participate in the traditional Chinatown social structures, which have begun to erode in recent years. Strauss (1998, p. 108) noted that because of the increased immigration to Chinatown of speakers from Hong Kong and other parts of South China and Southeast Asia, the "Chinatown lingua franca" after the 1970s has shifted from the Toisanese dialect of Cantonese to a more standard Guangzhou city Cantonese. It has been estimated that 20 years ago, 90% of new immigrants to the Chinatown area spoke some dialect of Cantonese, but that today only half of the new residents speak Cantonese, the remainder speaking some other Chinese dialect, with Mandarin as a first or second dialect. (Adler, 2000). Printed signs in stores and restaurant menus usually are written bilingually in Chinese and English as are official governmental public notices, whereas handwritten signs and publicly posted notices such as those announcing apartments for rent and job advertisements are handwritten in Chinese only. Both Chinatowns now provide a wide variety of services in Chinese directed at Chinese-speaking clientele. Public and private Chinese-run enterprises such as stores, travel agencies, driving schools, law offices, doctors' offices, social service agencies, and banks all employ staff who speak Cantonese and whatever other Chinese language or dialect local customers are likely to speak: Mandarin, Chaozhou, and Fujianese. The banking slips and materials in the Chinatown branches of various banks are printed in both Chinese and English. The Chicago Chinese Yellow Pages telephone book, updated yearly, contains more than 200 pages of listings and advertisements in Chinese and English for a wide variety of goods and services in the Chicagoland area, plus an additional 120 pages of similar material for Colorado, Michigan, Missouri and Ohio. Nevertheless, the common language and cultural background that these new immigrants share with those already in Chicago's two Chinatowns and the public and private social services located there do continue to provide a cultural "bridge" for these immigrants, as they did for the Southeast Asian refugees in the 1970s.

A smaller number of "long-lost" relatives of those refugees who had fled (often through Taiwan) from other parts of mainland China in the early 1950s now join their more educated Mandarin-speaking Chinese relatives in the Chicago suburbs. As with the Taiwanese in the 1970s, however, the majority of educated immigrants from the Peoples Republic of China come on student visas for postgraduate study in the United States, usually graduating with degrees in engineering, computer science or accounting from the University of Chicago, Northwestern, the University of Illinois at Chicago, the Illinois Institute of Technology, or other Chicago-area or U.S. universities. 17 They then follow the path pioneered by the Taiwanese to the many "high-tech" companies located in the suburbs surrounding the city of Chicago. As college-educated speakers of Mandarin, in graduate school they coexist with their fellow graduate students from Taiwan, whom they now outnumber, occasionally forming superficial friendships, but more often remaining separated by more than half a century of political differences, suspicion, and economic and cultural differences. (Generally speaking, students from mainland China, Hong Kong, and the two different language communities from Taiwan—native Taiwanese and "Mainlanders"—have separate social organizations on U.S. campuses and do not socialize across group boundaries. These social separations tend to continue after graduation for those who stay in the United States.) In recent years, many of these American-educated immigrants from China have also sought employment and moved to Chicagoland's surrounding suburbs after graduation, and like the Taiwanese before them, they have now set up their own separate part-time Saturday schools (called "Xilin Chinese Language Schools") for their children, assisted by the Chicago consulate of the Peoples Republic and staffed by volunteer teachers with a teaching background from among their number.[18]

With the opening up of American society to its economically deprived ethnic "minorities," residents of Chicago's two "Chinatowns," including some of the newer immigrants who have been successful, have begun to send their children for higher education, and they or their children have begun to move to other areas of the city or to the suburbs. Beyond the boundaries of the City of Chicago proper there is a continuation of this pattern of dispersion. By 1980 there were nine cities, towns, and villages in the remainder of Cook County with more than 100 residents identifying themselves as Chinese. The largest was Skokie Village, which had 721 Chinese in 1980. In Dupage County, there were four cities or towns with more than 100 Chinese. Lake Country had just over a 1,000 Chinese, and Kane, McHenry and Will Counties each had fewer than 300 Chinese residents apiece in 1980. In contrast, by 1990 there were 21 cities, towns, and villages in Cook County beyond the Chicago city limits with more than 100 Chinese residents each. The largest was still Skokie, followed by the city of Evanston. (These statistics usually do not include foreign students at universities.) In Dupage County there were 15 cities or towns with more than 100 Chinese and more than 1,000 Chinese residents living in the western suburb of Naperville.

The 1990 U.S. Census showed that the 49,936 Chinese living in Illinois gave Illinois the sixth largest Chinese population of any state in the union, and the largest concentration of Chinese (as well as of many other Asian groups) in the Midwest (Moy, 1995, p. 408). More than 43,000 (86%) of Illinois Chinese live in the Chicagoland area. In the 1960s and 1970s the rate of growth of the Chinese population in the Chicagoland area surpassed the increase of Chinese in the United States as a whole. Between 1960 and 1970, the U.S. Chinese population almost doubled, growing from 237,292 to 435,062. During the same period, the Chicagoland Consolidated Metropolitan Statistical Area (CMSA) Chinese population grew from 5,289 to 12,653, a per annum increase of 9.11%. As a result, between 1960 and 1970, the proportion of all Chinese living in the Chicagoland CMSA rose from 2.23% to 2.91% of the total population in the area. Although the rapid growth of the Chicagoland Chinese community slowed to 6.94% a year in the 1970 to 1980 decade, it was still higher than the overall U.S. Chinese growth rate of 6.34%. By 1980, the Chicagoland Chinese community included 3.01% of all the Chinese in the United States.

Since 1950, the Chinese population in the City of Chicago proper has increased, as opposed to the general trend toward suburbanization of the population in northern Illinois and most other metropolitan areas in the United States over that time. While Chicago proper lost about 2% of its overall population to the suburbs during the 1950–1960 period, its Chinese population grew by 74%. In the following decade, the City of Chicago lost another 5% of its total population, whereas its Chinese population again grew by 84%. In the following decade, between 1970 and 1980 the City proper lost an additional 10% of its population, whereas the Chinese population doubled, standing at 13,638 in the City (and 24,755 in the overall CMSA) by 1980. As a result of these demographic changes, the proportion of Chinese in Chicago's total population rose sixfold from 1940 to 1980, increasing from 0.1% to 0.6% of the City's population. However, during the 1980–1990 decade, the total population in the City of Chicago as a whole increased at a rate of 7.63%,[19] whereas the Chinese population within the City grew only at a rate of 5.80% per year. On the other hand, the rate of Chinese population growth in the suburban regions of the Chicago CMSA (6.68% per year) grew faster than that in Chicago City (5.04% per year). This shows an increasing trend of diverging settlement and suburbanization of the Chicagoland Chinese population as they become more affluent and educated.

The educational level of Chinese living in the Chicagoland area continues to improve. Recent immigrants from China, Hong Kong, and Taiwan are better educated than previous immigrants because of a gradual improvement in economic and educational conditions in those places. In addition, of course, many legal immigrants to the United States who do not have relatives here must demonstrate professional expertise, which presupposes a high level of education. By 1990, most Chinese in South Chinatown had achieved either basic schooling (9 years) or some middle-level schooling (9 to 12 years). But in 1990 in the core South Chinatown area (census tracts 3402, 3403, and 3404) only 12.7%, 20.3%, and 25.3%, respectively, of the Chinese living there had obtained a bachelor's degree or higher, which was far lower than the same figure for Cook County in the same time period (46.5%). This is possibly accounted for by the continuing immigration into the South Chinatown area of more relatively undereducated people, and the out-migration to the suburbs of those who have become more educated as noted earlier. In contrast to the overall figure of 46.5% of college graduates in Cook County just cited, in Evanston, where many Chinese reside, 77.9% of the population have bachelor's degrees or higher, and in neighboring Skokie, another high Chinese residency area, the figure for college graduates is 51.2%. Similarly, suburban Chinese report a much higher level of English proficiency: The proportion of the population of Chinese older than 17 years who are reported as "not speaking English well" ranges from a low of only 2.6% in the far south suburb of South Holland to a high of 32.9% in the nearby northwest suburb of Norridge. Early results from the 2000 census show that U.S. population growth resulting from immigration is at the highest rates since the 1930s, with most of the growth concentrating in the major urban areas, including Chicago, and that the number of English-only households continues to decline, so figures may well increase in the detailed 2000 census and in the first decade of the 21st century. (See author's note on p. 354.)

The increasing influx of Chinese-speaking immigrants particularly into the Chicago City public schools has necessitated the development of special bilingual education programs for these children. (Federal and state laws require that schools having a certain number of non-English speakers from one language background must provide instruction in that language. Because of this, four of the elementary schools in the South Chinatown area (Haines, Healy, Sheridan, and James Ward) provide bilingual education classes in Chinese. In practice, this means Cantonese, and in more recent years Mandarin for children from other Chinese-speaking areas. In addition, the Kelly and Curie high schools adjacent to South Chinatown also provide similar bilingual education classes in Chinese. In support of these efforts, the Office of Language and Cultural Education of the Chicago Board of Education makes available a "Chinese Language and Culture Curriculum" produced by the Illinois State Board of Education, as well as a 294-page Chinese Heritage Curriculum Resource Guide. In addition, St. Therese elementary school run by the Catholic Archdiocese of Chicago in the heart of South Chinatown also provides similar bilingual education instruction, as well as Chinese language and culture classes. English as a Second Language and other classes for adults are provided by two state and federally funded social agencies, the Chinese American Service League in South Chinatown and the Chinese Mutual Aid Association in North Chinatown and in Westmont,[20] as well as by some smaller church-affiliated groups.

CHINESE LANGUAGE EDUCATION IN CHICAGOLAND

Mention has already been made of the part-time "heritage" or "Saturday schools" set up by educated immigrant parents from Taiwan and the similar *Xilin* Saturday schools more recently set up by educated immigrant parents from mainland China for their respective children. Both of these types of schools, as well as a few similar ones set up in the Chinatown communities, are supported by either the offices of the Republic of China on Taiwan in Chicago or the consular offices of the Peoples Republic on the mainland of China, depending on the origin of the group running the school. As we have noted, in the suburbs, the language of instruction and the object of study is spoken and written Mandarin Chinese, the official national language of both governments. In the few Chinatown heritage language schools, the language of instruction may be Cantonese, at least at the beginning levels, but the ultimate object is still literacy in standard Chinese and some command of Mandarin Chinese, which is everywhere considered to be the national standard, and also useful for business dealings with Chinese from the suburbs and elsewhere.

One significant difference between the Saturday schools run by Taiwanese or Hong Kong immigrants and the newer *Xilin* Chinese language schools supported by the Peoples Republic lies in the type of Chinese *characters* which are taught and in which the supplied materials are printed. Although both governments (and the Hong Kong educational system as well) recognize Mandarin Chinese as the official national language of China, there is in fact a small but significant difference between the "old style" Chinese characters used to write and print modern Chinese in Taiwan and Hong Kong (even after 1997) and the new-style "simplified characters" used to write and print Chinese in the Peoples Republic. In the 1950s, in an attempt to facilitate widespread literacy throughout the mainland of China, the newly established government and educational authorities of the Peoples Republic undertook to "simplify" the printed and written forms of about 40% of the traditional Chinese character forms. Notably, the thousands of different characters used to print and write Chinese are not *alphabetic,* but rather, may (for simplicity's sake) be thought of as part "ideographic" and part "phonetic," having evolved out of ancient pictographs and ideographs. They often require writing quite a number of complex strokes in small boxlike shapes, one separate character for each syllable of a spoken word. In the early 1950s the educational leaders of the newly established government of the Peoples Republic of China researched and then promulgated a number of simplified forms of many of the traditional Chinese characters, abandoning the older forms still used by Chiang Kai-shek's refugee government on Taiwan, in Hong Kong, and in all the overseas Chinese communities throughout the world, as well as in most Western universities teaching Chinese. To repeat, although the Chinese characters are in fact *not* alphabetic, the resulting simplification was "*sumwat unalogus tu raiting Ingliš dis wey*," confusing to the uninitiated used to the traditional English writing system, but transparent to native speakers willing to make the effort to adjust to it (Rohsenow, 1991).

Unfortunately, but perhaps understandably, this attempt to "simplify" the burden of learning thousands of complex shapes in order to facilitate the education of millions of illiterate Chinese was taken by the exiled government on Taiwan and by many other refugees from China to be a "communist plot," a deliberate attempt to cut off China's people from thousands of years of traditional Chinese culture and values. Thus materials printed in the new simplified Chinese characters were for many years banned in Taiwan and in the United States, and simplified characters were not taught outside the Peoples Republic, except as a variation to be learned by a few specialists doing intelligence work on Communist China.

After the Peoples Republic replaced the Republic of China (Taiwan) in the United Nations in the 1970s, technically these simplified characters became the international standard, but in fact habit and years of social and political prejudice have prevented Chinese communities outside of mainland China from adopting them. Therefore all Chinese newspapers printed in the USA, in Hong Kong, and in most of the overseas Chinese communities whence Chinese immigrants to the U.S. have come do not use these PRC simplified characters. However, the new *Xilin* heritage language schools established throughout the Chicagoland area are provided by the PRC consulate with teaching materials written in these simplified characters, which Chinese from other Chinese communities in Taiwan and even (until recently) Hong Kong cannot or will not read.[21] One irony little commented on is that all Chinese newspapers and magazines printed in the U.S. (as well as all imported from Taiwan and most from Hong Kong) are printed in the "old style" Chinese characters. Most immigrant Chinese from mainland China who continue to read the American Chinese press (including the parents of children in the *Xinlin* schools) quickly accustom themselves to reading the older forms of the characters, primarily because they often find materials from PRC boring or propagandistic. A second irony is that many of these same PRC immigrant parents continue to insist that the heritage language schools their children attend teach the new "simplified" characters presently used only in the Peoples Republic, even though they themselves have quickly accustomed themselves to reading the traditional old style characters still used in all U.S. Chinese publications, in Taiwan, Hong Kong, and throughout most of the overseas Chinese communities throughout the world.[22]

The 1998–1999 Chicago Chinese Yellow Pages lists 33 Chinese language schools, eight in South Chinatown, one in North Chinatown and twenty-one in the Chicagoland suburbs,[23] not counting the five additional *Xilin* Chinese language schools in Chicago and the suburbs run by mainland Chinese immigrants for their children. As noted above, regardless of whether these "heritage language schools" are run by groups of parents, churches, or other Chinese social groups and whatever the home dialect of the parents (Cantonese, Taiwanese, Mandarin), all of these schools, like all schools in mainland China, Taiwan, and now Hong Kong, teach standard spoken and written Mandarin Chinese, the recognized national language of China. In addition, beginning in 1999 the Chicago Public Schools implemented teaching Chinese and Japanese in four elementary and seven high schools. The four elementary schools which offer Mandarin Chinese are Bell, Healy, McCormick and Solomon. The eight high schools which offer Mandarin are Clemente, Curie, Jones, Juarez, Kelly, Lindbloom, Northside College Preparatory, Payton College Preparatory, and Whitney Young.[24]

In recent years conflict has arisen in some New York and San Francisco area Chinese heritage language programs. These programs originally catered primarily to the children of immigrants from Taiwan, but since the mid-1990s increasingly include the children of the more recent immigrants from the Peoples Republic. Emotional conflicts have therefore arisen between the two groups of parents about whether old style traditional Chinese characters or the new "simplified" characters should be taught in those suburban public schools and even some of the private programs attended by children of both groups (Chao, 1997; Chen, 1996; Ni, 1999). The number of different heritage language schools dispersed throughout the Chicagoland area, each tailored to the needs and desires of its sponsors, may explain the absence of such conflicts here at least up to the present, but they perhaps may be anticipated in the near future.[25]

The American born Chinese children ("ABCs") of the earlier more educated, primarily suburban immigrants from Taiwan and Hong Kong are, as noted above, fluent and educated in English, and—if they attend such part time heritage language "Saturday school" programs at all as children— they often tire of them in their teen-age years or become involved in other more "mainstream" American activities. As the well-educated children of suburban professionals, they usually hope to attend the more prestigious American colleges and universities within Illinois or throughout the nation, and are welcomed by such institutions as members of a "model minority."

Thus, college students from Taiwanese or Mandarin speaking families in the suburbs, if they do not go out of state, often attend the University of Chicago, Northwestern, or the University of Illinois at Champaign-Urbana. A minority of these students who have completed one of the heritage language programs through the high school level may either "test out" of their college level foreign language requirement using Mandarin Chinese if their speaking and writing ability is adequate or at least place into second or third-year-level Mandarin classes by examination. On the other hand, those children of more recent adult immigrants (many of whom are immigrants themselves), who are usually Cantonese speakers, and who often live in or near one of the two Chinatown areas within the city are more likely to attend local institutions such as Roosevelt University or the University of Illinois at Chicago within the City itself. As with other "heritage language speakers" of Spanish, Polish, Hindi, Russian, and the like in the Chicago area and increasingly throughout the nation, if they have some level of spoken fluency in Cantonese, but no real command of Mandarin or the written language, they present a special problem in terms of their college foreign language placement. On the U.S. West Coast and in Hawaii, such cases are sufficiently numerous that they are often handled, at least in the larger public universities, the same way that nonliterate speakers of Mexican Spanish are handled in Illinois: they are put in special "heritage language learner" sections separate from nonnative speakers and taught literacy and standard grammar and usage on an accelerated track designed especially for them. Because the number of such Chinese students in Chicago is not as numerous as in San Francisco, Los Angeles, or Honolulu, and because the total number of students, both Chinese and non-Chinese, wishing to study Mandarin is not large, special arrangements must be made for them to satisfy their college foreign language requirement using either Cantonese or Mandarin Chinese.[26]

LITERACY IN CHINESE

Turning now to the question of literacy in Chinese in the various Chicagoland Chinese speaking communities, we must first examine the concept of "literacy" in the Chinese context, as well as the linguistic concept of differing types of "literacies" in a language community (Imber, 1990). It should be recalled again that the system of Chinese characters is not alphabetic, but rather, each syllable in a Chinese spoken word is represented by a different Chinese character. Most characters are usually partly "ideographic,"—that is, suggestive of the syllable's general meaning —and partly suggestive of the spoken word's pronunciation at some time in the far past. The problem is compounded in that every one of the thousands of characters has a differing pronunciation in each of the hundreds of "dialects" of the various Chinese language families and regionalects. The 20th century solution to this age-old Chinese problem is that (a) "Mandarin" Chinese (based on the dialect of Beijing [Peking], the national capital) has since the 1920s been recognized by all parties as the standard "National Language" (*Guoyu*), and (b) since that time, modern Chinese has been written using Chinese characters, but in a semiliterary style which approximates that new spoken standard. This has meant that Chinese newspapers (themselves basically a 20th century import) are in principle intelligible to all sufficiently literate Chinese, regardless of the Chinese language or dialect they speak.

The State Language Commission of the Peoples Republic of China has determined that a person knowing approximately 3,755 Chinese characters can read 90% of the characters normally occurring in ordinary newspapers, magazines, and other commonly encountered printed matter. A knowledge of 6,763 Chinese characters allows one to read approximately 99% of such commonly encountered printed material.[27] Given the need to learn to recognize and write thousands of different characters, combined in different ways in different (spoken) words, it is perhaps easy to see why nonliteracy or only functional semiliteracy restricted to one's immediate needs (e.g., business accounting) was and is rampant in China. The governments of the Peoples Republic of China on the Chinese mainland and the Republic of China on Taiwan are to be congratulated for their great strides in promoting both Mandarin as the standard national language and at least minimal literacy in Chinese characters among many of China's 1.4 billion people, but it is also easy to understand how the Chinese character literacy of immigrants to the United States may vary greatly, depending on the educational and regional background of the people in question.

As noted earlier, educated first-generation immigrants to Chicago's Chinatowns and suburbs who are literate in Chinese continue to read Chinese newspapers, but most prefer to read Chinese newspapers printed in the United States. In the Chicagoland area, Chinese read either the Midwestern editions of several U.S.-wide Chinese papers printed in New York or California and/or one or more of several Chinese papers printed in Chicago. The most popular U.S. nationwide Chinese paper is the *Shijie Ribao*

(World Daily News), which keeps local reporters in Chicago, carries national and local financial news and prints primarily advertisements from Chicago Chinese businesses in its Midwestern U.S. edition (circulation; 50,000 in the Midwest). It is the only Chinese newspaper sold on the street in vending boxes in the two Chinatowns, near those of Chicago's major universities, which many Chinese foreign students attend, and in the Chinese stores and supermarket complexes in the suburban Chicagoland area. Like most other U.S. Chinese newspapers, it carries national and international news of particular interest to the Chinese community, and now may be said to have a more or less neutral political position with regard to internal Chinese politics. It also has an associated weekly news and feature magazine, *Shijie Zhoukan* (World Weekly). A second national Chinese newspaper popular in the Chicagoland area is the *Qiao Bao* or (Overseas Chinese Daily), founded in 1991, briefly published in Chicago, and now relocated to New York. This paper, which claims a Midwest circulation of 10,000 copies, is similar in coverage to the World Daily News, but tends to lean more toward a viewpoint compatible with that of the Peoples Republic. A third less popular national paper is the Xingdao Ribao (Sing Tao Daily), published for American Chinese by a Singapore-based conglomerate in New York. There are also a number of other newspapers and magazines in Chinese printed both in the United States and abroad available for sale or by mail for those interested.

Finally, the *Peoples Daily—Overseas Edition*, published in Beijing (Peking) should be mentioned. This is a special overseas edition of the leading national daily in the Peoples Republic, published by the Chinese Communist Party for the benefit of its citizens overseas. It is now available only by subscription, and is usually only read by PRC nationals visiting the United States for a short time who intend to return to China, and whose interest lies in keeping abreast of the "party line" in internal PRC politics. It is interesting to note that from the late 1970s through the mid-1980s, this Overseas Edition of the *Peoples Daily* was deliberately printed in old-style traditional characters and distributed free overseas as a propaganda gesture toward the American Chinese community. Because of its parochial and propagandistic content, however, it was not well received, and therefore is now again printed in the simplified characters used throughout the PRC. It now is available only by subscription at a subsidized rate of 30 U.S. dollars a year.

Before the innovation of computerized typesetting and layout programs, Chicago had a number of Chinese printing businesses, which set up restaurant menus, advertisements, and other announcements in old-style Chinese characters to be printed by local printers. Now, with local Chinese newspapers and other materials formatted completely in Chinese by Chinese software computer programs, the layout is sent to local English-language commercial printers for final printing. Although new-style simplified character programs and even old-to-new-style character conversion programs are now easily available, material is formatted only in the new-style simplified characters on special order. In 1979, when the only Chinese news publication seen in Chicago from the Peoples Republic was the aforementioned-mentioned Overseas Edition of the *Peoples Daily,* especially printed in traditional old-style characters for free distribution in North America as a propaganda gesture, I enquired (in Mandarin) in one of South Chinatown's print shops on South Wentworth as to whether they also could print in mainland Chinese simplified characters. As the only mainland Chinese paper he had ever seen in those days was the Overseas Edition of the *People's Daily,* especially printed in old-style characters for overseas consumption, the owner-operator replied dismissively that there was no point in his investing in them. "They're giving those up," he said. "Look, even the *Peoples Daily* is printed in traditional characters!"

The growth of the Chicagoland Chinese community, coupled with the development of computer-assisted newspaper layout programs for Chinese in recent years, has made it possible for small groups of two, three, or four people each to produce local newspapers. There are currently four locally published Chinese papers of much smaller circulations in Chicago, dependent primarily on local advertising and distributed cheaply or free throughout the Chicagoland area in those restaurants, stores, and supermarket complexes that cater to the Chinese community. These include the *Meizhong Xinwen* (Chinese American News), an independent local paper started in 1989 with a circulation of about 3,000; the *Chen Bao* (China Star); the *Shenzhou Shibao* (China Journal—Chicago), a locally produced version of a California-based newspaper chain, and the *Zhijaige Shibao* (Chicago Chinese News), the local newspaper of the Dallas-based Southern Chinese Newspaper Group with affiliate Chinese papers in 11 U.S. cities. In addition to a few other locally produced "supermarket throwaway" papers, a number of other weekly newspaper-style publications are also distributed free in the Chicagoland area. In addition to the *Hongguan Bao* (Macroscopic Weekly), an economic overview from Taiwan printed in California, there are also the Buddhist *Tsu Chi World Journal*, published in California by a Taiwan-based Buddhist association; the *Zhen Fo Bao* (True

Buddhist News Weekly), also distributed throughout North America by another Taiwan-based Buddhist organization; and the Christian evangelical *Hao Jiao* (Herald Weekly), published by Chinese Christian Herald Crusades, Inc. in New York City.

For the reasons stated earlier (until very recently), all of the Chinese-language newspapers available in the United States are in old-style, traditional Chinese characters, but still differ in their physical format layout. Traditionally, Chinese characters were written and printed from right to left and vertically from top to bottom. More modern publications, including most contemporary books, newspapers, and magazines published in the Peoples Republic, follow the Western style in being printed in horizontal lines from left to right. Whereas all U.S. Chinese newspapers use the older traditional style characters and most of the older ones continue to follow the traditional right-to-left, vertical top-to-bottom format still used in Taiwan and Hong Kong, some of the newer ones follow the PRC horizontal right-to-left format. In 2002, the country's most widely circulated Chinese newspapers provoked great controversy within the American Chinese community nationwide by switching from the traditional vertical right to left format to the newer, PRC-style horizontal right to left format (Chen, 2002).

The 1998–1999 Chicago Chinese Yellow Pages lists 12 Chinese language bookstores in the greater Chicagoland area: three in South Chinatown, one in North Chinatown, one downtown in the Chicago Loop, one each near the University of Chicago and near Northwestern University in Evanston, and the remainder in those suburban areas with the greatest concentration of Chinese immigrants listed earlier. Catering to their more literate clientele, these bookstores primarily stock a wide variety of Chinese bestsellers, cook books, and the like, almost all from either Taiwan or Hong Kong, and thus all printed in traditional old-style characters. Those of such books permitted by the censors are now equally sought after in the Peoples Republic (often reprinted in simplified characters), whereas very few books published within Mainland China are of interest to Chinese readers outside the country. Any rare exceptions would quickly be converted by computer printers into old-style characters in Hong Kong or Taiwan for readers in those places and by overseas Chinese communities elsewhere.

The main branch of the Chicago Public Library, as well as the local branches of the CPL located in both South Chinatown and North Chinatown have Chinese dictionaries, general Chinese reference works, and a sizable collection of Chinese books similar to those sold in the Chinese bookstores just described. In the 1990s, the South Chinatown branch library has consistently had the highest circulation of all 76 branches of the Chicago Public Library, in part because of regular patrons coming there not only from all over the Chicagoland area, but also from northwest Indiana and southern Wisconsin.[28] Serious scholarly readers must find a way to access the East Asia research collections of the libraries at the University of Chicago or Northwestern University. Adjacent to the Di Ho Chinese supermarket complex (where one of the three Chicagoland branches of the World Journal Bookstore is located and all of the Chinese newspapers are available) the government of the Republic of China on Taiwan has for more than 20 years subsidized a Chinese Cultural Center for propaganda purposes. In addition to a fairly sizable free lending library of books published in Taiwan, this Center holds free classes and social activities, including Chinese heritage Mandarin language classes; sponsors Chinese-language visiting speakers from Taiwan and speaking contests and Mandarin language camps in the Midwest and Taiwan for children; and promotes Taiwan satellite television subscriptions. As Taiwan recognizes dual citizenship, which the PRC does not, every year, sympathetic representatives from all three Chicagoland communities are invited to join representatives from other U.S. Chinese communities as all-expense-paid "overseas Chinese" guests in Taipei, Taiwan on October 10th ("Double Ten"), the anniversary of the founding of the Republic of China by Dr. Sun Yat-sen in 1911. Both the Peoples Republic and the Republic of China on Taiwan make sure that a number of the diplomatic-level representatives in their Chicago offices speak either Cantonese or Taiwanese in addition to Mandarin. Both governments subsidize annual U.S. tours of popular Mandarin-speaking professional entertainers and amateur youth entertainment groups.

OTHER MEDIA IN CHINESE

The Chinatown community in the city, like many other Chicago ethnic communities, has long supported "Global Radio," a commercially available Chinese radio station, until recent years, mostly all in Cantonese, which is accessed by purchasing a specially programmed radio set to receive broadcasts over a restricted frequency. This service has recently expanded its broadcasting range to a 60-mile-wide radius from downtown

Chicago, and added some programming in Mandarin Chinese for the benefit of the increasing number of suburban listeners. A few hours per week of Cantonese language programming is also available free over two local radio stations specializing in ethnic programming.

Beginning in the late 1970s, the Taiwan government provided 2 hr weekly of Mandarin language television programming from Taiwan to be shown over a local for-profit ethnic programming station (WFBT-TV), with local Chicago advertising in Cantonese or Mandarin Chinese. In the 1990s, similar programming from mainland China became available, and for a few years in the late 1990s, 90 minutes of Mandarin news and features from the PRC were made available every evening, plus 2 hr on Sunday afternoon, while the Taiwan news retreated to ½ hr of news in Mandarin in the late evening. With the advent of Chinese television programming on cable in some of the (affluent) western Chicagoland suburbs and by satellite throughout the Chicagoland area in the late 1990s, early in 2001 the subsidy for the ½ hr of free nightly television news from Taiwan was ended by the Taiwan government. However, the same late evening time slot continued to be filled with news from Taiwan and the local Chicagoland Chinese community, supported by a local Chinese newspaper, *Meiguo Xinwen*. In early 2002, the China Star Media Corporation, publishers of the Chicago-based *Chen Bao*, began 24/7 broadcasting of PRC supported news and features on a new (free) television station, WOCK-CA TV. Satellite television news and entertainment programming directly from Taiwan and the PRC in Mandarin and from Hong Kong in Cantonese are now commercially available 24 hr a day, making the free, often more propagandistic television programming from mainland China increasingly less attractive to viewers. With the advent of less expensive computer graphics, commercial programming for the free PRC television news and feature programming can be produced locally. It is here that those who purchase and repackage these television news and feature programs from Taiwan and the PRC make their profit advertising Chicagoland's numerous Chinese goods and services to local viewers in either Cantonese or Mandarin.

Unlike larger Chinatowns in North America, Chicago's Chinatown has not been able to support a permanent Chinese movie theater, although sometimes Cantonese operas and popular films in Cantonese are shown in nearby theater or other rented space on a limited basis. This lacuna has of course been satisfied by the increasing availability, first of video-taped movies, and now VCD and DVD disks.[29]

Both Chinatowns as well as most of the stores and supermarkets in the Chicagoland suburbs that cater to the Chinese immigrant community have video rental sections or stores. As both Hong Kong and Taiwan are among the world's largest film-producing areas, hundreds of films in Cantonese and Mandarin are now easily available to overseas Chinese communities throughout the world. And because almost all of these films, music videos, and the like. are shown and exported to various overseas Chinese communities all over the globe, the majority have printed subtitles (in old-style characters) at the bottom of the screen, in recognition of the wide variety of spoken Chinese languages and dialects, and the shared common written language within these communities described earlier. On some of the newer DVD disks, however, viewers may choose from a menu whether to hear the film in the original Cantonese or dubbed into Mandarin, and whether to have the subtitles in old-style characters, new-style characters, or English translation. The latest award-winning films from Hong Kong, Taiwan, and the PRC are now shown (subtitled in English and Chinese) on a limited basis at the annual Chicago Film Festival and replayed at the city's local art house cinemas, usually attracting a mixture of non-Chinese interested in foreign films and a small number of local Chinese students and intellectuals. Professor. Barbara Sharres, the Director of the Film Center of the School of the Art Institute of Chicago, has a done a great deal to organize retrospectives of the major Chinese directors from those three areas, and she has shown a special concern for promoting the better films from Hong Kong. Chinese films supplied by the government offices of the PRC and Taiwan are also sometimes shown at the major local universities for their respective Chinese student groups.

OTHER CHINESE LITERACIES

As a sociolinguistic term, "literacy" or "literacies" is used to refer to sets of cultural practices that readers said to be "literate" in some language (or other set of symbols) bring to material written in that language allowing them to interpret those materials in a culturally appropriate and meaningful manner (Imber, 1990; Street, 1984). It is therefore possible to speak of "religious literacy," "musical literacy," "numeracy" (i.e., ability to deal with systems of written numbers), and a variety of other such specialized "literacies" within various groups. In this context, we may note a number of such literacies in the Chinese-speaking communities in Chicago.

One such specialized type of literacy found in America's Chinese communities is religious literacy. It should first be understood that traditional religious practices have been under some siege in mainland China for at least the last half century. But many immigrants from more traditional Chinese communities in Taiwan, Hong Kong, and Southeast Asia may bring with them their knowledge of the specialized literacies of Buddhism, Taoism, and local folk beliefs or religions. This may be termed a specialized literacy in the sense that certain terms, both spoken and written, are not always intelligible to those uninitiated in one or another of those particular belief systems, particularly given the deliberate attack on all such religious practices, native and foreign, carried on by the Chinese Communist Party within the Peoples Republic of China since its founding in 1949. Because of this, not only are certain spoken terms, locutions, and concepts often understood only by those who have been initiated in one set of practices or another, but also certain special Chinese *characters* or specialized *combinations of* normal Chinese characters may not be understood. (One might be able to sound out these latter combinations, but the meanings of the words would not make any sense to anyone not "literate" in that particular religious culture.) Thus the religious instruction classes held at the Taiwan Ling Shen Ching Tze Buddhist Temple in Bridgeport or the newer Southeast Asian Chanh-Giac-Tu Buddhist Temple on North Broadway near North Chinatown consist largely of teaching new characters and new combinations of characters or "words" with new meanings to converts. This is even more true of Chinese Christianity, which because it is a religion imported from the West, has some special madeup Chinese characters and imported names, concepts, words, and locutions in its rituals that simply do not make an sense to non-Christian Chinese. It should also be mentioned that some Chicagoland Chinese Christian groups hold their services in spoken Cantonese or Taiwanese, and sometimes use printed materials that contain some special Chinese characters used only in writing those dialects that ordinary educated readers and writers of standard Chinese do not understand.

Another type of specialized literacy is traditional Chinese musical notation, different from Western musical notation, which is sometimes used in hymnals and sheet music for popular singing and by some of the seven Chinese music and choral groups listed in the Chicago Yellow Pages, plus other such singing groups on local university campuses. Yet another specialized literacy involves the ability to read a kind of "numerical code" used to write prices of popular dishes on slips of papers pasted on the walls of Chinatown restaurants, which cater primarily to local residents. Instead of using either Arabic numerals (as Chinese often now do, even in China) or regular Chinese number characters, Cantonese restaurants may use this numerical shorthand, originally designed to display prices in Chinese currency in China, to refer to the price in U.S. currency. Other sets of coded Chinese characters or symbols are sometimes used on Chinese lottery tickets sold in lotteries in American Chinatowns. Even more esoteric are certain Chinese characters and "gang symbols" long associated with Chinese "secret societies," "triads," and gangs, many of which long ago crossed the Pacific Ocean and continue to do so. As with other ethnic gangs in Chicago, these specialized locutions, symbols, and combinations of symbols are used for mutual recognition and solidarity among the initiated, and members usually swear a blood oath upon initiation not to betray them to outsiders. Naturally, for a variety of reasons these are not normally discussed in the Chinese community, and especially not with outsiders.

THE FUTURE OF CHINESE LANGUAGE USE IN CHICAGOLAND

Chinese language use in Chicagoland, as in the rest of the world's Chinese communities, has been greatly affected by the development of global, "transnational" communities among what has been called the "Chinese diaspora." In a world of increasingly permeable borders, with greatly facilitated intercontinental transportation and instant global communication, Chinese communities in Chicagoland and throughout the world find themselves in a new context that greatly affects patterns of Chinese language use. This new context includes increased facility of immigration to the U.S. and international travel back and forth; ubiquitous telephone credit cards with discounted long distance rates to Hong Kong, Taiwan, and mainland China; the rapid spread of cell phones in those areas; and simultaneous satellite and cable broadcasting of television programming from those three areas and from other larger Chinatowns within the United States. All of these new facts of transportation and communication mean that Chinese speakers, both adults and children, resident in any of Chicagoland's Chinese communities are no longer linguistically and culturally isolated from ongoing participation in mainstream Chinese culture. The development of Chinese software and instant Internet access to all types of information in Chinese, from the daily news and the latest Hong Kong music videos to university classes from both within and without the

United States, all promise unlimited cyberspace possibilities, but do require literacy in Chinese characters. More tolerant and sophisticated bilingual education programs and services in the Chicago public schools and social service agencies do not discourage the use of their Chinese language(s) within the community. All these factors allow and even encourage immigrants and their American-born children to maintain their Chinese language skills. In business and diplomatic dealings with Chinese communities in Asia, the ability to read and write Chinese and familiarity with traditional Chinese culture and behavior provides a natural advantage. At the same time of course, the level of English teaching in Hong Kong, Taiwan, and the Peoples Republic continues to improve as English continues to be the "world language" of commerce and communication. Traditional pressures on all immigrants to U.S. society to "assimilate" into "mainstream" American society also continue to entice and even force them to develop their English language abilities, both spoken and written. In the increasingly fluid transnational world of the globalized 21st century, members of U.S. Chinese communities will continue to participate as bi- and multilingual members of multiethnic America's increasingly pluralistic culture.

ENDNOTES:

1. I thank Sarah Caldwell and the Chinese Mutual Aid Association of Chicago, Ling Aronsen, Richard Barrett, Marcia Farr, Dell Hymes, Jennifer Lee, Annie W. Liu, Michael Luo, Susan Lee Moy, Rachel Reynolds, Piotr Sromek, Daniel Strauss, Chinliang Wang, Wei Wang, Shawn Zhang and Lisa Zhao for assistance with this chapter. Interviewing was conducted under UIC IRB Research Protocol #2000-0405. No humans or animals were harmed in research for this article.
2. For the history of Chicago's Chinese community, see Moy (1995) and McKeown (2001).
3. Chinese place and dialect names are given in the now standard Hanyu Pinyin romanization with the more traditional Wade-Giles romanization immediately following in parentheses. However, following customary practice and for ease of understanding, Cantonese and other traditional names for places, dialects, and the like, commonly encountered in English (e.g. Toisan; Canton[ese]) will be substituted where appropriate.

4. Specifically, census tract 3402. These and all subsequent statistical data are from the *Statistical Abstract of the United States,* (1996) and the *Chicago Fact Book*—1990. I am grateful to Ms. Wei Wang and Prof. Richard Barrett of the University of Illinois at Chicago for assisting me in obtaining and interpreting much of the following census data.

5. *Chicago Fact Book*—*1990,* 381, 399.

6. Census tracts 3401–3404 in *Chicago Fact Book*—1990, 121.

7. *Chicago Fact Book*—*1990,* 175.

8. *Chicago Fact Book*—*1990,* 176.

9. *Chicago Fact Book*—*1990,* 384, 402.

10. Adler (2000). These and other census figures of those listing themselves as "Chinese" probably underestimate the actual number of Chinese speakers because of "the reluctance of respondents to report an ethnic identification that still carried a social stigma, as well as the inability or unlearned people to understand the complex questionnaires. ... Others did not respond or could not respond. ... because they feared any contact with the federal government" (Tsai, 1986, p. 151).

11. Historically, S. L. Moy notes that a small percentage of Chinese born in the United States were sent back to be educated in China from the late 19th century until the enforcement of the Chinese Exclusion Laws. This "reverse immigration" was prominent among the merchant class of Chinese immigrants who valued education and who felt that their sons should be educated in the Chinese classics if they were to become successful and respected among their peers and family. Although a majority of the early immigrants were illiterate, they worked hard to provide funds for their children to become educated in China. Later immigrants from the 1920s on were more educated, and many enrolled in English classes offered at the local Chicago Baptist churches across Chicago. These Chinese Sunday Schools used English lessons to preach Christianity to these immigrants (S. L. Moy, personal communication).

12. An exception was the small number of Chinese students from more educated families who attended the University of Illinois at Urbana during the 1920s through the 1940s who remained in the United States to become active members of the Chinese community. Because of their status as students, they were able to bring their wives and children to America and were exempt from the Chinese Exclusion Laws (S. L. Moy, personal communication).

13. There also exists a minority of speakers of another Chinese language "Hakka" (Kejia) and a very small minority of speakers of the non-Chinese languages of the aboriginal peoples who inhabited Taiwan before the large migration of Han Chinese from neighboring Fujian province across the straits to Taiwan in the 1600s, but these are not statistically significant for this discussion.

14. Under "Associations" the 1998–1999 bilingual Chicago Chinese Yellow Pages lists 15 Chinese social organizations in the North Chinatown area, including the Fukien Association and the Teo Chew [Chaozhou] Mutual Assistance Association, whereas there are 51 such associations listed in the South Chinatown area.

15. For a fascinating study of the complex linguistic history of many of these immigrants, their varying command of different Chinese languages and dialects, and their ability to "code switch" between them, see Strauss, (1998), especially chapter 6, pp. 106–139.

16. *Chicago Fact Book–1990,* 387, 395–396, 404. It is possible that some additional ethnic Chinese speakers may have identified themselves by the Southeast Asian country whence they had emigrated. Also see endnote 10.

17. In 1999 international student enrollment at Illinois colleges and universities climbed 8% to 22,807, and Cook county, Illinois had the third highest foreign student enrollment of all U.S. counties, at 12,322, the majority of whom were from China, India, South Korea, Japan and Taiwan. ("Open Doors," Institute of International Education, Washington, D.C., November 13, 2000.)

18. The PRC government is not as generous to its emigrants as the Taiwan government, providing only books printed in mainland Chinese "simplified characters" (see later) and the now standard Hanyu Pinyin romanization used in the PRC, but not teacher training and supplements, trips to the home country, or subsidized "Chinese summer camps" in the United States and Taiwan, which the Republic of China government on Taiwan continues to provide to its emigrants for propaganda purposes.

19. *Statistical Abstract of the United States* (1996).

20. In recognition of the growing number of Chinese in the Chicagoland suburbs, the Chinese Mutual Aid Association in North Chinatown opened a branch next the DiHo Chinese supermarket complex in Westmont in January, 2001.

21. As in mainland China, PRC teaching materials also use a version of the Latin alphabet known as *Hanyu Pinyin* as a sort of "Initial Teaching Alphabet" to assist Chinese children in learning the ac-

tual pronunciation of the Chinese characters, whereas teaching materials from Taiwan continue to use a somewhat cumbersome older system invented in the 1920s that employs a specialized set of Chinese phonetic symbols (not characters) something like the Japanese *kana* syllabary to teach Taiwanese children how to pronounce Chinese characters. One of the many debates between the two immigrant groups is whether the additional "burden" of learning this specialized set symbols is better or worse than having the children become "confused" between the phonetic values of the Latin-based *Hanyu Pinyin* initial teaching alphabet and the sound values of those same Latin letters that they are learning in their regular American school classes.

22. Interestingly, the tiny but influential island Republic of Singapore, which is dominated by a large overseas Chinese community ever mindful of future business opportunities in Asia, teaches mainland simplified characters in the majority of its schools.

23. A partial annotated listing of many of these schools appeared in the 1993 Chicago Chinese Yellow Pages telephone book (Chen, 1993, pp. 55–60).

24. S. L. Moy (personal communication, February 19, 2001).

25. Because a large number of female babies from the Peoples Republic were adopted by suburban U.S. parents in the 1990s, a small number of the White parents have been sending their adopted Chinese children (adopted at too early an age to speak any language at all) to the beginning levels of these Saturday schools so that these China-born children can be "exposed to their native language and culture."

26. In Chinese language classes at the University of Illinois at Chicago over the post 20 years, in addition to the 10 to 20 local students per year who satisfy their 2-year foreign language requirement based on their knowledge of either spoken Mandarin or spoken Cantonese and their command of the written language, there are usually about 40 students in the first-year Chinese class and about 20 in second-year class, 75% of whom are of Chinese ancestry, but not all of these students know Cantonese or any other Chinese language or dialect.

27. These figures are in fact for the new "simplified" characters used in the PRC, but there is no significant difference in these figures for materials printed in the "old-style" Chinese characters used in Taiwan, Hong Kong, and all U.S. Chinatown newspapers.

28. Chahee Stanfield, Chicago Public Library (personal communication).

29. Video compact disks (VCDs) are a cheaper video format popular in Asia not common in the United States because of their poorer sound and picture quality.

AUTHOR'S NOTE

According to data available from the 2000 census in March, 2003, of the entire population of the state of Illinois, 50,705 or slightly less than 0.41% of the state's population were born in China. These make up 3.3% of the state's foreign born population, with 36,586 (2.39%) of these born in mainland China, 5,767 (0.37%) born in Hong Kong and 8,352 (0.55%) born in Taiwan. In Illinois, 65,251 people gave "Chinese" as their language spoken at home, 9,678 of these aged 5–17 years old, and 55,573 aged 18 or older. In Illinois 76,725 persons or 0.6% of the state's population gave their "race" as Chinese; in the city of Chicago proper 31,813 or 1.1% of the city's population listed their race as Chinese, and in Cook county, which contains the city of Chicago, 48,058 or 0.9% of the county's population listed their race as Chinese. In the northwestern suburb of Arlington Heights 757 persons (1.0% of that city's population) gave their race as Chinese; in the city of Evanston bordering Chicago to the north, 1,426 people (1.9% of the city's population) declared themselves as Chinese; in the far western suburb of Naperville 4,198 persons (3.3% of the population) listed themselves as Chinese.

In the core census tracts of South Chinatown in the Amour Square section of Chicago the percentages of each census tract's population aged five or older "speaking a language other than English at home" were: 82.8% (census tract 3401), 83.2% (3402), 70.4% (3403), 77.9% (3404), and the percentages of those characterized as "speaking English less than well" were 48.6% (3401), 65.9% (3402), 48.5% (3403), and 51.3% (3404). In those census tracts in the Bridgeport section of Chicago bordering South Chinatown, (where many Chinese speakers live, but which also has a Mexican population), the percentage of those listed as speaking a language other than English at home were 38% (census tract 6001), 58% (6002), 47.9% (6003), 64.2% (6004), 64.1% (6005), 59.6% (6006), and 43.1% (6007), and the percentages of those speaking English less than well in these areas in Bridgeport were 30.2% (6001), 36.8% (6002), 38.1% (6003), 42% (6004), 43.3% (6005), 37.3% (6006), and 26.1% (6007). In the two census tracts in the Uptown section of Chicago which contain the City's northern Chinatown (composed of many ethnic Chinese from Southeast Asia as well as other immigrants from Southeast Asia), the percentages of those speaking a language other than English at home were 49% (0311) and 50.5% (0312), with 30.1% (0311) and 32.5% (0312) speaking English less than well.

REFERENCES

Adler, J. (2000, October 8). Family ties: Former residents of Chinatown find roots pulling them home. *Chicago Tribune*, p. 16: 1, 7.

Chao, J. (1997, March 2). Chinese school days: Language links kids to culture: But which form of characters they learn a is question of politics. *The San Francisco Examiner*, p. B-1.

Chen, D. W. (1996, November 29). In learning Chinese, less is more complex; Westchester parents are divided between tradition and simplicity. *The New York Times*, p. B-1.

Chen, D. W. (2002, March 25). Chinese papers really change direction. *The New York Times*, p. A-19.

Chen, H. (1993) *Meizhong Zhongwen Xuexiao Xiehui Jianjie* [A brief introduction to the Association of Midwest Chinese Language Schools]. In *1993 Chinese Yellow Pages / Chicago–Mid-U.S.A.* (pp. 55–60). Chicago, IL: Chinese American Newspapers Company.

Chicago Fact Book Consortium. (1984). *Local community fact book: Chicago metropolitan area–Based on the 1970 and 1980 censuses.* Chicago, IL: Author.

Chicago Fact Book Consortium. (1995). *Local community fact book: Chicago metropolitan area–1990.* Chicago, IL: Author.

1998–1999 Chinese Yellow Pages /Chicago/Mid-U.S.A. (1998). Chicago, IL: Chinese American News.

2000–2001 Chinese Business Directory (Chicago/Midwest edition). (2000). Whitestone, NY: World Journal Press.

Gates, H. (1987). *Chinese working-class lives.* Ithaca, NY: Cornell University Press.

Groark, V. (2002, September 4). Chinese speakers get help at polls. *Chicago Tribune*, pp. 2:1, 6.

Imber, B. (1990). *Official and popular literacies in the Peoples Republic of China: A search for shared perspectives.* Unpublished doctoral dissertation. The University of Michigan, Ann Arbor, MI.

Kiang, H. (1992). *Chicago's Chinatown.* Lincolnwood, IL: The Institute of China Studies.

Kennedy, K. (2002, February 20). Chinatown returns to center stage. *Chicago Tribune*, p. 16:1, 4.

McKeown, A. (2001). *Chinese migrant networks and cultural change.* Chicago: The University of Chicago Press.

Moy, S. L. (1995). The Chinese in Chicago: The first one hundred years. In M. G. Holli & P. Jones, *Ethnic Chicago* (4th ed., pp. 378–408). Grant Rapids, MI: Wm. B. Eerdmans.

Ni, C. C. (1999). Which character to teach? School's class in Chinese splits. *Newsday* (Nassau and Suffolk editions). May 2, n.p.

Norman, J. (1988). *Chinese.* New York: Cambridge University Press.

Ramsey, S. R. (1987). *The languages of China.* New York: Cambridge University Press.

Rohsenow, J. S. (1991). Can Taiwanese read simplified characters?" *Sino-Platonic Papers, 27,* 183–197.

Statistical abstract of the United States 1996. (1996). U.S. Department of Commerce Economics and Statistics Administration, Bureau of the Census, Washington, D.C.

Strauss, D. M. W. (1998). *Chinese multilingualism in Chicago.* Unpublished doctoral dissertation. Northwestern University, Evanston, IL.

Street, B. V. (1984). *Literacy in theory and practice.* New York: Cambridge University Press.

Tsai, S. S. H. (1986). *The Chinese experience in America.* Bloomington, IN: The University of Indiana Press.

Wang, X. (1996). *A view from within: A case study of Chinese heritage community language schools.* Washington, DC: National Foreign Language Center.

Photograph by Laura Miller

14

Consuming Japanese Print Media in Chicago

Laura Miller
Loyola University, Chicago

In *The Gutenberg Elegies: The Fate of Reading in an Electronic Age*, Sven Birkets (1994) said of books: "I now see each one as a portable enclosure, a place I can repair to to release the private, unsocialized, dreaming self" (p. 164). It is easy to take for granted the type of written refuge Birkets noted, but what if one lives in an environment wherein one must purposely hunt for reading materials? Specifically, what if you are in Chicago and want to enclose your private self in a Japanese book? What books and other types of writing in the Japanese language is it even possible to find in Chicagoland? After introducing some background on the Japanese writing system and settlement in Chicago, this chapter surveys a spectrum of locally found Japanese print media, including imported and domestically produced books, magazines, newspapers, newsletters, and ephemera such as advertising flyers and notes posted on community message boards. From the *Chicago Shimpô*, a home-grown Japanese-language newspaper published since 1945, to *Fine Boys,* a new imported magazine devoted to male beauty work, the variety of available Japanese-language

357

materials indicates a diversity of readerships. Consumers of Japanese include expatriate business people and their families, scholars and students, heritage communities, and popular culture fans. In some cases, Japanese trends in media consumption, such as the recent explosion in confessional and self-help books for women, are mirrored in Chicago's offerings. On the other hand, the prevalence of special genres of print media and the rarity of others reflects the particular makeup and interests of Chicago readers of Japanese. The range and diversity of print media available illustrate the important role they play in creating a sense of place for an otherwise marginalized group.

A little more than a century ago, there were only 68 Japanese living in Chicago (Chicago Public Library, 2000), but these days one finds an established community of second-, third- and fourth-generation Japanese Americans (called *nissei, sansei,* and *yonsei* respectively) who are either bilingual in English and Japanese or monolingual in English. The earliest Japanese Chicagoans owned small shops or restaurants during the 1880s. According to a local historian, Ryôichi Fuiji (Osako, 1995, p. 422), one of these was Kamenosuke Nishi, the proprietor of a gift shop at the corner of Cottage Grove and 27th Street. Another early arrival was Jun Fujita, a photographer born in Hiroshima in 1888 who eventually settled in Chicago. Fujita worked for the *Chicago Evening Post*, published poetry in English, and started his own photography business (Flanagan, 1996). By the 1930s Nishi and Fujita had been joined by at least 400 other Japanese immigrants.

A big infusion of Japanese Americans, however, came after 1942. There are different figures for how many migrated to Chicago as a result of forced relocation and camp internment, ranging from 20,000 (Brooks, 2000, p. 1655) to 30,000 (Osako, 1995, p. 423). Many of these formerly impounded people returned to live on the West Coast, and the approximate number of Japanese American residents fell to perhaps 16,000 in the Chicago metropolitan area by the 1960s. These first generations of Japanese Americans settled in the South Side (Hyde Park–Kenwood area) and the near North Side near Clark and Division. Osako (1995) attributed their initial residence in racially transitional and industrial areas to difficulty obtaining housing elsewhere because of discrimination. The Midwest Buddhist Temple, built in 1972 at Menomonee and Hudson streets, is still the center for seasonal festivals and events for many of Chicago's Japanese Americans. In later decades, assimilated and successful Japanese Americans dispersed throughout the city and moved into the suburbs of Skokie, Evanston, Niles,

Mt. Prospect, and Des Plaines. According to Osako (1995, p. 431), one in four Chicago Japanese American households is now in the suburbs.

The reading needs and expectations of this heritage population are quite different from those of the largest group of Japanese readers: the nonpermanent, long-term Japanese residents. Aside from visiting Japanese university students and a scattering of non-Japanese popular culture fans, students, and scholars, the primary readers of Japanese texts are these expatriate nonpermanent residents. In 1999, Illinois had 7,570 nonpermanent, long-term Japanese residents and 2,536 permanent new immigrants, most of them in Chicago and area suburbs such as Evanston, Wilmette, and Arlington Heights (there is also a sizable community in Normal where the Mitsubishi plant is located). Together with the thousands of tourists who visit each year, there are more than 10,000 Japanese nationals in the area. Chicago is often classified by marketeers as sixth in the top 10 Japanese markets in the United States, after Honolulu, Los Angeles, San Francisco, New York, and Seattle.

JAPANESE WRITING AND MASS LITERACY

Although they have one of the clunkiest written languages imaginable, Japanese have been prolific readers and writers ever since the introduction of the Chinese script during the fifth and sixth centuries. At that time, Chinese books, mainly on philosophy and religion, were avidly imported and rigorously studied. Over time, Chinese writing began to be used to represent the Japanese language, no easy task given their distinct genetic unrelatedness, and by A.D. 927 we find small Chinese characters, or *kanji*, used phonetically to represent Japanese place names, proper names, grammatical inflections, and particles (Habien, 1984). The eventual development of two native phonetic syllabaries subsequently enabled the creation of a written vernacular language for the writing of tales, poetry, diaries, and other texts in the private domain.

Today's written language is therefore a combination of four different scripts: *kanji* (Chinese logographs), two *kana* syllabaries (*hiragana*, the primary cursive syllabary, and *katakana*, a more angular syllabary mostly used for onomatopoetic words, foreign words, and emphasis), and *rômaji*, or the Latin alphabet. A typical Japanese text, for example, will have some free morphemes written entirely in *kanji*; some words with the stem morphemes written in *kanji* but the inflectional endings or other suffixes written in *hiragana*; stand-alone words, particularly auxiliary verbs, all written in *hiragana*; exclamations and foreign words written in *katakana;* and words and acronyms such as OL (short for "Office Ladies" or female clerks) written in *rômaji*.

Despite this cumbersome system, Japan is said to have one of the highest literacy rates in the world.[1] Before a society can have strong mass literacy, however, it needs to have a mass educational system coupled with the idea of a unified language. Before the major sociopolitical reforms undertaken during the Meiji period (1868–1912), a national consciousness of one unified language was weak, if not absent. There was also a gap between colloquial spoken speech and the language of the classical literary tradition. The Meiji leaders instituted a campaign for the unity of the written and spoken languages, for which they imposed one dialect (Tokyo) as the basis for the creation of a "standard" language for the nation. Today this oral and written standard as taught in schools and used in mass media overlies a wide diversity of regional and social dialects that continue to be used.

It was only after the Pacific War that mass literacy became accessible to virtually all Japanese. The rise of mass media and the proliferation of newspapers and magazines stemmed from postwar implementation of universal coed education. There are only 9 years of compulsory Japanese education, yet 95% of all Japanese continue on to high school. The Japanese educational system is highly gendered, and junior colleges are attended primarily by women, where they study liberal arts and secretarial skills. The majority of college-bound men are funneled off to the more prestigious and rigorous 4-year universities. Of those who complete high school, 21.9% of the women and 2.3% of the men go on to junior colleges, and 27.5% of the women and 44.9% of the men continue studying at 4-year universities (Asahi Shimbun, 2000, p. 248). The establishment of this compulsory education system is credited with maintaining Japan's enormous publishing industry.

Although a large dictionary might contain up to 50,000 *kanji*, and a particularly erudite author may know and use as many as 3,000 characters, the actual number of characters one needs to know to read a daily newspaper is considerably fewer. One scholar goes so far as to claim that with knowledge of only the *kana* and 500 *kanji*, 75% of most media can be read (Crowley, 1990, p. xviii). In 1946, the Ministry of Education composed "official" lists of characters deemed necessary for reading and writing. Other reforms included the modernization of *kana* usage, the simplification of Chinese characters, and some rationalizations for their use. By the sixth grade, students were expected to have learned all the *kana* (46 *hiragana*, and 46 *katakana*, plus secondary *kana* formed with diacritic marks)[2], as well as 996 basic "Educational Characters" (*kyôiku kanji*). By the end of the ninth grade they should have learned all 1,850 characters on the List of Characters for Interim Use (*tôyô kanjihyô*). It was also stipulated by government decree that all official legal documents, including school textbooks, must contain no characters not on this list. It was urged that published mass media for the general public also limit their use of characters. There were ongoing debates about such script restrictions (Gottlieb, 1994; Seeley, 1984,1991), particularly among elite intellectuals and ultranationalists, who claimed it was censoring their freedom of expression and diluting the "special" nature of the Japanese cultural heritage. After decades of political dissent, the number of "official" characters judged appropriate for general use and media was revised in 1981. The new Ministry-approved list, renamed the List of Characters for General Use (*jôyô kanjihyô*), increased the target number of characters necessary for government-defined literacy from 1,850 to 1,945, plus some 284 supplementary characters approved for the use of personal names. There had been campaigns for script reform for decades before 1945, but it was the government's linking of script reform to efforts to promote democracy and improve education that ensured acceptance of the restrictions.

With mass education and script reform behind them, virtually all Japanese nationals who end up in Chicago will be literate. Among Japanese Americans there is a high degree of literacy in Japanese for older generations, and some partial literacy for younger generations, who easily learn to read the two *kana* syllabaries, and may also master some rudimentary characters. For example, while browsing through the video rental section at the Sea Ranch Market, where all the titles are in Japanese, two young Nisei women asked my help in reading and selecting a video suitable for family viewing. They could speak Japanese, but could not read more than the *kana* and a few *kanji*.

CONSUMERS OF JAPANESE PRINT MEDIA IN THE CHICAGO AREA

The local market for Japanese print media is, for the most part, driven by the reading desires of the prolonged expatriate Japanese nationals. This group is predominantly made up of male managers or business professionals in their midcareers, who bring their wives and children with them to their temporary transfer postings, and stay an average of 2 to 5 years. Many are employed by more than 450 or so Japanese companies located in the Chicago area. This well-educated high-income group has engendered a variety of businesses that cater to their needs: restaurants, karaoke bars, translation services, travel agencies, food markets, and bookstores. They are not deprived of *nattô*, fermented soybeans, or *takuan*, yellow radish pickles, nor of their favorite reading materials. Magazines such as *Wink Up Hyper Visual Magazine for Girls*, and books with titles like *A Century of Brand Names* (Yamada, 2000) or *The Japanese Face* (Hanihara, 1999) all can be purchased in the Chicago area.

One primary concern of the expatriate community of Japanese is the schooling of their children. The great emphasis placed on a person's educational background is expressed in a term often used to describe Japanese society, *gakureki shakai* (the education credentials society). Once they return to Japan, children who have lived abroad are labeled *kikokushijo* (overseas returnee children), a term coined by the Japanese media in the 1970s. As detailed by Goodman (1993), the returnee children are subject to a variety of institutionalized and social measures meant to cleanse them of their foreign experience and get them back into the educational hustle. The Japanese government also sponsors overseas Japanese schools, both regular and extracurricular, in an effort to keep *kikokushijo* from falling behind, especially in the area of their Japanese language skills. Flyers and promotional materials in Japanese that advertise educational counseling and courses through supplementary schools or private lessons are found in all Chicago area Japanese bookstores, some Japanese markets, and even a few restaurants. One of these supplementary schools, Kumon, offers courses in Japanese language, math, and English for all grades at 19 branches in the Midwest. It is not surprising, therefore, that when searching for print media in Chicago, Japanese parents have not only themselves, but also their children in mind as consumers. Anywhere there are Japanese reading materials, there will be something targeting children as well. For example, many bookstores sell Kumon's series of study guides for children.

CONSTRUCTING COMMUNITIES IN PRINT

One of the most commonly read forms of print media is the newspaper. In Japan the top five daily newspapers, which are national, are the *Yomiuri Shimbun* (published since 1874), *Asahi Shimbun* (published since 1879), *Mainichi Shimbun*, *Nihon Keizai Shimbun*, and the *Sankei Shimbun*. Japanese readers love their daily papers, and circulation in Japan exceeds that in the United States, where it was only 60,164,000 in 1992, as compared with 71,690,000 for Japan (Asahi Shimbun, 1998, p. 265). Not surprising, Japanese living in the Chicago area want to continue getting their daily infusion of news, so home delivery subscription services, while expensive, are easily available. Subscription information for the top three daily newspapers is found just about everywhere—in flyers at Japanese bookstores and super-markets, and in community newsletters. In Chicago, copies of *Yomiuri Shimbun* and *Asahi Shimbun* are sometimes sold in mega-bookstores such as Borders or Barnes and Noble. Japanese newspapers also can be read for free by going to the periodicals sections of the major university libraries in the area. It used to be that editions of Japanese newspapers arrived in the United States a day late, but with new forms of technology, many newspaper companies have been printing satellite editions issued simultaneously with those in Japan. *Asahi Shimbun* began this practice in 1986, followed by *Nihon Keizai Shimbun*, considered the "Wall Street Journal" of Japan, which began publishing their American editions in 1987.

In addition to newspapers from Japan, there is a long history of newspaper publishing in the United States by Japanese Americans. Japanese journalism arose in San Francisco with the 1892 publication of *Soko Shimbun*, a daily Japanese-language newspaper (Chiu, 1997). Japanese immigration peaked around 1900, and it is during this period that we see the inception of many other domestically published Japanese newspapers. Beginning in 1892, *The Nippon Shubô*, later renamed *Nippu Jiji*, was published in Honolulu. Los Angeles has had, and still has, the *Rafu Shimpô* since 1903. Chicago's first Japanese-language newspaper is the *Chicago (Skikago) Shimpô*, which began publishing in 1945. It features bilingual reporting and coverage of local and international (mainly Japan) news. It is published twice a week and has a circulation of about 5,000.

The *Chicago Shimpô* has an interesting bilingual format, with the Japanese text begining on what Americans would consider the "back" page. Traditionally, Japanese writing is printed or written in vertical lines from top to bottom, starting at the right side of the page. If written horizontally, the direction is usually from left to right (but print media before 1945 often has horizontal writing that runs from right to left). The English text of the *Chicago Shimpô*, which has some overlap with the main stories in the Japanese text, begins on what a Japanese would consider the "back" page, and usually takes up no more than 2 pages of the 12-page paper. Only a few of the English items are translations of the Japanese section, so each language section has material not found in the other.

The *Chicago Shimpô* has a difficult task trying to unite different multigenerational communities of both Japanese nationals and Japanese Americans. It offers bread and butter community coverage in a section entitled "Chicagoland News," yet it also reports on the results of sumo matches and high school baseball playoff games in Japan. One of the regularly running columns is *wârudo etosetora*, a direct transliteration of English "World, Etcetera," in which human interest stories from Japan, the United States, or elsewhere in the world are clumped together. The primary readership for the paper comprises those who consider Chicago and its environs their home, not a temporary posting. Although the English section occasionally carries editorials by well-known Japanese Americans, such as George Yoshinaga, a columnist for the Los Angeles *Rafu Shimpô*, the orthodox reporting mainly features local business personages and their charity activities, advocacy group activities, current political events in Japan, and short international news briefs. Unlike newspapers published in Japan, there is no nudity, none of the covert advertisements for sex-for-sale services, and few of the satirical or tongue-in-cheek stories that would spice up a morning read in Osaka. A tabby to *Asahi Shimbun's* tiger, this paper is loved not for its insightful news or witty writing, but for its metastatement about identity. *Chicago Shimpô's* presentation of short, not too keenly analyzed doses of what's going on in Japan reflects community pride in heritage and language that is superseded by affective networks and ties to the local area.

The difference between the established Japanese American community and the more transient Japanese expatriates is seen in other domestically produced Japanese-language publications available in the Chicago area, such as *RyugakUSA, NetLife Internet Magazine, Mainichi Kodomo Shimbun*, and *Prairie Message and Information Magazine*. Unlike the Japanese American newspapers, these are geared to an audience of Japanese who fully intend to return to Japan someday. Their aim is to offer advice and information on how to get on in a foreign culture, and the best places to go to buy Japanese goods and services. *RyugakUSA* (the title uses a clever play on the word *ryûgaku*, study abroad, with the final "u" used as part of the acronym "USA") is published in Santa Monica and targets Japanese university students. It profiles students and their first-hand reports on life at an American college. There are also pieces on job hunting strategies, travel, and the use and purchase of computer software. *NetLife Internet Magazine*, published in Torrance, California, is a compendium of product ads, columns on software, computer troubleshooting tips, online manners, useful Web sites, and a directory of stores in the United States that sell Japanese software. *Mainichi Kodomo Shimbun* (Daily Children's Newspaper), published in Santa Monica, is for children of all ages. Given uneven degrees of reading competency, the newspaper runs varied pieces on life in the United States, sports, and "fun" activities, each geared to different age levels. Articles for younger children use Chinese characters with *furigana,* which are small *kana* giving the phonetic readings printed next to each character (Fig. 14.1).

The intent of the paper is to turn the time spent in American society into an educational experience, and to aid in the socialization of children into proper readers of Japanese.

Japanese efforts to domesticate the Midwest are seen in a magazine published in Elk Grove, Illinois, named *Prairie Message and Information Magazine* (the English word "Prairie" is oddly written in *hiragana* rather than the usual *katakana*). It targets Japanese living in Ohio, Indiana, Michigan, Illinois, and Wisconsin, and contains ads for local Japan-related businesses, specifies points of interest in each state with brief notes in Japanese, runs many classified ads, and carries short pieces on topics such as car maintenance, how to get Viagra, and hairstyling.

Closely aligned with community newspapers are the Japanese-language newsletters published by various Chicago cultural groups and organizations. Although similar in their focus on the local, the aim of these newsletters is to document the presence and activities of more self-conscious groups. One assemblage is the Japanese Chamber of Commerce and In-

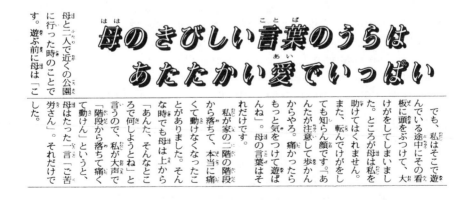

Fig. 14.1.　Domestically published children's newspaper text with small *furigana* readings given in Chinese characters. Reprinted with permission of Mainichi International Inc.

dustry of Chicago (JCCC), an organization founded in 1966 by Japanese business people. It currently has approximately 530 members and publishes a monthly newsletter, a directory, and member magazines in Japanese. The JCCC also manages one of the Japanese schools for expatriate children, the Chicago Futabakai Japanese School in Arlington Heights. The status-forming texts published by the group promote their many charity events, seminars and surveys, highlighting the elite nature of their business and social networks. Less business-oriented and not as class proscribed is the newsletter published by the Mid-America Japanese Club and Japanese American Association of Chicago. This publication runs announcements of local events, hands out business advice, and tracks the activities and achievements of its members. There are homey pieces by amateur writers about their efforts to explain Japanese culture to their American friends, accounts of harmless mishaps of the intercultural variety, and a monthly welcome column that provides information on the new Japanese couples and families who have arrived in the area.

Japan anthropologist Ebuchi (cited in Goodman, 1993, p. 36; see also Ebuchi, 1994) proposed two models to describe Japanese communities overseas, which he calls the "North American model" and the "Asian model." Those communities that follow the Asian model, most often in places such as Singapore or the Philippines, are said to live in isolated enclaves having no contact with the local people or culture. In contrast, those Japanese communities that follow the North American model are said to be much more absorbed into the local societies, expressing a degree of behavioral assimilation, participating in the host culture, and perhaps even intermarrying. Other studies suggest that Ebuchi's model is overly simplistic, and that it fails to account for the great diversity one in fact finds (Befu & Stalker, 1996; Goodman, 1993; Suzuki, 1984).

Chicago's expatriate Japanese community does, however, resemble the North American model, although there is still a degree of enclaving. There is a sincere campaign to participate in many of Chicago's cultural events and lifestyles, and to promote charity and other occasions meant to foster understanding. Yet one also sees in these good efforts the idea that Japanese in Chicago are cultural brokers who have an obligation to "explain" Japan to the unenlightened Midwest, and the flow is decidedly one way. The writing and events promoted in the newsletters reflect what might be called a "*nihonjinron* sensibility." *Nihonjinron*, literally "theories about the Japanese," is a distinct genre of mass media writing that emphasizes the "unique" or unusual aspects of Japanese language and culture, in contrast to "the West," which is almost always an unstated America. The Japan reflected in the newsletters is one of elegant tea ceremonies, delicate flower arrangements, and a nostalgic recreation of a longed-for but imagined "traditional" Japan (Ivy, 1995). From reading these pages, a reader would never know that the majority of young Japanese dye their hair, or that eyebrow plucking is a *de rigeur* fad among trendy urban young men. It would take a visit to a Chicago area Japanese bookstore to find media that describes the vibrant, constantly shifting culture of contemporary Japan.

PUBLIC SERVICE PRINT MEDIA, BULLETIN BOARDS, AND BEYOND

In addition to newspapers and newsletters, one can find other forms of locally produced Japanese print media throughout the Chicago area. World Business Chicago, a local civic organization, publishes a Japanese-language brochure to promote international business, and the Chicago Office of Tourism publishes a map of Chicago intended for Japanese readers. The map itself is actually in English, but a few cultural institutions, touristic sites, bus tour firms, and sport's venues are described in Japanese. Although the map is free, few downtown Chicago hotels bother carrying it. When I asked for one at hotels such as Summerfield Suites, Windham Chicago, and the Radisson, the clerks insisted that such a map does not even exist.

A much more interesting Chicago area map is published by Tsuruki Promotions, a Chicago-based publishing firm that produces many local newsletters and brochures. Tsuruki's map has more description in Japanese of local sites. For instance, Oak Street is described as "Chicago's hot fashion spot," and the area around Superior Street and Clark is described as "Chicago's Roppongi!" (Roppongi is a district in Tokyo noted for its high-octane night life for young people.) There are also Japanese-language telephone directories for Chicago.

Yellow Pages Japan in USA: Chicago/Detroit Edition is published in Los Angeles, but lists hundreds of Japanese businesses and services in the Chicago area such as dentists, lawyers, and astrologers. There is also a front section with useful information on transportation, first aid, measurement conversions, visas, postal rates, time zones, and the education of returnee schoolchildren. The *Chicago Shimpô* also publishes a Yellow

Pages, the *Shikago Seikatsu Denwa Hayamichô* (Chicago Japan Telephone Directory).

In addition to public service literature, there are many types of ephemera such as advertising flyers, brochures, and bulletin board postings. During a 2-month period, I collected printed or handwritten Japanese flyers or brochures for such things as cram schools and private tutoring lessons, a Japan Music Festival, subscriptions for *Asahi Shimbun*, chiropractic and acupuncture services, Mitsuwa Marketplace service cards, hairstyling care, a JCCA charity event featuring a *rakugo* (comic storytelling) performance, a new Palm Pilot in Japanese, the Japan Christian Church, a karaoke bar, All Nippon Airways special discount fares from Japan, English classes at Glenview Christian Church, Mitsuwa Marketplace's Gift Service for exotic souvenirs such as beef jerky and macadamia nuts, Shiseido UV White skin-lightening products, an information guide for Japan TV, Dr. Mouse software, and a Buddhist prayer (at the Buddhist Temple of Chicago).

Many Japanese stores provide message boards for the exchange of information. Sea Ranch Market in Wilmette has one, but the largest I have seen is at Mitsuwa Marketplace (Fig. 14.2). On that one, postings are lim-

FIG. 14.2.   Information bulletin board at Mitsuwa Marketplace.

ited to 2 weeks, and all material must be signed and dated by the store manager. Private individuals advertise exercise classes, housing and subleasing, moving sales, used cars, martial arts lessons, English lessons, piano lessons, and used golf clubs.

Occasionally, writing, which is domestically produced, is modified to suit local linguistic norms and functions. English punctuation practices clearly have had an influence, as there is use of hyphens or separation spaces between words, when Japanese normally is written without these. (An example of word separation is *chariti ibento* [charity event] in Table.14.1.) When addresses are given, they are rarely transliterated into *katakana*, but are written in the Latin alphabet. This results in interesting cases of script mixing, as in a flyer for a free seminar that has "Biesterfield *to* Wellington Avenue *no nansei kado*," (at the southwest corner of Biesterfield and Wellington Avenue"), in which Biesterfield and Wellington Avenue are written in the alphabet, but the Japanese connective particle *"to"* and the rest of the sentence are written in *hiragana* and *kanji*. Another example is a sublease notice, in which the words "Algonquin," "Busse," and "studio apartment" in the sentence "Algonquin *x* Busse *no chikaku ni aru* studio apartment *de rokugatsu kara sumeru kata o sagashite imase"* [looking for someone who can stay in a studio apartment near Algonkian and Busse from June] are written in the alphabet rather than in *katakana*, the syllabary usually used for foreign words.

Words and concepts important in American culture but not found in Japan are not always translated, but just transliterated directly into *katakana*. For instance, a notice in the *Chicago Shimpô* for the United States Census used the term *nihonjin komyunitii* [Japanese community], in which "community," a notion that would be odd to use in Japan in a way

TABLE 14.1
American concepts

Japanese community	*nihonjin komyunitii*	日本人コミュニティー
start at eight dollars	*hachi doru de sutâto shimasu*	八ドルでスタートします
two bathrooms	*ni basu*	ニバス
two-car garage	*ni kâ gareji*	ニカーガレジ
charity event	*chariti ibento*	チャリティ イベント
family room	*famirii rumû*	ファミリールーム
no charge	*fūrii desu*	フーリイです

other than local or regional boosterism, is not translated, and a flyer for a
Japanese Chamber of Commerce and Industry-sponsored affair used the
term *chariti ibento* [charity event].[3] Mitsuwa Marketplace frequently uses
transliterated English in grocery ads, such as one put out in January that
used *niyûiyâzu sêru* for "New Year's sale" rather than Japanese *oshôgatsu*
[New Year]. In another case, a posted help-wanted ad said *hachi doru de
sutâto shimasu*, [start at 8 dollars' an hour], borrowing the English verb
"start," transliterated into *katakana*, instead of using a Japanese verb.
Housing notices often have references that would be uncommon in Japan, such as one for a townhouse in Wilmette with *ni basu* [two bath-
rooms] and *famirii rûmu* [family room] (Fig. 14.3). Another housing flyer
lists a two-car garage, and in place of *nidai shako* in Japanese, it is written
in *katakana* as *ni kâ gareji*. "Two baths" and "two-car" violate Japanese

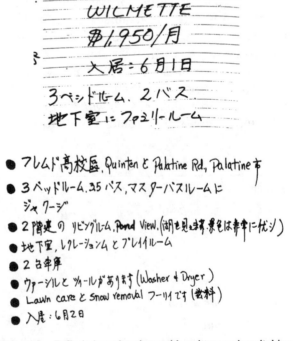

FIG. 14.3.   Bulletin board notices with written codeswitching.

grammatical rules for counting, which requires the use of a counter suffix attached to numbers, so usages such as these reflect English-derived numeration practices. Another instance is a sign for a moving sale in which the dimensions for an audio rack are given as the *saizu* [size]. Finally, the idea that something is gratis is occasionally rendered as "free," as in a rental notice offering "lawn care *to* (Japanese connective particle) snow removal *furii desu*" [no charge for lawn care and snow removal] (Fig. 14.3). These written communications for Japanese readers living in an English-speaking world might constitute a new genre of writing that is the counterpart of oral bilingual codeswitching.

Locally produced print media usually gives measurements in the American system (e.g., pounds, gallons) instead of the metric system, which is used in Japan. Since 1872, most Japanese publications use the Western calendar for dating years, but also retain the practice of using period names for years that coincide with the reigns of each Emperor. The reign of the current Emperor is called Heisei, and a date such as 1999 would be written as Heisei 11 on a Japanese publication. The *Chicago Shimpô* provides both dates, but most other locally printed publications do not.

FEEDING THE MEDIA DIET: BUYING BOOKS AND MAGAZINES

During the later part of the Tokugawa period (1603–1868), Japan's urban centers were home to bookstores and commercial lending libraries that provisioned merchants, samurai, and even some literate farmers with romantic novels, satires, poetry, encyclopedias, and other things to read (Morris-Suzuki, 1994, p. 33). Today, the Japanese publishing industry is one of the largest in the world, with 6.48144 billion books and magazines published in 1 year alone (Asahi Shimbun, 2000, p. 260).

The largest Japanese bookstore in the Chicago area is Asahiya, located in the Mitsuwa Marketplace (formerly called Yaohan Plaza) in Arlington Heights. Mitsuwa Marketplace is a 35,000-ft^2 complex that houses a pottery and ceramics store, liquor store, travel agency, food court, supermarket, bakery, video rental store, "fancy goods" store, and souvenir shop. Soon after it opened in 1991, it became a center for Japanese cultural activities, and is currently the site of an annual festival in the summer. On Sundays it is packed with families and couples shopping, eating, hanging out, and refueling the inner landscape with a stop in the bookstore.

Asahiya faithfully reproduces the sort of bookstore one might find in a Tokyo neighborhood, with books and magazines classified in a similar manner. At one time, the store's clerks even managed payment transactions in the same ritualized way one finds in Japan, with crass money passed discreetly via a small platter. Recently, however, they seem to have given up this practice and actually hand customers receipts and cash directly. One behavior that has not changed is the acceptance of browsers who spend hours standing around reading, often without buying anything. Termed *tachiyomi* [standing-reading], this habit is much tolerated in Japan, and I have never seen a clerk at Asahiya or in any other Japanese bookstore in Chicago attempt to instill guilt in customers with the "Are you looking for something?" tactic. The primary difference between Asahiya and bookstores in Japan is in the relative numbers of some types of books and other materials. In the United States more shelf space is given over to dictionaries, language manuals, TOEFL (Test of English as a Foreign Language) guides, travel guides, cookbooks, and children's books than usual. Although the largest percentage of Japanese books published each year are in the social sciences, in Chicago there are considerably fewer of these and other highbrow books on literature, art and design.

Asahiya's "Business" section has selections an American might not think of in that context, but which make perfect sense to a midlevel Japanese manager. There are books by and about corporate idols, especially Bill Gates, whose book *The Road Ahead* (1995), although not a great commercial success in the United States, made it onto the top 20 best-seller list in Japan soon after it was translated. Another optimistic self-improvement book, Richard Carlson's *Don't Sweat the Small Stuff* (1999), originally published in 1961 but only recently translated into Japanese, soon rose to the top 10 best-seller list in 1999. Of course, there is always the durable *How to Stop Worrying and Start Living* (1984) by Dale Carnegie, originally published in 1948, fitting right in with similar works by Japanese authors. In this section, too, we find some of the obligatory *nihonjinron* (theories of the Japanese) classics, books that contrast Japanese culture with the rest of the world, always in search of unique and separate qualities. Many of the books carry the word *sarariiman* (salaryman or white-collar worker) in their titles, such as Omae's *Salaryman Survival* (1999), the number one business book in 1999.

Asahiya has a "Current Events" table and a "New Books Corner" where we find books on golf, economic trade problems, and Golden's *Memoirs of a Geisha* (1999), translated into Japanese with the new title *Sayuri*. During the 1990s there was a dramatic increase in the number of books by and about women. Suddenly, bookstores in Japan began to set aside areas for female fiction, confessionals, self-help, biographies, and exposés. A subgenre of these were dedicated to young working women or "Office Ladies." I found titles such as *Fundamental Checklist of Office Lady Manners* (Nakamura, 1993) and *Anthology of Office Lady Taboos* (Zennikkû Eigyôhonbu Kyôikukunrenbu, 1991) at Asahiya a few years ago, but it was not until 1999 that the store rearranged its book displays and created a new women's section, one that is different from the prosaic and still-intact housewife section (in which there are books on cooking, child care, sewing, and hobbies). This new section has titles such as *Love is Fine, But I Like Books, Too* (Kishimoto, 2000), *The Tale of Being Thirty Years Old* (Kishi, 1999), *55 Ways to Have a Likeable Self* (Satô, 2000), and *The Sociology of Gender* (Ehara, 1999). This suggests that the businessmen's spouses and female workers in the recent influx have strong identities separate from their roles as wives or mothers.

Perhaps as much as one fourth of Asahiya's floor space is set aside for magazines. Each year 3,271 different monthly magazines, and 88 weekly magazines are published in Japan (Asahi Shimbun, 1998, p. 268). In the United States, the majority of magazines are obtained through subscription, whereas in Japan, most are purchased at newsstands, train station kiosks, convenience stores, small general stores, and vending machines (which even sell pornographic texts). Here in the Chicago area, many of the Japanese bookstores keep afloat through a lucrative subscription service for hundreds of the most popular magazines. Even so, Asahiya carries a respectable representative sampling of this important segment of the publishing industry. It carries some titles that Japanese bookstores in areas of the country with a higher concentration of Japanese consumers do not stock. For example, I couldn't find *Bidan*, a men's beauty work magazine, at the Kinokuniya Japanese bookstore in the Little Tokyo section of Los Angeles, but did see it at Asahiya. Other young men's fashion and beauty magazines sold at Asahiya are *Bart, Men's EX, Get On, Cool*, and *Fine Boys*. Sometimes non-Japanese Asian men and Japanese American men who do not read Japanese can be seen riffling through these.

The market for Japanese magazines expanded rapidly in the 1970s, and sales surpassed that of books during the following decade (Skov & Moeran, 1995, p. 58). Magazines focusing on cooking, hobbies, fashion, lifestyle, travel, gossip, entertainment, music, and other areas are sold according to several different age and gender cohorts. In 1985, 245 new magazines were launched (Asahi Shimbun, 2000, p. 265), many of them targeting a female audience. Asahiya sells most of the main women's magazines, which often have Western-sounding names, such as *Frau, Miss, Classy, Sassy, With, Can-cam, JJ, An-an, Say, Non-no, Olive, Sassy, McSister*, and *Cutie* (Fig. 14.4). They also carry specialty music magazines for young girls, such as *Duet Pretty Up Live Magazine* and *Myôjô* (Venus). In the housewife section of the store are magazines such as *Sutekina okusan* (Cool Housewife), *Katei gahô* (Household Graphics), *Shufu no tomo* (Housewives' Friend, first published in 1917), *Ohayō okusan* (Good Morning Mrs.), and *Madam*. Current issues of some magazines disappear from the shelves quickly, so readers make special trips to Asahiya each month to ensure that they get the ones they want, or ask the clerks to set aside a copy for them. Given how expensive some of the magazines are (a single issue may cost from $14.00 to $19.00 in Chicago), readers often participate in a practice named *mawashiyomi*, the custom of passing media along to friends.

On the list of best-selling magazines for 1999, we find two weekly television magazines and two women's magazines, but the majority fall into a category called *shûkanshi*, (weekly magazines) (Shōgakukan, 2000, p. 492). The weeklies cover gossip about singers, actors, politicians, and sports

FIG 14.4.   Women's magazines at Asahiya.

figures, and range from the reputable to the unapologetically trashy. These usually contain blurry shots of celebrities going into or out of love hotels with those to whom they are not married, ads for breast enlargement products, and smarmy photos of the royal family. The scandal weeklies are also gendered, with several targeting women readers, such as *Josei jishin* (Woman Herself) and *Josei seben* (Woman Seven). The weeklies for salarymen, such as *Shûkan posuto* (Weekly Post) and *Shûkan gendai* (Weekly Modern Times) carry photographs of undressed women, whereas others such as *Friday* or *Focus* are almost all photographs. A few of the reputable weeklies, such *Aera*, are similar to *Newsweek* or *Time* in their coverage of current events. All of these weeklies are sold at Asahiya, and many are available at the other area bookstores.

Thomas Jefferson, in a 1815 letter to John Adams, said "I cannot live without books." For a contemporary Japanese, this might better be stated as "I cannot live without *manga*." *Manga* is usually translated as "comics," although what Americans consider comics does not come close to describing this Japanese genre. As a leading *manga* scholar said "*Manga* are read by nearly all ages and classes of people today; references to them permeate Japanese intellectual life at the highest level, and they are increasingly influencing Japanese art and literature" (Schodt, 1996, p. 21). *Manga* are published weekly, biweekly, and monthly and usually contain a number of different serialized story narratives, some of which can go on for decades. According to Schodt (1983, p.12), Japan uses more paper for its comics than it does for its toilet paper. It is comfort reading, and generally has fewer characters than other writing, so is easy to digest quickly. There are different subgenres of *manga*, usually divided into four categories: boys comics (*shōnen manga*), girls comics (*shōjô manga*), youth comics (*seinen manga*), and adult comics (*seijin manga*). There are more than 40 different *shōjô manga*, and Asahiya sells many of them, including *Ribbon*, *Nakayoshi*, *Margaret*, and *Shōjô komikku*. A good proportion of the *manga* sold at Asahiya are, however, the adult comics, which are lavishly illustrated with bizarre depictions of sex, violence, and scatology. Given the cultural milieu of American society, *manga* sold at Asahiya are usually shrink-wrapped to prevent the unwary or voyeuristic from flipping through them. A disturbing number of adult comics fall into a subcategory some call *rorikon manga* (Lolita complex comics) in which very young girls serve as sexual objects, a situation that has drawn the attention of more than a few scholars (Allison, 1996; Shigematsu, 1999). There is also a separate subgenre of adult comics for women, some of them quite racy, called *redikomi* (ladies comics). At Asahiya, these fill up one entire side of a display case, and include a selection of the 57 or so titles in this category, such as *Silky*, *Be Love*, *Petit Flower*, *Lady's Comic You*, and *Merodei* (Melody). Interestingly, the sex featured in these often includes sugary scenes of gay love and romance.

The garish covers of so many comics often creates a distinctive visual feel to a Japanese bookstore. Unlike the muted mauves and hunter green characteristic of places such as Borders, a *manga*-drenched bookstore screams with magenta and pink.

A very noticeable difference in the consumption of *manga* in the United States is that one never sees a Japanese reading this form of vernacular culture in public. No embarrassment accrues to reading *manga* in Japan, and people of all ages and socioeconomic classes read them everywhere, in restaurants, in offices, and openly on trains and subways. During the late 1990s, there was an increase in the number of "*manga* coffee shops," coffee shops stocking enormous quantities of comics that customers may read for free with their purchase of something to eat or drink. One café in Shinjuku is said to have more than 20,000 *manga* on hand. The reason this typical reading behavior is modified while in Chicago is most likely because Americans view comics as a juvenile form of entertainment, and also, of course, due to the massive level of sex and violence one finds in them.

Japanese animation (*anime*) dubbed into English has firmly penetrated American popular culture. There are now thousands of American *anime* clubs, conferences, Web sites, and English fanzines, such as *TokyoPop* magazine. The spread of *anime* has fueled interest in related media such as *manga* and Japanese popular music, called "J-Pop." Media that is everyday fare in Japan has achieved a cult status in the United States, and many Americans who cannot read Japanese nevertheless seek out Japanese print media such as *manga* and J-Pop music magazines. Tower Records in Lincoln Park sometimes carries *manga* in its book section, but these are quickly grabbed up as novelties and do not stay on the shelves long. At the video rental store in the Mitsuwa Marketplace complex, I once heard a young non-Japanese fan grilling the clerk. When the clerk asked him if he liked Japanese videos, he answered "Yes, I really like them even though I can't understand them." Japanese and non-Japanese fans of J-Pop often visit Asahiya to pick up CDs or music magazines and books. Asahiya carries Japanese-language music magazines such as *Cool Up*, *J-Rock*, *Jazz Life*, *Rhythm and Drums*, *Gigs*, *Groove*, *Backstage Pass*, *What's IN?*, *Black Music*

Review, *Indies Magazine*, *Arena 37°C*, *GirlPop*, and *Hip Hop Style Bible*. One of Japan's hottest groups these days is GLAY, and books by and about them have proliferated. In addition to many other books on popular music artists, Asahiya sells many of the crop of GLAY books (Ôshima, 1998; Sanninbashi, 2000; Shimizu, 1999; Take, 1999), attesting to the local market demand for J-Pop media.

Although Asahiya is not the only Japanese bookstore in the Chicago area, nor the only place at which Japanese language materials are available, it is the largest and most comprehensive. Even so, two other area bookstores, Japan Books and Records on Peterson, and JBC Books on Golf, have succeeded in carving out their own niches. Japan Books, which is owned by a Korean family who also owns the adjacent Korean bookstore, has been in business for about two decades. The majority of the customers who visit are elderly Japanese Americans who occasionally stop in to pick something up and to chat with the Japanese clerks. At least half of the store is taken up with videos, and the claustrophobic arrangement, together with the fact that most of the books and magazines are used and dusty, does not inspire much browsing. But the store provides an important resource by running an efficient subscription service for magazines and videos. It publishes its own Japanese-language newsletter, which contains announcements of new books, with prices in dollars; book summaries; and magazines subscription lists. JBC Books is also a used bookstore, but with a younger Japanese clientele. It carries few magazines but much fiction and *manga* in a small but fresh atmosphere. There are always readers engaged in *tachiyomi* [standing-reading]. Used books can also be purchased at the Sea Ranch Market in Wilmette. Beginning in 2000, the market began to augment its selection of cookbooks, scandal weeklies, and women's magazines with a few shelves of used fiction and *manga*.

For a Japanese person, one of the hardships connected with living abroad is the extra effort required to obtain print media that one habitually finds in all environments back home. Without fresh books or magazines, the expatriate is always adrift in an alien world, with fewer opportunities to suspend the self in the written language. A Japanese bookstore crammed with books and garishly hued magazines and comics provides a temporary re-emersion in home territory. Unlike a Japanese restaurant, in which things are changed to suit American tastes (for instance, *miso* soup made with chicken broth, served as a "first course" with a spoon), a bookstore offers a space that is more resistant to American cultural infringement.

Back in the pages of one's own language, awareness of the alien culture is shoved onto another plane as the written word cocoons the reader. "The page is our platform, the beginning place. When we lift our eyes away we carry the energies of the book inside ourselves as a kind of subsidiary momentum" (Birkets, 1994, p. 101). For Japanese Americans and Japanese living in the Chicago area, print media is a primary repository of cultural memory, one that provides a critical material resource for the construction and maintenance of identities.

ACKNOWLEDGMENTS

Thanks are extended to Jan Bardsley, Kuei Chiu, Marcia Farr, Jacquetta Hill, James Stanlaw, and Nobuko Adachi for their suggestions or comments.

ENDNOTES

1. The problem of what constitutes literacy in Japanese deserves a separate study. Literacy is not a uniformly agreed on concept, with different types of literacy (e.g., functional, basic, minimal, conventional, vernacular, restricted) proposed by many researchers (Wiley, 1996). Official statistics on Japan's literacy rate are unrealistically based on the assumption that all children who complete the compulsory education system have learned everything they are supposed to have learned.
2. The number of *kana* may vary depending on which types are included in the count. Each of the two syllabaries represents 5 monosyllabic vowels, 40 consonant–vowel syllables, and 1 nasal, but additional voiced syllables are represented with the use of tick marks or tiny circles added to the top right of 25 of the *kana*, and through compound *kana*.
3. The result of a long history of English language borrowing (Stanlaw, 1982) and English-derived coinages (Miller, 1997) is the development of certain conventions for the orthographic representation of non-Japanese sound sequences. An example is the sound "ti", not found in Japanese, which is commonly written with the *kana* for "te" together with a smaller *kana* for "i", with the resulting reading intended as "ti". The non-Japanese sound "fa" is likewise represented with the *kana* for "fu" and small "a", with the reading "fa".

REFERENCES

Allison, A. (1996). *Permitted and prohibited desires: Mothers, comics, and censorship in Japan*. Boulder, CO: Westview Press.

Asahi Shimbun. (1998). *Japan Almanac 1998*. Tokyo: Asahi Shimbun.

Asahi Shimbun. (2000). *Japan Almanac 2000*. Tokyo: Asahi Shimbun.

Befu, H., & Stalker, N. (1996). Globalization of Japan: Cosmopolitanization or spread of the Japanese village? In H. Befu (Ed.), *Japan engaging the world: A century of international encounters*, (pp. 110–120). Denver, CO: Center for Japan Studies at Teikyo Loretto Heights University.

Birkets, S. (1994). *The Gutenberg elegies: The fate of reading in an electronic age*. Boston: Faber and Faber.

Brooks, C. (2000). In the twilight zone between black and white: Japanese American resettlement and community in Chicago, 1942–1945. *The Journal of American History, 86*, 1655–1687.

Carlson, R. (1999). *Chiisai koto ni kuyokuyo surunai!* [Don't Sweat the Small Stuff, M. Ozawa, trans.]. Tokyo: Sanmaku Shuppan. (Original work published 1961)

Carnegie, D. (1984). *Michi wa hirakeru* [How to stop worrying and start living, A. Kayama, trans.]. J. Osaka: Sogensha. (Original work published 1948)

Chicago Public Library. (2000). Chicago in 1900: A millennium bibliography. Available: http://www.chipubib.org/0004chicago/1900/pop.html Accessed May 5, 2001.

Chiu, K. (1997). Access to the past of a nation of immigrants: Asian language newspapers in the United States. *Journal of East Asian Libraries, 112*, 1–8.

Crowley, D. (1990). *The kanji way to Japanese language power*. Washington DC: The King's Business Publishers.

Ebuchi, K. (1994). *Ibunka-kan kyôikugaku josetsu* [Introduction to intercultural communication studies]. Fukuoka: Kyushu Daigaku Shuppankai.

Ehara, Y. (1999). *Jenda no shakaigaku* [The sociology of gender]. Tokyo: Hoso Daigaku Kyôiku Shinkokai.

Flanagan, E. (1996). Jun Fujita's Chicago. *Chicago History, 25*, 34–55.

Gates, B. (1995). *Biru Geitsu mirai o kataru* [The road ahead, K. Nishi, trans.]. Tokyo: Asuki Shuppankyoku. (Original work published 1995)

Golden, A. (1999). *Sayuri* [Memoirs of a Geisha, T. Ogawa, trans.]. Tokyo: Bungei Shunju. (Original work published 1997)

Goodman, R. (1993). *Japan's "International youth": The emergence of a new class of schoolchildren*. Oxford: Clarendon Press.

Gottlieb, N. (1994). Language and politics: The reversal of postwar script reform policy in Japan. *The Journal of Asian Studies, 53*, 1175–1198.

Habien, Y. S. (1984). *The history of the Japanese written language*. Tokyo: Tokyo University Press.

Hanihara, K. (1999). *Nihonjin no kao* [The Japanese face]. Tokyo: Kodansha.

Ivy, M. (1995). *Discourses of the vanishing: Modernity, phantasm, Japan*. Chicago: The University of Chicago Press.

Kishi, K. (1999). *Sanjûnen no monogatari* [The tale of being thirty years old]. Tokyo: Kôdansha.

Kishimoto, Y. (2000). *Koi mo ii kedoo, hon mo suki* [Love is fine, but I like books, too]. Tokyo: Kôdansha.

Miller, L. (1997). Wasei eigo: English 'loanwords' coined in Japan. In J. Hill, P. J. Mistry, & L. Campbell (Eds.), *The life of language: Papers in linguistics in honor of William Bright* (pp. 123–139). The Hague: Mouton/De Gruyter.

Morris-Suzuki, T. (1994). *The technological transformation of Japan*. Cambridge, UK: Cambridge University Press.

Nakamura, Y. (1993). *OL manâ kihon chiekku* [Fundamental checklist of Office Lady manners]. Isetan: Tokyo.

Omae, K. (1999). *Sarariiman sabaibaru* [Salaryman Survival]. Tokyo: Shogakukan.

Osako, M. (1995). Japanese-Americans: Melting into the all-American melting pot. In M. Holli & P. A. Jones (Eds.), *Ethnic Chicago: A multicultural portrait* (pp. 409–437). Grand Rapids, MI: William B. Eerdman's.

Ôshima, H. (1998). *GLAY Tokyo monogatari* [GLAY Tokyo story]. Tokyo: Line Books.

Sanninbashi. (Ed.). (2000). *GLAY the greatest kyôkyoku* [GLAY the greatest songs]. Tokyo: Shûgeisha.

Satô, A. (2000). *Sukina jibun ni naru 55 no hôhô* [55 ways to have a likeable self]. Tokyo: Kôdansha.

Schodt, F. (1983). *Manga! manga! The world of Japanese comics*. Tokyo: Kodansha International.

Schodt, F. (1996). *Dreamland Japan: Writings on modern manga*. Berkeley: Stone Bridge Press.

Seeley, C. (1984). The Japanese script since 1900. *Visible Language, XVIII*, 267–301.

Seeley, C. (1991). *A history of writing in Japan*. Leiden: Brill.

Shigematsu, S. (1999). Dimensions of desire: Sex, fantasy, and fetish in Japanese comics. In J. Lent (Ed.), *Themes and issues in Asian cartooning: Cute, cheap, mad and sexy* (pp. 127–163). Bowling Green, OH: Bowling Green State University Popular Press.

Shimizu, Y. (1999). *GLAY indeizu kaisôki* [GLAY indies reflection diary]. Tokyo: Core House.

Shôgakukan. (2000). *Dêtaparu: Saishin jôhô yôgo jiten* [DataPal: Up-to-date information and encyclopedia of terms]. Tokyo: Shôgakukan.

Skov, L., & Moeran, B. (Eds.). (1995). Introduction. In L. Skov & B. Moeran (Eds.), *Women, media, and consumption in Japan* (pp. 1–74). Honolulu: University of Hawai'i Press.

Stanlaw, J. (1982) English in Japanese communicative strategies. In B. Kachru (Ed.), *The other tongue: English across cultures* (pp. 168–197). Urbana: University of Illinois Press.

Suzuki, M. (1984). *Kaigai, kikokushijo no kyôiku* [The education of overseas and returnee children]. *Kyôikugaku kenkyû, 51*, 38–37.

Take, H. (1999). *GLAY Yume no chihei* [Glay's dream horizon]. Tokyo: Sony.

Wiley, T. (1996). *Literacy and language diversity in the United States*. Center for Applied Linguistics. McHenry, IL: Delta Systems.

Yamada, T. (2000). *Burando no seki* [A Century of Brands]. Tokyo: Magajin Hausu.

Zennikkû Eigyôhonbu Kyôikukunrenbu. (Ed.). (1991). *OL tabûshû* [Anthology of Office Lady taboos]. Tokyo: Goma Seibo.

Afterword

Words and Lives: Language, Literacy, and Culture in Multilingual Chicago

Robert Gundlach
Northwestern University

Students at the university where I teach can study many languages, including Arabic, Chinese, English, German, Greek, Hebrew, Hindi, Italian, Japanese, Korean, Latin, Polish, Portuguese, Russian, Spanish, and Swahili. At this university, with campuses in Chicago and nearby Evanston, it is common to characterize all of these languages—with the notable exception of English—as "foreign." In the Chicago area, it is assumed that English is the language people use.

The essays collected in this volume provided a valuable corrective view. Once one has read discussions ranging from Sharon M. Radloff's "Arabs in Chicago: The Accountant's Office as Language and Culture Mediator" to Carl Issacson's "They Did Not Forget their Swedish: Class Markers in the Swedish American Community," or contributions ranging from John Rohsenow's "Chinese Language Use in Chicago" to Daiva

Markelis's "Lithuanian and English Language Use Among Early 20th-Century Lithuanian Immigrants in Chicago," it becomes impossible to hold to the notion that Chicago is a monolingual city. As these and other studies in this volume document, Chicago is—and always has been—richly and complexly multilingual.

Other chapters in this collection demonstrate that English itself, as used in the Chicago, varies considerably in both form and use, among different groups of speakers. After one has read such contributions as Julie Lindquist's "Class Identity and the Politics of Dissent: The Culture of Argument in a Chicago Neighborhood Bar," Rachel Reynolds's 'bless this little time we stayed here': Prayers of Invocations as Mediation of Immigrant Experience Among Nigerians in Chicago," and Marcyliena Morgan's "Signifying Laughter and the Subtitles of Loud-Talking: Memory and Meaning in African American Women's Discourse," it becomes clear that English in Chicago is used in a variety of dialects, registers, and identity-inflected voices.

It is not entirely surprising then, as Elliot Judd argues in his overview of "Language Policy in Illinois: Past and Present," that the history of language policy in Illinois is, at least in part, a story of monolingual policies existing alongside the continuing practice of multilingualism in many institutions and agencies. Whenever language is observed closely and in context—when language use is studied "on the ground," as Marcia Farr and Rachel Reynolds phrase it in their introductory essay, "Language and Identity in a Global City"—the intricacies and subtleties of variation, whether across language or within a single language, are the aspects of language use that emerge most clearly.

In documenting a number of the ways in which Chicago is, and has long been, a multilingual American city, *Ethnolinguistic Chicago* joins an increasingly recognized body of scholarly work that illuminates and explores the multilingual character of the United States, both past and present. In the introductory essay to *Multilingual America: Transnationalism, Ethnicity, and the Languages of American Literature* (1998), another recent scholarly collection emphasizing that language in the United States is best understood not as "English only" but as "English plus," Werner Sollers observes that "many American languages have coexisted in great proximity, and some have shared the same city, the same newspaper, the same street, the same building, the same family, and the same individual" (p. 8). (On the phenomenon of different languages sharing "the same individual," see particularly the examples of code switching in Koliussi and Nardini, this volume.) At the same time, *Ethnolinguistic Chicago,* with its complementary emphasis on diversity in the ways English is used in Chicago's neighborhoods, contributes to scholarly work on what might be called the variousness of English as a language, not only in the United Sates but also across the world—see, for example, *Alternative Histories of English* (2002), a recent volume edited by Richard Watts and Peter Trudgill.

Along with contributing to our understanding of American multilingualism and sharpening our view of variation within English, the studies presented in *Ethnolinguistic Chicago* offer a distinct perspective of their own. With their close attention to the details of language use in everyday life, and especially with their emphasis on interplay of language use and social identity (e.g., Cho & Miller, Isaacson, Lindquist, Morgan, Moss, and Reynolds, this volume), the studies in this volume, taken together, point to the complexity of the processes of both language persistence and language change, particularly as these processes operate in a large American city at the beginning of the 21st century.

To judge from the studies gathered in *Ethnolinguistic Chicago,* it is apparent that the persistence of a given language in a multilingual city is the ongoing result of complex dynamics that vary from cultural group to cultural group, sometimes from neighborhood to neighborhood, and sometimes according to differences in extranational politics (see Markelis and Rohsenow, this volume). A particular language used in Chicago may be sustained—may be supported in its persistence—by various combinations and interactions of at least three different social processes. First, a language may be sustained across generations by the process of language socialization in families. Families as units for language socialization are often extended families, and can include non-family members of durable social networks (Ochs, 1988). In this process, children are cultural apprentices, and they learn the practices of their cultural mentors.

Second, a language may also be sustained by the continuity of its use in neighborhood institutions, or by institutions that serve as cultural gathering places for people attracted to them from several different places—that is, an institution that establishes a shared "cultural neighborhood" for people who may live in different geographic neighborhoods. These institutions might be places of religious observance, private schools, clubs and associations, bars and restaurants, shops, or business offices. Such institutions might also be part of the media marketplace, visited in a mediated sense by turning on the radio or television to channels broadcasting in a particular language favored by the community.

And third, the use of a particular language may be sustained by the use of materials written in the language. Written language is portable as textual object but can seem, as language, to remain fixed, inasmuch as a written utterance or text, once composed, holds its form and becomes retrievable in that form across time and space. Some linguists argue that elements of the "sound" of a spoken language are retrievable from texts written in that language, regardless of writing system (DeFrancis, 1989). In this respect, the practice of literacy may operate in a given community as a conserving or stabilizing force, helping to sustain the use of a language more widely spoken elsewhere (see Miller, this volume).

More generally, we see that, in a sense, the use of a particular language creates its own geography. A conversation is a place to be, a territory to inhabit. A book, newspaper, or letter offers a place apart from the immediate environment in which a reader reads. (For an engaging collection of photographs of readers reading in cities, see Kertesz, 1971.) A language persists in a multilingual city such as Chicago when the spoken and sometimes the written use of the language helps to create the space in which its users live. In a multilingual city, a particular language—whether Spanish or Japanese, English or Russian—is both practical tool and a dimension of the identity of the person who uses it.

Because a multilingual city is at once a collection of separate groups and a more or less coordinated set of interacting communities, the social processes that support language persistence can also promote language change. Language change—either change to the use of a new language or change in ways of using a familiar language—can be the product of children's language development, both in families and in broader contexts (Karmiloff & Karmiloff-Smith, 2001; Lightfoot, 1999). Language change can also be a response to the shifting demands of language use in insitutions that make up the complex discourse community of an entire metropolitian area (for a discussion of the "perennial disequilibrium" of urban spatial and social organization, see Kostoff, 1992, p. 298). Language change can be spurred, too, by literacy learning and both literate and oral language practices, whether language users are adapting to fluctuating cultural and economic values (Brandt, 2001), exploiting new technology (Gundlach, 2003), or improvising within the fundamental literary traditions of linguistic innovation and verbal art (Farr, 1994, 2000; Hymes, 2000; Reynolds, this volume).

In many patterns of immigration, language change is forced on language users, so that a person's need to learn the use of new linguistic tools precedes any sense of change in identity. Language users in a multilingual city can thus feel alienated from the sound of their own voices (Hoffman, 1989; Wennerstrom, 2001), even as they learn to use powerful new linguistic tools for conducting their lives in the city. A different, and in some respects contrasting, dynamic—the potential for change in identity leading to an exploration of new ways of speaking or writing—is suggested in literary terms by translator and poet W.S. Di Piero (2001), who observes, "A poet's memory is a whispering gallery of other poets' voices." Commenting on the poet Dante's self-fashioned apprenticeship to Virgil— Dante wrote in Italian, Virgil in Latin—Di Piero (2001) adds, "Who would not want as an early guide a great predecessor who does not get in the way, who launches the younger poet into the freedom of his own idiom?" (p. 352). In Chicago, some seven centuries after Dante, as in other multilingual and culturally complex contemporary cities across the world, it may be that some young language users experience a similar freedom as they invent their own idiom in their everyday lives, transforming the language—or languages—of those who have come before them into new linguistic forms, new strategies for argument, new voices for telling stories.

These dynamics of language persistence and language change seem especially promising as a focus for further inquiry that would build on the many specific insights and broader overall perspective offered by *Ethnolinguistic Chicago*. Learning more about the interplay between language persistence and language change would strengthen our understanding of cultural complexity in contemporary multilingual American cities. Stronger understanding on this level would in turn produce, as Farr and Reynolds suggest, a more accurate understanding of the relationship between the increasingly significant processes of economic globalization and cultural transnationalism.

Finally, this work also has implications for the study of language as it is conducted from the perspective of cognitive science. The basic human capacity for language, however singular when considered as a species-wide biological preparedness for acquiring and using language, expresses itself in many different forms. The research reported in *Ethnolinguistic Chicago* highlights this variety of linguistic forms in a single multilingual city and explores the interactions between various linguistic forms and speakers' cultural histories and current social identities. If, as Steven Pinker (1999) has argued, an explanation of what we know when we know when we know a language must take into account both words and rules—both individual bits of language and broader cognitive or linguistic principles that organize and guide their use—then the researchers whose work is represented in *Ethnolinguistic Chicago* could argue that a third crucial ingredient must also be taken into account: the linguistic knowledge embodied in cultural practices (see Gumperz, 1996; Hymes, 1972). It could be argued, that is, that the scope of what Ray Jackendoff (2002) has recently identified as "the foundations of language" extends not only to words and rules—not only to brain, meaning, grammar, and evolution, as Jackendoff outlines the current agenda of broad topics for linguistic research—but also, in the perspective offered by *Ethnolinguistic Chicago,* to the interplay of words and lives. The studies in this volume help us understand the cultural and linguistic experience that shapes what people know when they know a language. More precisely, this volume helps us understand the experience that triggers and shapes what people in a multilingual city know when they know a combination of languages and learn distinctive ways of using them, both to conduct the practical tasks of their lives and to express and continue to create who they are.

REFERENCES

Brandt, D. (2001). *Literacy in American Lives.* Cambridge, UK: Cambridge University Press.

DeFrancis, J. (1989). *Visible speech: The diverse oneness of writing systems.* Honolulu: University of Hawaii Press.

Di Piero, W. S. (2001). Our sweating selves. In. P. S. Hawkins & R. Jacoff (Eds.), *The poets' Dante* (pp. 344–353). New York: Farrar, Straus and Giroux.

Farr, M. (1994). *Echando relajo*: Verbal art and gender among *mexicanas* in Chicago. In M Bucholtz, A. V. Liang, L. A. Sutton, & C. Hines (Eds.), *Cultural performances: Preceedings of the third women and language conference,* April 8–10, 1994 (pp. 168–186). University California, Berkeley.

Farr, M. (2000). *¡A mi no me manda nadie!* Individualism and Identity in Mexican speech. In V. Pagliai & M. Farr (Eds.), Special issue of Pragmatics (10:1) on Language, Performance and Identity, 61–85.

Gumperz, J. J. (1996). The linguistic and cultural relativity of conversational inference. In J. J. Gumperz & S. C. Levinson (Eds.), *Rethinking linguistic relativity* (pp. 374–406). Cambridge, UK: Cambridge University Press.

Gundlach, R. (2003). The future of writing ability. In M. Nystrand & J. Duffy (Eds.), *Towards a rhetoric of everyday life: New directions in research on writing, text, and discourse* (pp. 247–263). Madison, WI: University of Wisconsin Press.

Hoffman, E. (1989). *Lost in translation: A life in a new language.* New York: Penguin Books.

Hymes, D. (1972). On communicative competence. In J. B. Pride & Janet Holmes (Eds.), *Sociolinguistics: Selected readings* (pp. 269–285). Harmondsworth: Penguin Books.

Hymes, D. (2000). Poetry. *Journal of Linguistic Anthropology, 9,* 191–193.

Jackendoff, R. (2002). *Foundation of language: Brain, meaning, grammar, and evolution.* Oxford, UK: Oxford University Press.

Karmiloff, K., & Karmiloff-Smith, A. (2001). *Pathways to language: From fetus to adolescent.* Cambridge, MA: Harvard University Press.

Kertesz, A. (1971). *On reading.* New York: Penguin Books.

Kostoff, S. (1992). *The city assembled: The elements of urban form through history.* Boston: Bullfinch/Little, Brown.

Lightfoot, D. (1999). *Language development: Acquisition, change, and evolution.* Malden, MA: Blackwell.

Ochs, E. (1988). *Culture and language development: Language acquisition and language socialization in a Samoan village.* Cambridge, UK: Cambridge University Press.

Pinker, S. (1999). *Words and rules: The ingredients of language.* New York: Basic Books.

Sollers, W. (1998). Introduction: After the culture wars, or from "English only" to "English plus." In W. Sollers (Ed.), *Multilingual America: Transnationalism, ethnicity, and the languages of American literature* (pp. 1–13). New York: New York University Press.

Watts, R., & Trudgill, P. (Eds.). (2002). *Alternative histories of English.* London: Routledge.

Wennerstrom, A. (2001). *The music of everyday speech: Prosody and discourse analysis.* Oxford, UK: Oxford University Press.

Author Index

Subject Index